ABRAHAM

ABRAHAM

JIMMY SWAGGART

Jimmy Swaggart Ministries
P.O. Box 262550 • Baton Rouge, Louisiana 70826-2550
Website: www.jsm.org • Email: info@jsm.org
(225) 768-7000

iii

ISBN 978-1-934655-90-0
09-119 • COPYRIGHT © 2013 World Evangelism Press®
13 14 15 16 17 18 19 20 21 22 23 24 / CW 1 / 12 11 10 9 8 7 6 5 4 3 2 1

TABLE OF CONTENTS

INTRODUCTION

"The Book of the Generation of Jesus Christ, the Son of David, the Son of Abraham" (Mat. 1:1).

In writing an introduction to this Book regarding Abraham, his person, his demeanor, who he was, what he did, the Call of God on his life, the position this man occupied and occupies in the great Plan of God, presents itself as a monumental task. In fact, I think one could say that Abraham occupies a place and a position in the Great Plan of God, in its own way, unequalled by anyone else or anything else. Every person who is Born-Again, with Jesus Christ as their Saviour and Lord, owes a debt of gratitude to Abraham. While that can be said to a certain degree regarding all the Bible characters, still, I think personally, that Abraham stands out as unique. In other words, I think one could say that he is in a category all to himself.

When I look at his Call and what it entailed, I realize that this Call by God given to this man some 4,000 years ago, included me and my family. The Lord in His Promise to him said:

"And I will bless them who bless you, and curse him who curses you: and in you shall all families of the Earth be blessed" (Gen. 12:3).

Thank God, my family got in. And as a result of this favored place and position afforded to me by the Lord and, in fact, every person who has ever come to Christ, we all share in this Blessing that was Promised to Abraham. In fact, the great Apostle Paul spoke of every Believer as being *"Children of Abraham"* (Gal. 3:7). We are that because of the *"Blessing of Abraham,"* which was and is *"Justification by Faith"* (Gal. 3:13).

BIBLE CHARACTERS

The names of the personalities in the Word of God,

with which we are well acquainted, such as Abraham, intrigue me. Who are they? What did they do, and why did they do it, whatever it may have been?

The Lord works with people, and these people, even as greatly as some of them were used by God, were human beings just like we are.

Sometime ago I was in a little village in Israel. The mayor of the small town had sent for us, asking if we would come out and see what he was doing in his area. It was somewhat of a commune, and to be sure, with the planting of the vineyard and all that he was carrying out, he had turned the place into a worthwhile project.

As we were standing and talking, he suddenly said to me, *"Brother Swaggart, those hills right in front of us is where the great Prophet Amos herded his flock of sheep"* (Amos 1:1).

Sometime ago I had the privilege of being in Hebron, where Abraham dwelt for a period of time, and, as well, was buried there along with Sarah, Isaac, Rebekah, Jacob, and Leah. According to Josephus the sons of Jacob, with the exception of Joseph, were buried there also.

As I stood there that day looking at the tomb of these individuals, realizing the great part that they had played in the Work of God and the Plan of God, and that me and my family were privileged to have a part in this great Work, presented itself as a sobering thought.

One day the Trump of God will sound, and all of these individuals buried in that tomb in Hebron, these great Bible characters that played such a part in my Salvation, their soul and spirit will come back with the Lord Jesus Christ, where they will be united with a Glorified Body, and that is the Blessed Hope.

JESUS SAID . . .

With a very short statement our Lord let us know

that Abraham had been given by the Holy Spirit the great Plan of Redemption. He said:

"Your father Abraham rejoiced to see My day: and he saw it, and was glad" (Jn. 8:56).

In the great Revelation of Justification by Faith given to Abraham by God, he was made to understand that this great Redemption Plan was wrapped up, not in a philosophy but rather a Man, the Man Christ Jesus, and what He would do at the Cross; the Patriarch rejoiced in that.

THE PERSON OF ABRAHAM

In this book, we will attempt to go with Abraham through his victories and through his defeats. We will attempt to feel what he felt, and see what he saw. Of course, we know that we can only go so far with that, but hopefully the Holy Spirit will help us in this endeavor, and that being the case, it will be, I think, a blessing to the reader. Anything that we can learn about these Bible Greats, and especially Abraham, helps us to learn not only about them, but ourselves as well, and above all about the Lord. The lives of these individuals help us to understand the Lord a little better, and anything that will do that is valuable, to say the least.

We will find that Abraham was human just like the rest of us. He grew discouraged at times! He failed at times, sometimes tragically so! But yet, we will be there with him in his victories, and thank God those victories overshadow all the failures.

THE BOOK OF GOD

This great Book of God, which incorporates every Believer who has ever lived, going all the way back to Abel, and continuing to be enlarged with the Salvation of every soul, should help us to realize how important all of this really is. Everything with God has eternal consequences. We have our part to play in this in which the Lord is doing, exactly as Abraham did. Ours may not be nearly as important as his Call and work, but nevertheless, nothing for the Lord must be taken lightly. It is all of extreme significance, irrespective as to how insignificant it may seem on the surface (Rev. 20:12).

Abraham lived about 2,000 years after Adam and Eve, and about 400 years after the Flood. He is now, as stated, with the Lord Jesus Christ, Whose Plan He furthered to such a great extent, awaiting the Trump of God.

"Thou Christ a burning, cleansing flame,
"Send the fire, send the fire, send the fire!
"Thy Blood-bought gift today we claim,
"Send the fire, send the fire, send the fire.
"Look down and see this waiting host,
"Give us the promised Holy Ghost,
"We want another Pentecost,
"Send the fire, send the fire, send the fire!"

"God of Elijah, hear our cry,
"Send the fire, send the fire, send the fire!
"He'll make us fit to live or die,
"Send the fire, send the fire, send the fire.
"To burn up every trace of sin,
"To bring the light and glory in,
"The revolution now begin,
"Send the fire, send the fire, send the fire!"

"'Tis fire we want, for fire we plead,
"Send the fire, send the fire, send the fire!
"The fire will meet our every need,
"Send the fire, send the fire, send the fire.
"For strength to ever do the right,
"For Grace to conquer in the fight,
"For Power to walk the world in white,
"Send the fire, send the fire, send the fire!"

ABRAHAM

CHAPTER

1

The Birth Of Abraham

THE BIRTH OF ABRAHAM

"These are the generations of Shem: Shem was an hundred years old, and begat Arphaxad two years after the Flood:

"And Shem lived after he begat Arphaxad five hundred years, and begat sons and daughters.

"And Arphaxad lived five and thirty years, and begat Salah:

"And Arphaxad lived after he begat Salah four hundred and three years, and begat sons and daughters" (Gen. 11:10-13).

Considering that Shem lived 500 more years after the Flood, means he was contemporary with Abraham for approximately 75 years; however, that number varies wildly with commentators. It is almost certain that Shem and Abraham were acquainted, and it is possible that Shem witnessed to Abraham.

At this time, about 400 years after the Flood, it is very much possible that there were several hundreds of millions of people on the Earth. And considering that Abraham was one of the most powerful men of his day, which we will deal with later, as stated, it's almost certain that Shem and Abraham were acquainted. If, in fact, that was the case, you can well imagine that Abraham plied Shem with every question concerning the Call of God on Noah's life, Shem's father. You can imagine that Abraham wanted to know about the building of the Ark, and everything about the Flood, etc.

As well, it is quite possible that Shem was used of God to witness to Abraham, but of that there is no record.

It is amazing, considering how the Lord used Abraham, that we have not one word in the Sacred Text as it regards how that the Lord spoke to Abraham. Did He speak to him personally, or did He use Shem?

It is believed that Noah was still alive when Abraham was born. Some even say that Abraham was two years old when Noah died. Noah lived three hundred and fifty years after the Flood, and could very well have been alive when Abraham was born. However, he would not have lived long enough to have witnessed to Abraham, at least there is no record that he did. But Shem lived some 500 years after the Flood and could easily have been well acquainted with Abraham, and could have been used, as stated, by the Lord to witness to the great Patriarch.

As it regards the genealogy of Genesis 11:10 through 26, some claim that this proved that all of these men lived for God. However, that may well be true, and, of course, we hope that it is, but there is no proof that even Shem served the Lord, even as much as we would like to think that he did. The fact of being in the Lineage of Christ, as wonderful and prestigious as that was, however, did not at all guarantee Salvation. In fact, the only man in this genealogy listed in Hebrews Chapter 11, the great Chapter of Faith, is Abraham.

THE BIRTH OF ABRAHAM

"And Serug lived thirty years, and begat Nahor:
"And Serug lived after he begat Nahor two hundred years, and begat sons and daughters.
"And Nahor lived nine and twenty years, and begat Terah:
"And Nahor lived after he begat Terah an hundred and nineteen years, and begat sons and daughters.
"And Terah lived seventy years, and begat Abram, Nahor, and Haran" (Gen. 11:22-26).

The early Verses of Chapter 11 of Genesis record man's effort to establish himself in the Earth and to make for himself a name; the Verses now under consideration show

God calling a man out of the Earth, namely Abraham, and giving him a name. Man said, *"Let us make us a name"* (Gen. 11:4). God said to Abraham, *"I will make you a name"* (Gen. 12:2).

When men throw in their lot with the Lord, they have then embraced that which is eternal, and in that which is *"more abundant life"* (Jn. 10:10). In fact, far too many Believers make their plans, and then ask God to bless those plans. He never will! The idea is that you let God make the Plans, and then those Plans are guaranteed of Blessing. Please understand the following:

God cannot accept anything that is conceived in the heart of man, even the godliest of men. If God accepts it, He must conceive it, give birth to it, and then guide, lead, and instruct. Sinful man cannot produce anything that God can accept and, as stated, and I repeat myself, that includes even the godliest, whomever they might be.

God has a Plan for every single Believer, a Plan that is tailor-made for the individual. And that goes for every single Believer, whoever that Believer might be. And if the Believer will ask the Lord what that Plan is, in other words, what the Lord wants that person to do, to be sure, the Lord will answer such a petition.

A PERSONAL EXPERIENCE

Back in the 1960's, I had the privilege of preaching several meetings with A.N. Trotter, who had, I think, the greatest Anointing of the Holy Spirit on his Ministry than any Preacher I had ever heard. He was many years my senior in those days, and I did everything I could to glean from him as much as would be possible.

I heard him relate a situation as it regarded his mother. She had been raised Baptist, was truly Saved, and truly knew the Lord; however, not having the Baptism with the Holy Spirit, there were many things she did not know.

He went on to relate how that his father had forsaken them, and left the family destitute. His mother began to cry to the Lord for help, and in answer to that prayer, the Lord baptized her with the Holy Spirit. And when that happened, she learned how to believe God for the impossible.

At any rate, in one particular prayer session, she was asking the Lord as to what He wanted her to do. She was a woman whose husband had forsaken her, and who had a house full of children, so what could she do for the Lord? But to be sure, the Lord had a Perfect Plan for her life.

He told her in answer to her petition, *"Raise the children."* Now at first glance that didn't seem to be very much. But what the Lord was talking about was far more involved than appeared on the surface. He was meaning that she should raise these children on Abraham, Isaac, and Jacob. On Paul, Peter, and John, etc. And that she did!

As stated, the Lord had much more in mind than what the simple statement, *"Raise the children,"* seemed to imply.

Her daughter, Brother Trotter's sister, married H.B. Garlock, who opened up West Africa to the great Pentecostal Message. His experiences in Africa, and that includes Sister Garlock, were straight out of the Book of Acts, even to the dead being raised.

Brother Trotter spent some twelve years in Africa, counting all the times he had gone there, and virtually every Preacher in several of the African countries pastoring Churches, were baptized with the Holy Spirit under Brother Trotter's Ministry. That's why the Lord said, *"Raise the children."* The Lord always has much more in mind than we realize. So, ask Him as to what He wants you to do, and to be sure He will answer.

AN IDOLATER

When the Lord called Abraham, then known as *"Abram,"* he was an idolater (Josh. 24:2); consequently, possessing no moral claim upon God, he was *"a Syrian ready to perish"* (Deut. 26:5). But He Who said to the Publican, *"Follow Me"* (Lk. 5:27), said to Abraham, *"Come with Me and I will bless you, and you shall be a blessing"* (Gen. 12:2).

With the family history of Shem, of Terah, and with the Call of Abraham is introduced the Divine Purpose of blessing families, as such, and bringing them into God's Kingdom upon Earth.

SARAI WAS BARREN

"Now these are the generations of Terah: Terah begat Abram, Nahor, and Haran; and Haran begat Lot.

"And Haran died before his father Terah in the land of his nativity, in Ur of the Chaldees.

"And Abram and Nahor took them wives: the name of Abram's wife was Sarai; and the name of Nahor's wife, Milcah, the daughter of Haran, the father of Milcah, and the father of Iscah.

"But Sarai was barren; she had no child" (Gen. 11:27-30).

We now come to the prelude before the Call of one of the greatest men of God who ever lived, Abraham (incidentally, except when quoting the Text, to keep it simple, we will refer to the Patriarch by the name which he is now known, Abraham).

As we look back through history, as given to us in the Bible, which, in fact, is the only reliable historic account given, we see that Millenniums or double Millenniums have marked a turning point in this history. For instance:

• About a thousand years after Creation, Noah was born. His life would mark an episode in history of staggering proportions — the Flood.

• About a thousand years after Noah, which would be about 2,000 years after Creation, we have the account of Abraham. This is another turning point in history, with God giving to this man the meaning of Justification by Faith, which would explain the Salvation process. From the loins of Abraham and the womb of Sarah would come the Jewish people, raised up for the express purpose of giving the world the Word of God, and, as well, serving as the womb of the Messiah, and also to evangelize the world. So from this, I think we can see how great this man Abraham actually was.

• About a thousand years after Abraham, which would be about 3,000 years after Creation, David is called by the Lord to be the King of Israel. Through his family, the Messiah would come, Who would be called *"The Son of David."*

• About a thousand years after David, making it about 4,000 years after Creation, Jesus was born, the Saviour of the world.

• From the Birth of Christ to this present time, which constitutes the Church Age, we can count approximately 2,000 years, making it about 6,000 years of recorded history from the time of the Creation. At this juncture, which should happen very shortly, the Rapture of the Church could take place at any moment, followed by the Great Tribulation, which will conclude with the Second Coming of Christ, which, without a doubt, will be the most cataclysmic moment in history, at least in the time frame of this 6,000 years.

SATAN

The Scripture tells us that Sarah was barren. Satan, knowing that it would be absolutely imperative for a male child to be born to this couple, that is, if the Seed of the woman was to be born into the world, would consequently make her barren, and God would allow him to do so. In this, we see one of the greatest tests of Faith, which brought about many failures on Abraham's part, but ultimately great Victory.

Of course, the Lord could have changed the situation of Sarah's barrenness in a moment's time; however, He would use the situation to teach Abraham and Sarah trust.

UR OF THE CHALDEES

"And Terah took Abram his son, and Lot the son of Haran his son's son, and Sarai his daughter-in-law, his son Abram's wife; and they went forth with them from Ur of the Chaldees, to go into the Land of Canaan; and they came unto Haran, and dwelt there.

"And the days of Terah were two hundred and five years: and Terah died in Haran" (Gen. 11:31-32).

It is said that Ur of the Chaldees, located a little north of what is now referred to as the Persian Gulf, was one of the most modern cities in the world of that time. So Abraham and his family would have left these modern conveniences — modern for that time — to go to a land to which they had never been, and to live a nomadic existence for the rest of their lives, because of a Revelation from God. How many would be willing to do that?

THE JEWISH TARGUMS

The Jewish Targums (Jewish historical commentaries of sorts) say that Abraham's family were idol makers. In other words, they made the idols, which represented the moon god *"Ur"* for which the city was named. They made them out of wood, out of stone, out of silver, out of gold, with some of them studded with precious stones, etc. In fact, at that time, Abraham was one of the most powerful men in the East, meaning he was one of the most powerful in the world. He had some 318 servants, and we speak of men servants alone, besides the women and children (Gen. 14:14). So, the entourage that left Ur at the behest of the Lord was quite large, counting the women and children, probably numbering about a thousand people.

Whether it is correct or not that Abraham and his family were idol makers, one thing is for sure, they definitely were idol worshippers. So we have to venture the thought that whatever Revelation it was that God gave to Abraham, it was so powerful, so obvious, and left such a mark upon the Patriarch, that he would never be the same again. To be sure, this is a conversion that so changes a man, that he will now forsake all that he has known all his life, all the comforts of the world of that day, to reach out by Faith, to something that he really could not see — except by Faith.

We know that Abraham had this Revelation when he was in Ur of the Chaldees. But how long he stayed there before he left for Canaan, with a stop in Haran, we aren't told. I suspect it would not have been very long, because as the First Verse of the next Chapter proclaims, the Command of the Lord was explicit.

He left Haran when he was 75 years old, as we shall see. Whether Terah, Abraham's father, accepted the Lord is not clear. There is some evidence that he did, in that he, as well, left Ur of the Chaldees and got as far as Haran, where he died.

"In the Book of God so precious,
"We are told of Pentecost,
"How the Blessed Lord's Disciples,
"Tarried for the Holy Ghost.
"Pentecostal fire fell on them,
"Burning up their sin and dross,

"Filling them with Power for service,
"Making them a mighty host."

"Pentecost can be repeated,
"For the Lord is just the same,
"Yesterday, today, forever,
"Glory to His Precious Name!
"Saints of God can be victorious,
"Over sin and death and Hell;
"Have a full and free Salvation,
"And the blessed story tell."

"When the Church of Jesus tarries,
"Pentecostal fire will fall.
"Sin and wrong will be defeated,
"Sinners on the Lord will call.
"She will march to glorious Victory,
"Over every land and sea,
"Lifting high the blood-stained banner,
"Holiness her motto be."

ABRAHAM

CHAPTER

2

The Call Of Abraham

THE CALL OF ABRAHAM

"Now the LORD had said unto Abraham, get out of your country, and from your kindred, and from your father's house, unto a land that I will show you" (Gen. 12:1).

THE REVELATION

The phrase, *"Now the LORD had said unto Abraham,"* if it is to be noticed, refers to instructions that had been given to the Patriarch sometime previously.

Chapter 12 of Genesis is very important, for it records the first steps of this great Believer in the path of Faith. There were Believers before him (a few), but the Scripture speaks of him as the father of all Believers who would come after him (Rom. 4:16).

While Abraham obeyed, it seems that family ties, at first, held him back. Though called to Canaan he, nevertheless, tarried at Haran till nature's tie was snapped by death, and then, with unimpeded step, he made his way to the place to which *"the God of Glory"* had called him.

All of this is very full of meaning. The flesh is ever a hindrance to the full Power of the Call of God. We tend to settle for less than that which God intends.

We are slow to learn that everything we need, and I mean everything, is found totally and completely in Christ. While we are quick to say *"Amen"* to the words I have just dictated, we are slow to actually come to the place of full surrender. *"Self-will"* hinders! The *"flesh"* hinders! However, we make excuses for all of this, by loading the flesh in self-will with religious phraseology.

THE CALL OF GOD

Whatever it is that God calls us to do, it is always beyond what we would, at first, see or think. Embodied in the Call, is not only a Work to be done, but, as well, the ingredients for Spiritual Growth. With the Holy Spirit, it is always growth. And to be frank, the growth must be brought about or the Work cannot be done. And here I would dwell, for a little, on the Cross of Christ. There is only one way all of this can be achieved, and that's by and through the Cross. If we do not understand the Cross, then we cannot really understand the Way of God. In fact, if the Cross is removed from Christianity, Christianity then loses its Power (I Cor. 1:18), and for all practical purposes, becomes little more than the religions of the world. While it might have a better ethic, it's an ethic that really cannot be reached without the Cross.

THE CROSS OF CHRIST

The Cross unfolds God as the sinner's friend. It reveals Christ in that most wondrous Character, as the Righteous Justifier of the most ungodly sinner.

Someone once asked me, *"Is it Who He is, or What He did, that makes the difference?"*

Only Christ could do what needed to be done to redeem fallen humanity; however, even though Christ is God and has always been God, on that premise alone, no one was redeemed. God would have to become Man and go to the Cross, if man was to be lifted out of his fallen state. So, in the final alternative, even though Who He was presents an absolute necessity, in reality, it was What He did, and we speak of the Cross, which guarantees Salvation for even the vilest of sinners.

THE INTRODUCTION OF THE CROSS

The Power of God, with all its Wisdom, Glory, Holiness, and Magnitude, but for the Cross, works against the sinner.

How precious, therefore, is the Cross, in this, its first phase, as the basis of the sinner's peace, the basis of his worship, and the basis of his eternal relationship with the God Who is there so blessedly and so gloriously revealed.

All that He has said, all that He has done, from the very beginning, indicates that the Cross was ever uppermost in His Heart. And no wonder! His dear and well-beloved Son was to hang there, between Heaven and Earth, the Object of all the shame and suffering that men and devils could heap upon Him, shedding His Life's Blood, all because He loved to do His Father's Will, and, thereby, redeemed the children of His Grace.

THE CROSS AND THE WORLD

The same Cross which connects me with God has separated me from the world. A dead man is, evidently, done with the world; and to be sure, every true Believer died with Christ as it regards His Death, Burial, and Resurrection (Rom. 6:3-5). Having risen with Christ, we are now connected with God in the Power of a New Life, even a New Nature. Being thus inseparably linked with Christ, we, of necessity, participate in our acceptance with God, and in our rejection by the world. The two things go together.

The former makes us a worshipper and a Citizen of Heaven, while the latter makes us a witness and a stranger on Earth. If the Cross has become between me and my sins, it has just as readily come between me and the world. In the former case, it puts me into the place of peace with God; in the latter, it puts me into the place of hostility with the world.

THE CROSS AND SEPARATION

The Believer cannot profess to enjoy the former of our heading, while rejecting the latter. If one's ear is opened to hear Christ's Voice within the Veil, it should be open also to hear His Voice outside the Camp; if one enters into the Atonement, which the Cross has accomplished, one should also realize the rejection that it necessarily involves.

It is our happy privilege not only to be done with our sins, but to be done with the world also. All this is involved in the Doctrine of the Cross. That's why Paul said:

"God forbid that I should glory, save in the Cross of our Lord Jesus Christ, by Whom the world is crucified unto me, and I unto the world" (Gal. 6:14). This means that Paul looked upon the world as a thing which ought to be nailed to the Cross.

CONSECRATION

The phrase, *"Get out of your country, and from your kindred, and from your father's house,"* proclaims the reason that many cannot be used of God. They refuse to separate themselves from certain things in this world and, therefore, unto God.

The following is what the Lord demanded of Abraham and, in effect, demands of us all:

• *"Get out of your country"*: The true Believer *"seeks a country,"* simply because that which the world offers can never satisfy and, therefore, simply will not do (Heb. 11:14). The things of this world lose their attraction. Money is a means to an end. The old song, *"This world is not my home, I'm just a passing through,"* becomes the song of the Redeemed. If one lays up treasures here, one's heart will be here, and simply because one's heart is where one's treasure is.

• *"Separate from your kindred"*: Now you belong to Christ. You are bought with a price, and a great price at that, and even though you continue to love your family, even love them deeply, Christ, and what He wants and desires, takes precedent over your family and anyone else for that matter. Regrettably, many aren't willing to do that.

• *"From your father's house"*: This refers to whatever future close loved ones have planned for you. As stated, you now belong to Christ. Anything and everything that might be detrimental in your *"father's house,"* must be laid aside. In effect, you leave everything, and do so for the sake of Christ.

Now, as stated, many simply will not do that. And, as a result, God simply cannot use them. Or else, they quit altogether, which tragically is the course it seems, for many.

• *"Unto a land that I will show you"*: This refers to the fact that Abraham had no choice in the matter. He was to receive his orders from the Lord, and go where those orders led him.

In many ways, living for God is similar to the military. While personally, I've never served in the military, still from what I see, there isn't a lot of difference, or at least it shouldn't be a lot of difference, in the Army of this nation and the Army of our Lord.

A GREAT NATION

"And I will make of you a great Nation, and I will bless you, and make your name great; and you shall be a blessing" (Gen. 12:2).

The phrase, *"And I will make of you a great Nation,"* pertains to Israel and all of its people, and for all time. The Nation of which God was speaking did not exist at this time. And besides that, Sarah was barren.

And yet, this Nation would be totally unlike any nation the world had ever known. Some 400 years later, a wayward Prophet would say, and by the Spirit of God, *"For from the top of the rocks I see him, and from the hills I behold him: lo, the people shall dwell alone, and shall not be reckoned among the nations"* (Num. 23:9). This means that Israel would be totally unlike any other nation that had ever existed.

The wayward Prophet then said:

"He shall pour the water out of His Buckets, and His Seed shall be in many waters, and His King shall be higher than Agag, and His Kingdom shall be exalted" (Num. 24:7).

MONOTHEISTIC

In fact, in Old Testament times, Israel was the only Nation in the world that was monotheistic, meaning she worshipped one God, Jehovah. All the other nations were polytheistic, meaning they worshipped many gods, in essence demon spirits. So, Israel was the only Light in the world of her day.

Under David and Solomon, Israel became the most powerful Nation on Earth and, as well, the richest; however, the true riches were in their relationship with God. They would give the world the Word of God, which has blessed the world immeasurably. And even greater than that, they served as the Womb of the Messiah, so to speak, even though they did not know Him when He actually came.

Due to crucifying their Messiah and the world's Saviour, at their request, the Lord took His Hand of Blessing away from them. Consequently, in A.D. 70, they, in effect, ceased to be a nation, totally destroyed by the Roman Tenth Legion under Titus.

As strangers, they have wandered the world for about 1,900 years, when once again establishing themselves in their ancient homeland, and once again becoming a Nation. And yet, they have some dark days ahead, in fact, darker than anything they have seen in the past. Jesus said so (Mat. 24:21). It will take that for them to finally accept Christ, the One they have rejected. This they will do (Zech. 13:1, 6). Israel will then be restored, never to lose her way again (Rom. 11:26-27).

A BLESSING

The phrase, *"And I will bless you, and make your name great,"* claims the Favor of God. According to Scripture, *"to bless"* means *"to increase."* Abraham would be blessed, and so would Israel.

These words, *"I will bless,"* indicate relations very close between Jehovah and Abraham, whereby the friends and enemies of the one, become so equally to the other.

The phrase, *"And you shall be a blessing,"* concerns itself with the greatest Blessing of all. It is the glory of Abraham's Faith. God would give this man the meaning of Salvation, which is *"Justification by Faith."* This Blessing, the great Patriarch would pass on to the entirety of the world.

Of course, the greatest Blessing of all, and by far, is that Israel, as we have stated, would serve as the Womb of the Messiah, the Saviour of Mankind, the King of kings and the Lord of lords, the One Who is All in all. Regrettably and sadly, Israel did not know her Redeemer when He came and, in fact, crucified Him, which was the most dastardly deed ever carried out by wicked hearts. But thank God, and not too very long into the future, they are going to accept the One Whom they rejected. It will be at the Second Coming, and to be sure, He most definitely is coming back.

THE BLESSING AND THE CURSE

"And I will bless them who bless you, and curse him who curses you: and in you shall all the families of the Earth be blessed" (Gen. 12:3).

The phrase, *"And I will bless them who bless you, and curse him who curses you,"* holds true not only for Israel, but, as well, for Spiritual Israel, i.e., *"the Church,"* i.e., *"those who are truly Born-Again."* Let's look first at Israel.

At least part of the reason that America has experienced such Blessings is because of our protection of Israel. This Promise given to Abraham by God nearly 4,000 years ago holds true even unto this hour and, in fact, will ever hold true.

It holds true for Israel; and it holds true for the Church as well, and I speak of the True Church. All those who bless the Work of God can expect Blessings from the Lord, and it doesn't really matter who they are.

As well, if a nation or a people oppose Israel, or the Work of God presently, God has said that He will Personally curse that nation or people. And please understand, if God curses anything, which means to hinder that nation or person, to be sure, trouble will be their continued lot. Of all the problems which presently beset our nation at this particular time, the worst of all is, that it seems like the Obama Administration is giving Israel precious little help. Although little understood or recognized by most of the general public, to be sure, it is recognized by God, and if continued, will cut off the flow of Blessings to this nation. To be sure, God meant what He said, and said what He meant, when He said, *"I will bless them who bless you, and curse him who curses you."* If we forget this, we do so at our peril.

ALL THE FAMILIES OF THE EARTH

The phrase, *"In you shall all families of the Earth be blessed,"* concerns a Blessing of unprecedented proportions.

It speaks of Israel giving the world the Word of God, and more particularly bringing the Messiah into the world. Through Christ, every family in the world who desires Blessing from God can have that Blessing. While the word *"Blessing"* covers a wide territory, the greatest Blessing of all, would be, and is, *"Justification by Faith,"* which is made possible to every believing soul as it regards the price paid of the Lord Jesus Christ at the Cross of Calvary.

A PERSONAL BLESSING

First of all, I want to say how much I thank God that my family got in on this Blessing, this Promise given to Abraham so long, long ago.

In fact, every time I read this Third Verse of the 12th Chapter of Genesis, I think of the time this *"Blessing"* came to our house.

I was born into a home on March 15, 1935, who did not know God. In fact, until my Dad was 25 years old, he had never been inside of a Church, not one single time. He had never heard a Gospel song and, in fact, had never even seen a Bible, much less having read one. My Mother's experience was very similar. They tried to be good moral people, but without God, such is a fruitless task.

And then two women, a mother and her daughter, came to our little town to build a Church. The year was 1939. The lady and her daughter were the mother and sister of Lester Sumrall.

A small Church was built. In fact, my Uncle, who was a millionaire, in whose home I was born, loaned the money to build the Church.

My entire family was Saved in that Church. And, as a result, I accepted Christ when I was 8 years old. I was baptized with the Holy Spirit a few weeks later. I do not know all the reasons that this great Gospel of Jesus Christ was brought to our town, and ultimately to our family. But, by the Grace of God, this Blessing came to us; consequently, I feel as Paul said so long ago, *"I am debtor"* (Rom. 1:14). I must do everything within my power to help take this Glorious Gospel to others. As I had the privilege to hear, they must have the privilege to hear as well!

ABRAHAM DEPARTED

"So Abram departed, as the LORD had spoken unto him; and Lot went with him: and Abram was seventy and five years old when he departed out of Haran" (Gen. 12:4).

So Abraham starts for the better land. This was his first surrender; there were seven in all:

- He surrenders here his native land (Gen. 12:1).
- He surrenders his family (Gen. 12:1).
- He then surrenders the *"plain of Jordan"* (Gen. 13:9-11).
- He then surrenders the riches of Sodom (Gen. 14:21-23).
- He surrenders self (Gen. 17:4-8).
- He then surrenders Ishmael (Gen. 21:9-21).
- And lastly, he surrenders Isaac (Gen. 22:9-14).

Each painful surrender was followed by increased Spiritual Wealth.

The Holy Spirit, through Moses, calls attention to the fact that Abraham was 75 years old when he departed out of Haran.

Why does He note this?

From the time that God revealed Himself to Abraham, to the time he obeyed the Command, might have been several years. Maybe there was a struggle there of which we aren't aware. We know that he did not leave Haran until his father, Terah, died. That seems to be the lot of many Christians. They go halfway; in other words, while they obey partially, they never quite obey totally. They make it to *"Haran,"* but they never quite make it all the way to Canaan, or else they arrive late.

CANAAN

"And Abram took Sarai his wife, and Lot his brother's son, and all their substance that they had gathered, and the souls that they had gotten in Haran; and they went forth to go into the Land of Canaan; and into the Land of Canaan they came" (Gen. 12:5).

From Haran to Canaan was approximately 350 miles. Abraham had 318 trained men with him (Gen. 14:14), meaning that they were trained to fight as soldiers. They were totally loyal to Abraham, actually born in his household. In fact, there may have been as many as a thousand people, as previously stated, in this entourage.

Also, Abraham was extremely rich in silver and gold, as well as flocks and herds. In other words, he was a mighty man, and quite possibly, one of the richest men in the East and, thereby, the world. And yet, as far as the comfort of Ur was concerned, he willingly left it all. In the leaving, he did not cease to be rich, and he did not cease to be mighty, but he gained the greatest riches of all, the Knowledge of Jehovah.

THE CANAANITE

"And Abram passed through the land into the place of Sichem, unto the plain of Moreh. And the Canaanite was then in the land" (Gen. 12:6).

At long last, Abraham now finds himself in the Promised Land. Thus it is presently. The Holy Spirit says, *"Believe on the Lord Jesus Christ and you shall be Saved."* The sinner believes and he is Saved. Into *"the Land of Canaan"* he comes, the Promised Land. This is the first step in the life of Faith.

But, what an unexpected experience for Abraham! He finds the hateful, impure, and hostile Canaanite in

God's land. This was Faith's first trial; his heart would be tempted to question the fact that this was God's land, for how could the Canaanite be in God's land?!

So, in the present day, the young Believer, expects after conversion, to find nothing in his nature hostile to Christ, but is distressed and perplexed very soon to painfully learn that, alas, the Canaanite is in the land, and he is now commencing a lifelong battle with what the New Testament refers to as *"the flesh."*

"They were in the court of Gentiles,
"They were all with one accord,
"When the Holy Spirit descended,
"As was promised by our Lord."

"Yes, this is Power from Heaven descended,
"With the sound of Rushing Wind;
"Tongues of fire came down upon them,
"As the Lord said He would send."

"Yes, this old time Power was given,
"To our fathers who were true;
"This is promised to Believers,
"And we all may have it too."

"O Lord, send the Power just now,
"O Lord, send the Power just now,
"O Lord, send the Power just now,
"And baptize everyone."

ABRAHAM

CHAPTER

The Altar

THE ALTAR

"And the LORD appeared unto Abram, and said, Unto your seed will I give this land: and there built he an Altar unto the LORD, Who appeared unto him" (Gen. 12:7).

The phrase, *"And the LORD appeared unto Abram,"* tells us the following.

Though the hostile Canaanite was in the land, the Lord was there as well.

The Bible doesn't say that the Lord appeared to Abraham while he was in Haran, because this was only a partial obedience. God reveals Himself only when the obedience is total. As we have previously stated, the only thing that a person can really do, as it regards doing, is to present to the Lord a willing mind and an obedient heart. There is really nothing else the Believer can do as it regards this great Salvation and, as well, this great Sanctification. But the Lord wants a fully obedient heart, not a partially obedient heart.

THE STRUGGLE OF FAITH

All of this is full of instruction for us. The Canaanite in the land is the expression of the Power of Satan; but instead of being occupied with Satan's power to keep us out of the inheritance, we are called on to apprehend Christ's Power to bring us in. This means that the very sphere into which we are is the sphere of our conflict. Should this terrify us? By no means.

We have Christ — a Victorious Christ, in Whom we are *"more than Conquerors."* We will find that strangely enough, the *"Altar"* is the manner in which Christ gives us the Victory. In fact, as there is no Salvation outside of the Cross, likewise there is no Victory outside of the Cross. If the Cross of Christ is removed from our thinking, our theology, our Faith, there is nothing left then but a vapid philosophy. The Cross of Christ is the hinge, one might say, of everything. While Jesus Christ is the Source, it is the Cross that is the Means for all things that are given unto us. And when I speak of the Cross, I am not speaking of the wooden beam on which Jesus died, but rather for what He there accomplished.

IS IT WHO HE IS OR WHAT HE DID?

I had someone to ask me that question once, whom I knew to be asking in sarcasm. In other words, he was saying that the Cross was inconsequential. It was Who Jesus was, he maintained.

Of course, Who Jesus was, the Son of the Living God, actually God manifested in the flesh, was absolutely imperative. He is the only One Who could have done what needed to be done. No one else could. So, Who He was and Who He is, is of such significance as to defy all description. But stop and think about this a moment.

Jesus has always been God. As God, He had no beginning, always was, is unformed, unmade, uncreated, is now, and ever shall be. But, as that alone, no one was Saved. Redemption was not afforded or accorded. For there to be Redemption, for Eternal Life to be given to men and women, for Justification by Faith to be made possible, in other words for God to justify obviously guilty man and retain His Justness, God would have to become Man, and to do so for the sole purpose of going to the Cross. Jesus Christ was not a martyr. He was a Sacrifice. He came to this world to go to the Cross. That was His Destination. It had been planned from before the foundation of the world (I Pet. 1:18-20).

When Simon Peter attempted to deny the Cross, Jesus *"turned, and said unto Peter, You get behind Me,*

Satan: you are an offense unto Me: for you savor not the things that be of God, but those that be of men" (Mat. 16:23). In other words, Jesus was saying that anything other than the Cross is *"an offense unto Him,"* and, as well, is *"not of God,"* but that which is of men. So, the Altar built by Abraham, as we shall further see, was, in effect, the title deed given in promise of the great Plan of God. The Cross says, *"I have given it, I am giving it, and I shall give it."*

YOUR SEED

The phrase, *"And said, Unto your seed will I give this land,"* proclaims in this short statement that Abraham will have a son who will be the progenitor of the Redeemer of all nations. It didn't matter that Sarah was barren, God has promised a son. And, as well, this son will lead to the coming of the Messiah. So we're speaking here of something that is outsized regarding significance. In fact, there is nothing in the world more important.

The *"land"* of which the Lord spoke was the land of Canaan. The Muslims should read this Passage. The Lord said that He was giving this unto Abraham's seed, and He later would say that Isaac was that seed, not Ishmael (Gen. 21:12). The Lord didn't say that He would give this land to the Muslims or anyone else for that matter, but rather to the seed of Abraham through Isaac.

If it is to be noticed, the Lord didn't say that He would give this land to Abraham directly, but rather to *"your seed,"* which spoke of coming generations. In fact, Stephen stated, and concerning this very moment, *"And He* (God) *gave him* (Abraham) *none* (no) *inheritance in it, no, not so much as to set his foot on"* (Acts 7:5). Therefore, this Promise agreed with that which Abraham had been given before, namely that he was to become a great people, for the land was promised not to him personally, but to his descendants.

THE ALTAR

The phrase, *"And there built he an Altar unto the LORD, Who appeared unto him,"* proclaims a step of Faith that tells us several things:
• That the Canaanites should be dispossessed, and the entirety of their country given to the offspring of a childless man already over seventy-five years old, demands a great leap of Faith. The apparent improbability of it ever being accomplished presented itself as a constant test of Faith throughout the entirety of the life of the Patriarch.
• The rearing of an Altar in the land was, in fact, a form of taking possession of it on the grounds of a right secured to the exercises of his Faith. It is often said of Abraham and the Patriarchs that they built Altars to the Lord; it is never said that they built houses for themselves.
• All of this proclaims to us, and we're speaking of the building of the Altar, that the Cross of Christ must ever be the Object of our Faith. Nothing is more important than this.
The problem with the modern church is not a lack of faith, but rather faith in the wrong thing. Let us say it again, and even more sharply:
If one's faith is not anchored squarely in the Cross of Christ, irrespective in what else it might be anchored, and no matter how Scriptural the other thing might be in its own right, the upshot is, God will not honor such faith. He honors Faith alone which is in the Cross of Christ.
• The Believer must understand, and without reservation, that everything we receive from the Lord, and that means everything exclusively, comes to us by the Means of the Cross. It is the Cross of Christ that has

made it all possible. As well, and as equally important, the Holy Spirit Whom we cannot do without, and Whose Power and Help we must have, Works entirely within the parameters, so to speak, of the Finished Work of Christ (Rom. 8:1-11).

• The Altar, and in every case, represented the coming Crucifixion, where the Son of God would give Himself in Sacrifice, in order to atone for all sin, past, present, and future, at least for all who would believe (Jn. 3:16).

SIN

The *"Altar,"* in essence, said that mankind's gravest problem, in other words, the problem that was the cause of all other problems, was and is sin. And sin can only be handled and, in fact, was handled, at the Cross, and the Cross alone. This means that all of these great Promises given by God to Abraham, which are: him having a son, a great nation being raised up from his loins, all the families of the world being blessed through him, him being a blessing to all nations, and his descendants acquiring the entirety of this land of Canaan, all and without exception, were for but one purpose, and that was to ultimately pave the way for the Redeemer to come into this world, in order to handle this terrible problem of sin.

The problem with the modern church is we get our eyes on the temporal aspects of the Promise. The *"land"* becomes very important to us, but not in the right way. Even the answer to prayer becomes very important, but again, all in the wrong way.

The center of gravity, so to speak, as it regards Christianity, is always the Cross, and nothing but the Cross. Paul nailed it down when he said:

"Christ Jesus came into the world to save sinners; of whom I am chief" (I Tim. 1:15).

In this short statement, the Holy Spirit, through Paul, tells us Who the Saviour is, the great problem facing the world, which is sin, and that I personally am in need of Redemption, just as much as anyone else, or more!

THE REVELATION

The Seventh Verse plainly says, even twice, that the Lord appeared unto Abraham. Exactly what this means we aren't told. Taking it at face value, it means that the Lord appeared to Abraham in visible form.

Some may say that if the Lord presently would do that for them, appear in visible form, they could then do great and mighty things, etc.

The truth is, the Lord has done even more. Paul said:

"God, Who at sundry times and in divers manners spoke in time past unto the fathers by the Prophets,

"Has in these last days spoken unto us by His Son, Whom He has appointed Heir of all things, by Whom also He made the worlds" (Heb. 1:1-2).

When we read the four Gospels and the Epistles, for that matter, we are reading what God has spoken unto us by His Son. It fulfills all the Old Testament Promises. Paul said:

"For Christ is the end of the Law for Righteousness to everyone who believes" (Rom. 10:4).

Jesus went to the Cross and there He atoned for all sin, past, present, and future, at least for all who will believe (Jn. 3:16). He satisfied the demands of the broken Law, by giving of Himself as a Sacrifice. Sin being the legal right that Satan had to hold man in captivity, that legal right is now broken, because all sin has been atoned, at least for all who will believe. When Jesus paid the terrible sin debt and paid it in full, this put Believers in a brand-new status (Col. 2:10-15).

THE HOLY SPIRIT

Due to the sin debt being completely lifted, in other words, man no longer owes a debt to God due to what Jesus did at the Cross, the Holy Spirit, Who could only Work in a limited way before the Cross, can now come into all Believers, which He does at conversion, and does so to abide forever (Jn. 14:16-17). As well, Believers, by and through Jesus Christ, can now receive the Baptism with the Holy Spirit, which is a Baptism of Power, in order to carry out the Work of the Lord. As well, this Gift is always accompanied by speaking with other Tongues (Acts 1:8; 2:4; 10:45-46; 19:1-7). Due to the fact that the Holy Spirit abides within us, and does so forever, He is there to lead us and guide us constantly, giving us the direction that we need (Jn. 16:13-15). Having such constant leadership of the Holy Spirit is far better than having the Lord to appear to us Personally at abbreviated times.

THE CROSS OF CHRIST AND
THE HOLY SPIRIT

Even though the Holy Spirit is definitely present at all times with all Believers, even the weakest Saints, His Leadership, Guidance, and Power are seldom known in their fullness because of two things. In other words, most Saints experience very little help from the Holy Spirit, when in reality, He desires to do much more and, in fact, will do much more, if we follow God's Prescribed Order.

The first part of that Order has to do with the Cross of Christ. The Holy Spirit Works exclusively within the boundaries of the Finished Work of Christ. In other words, every single thing He does for us is done exclusively according to what Jesus did for us on the Cross

(Rom. 8:1-2, 11). This is what gives Him, as stated, the legal right to do all the things which He does. As also stated, the sin debt has now been lifted, paid for by Christ at the Cross, which gives the Holy Spirit great latitude in which to work. That's the reason that He couldn't come into hearts and lives to abide forever before the Cross. But after the Cross, it is now an entirely different story (I Cor. 1:17-18, 21, 23; 2:2, 5).

THE CROSS OF CHRIST IS THE MEANS

The Holy Spirit doesn't ask much of us, but He does demand that we place our Faith exclusively in the Cross of Christ (Rom. 6:3-5; 8:2; I Cor. 1:17-18; 2:2; Gal. 6:14; Col. 1:20; 2:14-15). We as Believers must understand that everything that comes to us from God does so exclusively through and by what Jesus did at the Cross, all on our behalf. In other words, He came to this world for the express purpose of going to the Cross. That was His Mission, His Purpose, and, in fact, that which had been decided from before the foundation of the world (I Pet. 1:18-20). Actually, the entirety of the Bible, and in every capacity, is the story of man's Fall and Redemption, and the Cross is how the Redemption process was brought about. So the point I'm attempting to make is this:

The Believer needs to understand the Cross, meaning that the Cross was not only necessary for our initial Salvation experience when we were Born- Again, but, as well, plays just as much of a part in our everyday living, and in every capacity. In other words, unless you the Believer, put your faith exclusively in the Cross of Christ, ever making it the Object of your Faith, you cannot have all the Help, Leading, Guidance, and Empowerment of the Holy Spirit, which means that no matter how hard you try, you're going to fail.

ABRAHAM AND JESUS

Now in a limited way, all of this of which we speak, is that which the Holy Spirit showed to Abraham. Concerning this, Jesus Himself said of Abraham, and speaking to the Jews, *"Your father Abraham rejoiced to see My day: and he saw it, and was glad"* (Jn. 8:56).

THE OBJECT OF OUR FAITH

It is absolutely imperative that you, as a Believer, ever make the Cross the Object of your Faith (I Cor. 1:17-18, 23; 2:2; Gal. 6:14). Concerning this very thing, Paul said:

"Blotting out the handwriting of Ordinances that was against us, which was contrary to us, and took it out of the way, nailing it to His Cross;

"And having spoiled principalities and powers, He made a show of them openly, triumphing over them in it" (Col. 2:14-15).

This Passage bluntly tells us that everything was done at the Cross; consequently, inasmuch as the Lord Works exclusively on the basis of Faith, we must understand what the Object of Faith must ever be.

CORRECT FAITH

Every Christian has faith; in fact, every person in the world has faith. The problem is, it's not faith in God or His Word. No unsaved person has Faith in God, while some few may have such in a rudimentary way, it would only be what they were taught by Christian parents, etc. But, actually, it's impossible for the unredeemed to have Faith in God or His Word, inasmuch as they are spiritually dead. As stated, while they have faith, it's not faith that God will recognize.

However, even Christians, most of the time, do not know and understand what their faith really is. All claim to have faith, and in truth that is correct; but most don't have the faintest idea as to what the Object of their Faith ought to be. They think they know, but in actuality, they don't.

If asked this question, most would claim that they have Faith in God or their Faith is in Christ, or they have Faith in the Word, etc. While all of these statements are correct, they really don't say very much.

The statement I'm about to make will be strong, but I believe it to be true. The type of faith that most Christians have, is really the same type of faith that demons have. Listen to what the Scriptures say:

"You believe there is one God; you do well: the devils (demons) *also believe, and tremble"* (James 2:19).

The entire Foundation of Christianity is the Cross of Christ. So, unless the Christian has, as the basis of his Faith, the Cross of Christ, in other words, what Jesus actually did there, it's really not faith that God will recognize.

THE MODERN CHURCH AND FAITH

In the last several decades, the Church has been inundated with teaching on faith, which claims to be Faith in the Word. The adherents to this doctrine, and I speak of the Word of Faith doctrine, so-called, do not at all believe in the Cross. In fact, they refer to the Cross as *"past miseries,"* or *"the most horrible defeat in human history."* So, they place no credence in the Cross, which means that what they are teaching is heresy.

They claim to be great students of the Word, to base everything on the Word, etc. Because of making these statements and quoting some Scriptures, most of the Church is deceived into believing that these people truly are sticklers for the Word. But, in fact, the very opposite is true.

They teach that the way to *"put the Word to work for you,"* which is the way they label it, is to find several Scriptures that seem to address your need or problem, whatever your problem might be, then quote those Scriptures over and over again. They teach that this creates some type of spiritual energy, and I speak of the constant quotation, which then has an effect in the spirit world, and will bring about the desired answer.

WHITE MAGIC

The truth is, this is no more than white magic. It is trying to use the Scriptures as some type of magic formula, which will bring about whatever one desires. Nothing could be further from the truth. God will not allow His Word to be used against Himself.

In the first place, these people teach that whatever they desire is the Will of God. In other words, they teach that they do not now need the Leading of the Spirit, inasmuch as they are new creation people. Whatever they do is right in the Eyes of God, whatever that might be. In other words, they totally ignore the Will of God, in effect, claiming that whatever they do constitutes the Will of God. Again, nothing could be further from the truth!

For a Believer to properly know and understand the Word of God, the Believer must realize that the Word is the Story of Jesus Christ and Him Crucified. Now think about that for a moment! Listen to what John said:

"In the beginning was the Word, and the Word was with God, and the Word was God" (Jn. 1:1). This tells us that Jesus is the Living Word. So, to divorce the Word from Christ, which means to not recognize Who He is and What He has done, is to do great violence to the Word. The Spirit then says:

"And the Word was made flesh, and dwelt among us, (and we beheld His Glory, the Glory of the only Begotten of the Father,) full of Grace and Truth" (Jn. 1:14).

Now the Story of the Word is the Story of Christ, which refers to God becoming Man, as the Scripture says, *"was made flesh, and dwelt among us."*

We now learn as to why the Word (Christ) was made flesh. The Scripture now says:

THE LAMB OF GOD

"The next day John sees Jesus coming unto him, and said, Behold the Lamb of God, which takes away the sin of the world" (Jn. 1:29). If it is to be noticed, John the Baptist referred to Jesus as *"the Lamb of God,"* Who would *"take away the sin of the world."*

John referred to Jesus as the Lamb of God, simply because His very Purpose for coming to this world was to die on the Cross, of which the untold millions of lambs previously offered through the many centuries, were Types and Shadows of the One Who was to come. He would *"take away the sin of the world,"* by what He did at the Cross.

So we have the Word put before us, and we are made to understand that this *"Word"* is Jesus, and that His Purpose was to go to the Cross in order to *"take away the sin of the world."* Now, let us bluntly make the following statement, so there will be no misunderstanding.

If the Believer doesn't understand the Word of God according to the Cross, then the Believer really doesn't understand the Word. That being the case, he can claim all he desires that he is a *"Word person,"* but in reality he isn't. Memorizing a few Scriptures and quoting them over and over doesn't make one a *"Word person."* A true *"Word person"* is one who understands the Word in relationship to Christ and what He did for us at the Cross, understanding, in effect, that Christ and the Cross are one and the same, one might say. That's why Paul said, *"One Lord, one Faith, one Baptism"* (Eph. 4:5).

ONE LORD, ONE FAITH, ONE BAPTISM

First of all let's understand that all of this we are giving, which is New Testament theology, actually the meaning of the New Covenant, all and without question, was represented in Abraham's Altar. When he built the Altar, which he was directed to do by the Lord, even though the Altar was only a Symbol, still it represented everything as to what Jesus would do in order to redeem humanity.

What did Paul mean by the statement, *"One Lord, one Faith, one Baptism"?*

Actually, to fully understand this Passage, we must also include Verses 4 through 6. In these three Verses 4, 5, and 6, Paul deals with the *"one"* aspect, and does so seven times. Let's look at it one by one.

ONE BODY

The *"One Body"* speaks of the True Church, into which one becomes a part of by being *"born again"* (Jn. 3:3). This is done by the believing sinner evidencing Faith in Christ and what Christ did at the Cross, in effect, accepting Christ as one's personal Saviour. Admittedly, the believing sinner doesn't understand anything about Christ, the Cross, or the Bible upon being Saved. The Lord doesn't require them to know that much, only to believe the Lord, which is done by the individual calling on Him. In fact, Paul said:

"For whosoever shall call upon the Name of the Lord shall be Saved" (Rom. 10:13). But after that person comes to Christ, of course, the Holy Spirit desires and strongly, that the person learn the Word.

ONE SPIRIT

Of course, this refers to the Holy Spirit, Who is the active Agent in all that is done as it regards the Godhead, and Their dealing with humanity. In other words, every single thing done by the Godhead on Earth, is done through the Person, Purpose, Work, Office, Ministry, and Power of the Holy Spirit (Acts 13:2, 4, etc.).

ONE HOPE

This great Hope held by every Saint of God pertains to what Jesus did at the Cross on our behalf. It refers to the fact that we are now washed, sanctified, and justified (I Cor. 6:11). As well, we have the Blessed Hope that soon we will be *"Glorified."* And please understand, the word *"Hope"* as used in the Bible is totally different than the way it is presently used. Now it means maybe or maybe not! The Biblical word *"Hope"* means that what is going to happen is guaranteed, but we just don't know exactly when.

ONE LORD

There is one Christ Who has Saved us, and He did so by what He did at the Cross. The title *"Lord,"* in effect, means *"Lord of the Covenant."* The Covenant of which it speaks goes all the way back to Genesis 3:15, where it speaks of the Seed of the woman bruising the head of the serpent. This was done by Christ at Calvary. As an aside, this means that all pretenders are just that, pretenders! I'm speaking of Mohammed, Joseph Smith, Confucius, and any other pretended light. There is only *"One Lord,"* not two, just one, and He is the Lord Jesus Christ.

ONE FAITH

If it is to be noticed, I am constantly using the terminology that the Believer must ever have as the Object of His Faith the Cross of Christ. In fact, if we place our Faith in anything else, we are abrogating the Word of God. There aren't ten faiths, or two faiths, but only *"one Faith,"* and that is, *"Jesus Christ and Him Crucified"* (I Cor. 2:2).

ONE BAPTISM

This does not refer at all to Water Baptism as most think. It refers to the Baptism into the Death of Christ on the Cross (Rom. 6:3). When Jesus died on the Cross, He did so as our Substitute. Whenever we, as the sinner coming to Christ or the Believer already in Christ, evidence Faith in Him, in the Mind of God we are literally in Christ, and because of that Faith. We are in Him to such an extent that the Holy Spirit used the word *"baptized into His Death"* (Rom. 6:3-5). It is this Baptism alone which saves. Unfortunately, most people in reading this statement by Paul, think he is speaking of Water Baptism. He isn't! He is speaking of us when we got Saved, being *"baptized into the Death of Christ, Buried with Him by Baptism into Death, and raised with Him in Newness of Life"* (Rom. 6:3-5).

ONE GOD

This, as should be obvious, speaks of God the Father (Eph. 4:6). We can know Him only by our acceptance of His Son, and our Saviour, the Lord Jesus Christ, and according to what He did for us at the Cross. Jesus said:

"I am the Way, the Truth, and the Life. No man comes unto the Father, but by Me" (Jn. 14:6).

In one way or the other, every single one of these things listed by Paul pertains to the Cross. Please note the following:

• The only way to God the Father is through Jesus Christ (Jn. 14:6).

• The only way to Jesus Christ is, by and through, the Cross of Christ (Lk. 9:23; I Cor. 1:17).

• The only way to the Cross is a denial of self (Lk. 9:23-24).

THE HOUSE OF GOD AND THE HEAP OF RUINS

"And he removed from thence unto a mountain on the east of Bethel, and pitched his tent, having Bethel on the west, and Hai on the east: and there he built an Altar unto the LORD, and called upon the Name of the LORD" (Gen. 12:8).

Abraham is now on a mountain east of *"Bethel"* which means *"House of God,"* and west of *"Hai"* which means *"the heap of ruins."*

The *"Altar"* and the *"tent"* give us the two great features of Abraham's character. He was a worshipper of God, hence, the Cross, and a stranger in the world, hence, the tent.

The modern Believer, as all before us, finds himself in this same exact spot. Bethel, the House of God, is on one side, while Hai, the heap of ruins, is on the other. If the Believer stays with the Altar, *"Christ and Him Crucified,"* our lot will be the House of God; otherwise it will be the *"heap of ruins."* Incidentally, Hai is the same city which Joshua would attack some 470 years from this time (Josh., Chpts. 7-8).

The *"Altar"* as it regards Abraham, represented the fact that he knew that his mission in life was the coming

Redeemer. For the Seed of the woman to come into the world, God would have to raise up a people, which He would do from the loins of the Patriarch and the womb of Sarah. A land would have to be obtained for these people, and that land would be where he was now encamped — Palestine. His business was to claim it and, in effect, take it by Faith, which he did! As well, a son would have to be born to him and Sarah, which ultimately would come to pass also.

THE TENT

A *"tent"* speaks of temporary quarters. And by Abraham using a tent for a house, this proclaimed the fact that he knew all of this. In effect, he was a pilgrim and a stranger (Heb. 11:8-9, 13).

In essence, Abraham is a prototype, so to speak, of every Believer. That's why Paul referred to him as the *"father of us all"* (Rom. 4:16).

We must recognize that this world is not our home. We are, in effect, only passing through. While it was Abraham's mission in life to prepare for the coming of the Redeemer, even though that coming would be distant years in the future, actually some 2,000 years, it is our mission to tell the world that He has come. And one way or the other, every Believer fits into this category. Spiritually speaking, our domicile is to be a *"tent,"* which refers to our roots being in Heaven, instead of on Earth. While we may work at particular occupations to make a living for our families, our main business is the Lord Jesus Christ and His Power to save. If the Lord helps us to make sizeable amounts of money, we must use it for the Glory of God, and not for selfish purposes. If the *"Altar"* and the *"tent"* be our characteristics, then the *"House of God"* will be our destination. Otherwise, and there are no exceptions, there will be a *"heap of ruins."*

THE ALTAR

The phrase, *"And there he built an Altar unto the LORD,"* portrays the Object of His Faith. The *"Altar"* represents the Death of Christ on the Cross, and the giving of Himself in Sacrifice. Abraham would have offered a lamb on this Altar.

He would have slit the throat of this little animal with a knife, with the hot blood pouring out, typifying the Blood that would be shed by Christ on the Cross. He would then remove the skin from its body, showing that sin is more than just a surface problem, but goes to the very vitals.

Inasmuch as this was a Whole Burnt Offering, quite possibly he would not have taken the entrails from the body, but would have offered the entirety of the lamb. But yet, he very well could have taken the entrails and burned them separately on the Altar.

The Whole Burnt Offering signified that God would give His All, in reference to the Salvation of our souls, and that we in turn should give Him our all. In effect, it was a Consecration Offering, the same that we are to give today in our consecration to the Lord, and do so by Faith. Then, it was a lamb and Faith, while now, it is still a Lamb and Faith, with the Lamb being Christ and what He did for us at the Cross.

Surely the reader can see that throughout the Old Testament we see the Altar. It began, as far as we know, with Abel, as portrayed in the Fourth Chapter of Genesis. It continued unto the Coming of Christ, Who Himself became and, in fact, was that which the Sacrifices represented. He was the Lamb of God Who took away the sin of the world, and did so by going to the Cross (Jn. 1:29).

THE NAME OF THE LORD

The phrase, *"And called upon the Name of the LORD,"* implies public worship. It is evident, I think,

that Abraham's servants joined in the worship as well
(Gen. 24:12, 26-27). What Abraham did was also a
witness to his Canaanite neighbors, which let them
know he was a Friend of God (II Chron. 20:6-7; Isa.
41:7-8; James 2:23).

The idea of Abraham building the Altar and calling on the Name of the Lord is that he made known to
those around him the Redeemer, Who was to remove
the Divine wrath and restore the Blessing, which man
had lost in the Garden of Eden. This was ever before the
Patriarch, and we speak of the terrible need of man, and
that the need could be met only by the One Who was to
come. And the way that He would meet the need would
be to go to the Cross, of which the Altar was a Type.

And thus, we have the story of the Word of God.
The Fall took only minutes, while Redemption took
several millennia.

PARADISE LOST

Sometime ago in a museum in Washington, D.C., I
had the occasion to see the famous painting by Milton,
"PARADISE LOST". Milton powerfully portrayed the
Fall of man, showing the sublime heights from which
he had fallen, and the lowest depths to which he fell. It
was the most moving painting I have ever witnessed.

The only manner in which the depth of that Fall
can be evaluated is the price that was paid to redeem
man from his perilous position. The price was the
Cross, and if we attempt to make something else the
price, which to be sure is Satan's greatest effort, we
blaspheme! I think it cannot be judged in any other
fashion. It is ever the Cross! The Cross! The Cross!
Cannot we see it in every Book of the Bible? Every
Chapter? Every Verse? Even every line? And in reality, every Word?

THE CHURCH

The Church must come back to that which has redeemed us, or else the Church is doomed! The individual Believer must ever make the Cross the Object of his Faith, or else he is doomed as well! In fact, if we call upon the Name of the Lord, we can only do so on the basis of the Finished Work of Christ. If we attempt to do so from any other position, even though we may call it Faith or whatever name or label we would choose, the truth is, God will not hear such a petition. He will hear only that which anchors itself in the price that Christ paid at Calvary. The Holy Spirit will Work on no other platform or basis (Rom. 8:1-2, 11).

"Lord, as of old at Pentecost,
"You did Your Power display,
"With cleansing, purifying flame,
"Descend on us today."

"For mighty Works for You prepare,
"And strengthen every heart;
"Come, take possession of Your Own,
"And nevermore depart."

"All self consume, all sin destroy!
"With earnest zeal endue,
"Each waiting heart to work for You;
"O Lord, our Faith renew!"

"Speak, Lord! Before Your Throne we wait,
"Your Promise we believe,
"And will not let You go until,
"The blessing we receive."

ABRAHAM

CHAPTER

4

The Famine And Egypt

THE FAMINE AND EGYPT

THE FAMINE

"And Abram journeyed, going on still toward the south.

"And there was a famine in the land: and Abram went down into Egypt to sojourn there; for the famine was grievous in the land" (Gen. 12:9-10).

Abraham journeys further south. It will not be uneventful. Faith has its trials as well as its answer.

Faith must be tested, and great Faith must be tested greatly.

Abraham went south. While there is nothing wrong with the direction of *"south,"* there is definite wrong in where this particular south will lead, which is Egypt. The Lord had told Abraham to come to Canaan, not Egypt! There is no record that Abraham truly sought the Lord about this matter. In other words, Abraham going into Egypt was something the Lord did not generate or desire.

As a Believer, we must be very careful that we have the Mind of the Lord in all things. Actually, everything that the Lord does with us is to teach us this great Truth. Regrettably, it's not a Truth that is quickly or easily learned. If one such as Abraham, and he was one of the great Faith giants of the entirety of all time, could go astray, where does that leave us? This shows us that it doesn't matter who we are or how much Faith we might presently have, if we step outside of the Will of God, even to the slightest degree, we are then functioning in Satan's territory, which can lead to disastrous consequences. As Believers, if we feel we do not yet have the Mind of the Lord in a certain thing, we must stand still until we do have the Mind of the Lord, and refuse to move until that particular direction is perfectly ascertained.

God leaves nothing to chance. The Scripture tells us:

"The steps of a good man are ordered by the LORD: and he delights in His (God's) *Way"* (Ps. 37:23). If the Lord even minutely orders the steps of His Children, well then, we certainly should know that He orders the direction.

EGYPT

"And there was a famine in the land: and Abram went down into Egypt to sojourn there; for the famine was grievous in the land" (Gen. 12:10).

The famine is engineered by Satan, and done so with a particular goal in mind, which goal was to prevent the Birth of the Messiah.

Through the famine he would drive Abraham into Egypt, and with plans already laid for Sarah to be taken into Pharaoh's house, in order that she might become the mother of a child by the Egyptian king, thus defeating the Messianic Promise made to Abraham. But for the intervening Hand of God, the plan would have been successful up to a point. Sarah was barren, but Pharaoh didn't know that. So what are we saying?

We are saying that God goes with His Children, even when they are going in the direction that's not His Will. Thank God He does! Were that not the case, all of us would have been destroyed a long, long time ago.

But yet, even though the Lord does go with us, there is always a penalty attached to failure. While it is true that oftentimes we learn more things from our failures than we do our victories, still the lessons are very expensive.

A TEST OF FAITH

At the same time, we know that God could have overruled Satan as it regards the famine. But the Lord didn't do that. Instead, He would use the famine as a test of Faith. In other words, He would allow Satan certain latitude, even as He constantly does with all Believers, all in order that we might grow in Grace and the Knowledge of the Lord.

THE MODERN FAITH TEACHING

The church in the past several decades has been inundated with teaching on Faith, but if the truth be known, almost all of this particular teaching is wrong. The modern Faith teaching claims that the new creation man, the Born-Again man, can bring anything he so desires into existence. In other words, he now has the power to create. To be sure, there is a touch of truth in this; but here is where the true teaching of Faith parts from the false teaching.

The true Believer, operating on true Faith, which always speaks of the Cross of Christ as its Object, can definitely create certain things, but only in the Will of God. The false Faith teaching proclaims that the Will of God is whatever the new creation man says it is, in effect, committing the same sin that Adam and Eve committed in the Garden by listening to Satan, and perverting the Word of God. And, to be sure, the so-called Faith teaching of the *"Word of Faith"* people is definitely a perversion of the Word of God.

THE CONFESSION PRINCIPLE

They teach that the Believer's power of creation is wrapped up in his confession. In other words, as we have recently stated, whatever problem he thinks he faces, he must choose several Scriptures, which seem to address that problem, quote them over and over which is supposed to create, by the constant recital,

some type of energy in the spirit world, which will ultimately bring to pass that which is demanded.

To the carnal ear, such thinking sounds right, and
simply because the Word of God is being used. However,
and as stated, while it is the Word of God which is being
used, it is being used in all the wrong ways.

As stated, God will never allow His Word to be used
against Himself, and what do we mean by that?

THE WORD OF GOD, THE WISDOM OF GOD,
AND THE WILL OF GOD

The Will of God is always the primary objective for
the Believer, or at least it certainly should be! But
sometimes, due to our own self-will, God's Will cannot
be carried out as it ought to, which then His Wisdom
will dictate another course.

Was it the Perfect Will of God for this famine to
grip the land of Canaan, which would put Abraham in
dire straits? No, it wasn't! However, it was definitely
His Wisdom that this be done, and for particular reasons. Is it the will of a godly, loving parent to have to
apply corporal punishment to a wayward child? No,
it's not; however, it is definitely his wisdom to do so,
and because of a prevailing circumstance.

The idea, as taught by the Word of Faith people, that
a proper confession can ward off all adverse circumstances, is not taught in the Bible. If we judge the
rightness of a path by its exemption from trials and
tests, this is a great mistake. The path of obedience may
often be found most trying to flesh and blood. Thus,
in Abraham's case, he was not only called to encounter the Canaanite in the place to which God had called
him, but there was also *"a famine in the land."* Should
he, therefore, have concluded that he was not in the
right place? Assuredly not! This would have been to

judge according to the sight of his eyes, the very thing which Faith never does.

A GREAT TRIAL

There is, no doubt, that this was a deep trial to the heart of the Patriarch, even an inexplicable puzzle to nature; nevertheless, all the Ways that God leads are not at first easily understood and known.

For instance, when Paul was called into Macedonia, almost the first thing he had to encounter was the prison at Philippi. Thus, to a heart out of communion, this would have seemed to have been a deathblow to the entire mission. But Paul never questioned the rightness of his position; he was enabled to *"sing praises"* in the midst of all, assured that everything was just as it should be, and so it was; for whatever Satan's plans were, they would not at all succeed.

EVERY ATTACK BY SATAN

It really doesn't matter what Satan's plans were as it regards Paul. The truth is, even as with Abraham, this attack by Satan at Philippi was meant to destroy, or at least seriously weaken the Faith of the great Apostle. In fact, every single attack by Satan, irrespective as to whether it is financial, domestical, physical, or spiritual, is always but for one purpose and reason, and that is to destroy our Faith, or at least seriously weaken our Faith.

In doing this, Satan is just as satisfied for us to move our Faith from the correct Object of the Cross, or in other words, *"Jesus Christ and Him Crucified,"* to something else. While the something else might be good in its own right, and even Scriptural, if we make that, whatever it might be, the primary objective, then we've lost our way. That's why Paul said the following:

"For Christ sent me not to baptize, but to preach the Gospel: not with wisdom of words, lest the Cross of Christ should be made of none effect" (I Cor. 1:17).

THE SHIFT OF FAITH TO SOMETHING ELSE

That which occasioned Paul to write these words was the emphasis of Faith being shifted from the Cross to something else, and in this case, Water Baptism. While Water Baptism is definitely important and definitely Scriptural, it, nor anything else for that matter, must never be the objective, but rather the Cross of Christ.

Abraham should have reasoned accordingly: despite the famine, he was in the very place (Canaan) in which God had sent him; and evidently, he received no direction to leave it. True, the famine was there; and moreover, Egypt was at hand, offering deliverance from pressure; still the path of God's servant was plain. *"It is better to starve in Canaan, if it should be so, than live in luxury in Egypt; it is far better to suffer in God's path, than to be at ease in Satan's; it is better to be poor with Christ, if such should needs be, than rich without Him."*

CIRCUMSTANCES

Let's look at circumstances for a moment!

Abraham had much responsibility, possibly even as many as a thousand people to look after. As well, he had great herds of sheep and oxen, etc.

Considering there was a famine in the land, which made it very, very difficult to feed all of these animals, the natural heart would, no doubt, say that he should take the road to Egypt. But remember this, and it is critically important.

Egypt was not the place of God's Presence. There was no Altar in Egypt, no Communion. And the moment we trade the Altar for other things, we have just lost our way, and the end result will never be good.

The fact is, God had put Abraham in Canaan, not in Egypt. And the great problem with the modern Child of God as well, is that he leaves God's appointed place, and because of circumstances, he goes elsewhere. Oh, to be sure, Egypt always looks enticing and inviting, but this is not where God had told Abraham to occupy himself. It didn't matter that there was a famine, that there was hardship, that there were difficulties, Canaan was where God had brought the Patriarch, and it was in Canaan, hardships or not, where God intended for Abraham to stay.

A WRONG DIRECTION!

Concerning this wrong direction, Mackintosh says:

"Nothing can ever make up for the loss of our communion with God. Exemption from temporary pressure, and the accession of even the greatest wealth, are but poor equivalents for what one loses by diverging even a hair's breadth from the straight path of obedience."

He went on to say, *"Let us, instead of turning aside into Egypt, wait on God; and thus the trial, instead of proving to be an occasion of stumbling, will prove an opportunity for obedience."*

And then, *"Shall we deny Him by plunging again into what from which His Cross has forever delivered us? May God Almighty forbid! May He keep us in the hollow of His Hand, and under the Shadow of His Wings, until we see Jesus as He is, and be like Him, and with Him forever."*[1]

THE TEST OF FAITH

As stated, while every attack by Satan against us, and irrespective of its direction, is always against our

Faith, as well, God is always testing our Faith. And, to be sure, great Faith always must be tested greatly.

While the Lord knows our Faith, its strength, its power, its weaknesses, etc., the idea is that we know as well. And to be sure, our Faith is never as strong as we think it is.

Pure Faith always has the pure objective of the Cross! But, when the test comes, as it always will, we find, to our dismay, that there is much *"self-will"* mixed with our Faith. It is this which the Lord seeks to eradicate in us, exactly as He sought to eradicate such in Abraham.

Since the Lord began to give this Message of the Cross to me, actually the same Message which He gave to Paul and which the Apostle gave to us in his fourteen Epistles, it has been most interesting not only to observe myself, but to observe other Christians in this Faith endeavor.

THE WAY OF THE CROSS

I have watched many embark upon this Way of the Cross (I Cor. 1:18), and then meet with tests, even as Abraham, in which they would forsake the Land of Canaan, the place where God wants them, and depart for Egypt. Their answer? *"The Cross,"* they say, *"doesn't work for me."* How utterly ridiculous!

No, it's not the Cross that has failed, for it can never fail. It is self-will, which came into the picture that caused the failure, whatever it might have been. But always remember this:

The failure was not so much in what you did that was wrong, whatever it might have been, but rather in the departing from true Faith, which is always Christ and Him Crucified (I Cor. 1:23; 2:2). That and that alone is Satan's objective. That and that alone is his goal — forsake the Cross, i.e., *"the Faith"* (Gal. 2:20).

A FAILURE OF FAITH?

Did Abraham's Faith fail?

Did Simon Peter's Faith fail regarding the denial of his Lord?

Jesus said this of Peter:

"Simon, Simon, behold, Satan has desired to have you, that he may sift you as wheat:

"But I have prayed for you, that your Faith fail not" (Lk. 22:31-32).

Faith does not fail as long as Faith does not quit. While Abraham and Peter and, in fact, every other Believer who's ever lived, had a failure in their Faith, or so they would have thought, the truth is, their Faith didn't fail. Had their Faith failed, they would have quit. In other words, Abraham would have turned his back on God, and so would have Peter. But they didn't do that!

Faith at times stumbles and falls exactly as unbelief. But the difference is: unbelief stays down, while Faith gets up and continues on its journey.

There is no such thing as a Believer who hasn't had a failure in one way or the other. But, one may rest assured that as long as one is believing, one's Faith actually has not failed.

EGYPT

"And it came to pass, when he was come near to enter into Egypt, that he said unto Sarai his wife, Behold now, I know that you are a fair woman to look upon" (Gen. 12:11).

It is not possible to go into Egypt, spiritually speaking, without partaking of Egypt. The Christian who thinks he can beat this game is only fooling himself. If we go into Egypt, we ultimately become like Egypt.

Much is at stake here, even the great Plan of Redemption. At this time, Sarah is about 65 years old, but yet a very beautiful woman. She would live to be 127 (Gen. 23:1).

Satan's plan was formidable. The entirety of Faith on the Earth at this time, at least as far as we know, is wrapped up in Abraham. To be frank, in a sense, it is the same presently.

Faith, and we speak of Faith as it regards leadership, is now ensconced in *"Apostles, Prophets, Evangelists, Pastors, and Teachers"* (Eph. 4:11). Now remember, we are speaking of leadership. All Believers have Faith, but it is not Faith for leadership, that ensconced, as stated, in the fivefold Calling. If this breaks down, and we continue to speak of Faith leadership, then the entirety of the church ultimately breaks down. And regrettably, that's exactly what has happened in the last few decades.

All Faith must be anchored in the Word of God, which in reality is the Story of the Cross. To be particular, our Faith must ever have as its Object the Cross of Christ (Rom. 6:3-11; I Cor. 1:17-18, 21, 23; 2:2, 5; Gal. 2:20-21; 6:14; Col. 2:14-15; I Pet. 1:18-20).

Satan's plan with Abraham was that he would leave Canaan as a result of the famine, which he did, go into Egypt, where the plan would then be set in motion for Pharaoh to impregnate Sarah, which was meant by the Evil One to thwart the coming of the Redeemer. It was quite a plan, and it almost succeeded. As stated, but for the intervening Hand of God, which we will study more in depth upon arriving at those Passages, he definitely would have succeeded.

And yet, I do not see how that Satan thought he could succeed in this, simply because Sarah was barren. It seems that the Scripture is clear that she could not conceive, whether by Abraham or someone else. We know that Abraham was not barren, simply because he was able to father a child through the servant girl, Hagar.

As well, Satan did not have any power to heal Sarah. So, for her to be impregnated by Pharaoh and to have a child, could not be; nevertheless, it seems this is what Satan was attempting to do.

DECEPTION

"Therefore it shall come to pass, when the Egyptians shall see you, that they shall say, This is his wife: and they will kill me, but they will save you alive.

"Say, I pray you, you are my sister: that it may be well with me for your sake; and my soul shall live because of you" (Gen. 12:13).

Concerning this, Matthew Henry said:

"Observe a great fault which Abraham was guilty of in denying his wife, and pretending that she was his sister. The Scripture is impartial in relating the miscarriages of the most celebrated Saints which are recorded, not for our imitation, but for our admonition; that he who thinks he stands, may take heed lest he fall.

"His fault was, disassembling his relation to Sarah, equivocating concerning it, and teaching his wife, and probably, all his attendants, to do so too, what he said about her being his sister, was in a sense true (Gen. 20:12), but with a purpose to deceive. He concealed a truth, so as in effect to deny it, and to expose thereby both his wife and the Egyptians to sin."[2]

By this deception, Abraham greatly placed in danger the entirety of the Plan of God. He seemed to think that the great Promise of God concerning *"his seed"* (Gen. 12:7), concerned him alone. In other words, as it regarded his thinking, Sarah didn't matter that much respecting the carrying out of this great prediction. He would merely obtain another woman, which showed up in him sinning regarding Hagar. In fact, the Lord would bluntly tell the Patriarch at a later time, *"As for*

Sarah your wife . . . I will bless her, and give you a son also of her . . . and she shall be a mother of nations; kings of people shall be of her" (Gen. 17:15-16). In all of this we find the following:

• God had a Plan: That Plan was for Abraham and Sarah to bring a son into the world, through whom ultimately the Messiah, the Redeemer of the world would come.

• Satan had a plan: That plan was to foil the Plan of God, and to do so through the weakness and cowardice of Abraham.

• Abraham had a plan: But Abraham's plan is not now the Plan of God, but is rather a plan of deception, which God can never honor.

PRESUMPTION

Abraham erroneously thinks that by offering his wife to the Harem of Pharaoh that he will save himself. He didn't seem to realize, at least at this time, that the Plan of God included Sarah, as much as it included him. Perhaps her being barren, not able to bear children, caused him to dismiss her in this capacity. But he was wrong, dead wrong!

All of this was presumption. The Patriarch merely presumed certain things, and because of an imperfect Faith.

True Faith will never sell God short, and true Faith will never resort to the deceptive machinations of mere man. True Faith always reaches for the impossible, and will settle for nothing less than God's Best. In fact, as it regards true Faith, it is either all or nothing! God would not condone any of the efforts of Abraham. It must be totally of God, or else it is not of Faith. Now let the reader understand that.

Anytime we mix our plans into the Plan of God, His Plan is instantly nullified. True Faith is always all of God and none of man. While man is the instrument, it is God Who does the doing, with man intended to be obedient.

SARAH'S BEAUTY

"And it came to pass, that, when Abram was come into Egypt, the Egyptians beheld the woman that she was very fair" (Gen. 12:14).

It is said by some that at this time, Egyptian custom demanded that any foreign prince coming into Egypt would have to give into the Harem of Pharaoh a daughter or a sister. This being done, it was supposed to guarantee the good behavior of such a one while in Egypt. Refusing to do such was considered to be an act of war.

So, Abraham would claim that Sarah was his sister, which would make her acceptable for the Harem of Pharaoh.

PHARAOH'S HOUSE

"The princes also of Pharaoh saw her, and commended her before Pharaoh: and the woman was taken into Pharaoh's house" (Gen. 12:15).

Whatever was the custom of those particular times regarding the question at hand, the Text seems to indicate that there was much more to the situation regarding Sarah, than for her to merely become a member of the Harem, which means that she was just one of many women.

The Text strongly implies that Pharaoh was looking for a particular woman, one whom he imagined to be of particular quality, who could be the mother of his child, and, therefore, the heir of the throne of Egypt. It's evident this was Satan's plan, devised to defeat the Promise of God, which would ultimately stop the coming of the Messiah into the world; consequently, we can see how fully Abraham fell into the trap, which was well laid for him. Even though he was a man of

Faith, in fact one of the greatest men of Faith who has ever lived, still his present position, strangely enough, is because of unbelief. Despite the famine, he should have remained in Canaan and trusted the Lord for deliverance. Resorting to Egypt, which he no doubt did with the entirety of his entourage, is never without its compromise and attendant results.

RICHES

"And he entreated Abram well for her sake: and he had sheep, and oxen, and he asses, and menservants, and maidservants, and she asses, and camels" (Gen. 12:16).

We find from this Passage that Pharaoh valued Sarah very highly. Even though she was approximately 65 years old, she evidently was beautiful, to say the least. It is not unlikely at all that the Lord had a hand in this, regarding her beauty, but most definitely which did not pertain to Pharaoh.

In this one Verse of Scripture, we have the position and problem of the modern church. It, as Abraham at this time, has joined Egypt and, in fact, has been enriched, however, as there was no Altar or Sacrifice or Communion with God in Egypt, there is none now as it regards the church and the world. While the church may be able to boast of riches, it can little boast of Power with God. Until Abraham went back to Canaan and back to the Altar, Revelation, and Communion with the Lord were stopped.

Revelation is found only at the Cross, and even then it comes *"precept upon precept, precept upon precept; line upon line, line upon line; here a little, and there a little"* (Isa. 28:10).

THE PLAGUE

"And the LORD plagued Pharaoh and his house with great plagues because of Sarai Abram's wife" (Gen. 12:17).

Concerning this, Matthew Henry said:

"Let us notice the danger Sarah was in, and her deliverance from this danger. If God did not deliver us, many a time, out of those straits and distresses which we bring ourselves into, by our own sin and folly, and which therefore we could not accept any deliverance, we should soon be ruined; nay, we had been ruined long before this. He deals not with us according to our deserts."[3]

In what manner Pharaoh came to know that the plagues falling on his house were because of Sarah, we aren't told.

Sarah was blameless in this, the fault being that of Abraham. From this Passage, we learn that the Believer can be a blessing or a curse; it all depends on his Faith, and at this time, Abraham was faithless, or he wouldn't have been there to begin with.

The cause of all problems is the Believer leaving the Cross, and the solution to all problems is the Believer going back to the Cross. When Abraham left Canaan to go to Egypt, he left the Altar (Gen. 12:8). When he went back to Canaan, he went back to the Altar (Gen. 13:4). It is always the Cross, of which the Altar was a Type.

WHAT HAVE YOU DONE UNTO ME?

"And Pharaoh called Abram and said, What is this that you have done unto me? why did you not tell me that she was your wife?" (Gen. 12:18).

Abraham had told those who were representing Pharaoh that Sarah was his sister. In fact, this was a half-truth. She was the daughter of his father, but not the daughter of his mother (Gen. 20:12). But because he intended to deceive, God looked at this episode as a *"lie."*

As a Child of God, even a man of Faith, and that despite his present situation, it lay within the power of Abraham to be a blessing or a curse. However, the curse comes only because of wrongdoing on the part of the Believer. It is not possible for a Believer to knowingly and willingly put a curse on anyone. Such activity is always of Satan; however, the Believer will definitely be accursed if his faith is in the wrong place, even as Abraham.

As we've already stated, in the path of Faith the Christian is a blessing to the world, but in the path of self-will, a curse.

QUESTIONS

"Why did you say, She is my sister? so I might have taken her to me to wife: now therefore behold your wife, take her, and go your way" (Gen. 12:19).

Pharaoh had three questions for Abraham:

- *"What is this that you have done to me?"*
- *"Why did you not tell me that she was your wife?"*
- *"Why said you, She is my sister?"*

At this time, Egypt is at least one of the most powerful nations in the world, which means that Pharaoh was one of the most powerful men in the world. Little did he realize the magnitude of these questions.

As he speaks this day to Abraham, little does he know, despite Abraham's present problems, that this is the man the Holy Spirit would refer to as *"the father of us all"* (Rom. 4:16). And yet, the picture that he would get of the Patriarch would be one of subterfuge, chicanery, and deception.

But before we criticize Abraham, we had best look at ourselves. Are we in the path of Faith or that of self-will? According to that answer, we will be a blessing or a curse!

DEPARTURE

"And Pharaoh commanded his men concerning him: and they sent him away, and his wife, and all that he had" (Gen. 12:20).

Because of Abraham, Pharaoh and his family are plagued with great plagues, and this heathen prince hurries this man of God out of his land as he would chase away a pestilence.

The implication here is, even though the Monarch was very unhappy concerning the turn of events, he knew within his spirit that this man Abraham was more than meets the eye. With anyone else he would, no doubt, have taken off their heads; however, with Abraham, the implication is that he was careful not to do anything to him, or even retrieve the animals which he had given to the Patriarch.

From the Scripture, we're given the bare bones of what actually took place. The mighty Pharaoh saw the Power of God, even though it was in a negative way. What effect it had on him, other than this which we see in the Scripture, we aren't told.

"Down at the Cross where my Saviour died,
"Down where for cleansing from sin I cried,
"There to my heart was the Blood applied;
"Glory to His Name!"

"I am so wondrously saved from sin;
"Jesus so sweetly abides within;
"There at the Cross where He took me in;
"Glory to His Name!"

"Oh, precious fountain that saves from sin!
"I am so glad I have entered in;
"There Jesus saves me and keeps me clean;
"Glory to His Name!"

"Come to this fountain so rich and sweet;
"Cast your poor soul at the Saviour's Feet;
"Plunge in today and be made complete;
"Glory to His Name!"

ABRAHAM

CHAPTER

5

Repentance

REPENTANCE

UP

"And Abram went up out of Egypt, he, and his wife, and all that he had, and Lot with him, into the south" (Gen. 13:1).

If Abraham went *"down"* into Egypt in Chapter 12, Grace brings him *"up"* out of Egypt in Chapter 13.

He went back to the mountaintop where his tent had been at the beginning, *"Unto the place of the Altar, which he had made there at the first,"* and there, doubtless with tears and shame, he called by Sacrifice, on the Name of the Lord.

His backslidings were forgiven, his soul was restored, and he resumes his true life as a pilgrim and a worshipper with his tent and his Altar; neither of which he had in Egypt.

In all of this we learn God's Way of Restoration, and God's manner of Restoration.

Even though the little word *"up"* refers here to a geographical setting, in this case north, it has a Spiritual connotation as well. To go to Egypt, Abraham had to go *"down,"* which, as well, even though geographical, presented a Spiritual Direction also. Whichever way we go as Believers, it is always either *"up"* or *"down."* So the question we must ask ourselves is, *"What direction am I travelling?"* Once again we come back to Faith.

To go *"down"* into Egypt, he did so because of a lapse in Faith. To come *"up"* out of Egypt, Faith is now regained, and will be proven by the Altar once again coming into view.

But yet, considering that Lot was with him, Abraham has not fully made the second surrender of leaving his kindred and his father's house, even as the Lord had demanded (Gen. 12:1). That surrender would come shortly.

RICH

"And Abraham was very rich in cattle, in silver, and in gold" (Gen. 13:2).

The truth is, Abraham could very well have been, one of the richest men in the world of his day. He had in his employ, 318 men which performed certain duties, and also were trained as soldiers. Many, if not most, of these men, were married, and, no doubt, had children. So the entire group headed up by Abraham, could very well have been approximately 1,000 people.

Strangely enough, we do not know how Abraham found the Lord. Did the Lord appear to him visibly so? Some think that it may have been Shem, the son of Noah, who witnessed to him. While that certainly is possible, we note in Hebrews, Chapter 11, that while Noah is listed there and so is Abraham, Shem is not mentioned. So, we are left clueless as it regards the manner in which the Lord revealed Himself and His Plan to the Patriarch. This we do know, however, whatever did happen with Abraham, as it regards that Revelation, it so shook him that he determined to carry out what God had told him to do, even packing up and leaving Ur of the Chaldees, which was one of the most advanced cities in the world of that time.

I suppose if the Holy Spirit had desired that we know the manner of Abraham's Conversion, that He would have told us. And yet, this man plays so prominently in the Salvation and our lives lived for God, as it regards the entirety of humanity. As we shall see, he was given the meaning of Justification by Faith, and there is every evidence, that the Lord showed him exactly as to the coming of the Redeemer, the Lord Jesus Christ, and the price that He would pay at Calvary's Cross. In fact, Jesus Himself said, and regarding this very thing:

"Your father Abraham rejoiced to see My day: and he saw it, and was glad" (Jn. 8:56).

Jesus, using the term *"My day,"* was speaking of His entire Mission, including Calvary and the Resurrection. It is obvious that He showed Abraham all of this, quite possibly in a vision.

IS IT PROPER FOR A BELIEVER TO DESIRE TO BE RICH?

No, it isn't proper!

It is very proper for a Believer to ask the Lord to bless him in whatever his endeavor may be, providing it is Scriptural. And, if the Lord chooses to bless one to the extent that it does make one rich, they should do two things:

• They should take care of their family.

• They should then support the Work of God to help take this great Message of Redemption, this Message of the Cross, to the entirety of the world.

The other day a businessman told Jim Woolsey, *"It's hard to find a place where it is proper to sow the seed of the Gospel."* And that brother was entirely right. But then he said to Jim:

"I think I have now found that place," and he was speaking of THE SONLIFE BROADCASTING NETWORK.

We are responsible not only to give to the Work of God, but, as well, to know to what and whom we are giving, and how our money is being used.

RESTORATION

"And he went on his journeys from the south even to Bethel, unto the place where his tent had been at the beginning, between Bethel and Hai" (Gen. 13:3).

We learn from this the true character of Divine Restoration. The first thing we must learn about this is that God does everything in a way entirely worthy of Himself. Whether He Creates, Redeems, Converts, Restores, or Provides, He can only act like Himself.

What is worthy of Himself is, ever and only, His Standard of Action.

The problem of humanity, even redeemed man, is to *"limit the Holy One of Israel."* Mackintosh says, *"And in nothing are we so prone to limit Him as in His restoring Grace."*[1]

From the cowardly escapade in Egypt, Abraham is brought back to where his tent had been *"at the beginning"* . . . unto the place of the Altar where he had made there *"at the first."*

Mackintosh commented on this, saying:

"We, in the self-righteousness of our hearts, might imagine that such an one should take a lower place than that which he had formerly occupied; and so he should, were it a question of his merit or his character; but inasmuch as it is altogether a question of Grace, it is God's prerogative to fix the Standard of restoration."

Mackintosh further said:

"He will either not restore at all, or else restore in such a way as to magnify and glorify the riches of His Grace. Thus, when the leper was brought back, he was actually conducted 'to the door of the Tabernacle of the congregation.' When the prodigal returned, he was sat down at the table with his father; when Peter was restored, he was able to stand before the men of Israel, and say, 'You denied the Holy One and the Just' — the very thing which he had done himself, under the most aggravated circumstances."[2]

The idea is, when God brings the soul back to himself, it is always in the full Power of Grace, and the full Confidence of Faith.

HINDRANCES TO RESTORATION

The three greatest hindrances to Restoration are *"legalism,"* *"license,"* and *"self-righteousness."* Strangely enough, these triple problems prove at the same time to be the greatest danger to the one restored.

It is impossible to restore the soul through legalism, and yet, that's where most of the church places its efforts. This pertains to the rules of men, rather than the Cross of Christ.

Or else, Restoration is looked at in a light way, concluding that sin is of little matter, which pertains to *"license."* If Grace abounds much more than sin, and it definitely does, then we might continue to sin that Grace may abound, some foolishly conclude (Rom. 5:20; 6:1).

Continuing with the problem of *"license,"* we are not restored in order that we may the more lightly go and sin again, but rather that we may *"go and sin no more."* Mackintosh goes on to say, *"The deeper my sense of the Grace of Divine restoration, the deeper will be my sense of the Holiness of it also."*[3]

Concerning this, David said, *"He restores my soul: He leads me in the paths of Righteousness for His Name's sake"* (Ps. 23:3).

John said, and dealing with the same problem, *"If we confess our sins, He is faithful and just to forgive us our sins, and to cleanse us from all unrighteousness"* (I Jn. 1:9).

The proper path and, in fact, the only path for the Divinely-restored soul, is *"the path of Righteousness."* To talk of Grace while walking in unrighteousness, is as the Apostle says, to turn *"the Grace of God into lasciviousness."*

SELF-RIGHTEOUSNESS

Mackintosh continues, *"If Grace reigns through Righteousness unto eternal life, it also manifests itself in Righteousness, in the outflow of that life. The Grace that forgives us our sins cleanses us from all unrighteousness. Those things must never be separated. When taken together, they furnish a triumphant answer to the legalism and the license of the human heart."*[4]

But possibly, an even greater problem than the problem of *"license,"* is the problem of *"legalism."* In simple terms, this is the formulation of laws, rules, and regulations, all made up by men, with the claim that abiding accordingly to such guarantees Righteousness and Holiness, etc. It doesn't! The self-righteous love to wield the legal stick of rules and regulations, once again, all made up by men. And let it be understood, any direction other than Christ and the Cross, whatever that direction might be, ever how religious it might be, always and without fail, leads to self-righteousness. In other words, if our Faith is in anything except Christ and the Cross, self-righteousness will definitely be the result. And it must be remembered, it was self-righteousness that nailed Christ to the Cross.

The greatest example of all of this was the *"Law of God"* given to Moses, and, thereby, to Israel. These were Laws designed by God, and which fit the human problem in every capacity. But despite their simplicity, men could not keep them because of our fallen nature.

However, Israel turned the effort into a form of righteousness, better known as self-righteousness. In other words, all of the efforts at law-keeping made Israel feel holy. As someone has said, *"The doing of religion is the biggest narcotic there is."*

Notice that we said *"the doing of religion!"* All of this has to do with legalism. Legalism is always *"doing,"* while Grace pertains to that which is *"done."*

So, men make up rules, and demand that other men live by them, and religious men do this more than all. It is claimed that the doing of such makes one acceptable. But, of course, the acceptance is in the eyes of other men, and never in the Eyes of God. The Lord cannot accept legalism or self-righteousness in any capacity. Paul plainly said, and bluntly so, *"If you be circumcised, Christ shall profit you nothing."*

He then said, *"Christ is become of no effect unto you, whosoever of you are justified by the Law; you are fallen from Grace"* (Gal. 5:2, 4). I don't know how much clearer it could be.

THE RESTORATION METHODS
OF THE MODERN CHURCH

Actually, Restoration, as it regards the modern church, is in name only. There is no restoration. Whenever we forsake the Bible and begin to devise our own ways, the results, as it regards Spiritual things, are always catastrophic. God has a Way that's found in His Word, and in His Word only, and if we depart from that we are then left with the foolishness of man, and foolishness it is.

For instance, in one particular Pentecostal denomination, if a preacher has a problem of any nature, he is forbidden to preach behind the pulpit in any church of that denomination, for a period of two years. He may preach in jails, prisons, nursing homes, and on street corners, and even preach to children or teens, but he cannot preach behind the pulpit in the main Sanctuary. How ridiculous can we be!

If it's wrong to preach one place, then it's wrong to preach any place. But when man starts to make the rules, thereby forsaking the Word of God, as stated, it becomes more and more ludicrous.

And then, all of these denominations, at least the ones of which I am aware, demand from six months to two years of psychological counseling. Pure and simple, this is a joke! The world of psychology holds absolutely no answers whatsoever to the Spiritual needs of man. For anyone to think it does, portrays, in a glaring way, one's Spiritual and Scriptural ignorance. I don't mean to be unkind or sarcastic, but I don't know any other way to state the case. When the church resorts to the likes of Freud to solve its spiritual problems, thereby forsaking the Word of God, it is in serious spiritual trouble indeed!

THE CROSS

To which we've already alluded, Biblical Restoration is very simple. The reason anyone fails is because their faith is in something other than the Cross of Christ. Consequently, such a person must be pointed to the Cross. Listen to what Paul said:

"But God forbid that I should glory (boast)*, save in the Cross of our Lord Jesus Christ, by Whom the world is crucified unto me, and I unto the world"* (Gal. 6:14).

Now notice that the Apostle said that the only way to Victory over the world, and one might quickly add, *"the world, the flesh, and the Devil,"* is by trusting in what Christ has done for us at the Cross. Let us say it again, the Cross of Christ is the answer to sin and, in fact, the only answer for sin.

To point anyone in that direction, and I speak of the direction of the Cross, is the only true Restoration there actually is (Gal. 6:1).

ENEMIES OF THE CROSS

Paul also said, *"For many walk, of whom I have told you often, and now tell you even weeping, that they are the enemies of the Cross of Christ:*

"Whose end is destruction, whose god is their belly, and whose glory is in their shame, who mind earthly things" (Phil. 3:18-19).

To present to the sinner seeking to be Saved anything except the Cross of Christ, simply means that the one doing such a thing is an enemy of the Cross.

For the ways of the world to be substituted for those who need Restoration in place of the Cross, once again, means that those who do such things can be labeled as none other than enemies of the Cross.

When Jesus said that this Way was a *"narrow way,"* He meant exactly what He said (Mat. 7:14). In fact, the exact width of this *"way,"* which leads to Glory is the width of the Cross.

The Cross of Christ is not something that is neutral. As well, it's not one of several ways. It is the only Way; therefore, it stands to reason if other ways are presented, that means the Cross has been rejected, which places such a one in the position of being an *"enemy."*

When the Lord first began to open up to me the Revelation of the Cross, which began in 1997, my immediate thoughts concerning the far greater majority of the church, and as it regards the Cross, were that ignorance was the culprit. While I'm sure that ignorance is the problem in many hearts and lives, I have since come to the conclusion that the major problem is unbelief.

Paul said, *"I am crucified with Christ: nevertheless I live; yet not I, but Christ lives in me: and the life which I now live in the flesh I live by the Faith of the Son of God, Who loved me, and gave Himself for me.*

"I do not frustrate the Grace of God: for if Righteousness come by the Law, then Christ is dead in vain" (Gal. 2:20-21).

All of this means that if any man can live a victorious life other than by Faith in Christ and what Christ did at the Cross, then Christ needlessly came down here to die on that Cross. But the truth is, Righteousness cannot come by any method other than Christ and what He did at the Cross, and our Faith in that Finished Work. That's why Paul referred to it as *"the Faith."*

THE ALTAR

"Unto the place of the Altar, which he had made there at the first: and there Abram called on the Name of the LORD" (Gen. 13:4).

Here we have it in black and white. When Abraham was walking in Victory, his trust, Faith, and confidence were totally and completely in the Cross of Christ (Gen. 12:7). And now Abraham, coming from a place of defeat back to Victory, must come back to the Altar, i.e., the Cross. There is no other way!

The Scripture plainly says that Abraham *"called on the Name of the LORD."* One cannot do this unless it is done in the spirit of the Cross. We must ever understand that every single thing we receive from the Lord comes to us exclusively, by and through Christ, and what He has done for us at the Cross. So when we call on Him, it must be with the idea in mind, regarding the price that He paid at Calvary. Prayer is answered only on that basis, and that basis alone! (I Cor. 1:17-18, 23).

VICTORY!

I want to make a statement, although very simple, it could very well be one of the most important statements you've ever read, as it regards our living for God. It is as follows:

"God cannot give victories to sinful men. He can only give Victories to His Son and our Lord and Saviour, Jesus Christ."

The idea is, the Lord has given total Victory, and in every capacity, to the Lord Jesus Christ, which, in essence, was done at Calvary. It was done at the Cross. Therefore, whatever Victory or Victories we might obtain must come exclusively through Him, which demands our Faith in Him, and in what He has done for us.

We must understand that everything Christ did was exclusively for us. He did nothing for Himself! He did nothing for Heaven! He did nothing for Angels! He did nothing for God, simply because God needs nothing. So what He did, and in all its capacity, was done exclusively for you and me.

As well, He paid a terrible price for all that He did. And considering the price that He paid, doesn't it stand to reason that He would want us to have all for which He died? Of course He does! So, if we don't have these Victories, the fault is ours and not His. That should be understandable from the beginning.

In one way or the other, the whole world, at least for all practical purposes, is calling on the Name of the Lord; however, almost none call on Him correctly. In other words, they call on Him in ways other than the Means of the Cross.

That particular Jesus, God will not recognize or honor, with Paul referring to such as *"another Jesus"* (II Cor. 11:4). And regrettably, that's where much of the modern church world presently is. Pure and simple, they are worshipping *"another Jesus."*

"I've been on Mount Pisgah's lofty height,
"And I've satisfied my longing heart's desire;
"For I caught a glimpse of Glory bright,
"And my soul is burning with fire."

"I will walk with Jesus, bless His Name,
"And to be like Him I every day aspire;
"For His Love is like a heavenly flame,
"And my soul is burning with the fire."

"I my all upon the Altar lay,
"As I to my closet lovingly retire;
"And the flame consumes while there I pray,
"And my soul is burning with the fire."

"By Faith's eyes I scan the ocean's foam,
"And beyond I see the haven I desire;
"There I view the beacon lights of home,
"And my soul is burning with the fire."

ABRAHAM

CHAPTER

6

Abraham And Lot

ABRAHAM AND LOT

"And Lot also, which went with Abram, had flocks, and herds, and tents" (Gen. 13:5).

As we shall see, the riches seemed to turn Lot's head; however, it didn't have that effect upon Abraham.

It is really never the riches that are at fault, but rather the individual involved. Why is it that Lot would allow such to turn his head from the Lord, even as it does millions today, and it had no such effect on Abraham?

Too oftentimes the church deals only with the symptoms instead of the real problem. Actually, that's just about the case for all time. The failure is actually the symptom, whatever the failure might be, but it's not exactly the real problem. In fact, it never is!

The church, for all practical purposes, has borrowed this thinking from the world of humanistic psychology. This nefarious system teaches that man's problem is environment, lack of education, or that which is hereditary. So they think if they can address these issues, man's problem will be solved.

It won't! These are all outward or external situations which have no bearing on what the real problem actually is.

SIN

The real problem is sin, whether personal, or sin in general, i.e., original sin, and we must ever understand that sin comes in many and varied forms. The only cure for sin is Christ and the Cross. But instead, we attack the symptom, instead of addressing the real problem. That's the reason that Jesus said:

"You shall know the Truth, and the Truth shall make you free" (Jn. 8:32). Man's problem is he believes a lie and that includes the church. Pure and simple, that's the problem.

What is Truth?

The Truth is Christ and what He did for us at the Cross. Listen to what He said:

"I am the Way, the Truth, and the Life: no man comes unto the Father, but by Me" (Jn. 14:6).

He then said:

"And I, if I be lifted up from the Earth, will draw all men unto Me" (Jn. 12:32).

Being *"lifted up"* spoke of the death that He would die on the Cross. As well, the only way that we can draw men to Victory is to draw them to Christ and the Cross. If we attempt to draw them in any other manner, we will draw them to that, other than the Lord. And that's what the majority of the modern Church is doing. It is drawing men to denominations, to Psychology, to preachers, to the promise of money, to all types of things. But, it is little drawing men to Christ.

DWELL TOGETHER?

"And the land was not able to bear them, that they might dwell together: for their substance was great, so that they could not dwell together" (Gen. 13:6).

Abraham had been told by the Lord to leave his kindred (Gen. 12:1). But he brought his kindred with him. It seems that his father Terah slowed him down in his obedience, until death took Terah out of the way. Lot followed Abraham on further, but it seems plain that Lot was, from the very beginning, borne onward rather by Abraham's influence and example, than by his own Faith in God. In other words, it seems that Lot functioned on borrowed Faith.

It does seem, however, that he made it at last, inasmuch as the Holy Spirit, through Peter, referred to him as *"that righteous man,"* and *"his righteous soul"* (II Pet. 2:7-8).

In no way do I want to demean Lot, but at the same time we must not overrate him.

THE CHURCH

In fact, Abraham and Lot and their families actually constituted the Church of that particular day and time. While this *"Church"* had its problems in the spiritual sense, at the same time, it had been blessed abundantly in a financial sense. Please allow me to make this statement:

We (and I speak of Jimmy Swaggart Ministries) preach a prosperity Gospel, but we do not preach a greed Gospel. They are two different things. We believe the Lord blesses and blesses abundantly. We believe that when a person comes to Christ, their entire situation including the finances, begins to improve. In fact, I believe that financial prosperity is just as much a part of the Gospel as Divine Healing. I believe we should preach that, because the Bible teaches it (II Cor. 9:6).

But the primary mission of the Church, at least that which the Lord desires of the Church, is not monetary enrichment. The primary purpose of the Church in Abraham's day was certainly not enrichment, even though God abundantly blessed the Patriarch, with Lot *"getting in on the Blessing."*

THE PLAN OF REDEMPTION

The primary purpose of the Church was and is the Plan of Redemption, which would be brought about by God becoming Man, and dying on the Cross of Calvary. Abraham was to play a tremendous part in all of this, and that was his mission. The Lord would show the Patriarch the great Doctrine of Justification by Faith (Gen. 15:6). He was to understand what that meant, and more particularly, to Whom it pointed, namely Christ. This was the mission and nothing else!

I'm afraid that the modern church has by and large forgotten its mission. In the hearts and lives of far too many, the idea is not Righteousness but rather Rolex's. The idea is not Salvation, but rather secular pleasure. The idea is not the true Moving and Operation of the Holy Spirit, but rather entertainment. The idea is not Holiness, but rather Heaven on Earth.

The *"substance"* of the modern church is *"great."* It no longer has to say *"silver and gold have I none."* But the sad fact is, no longer, as well, can it say, *"but such as I have give I thee: in the Name of Jesus Christ of Nazareth rise up and walk"* (Acts 3:6).

STRIFE

"And there was a strife between the herdmen of Abraham's cattle and the herdmen of Lot's cattle: and the Canaanite and the Perizzite dwelled then in the land" (Gen. 13:7).

The outward cause of Lot's foray into Sodom was the strife between his herdsmen and those of Abraham. But the fact is, when one is not really walking as one should, something will occasion his stumbling. The outward cause is merely the trigger, while the real problem lies elsewhere.

To Abraham, the strife between the herdsmen, as distasteful as it was, afforded an occasion for exhibiting the beautiful Power of Faith, and the moral elevation on which Faith ever sets the possessor thereof. Mackintosh said:

"However, the strife no more produced the worldliness in Lot than it produced the Faith in Abraham; it only manifested, in the case of each, what was really there."

He then went on to say:

"Thus it is always: controversies and divisions arise in the Church, and many stumble thereby, and are driven back into the world in one way or another. They then lay the blame on the controversies and division, whereas the truth is, that these things were only

the means of developing the real condition of the soul, and the bent of the heart. The world was in the heart, and would be reached by some route or another."[1]

THE CANAANITE AND THE PERIZZITE

The Holy Spirit made mention of these two heathen tribes for a purpose and reason. The idea is, whatever happened between Abraham and Lot was observed by these who knew not God. And the question is, what did they see?

They saw in Abraham a beautiful and gracious spirit. And, to be sure, events and circumstances, especially those that are negative, always tend to bring out what is in the spirit of the man. An outward show is one thing; however, pressure reveals what the container really holds.

What did they see in Lot? The details we aren't given; however, I think it is obvious that the spirit of Lot in no way resembled that of Abraham. As we have already stated, Lot, it seems, was functioning on borrowed Faith. Regrettably, that is the condition of much of the modern church presently. It has little faith of its own, but rather borrows from someone who genuinely has Faith, or else is thought to have faith. Unfortunately, the latter is the situation in most cases. The one being followed has no faith either.

FAITH

The Faith of which we constantly speak, and will continue to do so, is an anchored Faith in Christ and what He did for us at the Cross, i.e., *"The Finished Work of Christ"* (Rom. 6:3-14; 8:1-11; I Cor. 1:17-18, 23; 2:2; Col. 2:10-15). Faith that's not anchored solidly in the Cross of Christ, which is the story of the Bible, is

Faith that God will not recognize. In fact, such Faith always falls into the category of that possessed by Lot. It doesn't matter whether it's borrowed Faith, or whether it's Faith in the wrong object; the *"strife"* will always show it up for what it really is. As we've stated, the strife is only the outward symptom, while the real cause is the wrong kind of Faith. What is it that the world sees in us presently?

It is ironic that most of the world observes the antics, which take place under the guise of Christianity, and automatically know that it's wrong, while at the same time, most in the church don't seem to know. How? Why?

The whole debacle, and I speak of the modern greed Gospel or outright erroneous directions, stems from the wrong kind of faith, or more particularly, misplaced faith, which means it's faith in something other than Christ and the Cross. And, to be sure, the wrong type of faith mostly comes under the heading of unbelief rather than ignorance. And that is the greatest tragedy of all!

The Believer must understand that the story of the Bible is the Story of *"Jesus Christ and Him Crucified."* When you understand that, you understand the Word of God. But to talk about the Word of God and claim to have your Faith thereby placed, and rather ignore the Cross of Christ or actually register unbelief towards the Cross, one then has destroyed the Word, whatever their claims.

"In the beginning was the Word, and the Word was with God, and the Word was God" (Jn. 1:1).

BRETHREN

"And Abram said unto Lot, Let there be no strife, I pray you, between me and you, and between my herdmen and your herdmen; for we be Brethren" (Gen. 13:8).

Abraham reminding Lot that they were *"Brethren,"* proclaims the fact that the strife had gone beyond the herdsmen, and was in Lot's heart as well. The bent towards Sodom is now beginning to exert itself. It demands its *"rights,"* which demands to be able to choose for itself, which at the same time, means that it does not trust God to make the choice. This is very important as it regards the Child of God. Do we chart the course, or do we allow God to chart the course? Regrettably, there was contention in the Church of that time, but the contention was only in the heart of Lot; it wasn't in the heart of Abraham.

THE PEACEMAKER

"Is not the whole land before you? separate your-self, I pray you, from me: if you will take the left hand, then I will go to the right; or if you depart to the right hand, then I will go to the left" (Gen. 13:9).

Everything that faces the Child of God, and in whatever capacity, is a test. This was a test for both Abraham and Lot. Lot didn't fair very well and, in fact, his choice would lead to his ultimate ruin.

Mackintosh says:

"Why did not Abraham make the choice of Sodom? Why did not the strife drive him into the world? Why was it not an occasion of stumbling to him?"

He answers, *"Because he looked at it from God's point of view. No doubt he had a heart that could be attracted by 'well-watered plains' just as powerfully as Lot's heart, but then he did not allow his own heart to choose. He first let Lot take his choice, and then left God to choose for him. This was Heavenly wisdom. This is what Faith ever does: it allows God to fix its inheritance, as it also allows Him to make it good. It is always sat-isfied with the portion which God gives. It can say 'the lines are fallen to me in pleasant places; yes, I have a goodly heritage.' It matters not where 'the lines' fall; for in the judgment of Faith, they always fall 'in pleasant places,' just because God cast them there."*

Mackintosh continues:

"The man of Faith can easily afford to allow the man of sight to take his choice. He can say, 'If you will take the left hand, then I will go to the right; or if you depart to the right hand, then I will go to the left.'"[2]

THE PLAIN OF JORDAN

"And Lot lifted up his eyes, and beheld all the plain of Jordan, that it was well watered everywhere, before the LORD destroyed Sodom and Gomorrah, even as the Garden of the LORD, like the land of Egypt, as you come unto Zoar" (Gen. 13:10).

Given his choice, what did Lot choose? As stated, everything with the Child of God is always in the form of a test. What will you choose?

He chose Sodom, incidentally, a place that was about to be judged by God, and judged so severely that there is no trace of it left. That should be a lesson to all of us.

If we choose wrong, and I continue to speak of our life being lived for the Lord, the consequences are never good.

Why select such a spot as did Lot regarding the plain of Jordan, which was towards Sodom?

It was because he looked at the outward appearance, and not at the intrinsic character and future destiny. The intrinsic character of Sodom was *"wicked"*; its future destiny was *"judgment"* — to be destroyed by fire and brimstone out of Heaven.

Of course, one could counter by saying that Lot knew none of this. That is correct, and more than likely Abraham had no knowledge of this sort either.

But God knew, and had Lot allowed God to *"choose for him,"* even as did Abraham, the Lord, to be sure, would not have chosen a spot that He Himself was about to destroy. The truth is, Sodom suited Lot, though it did not suit God or Abraham.

THE FLESH

This entire episode presents a perfect picture and, as well, a perfect example, of what happens to the Believer when he allows his senses, i.e., *"the flesh,"* to choose for him. Outwardly, this looked like the place of prosperity, even though, admittedly, Sodom was a wicked place.

But Lot didn't see the wickedness of Sodom; he only saw the *"well-watered plains."* He saw the outward, and not the inward.

How many modern Christians are making the same choice presently? How many truly seek the Face of the Lord as it regards direction? How many only assume?

Woe is the Believer who makes his own choices, and is not led by the Lord. And woe is the Believer who thinks he's being led by the Lord, but in reality is being led by something else altogether!

SEPARATION

"Then Lot chose him all the plain of Jordan; and Lot journeyed east: and they separated themselves the one from the other" (Gen. 13:11).

At long last, that which God had originally told Abraham to do, *"Get thee . . . from your kindred, and from your father's house,"* is now done (Gen. 12:1).

From this we learn that the man of true Faith, Faith in Christ, and what Christ has done for us at the Cross, must separate himself from those in the church who have an improper faith. To be sure, this is definitely something that will come to pass without any overt action on the part of the one of true Faith. The two, true Faith and improper faith, cannot in any way mix. They are like oil and water! There must be a separation, even as there is a separation. The man of true Faith looks entirely to God, while the one with improper faith, looks to his own senses, mistaking that for Faith, when in reality, it's something else altogether.

Out of this we have the True Church and we have the apostate church. It has been that way from the very beginning, with Cain and Abel setting the first example. It has continued thusly ever since. Millions are in the church, but not in faith. Millions claim faith, but in reality, it is not Faith. And let the reader properly understand the following:

TRUE FAITH

The entirety of the Bible is the story of the Fall and Redemption of man. The Fall of man takes up only one Chapter (Gen., Chpt. 3), with the remainder devoted to the Redemption of man. The central core of the Redemption Plan is the Lord Jesus Christ, and what He would do at the Cross. Everything in the Bible points to Him; however, it points to Him in the realm of what He would do at the Cross on our behalf. It is always *"Jesus Christ and Him Crucified,"* always typified by the Sacrifices of the Old Testament, and the reality in the New (I Cor. 1:23; 2:2).

It is Faith in that Finished Work which guarantees Redemption for mankind, and Faith in the Finished Work alone, which God recognizes as true Faith (Jn. 3:16).

When Paul spoke of *"fighting the good fight of Faith,"* he was speaking of this *"Faith which was once delivered unto the Saints"* (I Tim. 6:12; Jude, Vs. 3). Satan's greatest effort is to move the Saint away from this Faith, that is, making the Cross the Object of his Faith, to something else. If he does that, he has succeeded. The Holy Spirit doesn't demand much of us, but He does demand that our Faith be explicitly in Christ, and what Christ has done for us at the Cross. Then and then only will He Work within our lives, and do the things which only He can do (Rom. 8:1-11).

The central theme of the Bible is Faith (Jn. 3:16; Heb. 11:6). But as stated, the Faith of which we speak, is Faith in Christ and what He has done at the Cross. That is *"the Faith"* (Rom. 1:5, 12; 3:3; Gal. 2:20).

SODOM

"Abram dwelt in the Land of Canaan, and Lot dwelt in the cities of the plain, and pitched his tent toward Sodom" (Gen. 13:12).

The first mistake on the part of Lot was the choice of direction, which was toward Sodom. The second mistake was that he *"pitched his tent toward Sodom,"* which means that soon he will be in Sodom, which he was.

The Scripture bluntly says, *"Abram dwelt in the Land of Canaan."* The idea seems to be, after the excursion into Egypt, he did not want a repetition of such. He puts his stakes down in Canaan, because this is where God had sent him. In fact, his dwelling in the land had far more to do with the Promises of God, which actually stretched into eternity, than the land itself. Actually, he never personally owned any of the Land of Canaan, except a burial place; however, all of that was of little consequence. How much of it he saw by Faith, we really do not know. He knew, of course, what God had told him the future would be, but even then the information was very scarce.

ISRAEL

In this land of Canaan, Israel will become a Nation. Ultimately the Prophets would come, and through them, the Word of God would be given, not only to Israel but also the entirety of the world. And then the greatest happening of all would take place, and we speak of the coming of the Messiah, which would fulfill the great prediction made by God to Satan through the serpent, concerning the *"Seed of the woman"* (Gen. 3:15). So Abraham would dwell in Canaan, because that's where God had sent him.

Lot pitching his tent toward Sodom portrays the fact that he little understood the great prophecies concerning the future of Canaan. They seem to have meant little to him. Were that not the case, he would not have moved toward Sodom, and ultimately into Sodom.

WICKEDNESS

"But the men of Sodom were wicked and sinners before the LORD exceedingly" (Gen. 13:13).

The Holy Spirit through Moses, as he wrote the Text, is very quick to characterize Sodom and its inhabitants.

Pulpit Commentary says concerning Sodom:

"Their vileness was restrained neither in quantity nor quality. As it passed all height in arrogance, so it burst all bounds in prevalence."[3]

The wickedness of the men of Sodom concerned itself, among other things, with the terrible sin of homosexuality. In fact, it is here that the name *"Sodomites,"* concerning homosexuality, came into being (Deut. 23:17; I Ki. 14:24; 15:12; 22:46; II Ki. 23:7). But yet, as wicked as this sin is, Jesus proclaimed that the rejection of the Gospel under the New Covenant, is far more serious even than the sins of Sodom and Gomorrah (Lk. 10:2-12). Considering the Cross, there is no sin greater than the rejection of Christ. If the *"men of Sodom were wicked and sinners before the LORD exceedingly,"* the rejection of Christ presently makes such a person more wicked.

Does that mean that those who reject the Cross of Christ are more wicked than Sodom?

I think it does!

"The great Physician now is near,
"The sympathizing Jesus;
"He speaks the drooping heart to cheer,
"Oh! Hear the Voice of Jesus."

"Your many sins are all forgiven,
"Oh! Hear the Voice of Jesus;
"Go on your way in peace to Heaven,
"And wear a crown with Jesus."

"All Glory to the dying Lamb!
"I now believe in Jesus;
"I love the blessed Savior's Name,
"I love the Name of Jesus."

"His Name dispels my guilt and fear,
"No other name but Jesus;
"Oh! How my soul delights to hear,
"The charming Name of Jesus."

ABRAHAM

CHAPTER

7

The Lord And Abraham

THE LORD AND ABRAHAM

REVELATION

"And the LORD said unto Abram, after that Lot was separated from him, Lift up now your eyes, and look upon the place where you are northward, and southward, and eastward, and westward" (Gen. 13:14).

Lot departing from Abraham, and the Lord appearing to the Patriarch after that departure, lets us know that the strife was far more serious than meets the eye. In effect, the Lord was telling the Patriarch that it didn't really matter what Lot or anyone else did, the Promise concerning the land had been given to Abraham, and now God verifies the Promise to an even greater degree. In essence, the Lord abrogated the portion claimed by Lot, and did so by giving it back to Abraham.

The Lord having done this, the Patriarch did not have to fight to defend it, or, in fact, to do anything. Let the reader remember this:

If God gives us something, man cannot take it away. To be sure, even as here, men will try, but men will not be successful.

FOREVER

"For all the land which you see, to you will I give it, and to your seed for ever" (Gen. 13:15).

Not only was the land of Palestine to be given to Abraham and his seed, which it definitely was, but the ownership was to be into perpetuity, i.e., *"forever."*

Now let the reader look carefully at these simple words, *"And to your seed forever"* for they spell certain doom to anyone or any nation, and irrespective as to how large or powerful they might be, who would seek to abrogate this Promise as given by the Lord.

Some decades ago, mighty Great Britain sought to stop the Jews from claiming their rightful possession. They did not succeed, and today Great Britain is only a shadow of what it once was. The former Soviet Union, with all of its monolithic power, set itself against Israel, but instead, saw herself disintegrated. This is an anvil on which many hammers have struck. The hammers break; the anvil remains.

At this present time, the Arab nations are demanding that the United States cease its protection of Israel; however, let the leaders of America understand, that if we ever lift a hand against Israel, and do so in any manner, we will incur the Wrath of Almighty God, a position in which no nation wants to find itself. The statement made by God some 4,000 years ago, *"I will bless them who bless you, and curse him who curses you,"* holds just as much Truth at the present, as it did when it was uttered.

And to be frank, as that particular statement was meant for Israel, it extends even unto Believers presently, and we speak of Gentiles, or anyone for that matter, who has accepted Christ. Those who bless Believers will be blessed; those who curse Believers will ultimately be cursed.

THE SEED

"And I will make your seed as the dust of the earth: so that if a man can number the dust of the earth, then shall your seed also be numbered" (Gen. 13:16).

Not only would the land be given to Abraham and his seed, but, as well, there would be so many seed that they would not be able to be numbered. Now remember this: at this particular time, Abraham did not possess one single foot of the land of Palestine, at least as far as personally owning it was concerned. As well, Sarah was barren, so in the mind of the Patriarch, as we shall see in his later experiences, he wonders how all of this can possibly happen.

We must never forget that there is nothing impossible with God. If He has promised it, to be sure, He will do it — irrespective as to what it might be. He is the One Who opens, and no man shuts; and shuts, and no man opens (Rev. 3:7).

WALK

"Arise, walk through the land in the length of it and in the breadth of it; for I will give it unto you" (Gen. 13:17).

This is a walk of Faith. With him walking the length and the breadth of the land presents his claim regarding this inheritance. It didn't matter to whom it belonged at the present; God said, *"walk it."*

God has the Power to give us anything; however, He will only give His treasures to men and women of Faith. And please remember that Faith is always attached to action in some way. We are to take possession of these gifts by Faith. This means, whatever the present circumstances, that we believe God. God said it, we believe it, and that settles it!

There would be many enemies in coming centuries who would try to stop Israel from possessing its land; however, despite their efforts, they were not successful — that is until the Lord allowed the land to be taken by others, and because of Israel's refusal to repent, and their wayward direction.

MOVE THE TENT

"Then Abram removed his tent, and came and dwelt in the plain of Mamre, which is in Hebron, and built there an Altar unto the LORD" (Gen. 13:18).

Hebron is a little over 20 miles south of Jerusalem, on the way to Beersheba. Actually, Hebron was built some seven years before Zoan, in Egypt, meaning it was one of the oldest cities in the world (Num. 13:22). It is elsewhere in the Bible styled *"Kirjath-arba,"* or the city of Arba (Gen. 23:2; 35:27). The fact of Abraham living in a tent portrayed his pilgrim nature. That which he sought was not to be found on this Earth, but rather in Heaven. *"He looked for a city which has foundations, whose Builder and Maker is God"* (Heb. 11:10). He looked for *"a better country, that is, an Heavenly"* (Heb. 11:16).

He moved his tent away from Sodom, even from its direction, bringing it closer to Jerusalem. There are many Believers, spiritually speaking, who desperately need to *"move their tents."* In fact, there are millions, as Lot, who have *"pitched their tent towards Sodom."* There is only disaster in that direction. The Blessing is as Abraham did, to move the tent ever toward Jerusalem, i.e., *"the New Jerusalem."*

So I suppose the simple question must be asked, *"Where is your tent?"*

The major denominations resort to humanistic psychology in order to address the needs of man, in which, incidentally, there is no help. It moves its tent ever toward Sodom! The modern greed gospel has repudiated the Cross, thereby, becoming an enemy of the Cross, which means it ever pitches its tent toward Sodom!

When the Church forsakes the Cross, and by and large it has forsaken the Cross, there is nowhere to go but to continue to *"pitch one's tent towards Sodom."*

THE CROSS

The phrase, *"And built there an Altar unto the LORD,"* proclaims the center of gravity, so to speak, as it regards Faith. I speak of the *"Altar,"* which is always a Type of the *"Cross."*

If there is to be Victory, if there is to be the Power of God, if there is to be Salvation, if there is to be a mighty Moving of the Holy Spirit, it all must be built on the Foundation of the Cross. The Holy Spirit will Function and Work in no other capacity.

If we try to build Faith on Denominationalism, particular churches, even particular doctrines, on good works, on preachers, etc., we have just placed ourselves in a position in which the Holy Spirit will not Work. He functions alone in the parameters of the Finished Work of Christ. Listen to what Paul said:

> **"For the Law** (*a Law devised by the Godhead in eternity past*) **of the Spirit** (*Holy Spirit*) **of Life** (*all life comes from Christ, but through the Holy Spirit*) **in Christ Jesus** (*referring to what Jesus did at the Cross*) **has made me free from the Law of Sin and Death"** (Rom. 8:2).

IN CHRIST JESUS

The words, *"In Christ Jesus"* proclaim the manner in which this *"Law"* operates and functions. It pertains to what Christ did at the Cross on our behalf, and it is that, and that alone, in which the Holy Spirit Works. As with Abraham, He demands that we place our Faith in the Finished Work of Christ, and that ever be the Object of our Faith. As previously stated, He doesn't demand much of us, but He does demand that. If we build on any foundation other than the Cross, He simply will not Work in that capacity, and that is exactly what is happening to the modern church. It desperately needs to go back and *"build there an Altar unto the LORD,"* i.e., *"reestablish our Faith in the Cross of Christ"* (Lk. 9:23-24; Rom. 6:3-14; 8:1-2, 11; I Cor. 1:17-18, 21, 23; 2:2, 5; Col. 2:10-15; I Pet. 1:18-20).

> *"I was lost in sin, but Jesus rescued me,*
> *"He's a wonderful Saviour to me;*
> *"I was bound by fear, but Jesus set me free,*
> *"He's a wonderful Saviour to me."*
>
> *"He's a Friend so true, so patient, and so kind,*
> *"He's a wonderful Saviour to me;*
> *"Everything I need in Him I always find,*
> *"He's a wonderful Saviour to me."*
>
> *"He is always near to comfort and to cheer,*
> *"He's a wonderful Saviour to me;*
> *"He forgives my sins, He dries my every tear,*
> *"He's a wonderful Saviour to me."*
>
> *"Dearer grows the Love of Jesus day-by-day,*
> *"He's a wonderful Saviour to me;*
> *"Sweeter is His Grace while pressing on my way,*
> *"He's a wonderful Saviour to me."*

ABRAHAM

CHAPTER

8

Abraham And War

ABRAHAM AND WAR

THE FOUR KINGS

"And it came to pass in the days of Amraphel king of Shinar, Arioch king of Ellasar, Chedorlaomer king of Elam, and Tidal king of nations" (Gen. 14:1).

If it is to be noticed, the Spirit of God occupies Himself with the movements of *"kings and their armies,"* only when such movements are in any wise connected with the people of God.

When we read all of these illustrations in the Old Testament, we should do so with the understanding that these things have to do with the Plan of God, and are always connected with the ever onward thrust of our ultimate Salvation. The conflicts here enjoined will ultimately involve Abraham and are, therefore, of our interest.

Some Jewish scholars claim that Amraphel was Nimrod; however, that is probably incorrect, because by now Nimrod probably had died.

This was about 400 years after the Flood, and despite that Judgment, brought by God, which destroyed all of mankind, with the exception of Noah and his family, we find that man is no better now than he was then. As there was only one family living for God before the Flood, and that family was that of Noah, we find now that this family has increased very little.

At this particular time, the only ones living for God, at least that are recorded, are Abraham and his family, and the great Priest-king Melchizedek. Lot could be said to belong to this number, but only in a limited way.

We find here four kings, led by Chedorlaomer, who sought to put down the rebellion of the five kings listed in Verse 2.

And how does this interest us presently?

It interests us simply because it is of interest to the Holy Spirit. And it is of interest to Him simply because it will involve Lot, who was a citizen of Sodom. While Lot is in serious straits spiritually, he is still attended to by the Holy Spirit, even as we shall see. This shows us the security of the Child of God, but it also shows the serious straits in which the Believer can find himself by engaging in disobedience.

THE FIVE KINGS

"That these made war with Bera king of Sodom, and with Birsha king of Gomorrah, Shinab king of Admah, and Shemeber king of Zeboiim, and the king of Bela, which is Zoar" (Gen. 14:2).

These five kings had been ruled by Chedorlaomer for some twelve years, and now they rebel. The king of Sodom, as we shall see, will be the principal in this confederation led against Chedorlaomer.

This is the first mention of *"war"* in the Old Testament, but, without a doubt, many wars had been fought before now.

REBELLION

"All these were joined together in the vale of Siddim, which is the salt sea.

"Twelve years they served Chedorlaomer, and in the thirteenth year they rebelled" (Gen. 14:3-4).

This is the first occurrence, as well, of the number *"thirteen"* in the Bible. It is the number of rebellion, and its subsequent occurrences in the Scriptures present the same feature.

The four kings of Verse 1 served Chedorlaomer for some twelve years. In the thirteenth year they rebelled, and in the fourteenth year, Chedorlaomer gathered his confederation in order to bring them back into line.

The *"Rephaims," "Zuzims,"* and *"Emims"* refer to giants. Satan is now doing the same thing he did before the Flood, fulfilling Genesis 6:4 which says, *"there were giants in the Earth in those days"* (before the Flood; and also after the Flood).

THE GIANTS

"And in the fourteenth year came Chedorlaomer, and the kings who were with him, and smote the Rephaims in Ashteroth Karnaim, and the Zuzims in Ham, and the Emims in Shaveh Kiriathaim,

"And the Horites in their Mount Seir, unto El-paran, which is by the wilderness" (Gen. 14:5-6).

These giants were the results of fallen Angels cohabiting with women. The Scripture says, concerning this, which first took place about 500 or more years before the Flood, *"That the sons of God saw the daughters of men that they were fair; and they took them wives of all which they chose"* (Gen. 6:2).

The *"sons of God"* portrayed here refer to fallen Angels, who had thrown in their lot with Lucifer, who led a revolution against God sometime in eternity past. In order to spoil the human lineage through which the Messiah would ultimately come, they would seek to corrupt that lineage, and to do so by marrying the *"daughters of men,"* thereby, producing a mongrel race, so to speak, of which at least some of these offspring turned out to be *"giants."* At any rate, all who were the result of such a union were tainted.

The term *"sons of God"* in the Old Testament, at least as it is used here, is never used of human beings, but always of Angels, whether righteous or fallen (Job 1:6; 2:1). In his short Epistle, Jude mentions these particular *"angels."* He said that they *"kept not their first estate, but left their own habitation"*; he then said what their sin was: *"going after strange flesh."* Concerning this, Jude also said that God *"has reserved* (them) *in everlasting chains under darkness unto the Judgment of the Great Day"* (Jude, Vss. 6-7).

The Scripture seems to indicate in Genesis 14:5-6, that the giants mentioned here were the last of their particular line, although not the last of the giants, that coming in the time of David.

SODOM

"And they returned, and came to En-mishpat, which is Kadesh, and smote all the country of the Amalekites, and also the Amorites, who dwelt in Hazezon-tamar.

"And there went out the king of Sodom, and the king of Gomorrah, and the king of Admah, and the king of Zeboiim, and the king of Bela (the same is Zoar;) and they joined battle with them in the vale of Siddim;

"With Chedorlaomer the king of Elam, and with Tidal king of nations, and Amraphel king of Shinar, and Arioch king of Ellasar; four kings with five" (Gen. 14:7-9).

We have here the mention of Sodom where Lot dwelt, which causes the interest of Jehovah, and points to the reason for all of this being included in these Passages.

It is obvious from the Text that Lot was not at all in proper relationship with the Lord; however, the Lord, despite that fact, continued to monitor his every move and, in effect, to exercise a form of Security and Protection for him, despite him having moved in with the Sodomites. However, let us quickly state, Lot did not join in with their homosexual activities.

Every Believer should understand the significance of all of this. We are bought with a price; that price is the Shed Blood of the Lord Jesus Christ on the Cross of Calvary. As a result, we belong to the Lord. And, as a continued result, He minutely watches over us.

FEAR

To be somewhat mundane, this is why it is so foolish for Believers to fear things. I get amazed at Christians who are afraid of flying or something of that nature. There is no way, that you as a Believer, are going to die before the Lord says so.

Now it is quite possible for Christians to be reckless and to do foolish things, which can shorten their lives; however, the greatest problem of all, the Scripture tells us, is Believers not properly discerning the Body of Christ. And what does that mean?

THE LORD'S SUPPER

Concerning our taking that Sacred Ordinance, which we refer to as the *"Lord's Supper,"* Paul said:

"Wherefore whosoever shall eat this bread, and drink this cup of the Lord, unworthily, shall be guilty of the Body and Blood of the Lord.

"But let a man examine himself, and so let him eat that bread, and drink of that cup.

"For he who eats and drinks unworthily, eats and drinks damnation to himself, not discerning the Lord's Body."

The Apostle then said, *"For this cause many are weak and sickly among you, and many sleep"* (I Cor. 11:27-30).

"Weak and sickly" explains itself, which refers to bodily sickness. The word *"sleep"* refers to dying prematurely. While these Believers are Saved, their lives are cut short, simply because they are not properly discerning the Lord's Body. And what does that mean?

To take the Lord's Supper, the Lord doesn't demand perfection. But He does demand Faith; however, the

Faith He demands, is Faith in Christ, *"and what Christ has done for us at the Cross."* The entirety of the Lord's Supper portrays the broken Body of our Lord and His Shed Blood. If we partake of the Lord's Supper and make something else other than the Body of Christ (Christ giving His Body on the Cross in Sacrifice) the object of our Faith, this means we are not properly discerning the Lord's Body, which also means that we *"eat this bread, and drink this cup of the Lord, unworthily,"* and, thereby, incur unto ourselves *"damnation,"* which in this case refers to harm, and not the loss of the soul.

THE CROSS

If the Believer places his Faith exclusively in Christ, and what Christ has done for us at the Cross, depending totally and completely upon that Finished Work, and conduct himself in a forthright, sensible manner, he doesn't have to worry about anything.

But, if the Believer, even as Lot, flirts with the world, he definitely can place himself in harms way, which can cause great problems, even as it did with Lot. Lot, in a sense, represents the apostate Church, while Abraham represents the True Church. Lot's attention and direction definitely were not on the Cross of Christ, but something else entirely. And regrettably, that's where most modern Christians are — they have made friends with the world.

LOT

"And the vale of Siddim was full of slimepits; and the kings of Sodom and Gomorrah fled, and fell there; and they who remained fled to the mountain.

"And they took all the goods of Sodom and Gomorrah, and all their victuals, and went their way.

"And they took Lot, Abram's brother's son, who dwelt in Sodom, and his goods, and departed" (Gen. 14:10-12).

Even though Lot was still under the protection of the Lord, at least to a certain degree, when we take ourselves away from the true Way of God, thereby devising our own way, even as did Lot, we incur upon ourselves great difficulties. The Way of the Lord is the only Way, and to be sure, Sodom was not that way. So, the Scripture says, *"They took Lot,"* along with *"his goods,"* etc.

THE WORLD

Becoming yoked up with the world, as stated, Lot could neither deliver Sodom nor himself. If we place ourselves in this position, as it relates to the world, and that means to become yoked up with its spirit, we will sooner or later be taken captive by the world, just as was Lot. Let the Christian read these words very carefully.

"They took Lot," and sooner or later, they are going to take you, that is, if you go in the wrong direction.

The Lord demands separation from the world; however, this doesn't mean isolation. Every Believer is *"salt"* and *"light"* to the world, which speaks of preservation and illumination (Mat. 5:13-14).

Williams says:

"Isolation is not separation. Isolation chills; separation warms. Isolation makes self the center; separation makes Christ the center. Isolation produces indifference to the need of others; separation fills the heart with love and interest for the needy and perishing. So soon then as Abraham hears of the captivity of his relative, he immediately sets out to save him. Such is the energy of love. Abraham's was the Faith that not only overcomes the world, but that works by love. Such is the nature of Divine Faith. It purifies the heart; it rescues the perishing; and it puts kings to flight!"[1]

LOT TAKEN CAPTIVE

"And there came one who had escaped, and told Abram the Hebrew; for he dwelt in the plain of Mamre the Amorite, brother of Eshcol, and brother of Aner: and these were confederate with Abram.

"And when Abram heard that his brother was taken captive, he armed his trained servants, born in his own house, three hundred and eighteen, and pursued them unto Dan.

"And he divided himself against them, he and his servants, by night, and smote them, and pursued them unto Hobah, which is on the left hand of Damascus" (Gen. 14:13-15).

Mackintosh says:

"The claims of a brother's trouble are answered by the affections of a brother's heart. This is Divine. Genuine Faith, while it always renders us independent, never renders us indifferent; it will never wrap itself up in its fleece while a brother shivers in the cold. There are three things which Faith does. It 'purifies the heart,' it 'works by love,' and it 'overcomes the world' (I Jn. 3:3; 5:4; I Cor. 13:2); and all these results of Faith are beautifully exhibited in Abraham on this occasion."[2]

What are we to do, as Believers, if we hear that our brother has been taken captive by the Devil?

Of course, we are to do exactly as Abraham, set about to rescue him.

However, we must realize that there is only one way that one can be rescued; that is by taking them to the Cross.

THE CROSS OF CHRIST

While there are many things which entered into this situation, the very reason that Lot had been taken captive by these heathen kings is because, in effect, he had left the Cross, i.e., *"the Altar."* There was no Altar, at least to Jehovah, in Sodom. And the very reason any Believer is taken captive by the enemy is because he leaves the Cross. In the Cross, and the Cross alone, is our protection. Our Faith and trust in the Finished Work of Christ is what gives the Holy Spirit latitude within our hearts and lives, and keeps us from *"works of the flesh"* (Gal. 5:16-25).

If the Believer is taken captive by the enemy, it is because he has left the Cross, and if he is to be brought back to a place of Victory, he must first of all be brought back to the Cross. The reason for failure is departure from the Cross, while regaining the Victory is being brought back to the Cross and remaining there.

WRONG DIRECTION

It is tragic that the modern church has, for all practical purposes, forsaken the Cross. As a result, almost all of the church, presently, is in the clutches of the enemy. The greater tragedy is, it is so deceived that it doesn't even recognize the position in which it now finds itself. It is only proper Faith in the Cross which keeps one from deception. Paul said:

"Now the Spirit *(Holy Spirit)* **speaks expressly** *(pointedly)*, **that in the latter times** *(the times in which we now live)* **some shall depart from the Faith** *(trust in Christ and what Christ has done for us at the Cross)*, **giving heed to seducing spirits** *(deception)*, **and doctrines of devils** *(demons)"* **(I Tim. 4:1).**

Lot departed from the Cross, so to speak, and Lot was deceived. As a result of his spiritual blindness, he could not see the terrible predicament in which he found himself. And neither can most modern

Christians. For all practical purposes, the church has forsaken the Cross, and for all practical purposes, it finds itself so deceived that it does not realize the clear and present danger.

Every evidence is that Lot was angry with Abraham as a result of the strife between the herdsmen (Gen. 13:7-8). But Abraham wasn't angry with Lot, only hurt by Lot's actions toward him. Never mind, this did not enter into the situation at present. Abraham must rescue Lot. He is Lot's *"brother."*

THE MODERN CHURCH

Unfortunately, the rescue attempts, if one would call it that, of the modern church, doesn't include the Cross. It has so adopted the ways of the world, that it uses the ways of the world to try to effect rescue, which, in effect, is no rescue at all. Let me ask the following question:

Could Abraham have rescued Lot if he had been captive of the kings also? Of course he couldn't have done so. He would have needed rescue himself. But, thankfully, that wasn't the case with Abraham; however, it definitely is the case with the modern church.

To the brother who has been taken captive by the enemy, does the modern church hold up the Cross as the solution to his problem? Unfortunately it doesn't. It rather holds up humanistic psychology, which provides no help at all, but rather harm. Let me give you an example.

Some years ago, someone sent me a copy of *The Pentecostal Evangel*, the weekly voice of the Assemblies of God. I did not keep the magazine; therefore, I cannot give the exact date of the issue.

Somewhere in the body of its contents, in addressing the problems we are discussing here, the writer of the article I was reading, boldly recommended the twelve-step programs of humanistic psychology. His statement was, if the church being attended, didn't have a good twelve-step program, the individual should find one that did.

By allowing such an article to be published, this means that the entirety of the leadership of that Denomination approved of this particular direction.

PSYCHOLOGY

It is impossible to trust in the Cross and humanistic psychology at the same time. To recommend the latter is to deny the former. One cannot have it both ways. To embrace this nefarious system of the world, is at the same time, to deny the Cross. While, of course, these religious leaders, so-called, would deny that, the simple fact is, one cannot embrace the world and its systems, and at the same time embrace the Lord and His Cross. One or the other must go. Paul plainly said:

"Be you not unequally yoked together with unbelievers: for what fellowship has Righteousness with unrighteousness? and what communion has light with darkness?

"And what concord has Christ with Belial? or what part has he who believes with an infidel?"

"Wherefore come out from among them, and be you separate, says the Lord, and touch not the unclean thing; and I will receive you" (II Cor. 6:14-15, 17).

Unfortunately, for every Christian who presently has a problem of any nature, the Church is holding up, at least for the most part, humanistic psychology as the answer to that dilemma. It has forsaken the Cross, and as such, it has forsaken all hope of rescue. Concerning this, Jesus bluntly said:

"They be blind leaders of the blind. And if the blind lead the blind, both shall fall into the ditch" (Mat. 15:14).

PSYCHOLOGY, THE RELIGION OF HUMANISM

Humanistic psychology is far more than a mere one hour a week talking to a psychologist, etc. It is rather the religion of humanism. It is a total way of life that completely denies the Word of God. In fact, most of the preachers standing behind pulpits Sunday morning, whether they realize it or not, will be, by and large, preaching psychology. In other words, even our vocabulary has become so enmeshed in this nefarious system that it has become a way of life. The Christian bookstores, so-called, are rather Christian in name only. Most of the books they offer are laced with psychology.

A Baptist preacher made the following statement the other day, which I feel the entirety of the Church world should read and heed.

He said, *"The world has become so psychologized, that it no longer believes in a coming judgment."* How right he is!

Psychology teaches that man is an innocent victim, that rather his problem is environment, lack of education, improper association, etc. The Bible teaches the very opposite, in fact, that every man is sinful and wicked, and, thereby, responsible for his own actions. I think it should be obvious that it's not possible for the two, the Word of God and humanistic psychology, to be wedded.

One particular Pentecostal leader (leader?) made the statement that modern man faces problems that are not addressed in the Bible, so he needs the help of psychology as well as the Bible. How so absolutely foolish when we read the statement of Simon Peter:

"Grace and Peace be multiplied unto you through the knowledge of God, and of Jesus our

Lord *(this is both Sanctifying Grace and Sanctifying Peace, all made available by the Cross)*,

"According as His Divine Power has given unto us all things *(the Lord with large-handed generosity has given us all things)* **that pertain unto life and godliness** *(pertains to the fact that the Lord Jesus has given us everything we need regarding life and living)*, **through the knowledge of Him Who has called us to Glory and Virtue** *(the 'knowledge' addressed here speaks of what Christ did at the Cross, which alone can provide 'Glory and Virtue')***:**

"Whereby are given unto us exceeding Great and Precious Promises *(pertains to the Word of God, which alone holds the answer to every life problem)***: that by these** *(Promises)* **you might be partakers of the Divine Nature** *(the Divine Nature implanted in the inner being of the believing sinner becomes the source of our new life and actions; it comes to everyone at the moment of being 'Born-Again')*, **having escaped the corruption that is in the world through lust.** *(This presents the Salvation experience of the sinner, and the Sanctification experience of the Saint.)*" **(II Pet. 1:2-4).**

RESCUE

"And he brought back all the goods, and also brought again his brother Lot, and his goods, and the women also, and the people" (Gen. 14:16).

Abraham not only rescued Lot, but all of his material possessions as well, along with all of the people who had been taken captive, and their goods also. In other words, every single thing that the enemy had taken was retrieved.

A proper restoration will, at the same time, retrieve everything that has been lost. As it regards evil, which is a type of the world, *"not one hoof must be left behind"* (Ex. 10:26).

Exactly how many others were with Abraham and his 318 trained soldiers, we aren't told. So we must come to the conclusion that the Lord greatly helped Abraham in this excursion. There is no record that he lost a single man.

Victories we win by our own ingenuity oftentimes come at great price. Victories we win by the Power of God come at no price at all on our part, but all on the part of God's Son and our Saviour, the Lord Jesus Christ.

VICTORY

The Believer must understand that God cannot give victories to sinful man. He can only give Victories, even as we've already stated, to His Son, the Lord Jesus Christ. And this Victory is given to Christ for us, due to what the Lord did at Calvary's Cross. In other words, there is no victory outside of the Cross.

Once our Faith and Trust are solely in Christ and His Cross, then the Victory which Christ has won becomes our Victory. But if we try to gain Victory in any other manner, we will fail every single time. John clearly said:

"This is the victory that overcomes the world, even our Faith" (I Jn. 5:4).

But never forget, the Faith mentioned here is, without exception, Faith in Christ and Him Crucified (I Cor. 1:23).

THE KING OF SODOM

"And the king of Sodom went out to meet him after his return from the slaughter of Chedorlaomer, and of

the kings who were with him, at the valley of Shaveh, which is the king's dale" (Gen. 14:17).

Everything has been retrieved by Abraham. The people who lived in the five cities were wicked; yet, for Abraham's sake, most, if not all of them, were saved from death. Thus, God honors His Saints, for He spares the most perverse ingrates on account of one or two Believers. In addition, these people received also their goods, which they could never have otherwise expected.

The same is true today and, in fact, has always been true. Whatever Blessings the world enjoys, it enjoys because of God's Saints on Earth. If it were not for God's People, and I speak of those who have been washed in the Blood of the Lamb, God would have utterly destroyed the whole world long ago.

All of this should have been a lesson to the Sodomites, which means they definitely should have repented, but they only increased in wickedness until they had to be destroyed, which they were, a short time later. This, which God allowed Abraham to do in rescuing all of these people and their goods, was the greatest sign of all of the Supremacy of Jehovah. But the Sodomites seemingly gave it little thought; they were only interested in their worldly goods.

"On the Cross Crucified,
"Great sorrow He died,
"The Giver of Life was He.
"Yet my Lord was despised,
"And rejected of men,
"This Jesus of Calvary."

"Price for healing was paid,
"As those cruel stripes were made,
"Within Pilate's judgment hall;
"Now His Suffering affords perfect healing for all.
"This wonderful Healer's mine."

"Came the leper to Christ,
"Saying surely I know,
"That You, Lord, can make me whole.
"When his great Faith was seen,
"Jesus said 'Yes, I will.'
"And touched him and made him clean."

"He has healed my sick soul,
"Made me every whit whole,
"And He'll do the same for you.
"He's the same yesterday and today and for aye,
"This Healer of men today."

ABRAHAM

CHAPTER

9

Abraham And Melchizedek

ABRAHAM AND MELCHIZEDEK

MELCHIZEDEK

"And Melchizedek king of Salem brought forth bread and wine: and he was the Priest of the Most High God" (Gen. 14:18).

Without fanfare or explanation, Melchizedek is introduced into this scenario. Who is he? What is he?

His name means *"King of Righteousness,"* and *"King of Peace"* (Heb. 7:2).

Some have thought he was a Canaanite, simply because he resided in Canaan, and was, in fact, king of Salem, an ancient name for Jerusalem. Some claim that he was, in fact, Shem, the son of Noah.

However, we do not know exactly who he was, and the Holy Spirit meant for it to be that way. He suddenly appears after the slaughter of the kings. Up till now, he has been hidden. The True Melchizedek is now hidden, but will appear in blessing, after the destruction of the kings of Revelation, Chapter 19. As King of Righteousness, the Lord Jesus Christ, as stated, the True Melchizedek, will judge the wicked, and as King of Peace He will bless the Earth. Peace does not displace Righteousness, but is based upon it. These are Millennial glories reserved for Israel and the redeemed nations; but the Church, being one with Him, will share all His Glories, whether Heavenly or earthly.

BREAD AND WINE

Melchizedek, at this meeting with Abraham, brings forth *"bread and wine,"* symbolic of the coming Crucifixion. At the Last Supper, the True Melchizedek brought forth bread and wine, symbolizing His Broken Body and His Shed Blood, necessary for the

Salvation of mankind (Mat. 26:29; Mk., Chpt. 14; Lk. 22:15; Rom. 8:21).

Melchizedek as a *"Priest"* also symbolizes the coming Christ, Who is our Great High Priest (Heb. 7:15-17).

Concerning this, David prophesied about 1,000 years after Abraham, *"The LORD has sworn, and will not repent, You* (Christ) *are a Priest forever after the order of Melchizedek"* (Ps. 110:4).

THE AARONIC PRIESTHOOD

Why after Melchizedek and not after Aaron the High Priest of Israel?

The Aaronic Priesthood of Israel was only meant to be temporal, while the Priesthood of Melchizedek is meant to be eternal. The former represented Israel only, while the latter represents the entirety of mankind, both Jews and Gentiles, and forever.

The Old Covenant was a Shadow of Heavenly things. Christ is their substance. He fulfilled all of the Old Covenant, thereby replacing it with the new. Consequently, He is the High Priest after the order of Melchizedek, and will be forever.

He was made such by the *"Most High God,"* i.e., *"El Elyon,"* and there is no greater authority than that.

While Abraham knew God in a glorious and wonderful way, he had not previously known Him as *"El Elyon"*; consequently, he now knows Him in even a higher and more blessed way.

THE BLESSING

"And he (Melchizedek) *blessed him* (blessed Abraham), *and said, Blessed be Abram of the Most High God, Possessor of heaven and Earth"* (Gen. 14:19).

We find here Melchizedek blessing Abraham, which means that the standing of Melchizedek was greater than that of Abraham. How could this be?

The Holy Spirit through Paul said of this situation:

"Now consider how great this man was (Melchizedek), *unto whom even the Patriarch Abraham gave the tenth of the spoils."*

He then said, *"And without all contradiction the less is blessed of the better"* (Heb. 7:4, 7).

Melchizedek stood in a higher position, simply because he was raised up by God to be a Type of Christ, and more particularly, the High Priesthood of Christ. Even though Abraham definitely represented Christ, it was this King-Priest who was a Type of Christ.

Concerning this position, the Holy Spirit through Paul further said:

"Without father, without mother, without descent, having neither beginning of days, nor end of life; but made like unto the Son of God; abides a Priest continually" (Heb. 7:3).

This Passage in Hebrews doesn't mean that Melchizedek didn't have a father or a mother, or that he wasn't born or that he didn't die, but rather that none of these things are recorded of him, because he was to be a Type of the eternal Priesthood of Christ.

JEWISH SCHOLARS

It is the common opinion of many Jewish scholars that Melchizedek was in fact Shem, the son of Noah. As we have stated, Shem was a contemporary of Abraham for a number of years, with some even thinking that possibly he outlived Abraham, dying just before Jacob went down into Egypt.

Considering that this man was referred to by the Holy Spirit as *"King of Righteousness,"* and *"King of Peace"* (Heb. 7:2), this means that he preached remission of sins through the coming Seed of the woman, the

Promised Redeemer. Since this Doctrine was unknown
to the world, or if known, despised by it, the pious people
at Salem (Jerusalem) chose this man to be their King.

Not far from him there ruled the kings of Sodom and
Gomorrah, who far surpassed him in riches, honor,
and power, and, no doubt, they greatly despised him
as a poor, though righteous king; nevertheless, to the
people of Jerusalem at that time, he was Melchizedek,
the King of Righteousness. The others were kings of unrighteousness, tyrants, and idolaters, for which reason,
God in His Righteous Wrath, punished them with war
and bloodshed. Shem, on the other hand, was king
of Salem, that is, king of Peace, which was thought by
some Jewish scholars (Heb. 7:2).

BLESSED OF THE BETTER

We find another Doctrine in this particular Verse
that should be attended closely.

While all Believers should *"pray for the other"* as we
daily seek the Lord, and while it's perfectly proper for
associate Ministers in the Church to lay hands on the
Senior Pastor (Acts 13:1-4), Believers who do not stand
in one of the fivefold Callings (Eph. 4:11) should never
take it upon themselves to lay hands on a Preacher of
the Gospel. All must ever understand that the better
is never blessed by the less. Such attitude smacks of
pride, and is seldom, if ever, of God.

Unfortunately, the land is full of self-called prophets,
etc., who have an exalted opinion of themselves and,
thereby, take it upon themselves to administer so-called
blessings, when in reality, they administer nothing.

The truth is, such action grieves the Holy Spirit,
and for the simple reason that such individuals are
refusing to recognize the Calling that God has placed
upon someone.

What if Abraham had haughtily proceeded to *"bless"* Melchizedek, instead of allowing the Lord to lead the situation? Abraham was the one who had been given the Revelation, had been called into Canaan, but the Patriarch never took a haughty, self-imposed position. He always allowed the Lord to lead in these particulars; consequently, the Word of God was always carried out. In fact, had Abraham not had this humble spirit, he would not have even been a footnote in Biblical history, much less the *"father of us all."*

THE MOST HIGH GOD

The Holy Spirit knows that a great temptation is about to fall upon Abraham, so through Melchizedek, the Lord reveals Himself to the Patriarch in a more exalted manner as *"the Most High God, Possessor of Heaven and Earth."* Abraham would now know Him as *"El Elyon,"* which, in effect, means *"The Most High."*

The king of Sodom, as we shall see, will attempt to entice Abraham with riches, but God is telling him here, through Melchizedek, that the One Abraham is serving is *"Possessor of Heaven and Earth"*; consequently, God can and will give him whatever he needs, which means he doesn't need the ill-gotten gains of the king of Sodom.

"El Elyon" describes God as the *"High, the Highest, the Exalted, the Supreme,"* and is sometimes used in conjunction with Jehovah (Ps. 7:18).

We find here that Melchizedek did not come forth when Abraham was in pursuit of Chedorlaomer, but when the king of Sodom was in pursuit of Abraham. This makes a great moral difference. Concerning this, Mackintosh said:

"A deeper character of communion was needed to meet the deeper character of conflict."[1]

TITHES

*"And blessed be the Most High God, Who has deliv-
ered your enemies into your hand. And he* (Abraham)
gave him (Melchizedek) *tithes of all"* (Gen. 14:20).

Melchizedek blesses Abraham and, as well, blesses
the Lord, giving Him praise and glory and, thereby,
the credit for delivering Abraham from his enemies.
This tells us that the Lord, which should be obvious,
greatly helped Abraham in this conflict. In fact, without this help, it would have been impossible for the
small army of Abraham to have defeated the army of
the enemy, which, no doubt, numbered many times
their size. So proper praise is given to the Lord.

After this blessing, Abraham gave tithes to
Melchizedek, which referred to a tenth, evidently of all
the goods he had taken from the enemy.

This is the first recorded instance of tithes being
given to the Work of the Lord, but it is obvious that this
practice had been carried out for a long, long time.

In Genesis 4:4, where it says that Abel brought *"of
the firstlings of his flock,"* some think that this could
have meant a tenth of the flock, or a tithe. If, in fact,
that was the idea, then the practice continued, and
comes down to us even unto this present time.

THE STANDARD

Abraham paying tithe to Melchizedek set the standard for this practice, and is meant to be continued
even now. Many erroneously think that tithing origi-
nated with the Law of Moses; however, I think it is
obvious that such was not the case. Tithing preceded
that Law, and continues unto this hour.

Abraham paid tithe to Melchizedek, who was a
Type of Christ; consequently, Abraham's children, who

make up the Church presently, are to continue to pay tithe to those carrying out the Work of God, of which Melchizedek was a Type. So we have two Types here.

Abraham was a Type of the Church (Rom. 4:16). Melchizedek was a Type of Christ (Ps. 110:1-4).

Under the Mosaic Law, which is not incumbent upon the Church, there were actually three particular tithes. They are as follows:

• The people were to pay their tithe to the Levites who attended the Temple. In fact, this was the support of the Levites, which included the Priests who attended to all the many duties of the Temple, which was a very involved process, and required many people (Lev., Chpt. 27; Num., Chpt. 18).

• Each family was to lay aside a second tithe (10%) to cover expenses for attending the national Feasts, conducted three times a year, and were all carried out at the Temple in Jerusalem (Deut. 14:22-26).

• There was to be a third tithe of sorts, carried out over three years, totaling three and one-third percent each year. This was for the strangers, fatherless, and widows. It was a special tithe for the poor, a charity tithe to relieve suffering, etc.

It was, as stated, to be given only every third year.

So all of this made up twenty-three and one third percent per year, which was the Mosaic Law.

PRESENTLY

Presently, it is ten percent of our income, and has been since the Day of Pentecost, which was the beginning, in essence, of the Church. Every evidence is that tithing, as a way and manner of the Lord, had its beginning at the very dawn of time, and continues unto this hour. There is no Passage in the Word of God, which abrogates this practice.

In II Corinthians, Chapters 8 and 9, the Holy Spirit through Paul gives the greatest dissertation on giving found in the entirety of the Word of God. And yet, in this dissertation, tithing is not once mentioned. Why? While tithing is incumbent upon the Child of God, that is, if he wants to obey the Lord, giving under the New Covenant is to go much further than ten percent. The idea is, everything we have belongs to God. It is at His disposal, and we are to be ever open to His Leading. In all of the teaching that the Apostle gives in these two Chapters, perhaps the entirety can be summed up in the following.

"But this I say, he who sows sparingly shall reap also sparingly; and he who sows bountifully shall reap also bountifully" (II Cor. 9:6).

"Oh, the joy of sins forgiven,
"Oh, the bliss the Blood-Washed know,
"Oh, the peace akin to Heaven,
"Where the healing waters flow."

"Now with Jesus crucified,
"At His Feet I'm resting low,
"Let me evermore abide,
"Where the healing waters flow."

"Oh, this Precious Perfect Love!
"How it keeps the heart aglow,
"Streaming from the fount above,
"Where the healing waters flow."

"Cleanse from every sin and stain,
"Whiter than the driven snow,
"Now I sing my sweet refrain,
"Where the healing waters flow."

ABRAHAM

CHAPTER

10

Abraham And
The Riches Of Sodom

ABRAHAM AND THE RICHES OF SODOM

"And the king of Sodom said unto Abram, Give me the persons, and take the goods to yourself" (Gen. 14:21).

Satan's ways are always very subtle. Abraham had performed a valuable service for the five kings, with the king of Sodom being the leading principal. So, in effect, Abraham having defeated the four kings who had attacked the five, which the five couldn't do, the five were in his debt.

It's perfectly satisfactory for the world to be in debt to the Believer, but never the Believer to be in debt to the world. Now when I say that, I'm not speaking of the normal and natural courtesy that every Believer should show any and all concerned, whomever they may be, for favors done, etc. It's the snare of which I speak, and that for which the Believer should be on guard.

Sodom was a doomed city, as well as several others of the five. In fact, their time was running out, even as the king of Sodom was speaking to Abraham.

It was another opportunity for this king to come to know the Lord. Without a doubt he knew that there was something different about Abraham. This man Abraham, as stated, with a small army, had defeated the confederation, of which they had been unable to do. He sought to appease his conscience by offering Abraham money, when the real problem was Spiritual.

ABRAHAM'S ANSWER

"And Abram said to the king of Sodom, I have lift up my hand unto the LORD, the Most High God, the Possessor of heaven and Earth" (Gen. 14:22).

Evidently much more went on here than meets the eye. It seems from the terminology used by the

Patriarch that the king of Sodom may have proposed an amalgamation of sorts with Abraham. But the Patriarch proclaims to all concerned that his allegiance is totally and completely to *"the LORD, the Most High God, the Possessor of heaven and Earth."* In this, he proclaims the fact that he is beholden to no man, but yet, gracious to all men, even as he was in delivering this king and his confederates.

Once again, that goes back to separation.

We are in the world, but, as Believers, we are definitely not of the world; however, separation does not mean isolation. Our lights are to shine before men that they may see our good works, and thereby glorify the Lord Who is in Heaven.

Abraham definitely performed good works and definitely glorified God, but he absolutely refused any entanglement with the world.

That should be our example!

THE GOLD OF SODOM

"That I will not take from a thread even to a shoe-latchet, and that I will not take anything that is yours, lest you should say, I have made Abram rich:

"Save only that which the young men have eaten, and the portion of the men which went with me, Aner, Eshcol, and Mamre; let them take their portion" (Gen. 14:23-24).

Abraham, lifting his hand to God and proclaiming to the king of Sodom that he would not take even so much as a thread or a shoelace, proclaims the fact that the Lord had instructed him in this capacity.

What a difference this meeting was than that in Egypt! There, Abraham, functioning from the position of fear, accepted all types of gifts from Pharaoh which was no credit to the Lord God of Glory. Now the Patriarch is operating in Faith, and because he is where God wants him to be, the story is now quite different. Faith is never fearful and Faith is never greedy.

At the same time, he made it known that the allies with him could be free to take what they so desired, and what the king of Sodom desired to give them.

LOT

It is noticeable that Lot is not mentioned in these proceedings. The reasons are obvious.

He has compromised himself with Sodom, and even now he hasn't learned his lesson, even as we shall see. So, the meeting with Melchizedek he will miss and, as well, the Revelation of God as *"The Most High."*

How much we miss when we miss God!

In all of this, Melchizedek may never have imagined how great was the dignity put upon him as a Type of Christ. Living a quiet, pure, and devoted life, he becomes accepted by his fellows as a Priest of the Most High, and becomes the Type of Him Who was to be the Saviour of the world.

FAITH

Faith, which Melchizedek exhibited, is always stronger, bigger, and greater than we could ever begin to imagine. In fact, anything from God always fits that category, but it's always Faith that allows us access to the Most High, and, more importantly, Faith in Christ and what Christ has done for us at the Cross.

Everything we see in these Chapters is a prelude to the main event, and that main event is always Christ and Him Crucified. That, and that alone, would bring mankind out of the terrible morass of evil, which now holds him in a vice-like grip. Jesus broke those chains!

Under the Jewish Dispensation, there was no one who, in his person, could represent the twofold character of Christ as the only High Priest and universal King. But in Melchizedek, both Offices are proclaimed!

A PERSONAL EXPERIENCE

If I remember correctly, the year was 1958. While Frances and I had begun Evangelistic work in 1956, we launched out full time in 1958. However, I must quickly add that launching out created no head-lines anywhere.

At any rate, I was preaching a meeting at our home Church in Ferriday, Louisiana. It was Sunday and, after the Service, there was a dinner on the grounds which was somewhat common in those days.

A table was set up at the back of the Church, and the ladies of the Church, what few there were, brought the food.

Frances and I were standing, eating, and enjoy-ing the fellowship, when all of a sudden, there turns off the main highway, onto the side road that led to the Church, a brand new Cadillac. It drove up very close to where I was standing and stopped. My Uncle quickly got out of the car. This was the dad of Jerry Lee Lewis. Elmo was his name.

My Uncle was a very likeable individual. If you met him, you liked him. It was that simple. He stood about six feet, six inches tall, and probably weighed about 200 pounds, if that.

At any rate, everyone was looking at that brand-new Cadillac, plus greeting him. In fact, this little Assembly of God Church in Ferriday, Louisiana, was the home Church of Jerry Lee's parents, along with my parents.

THE PROPOSAL

At any rate, after my Uncle had met and greeted the people, he hurriedly walked over to me and said, *"Jimmy, I have the greatest news."*

He went on to say, *"Sam Phillips has sent for you. Sun Records is starting a Gospel line, and you are to be the first artist."*

At that time, Sun Records was at least one of the largest labels in the world, having started Elvis Presley, my cousin Jerry Lee Lewis, Carl Perkins, Johnny Cash, and a host of others. To be sure, this was good news and I opened my mouth to say *I'm ready,* when the Holy Spirit checked me.

I must have looked a little strange, because my Uncle said to me, *"Jimmy, did you hear what I just said?"*

I looked at him for a moment and then said, *"Yes I heard you, and I am very, very grateful; however, I can't do it."*

He looked at me and said again, *"Jimmy, your car is falling all to pieces. Every time I see you, you've got on the same suit. As well, every time I see Frances, she has on the same dress."* He then said, *"A week from now, you could be driving a Cadillac exactly like the one I've got here."*

To be sure, this offer was very, very enticing. Besides that, how could it hurt, considering that it was Gospel music!

I didn't really know what to say to my Uncle, except what I had already stated. I didn't understand it myself. Why could I not go, considering, as stated, that it was Gospel music?

I retorted to him that he should thank Sam Phillips very profusely for the offer that was made. I tried to tell my uncle how much I appreciated it, because I didn't want to seem ungrateful.

At any rate, my Uncle, who really wasn't living for God, looked at me and said, *"Jimmy, I think I understand."*

WHY?

I wish I had the vocabulary to properly express exactly how I felt at that moment. My Uncle was right. Our car was falling to pieces, and we really did not know where the next dollar was coming from.

I overheard one of the dear ladies nearby say, *"Did you hear what he just did? He turned down that offer."*

I walked away, actually going into the little Church. There was a little broom and mop closet there, and I stepped inside of it, to get alone with the Lord.

TRUST ME!

For a few moments I poured out my heart to God, asking Him why I could not do this. It was Gospel music, and, on the surface, it seemed like an answer to prayer. Especially considering how much Frances and I needed the money. Yet the Holy Spirit had said, *"No."*

After a few minutes I sensed the Presence of the Lord, and He spoke to me in answer to my questions. He did so with just two words. He said, *"Trust Me!"*

That was all, just the two words. No explanation was given, no reasons why, just two words, *"Trust Me."*

Looking back these many, many years, I think I now know, at least somewhat, as to what the Lord was doing.

THE EXPLANATION?

From then until now, without signing with record companies, by strictly allowing the Lord to be our Arranger, Distributor, etc., we have sold some 16 million Recordings. And we give the Lord all the praise and all the glory for that. I believe the Lord was wanting to show me, even as Abraham said to the king of Sodom, that he didn't need the world or anything pertaining to the world to do what He wanted to do with the musical ability that He had originally given me.

We must understand that, at times, the Lord will tell us to do things or not do certain things, which of themselves aren't wrong; but the reason is, those things are not, whatever they might be, His Will. The Lord wants to Lead us, wants to Guide us, and we had better be careful that the offers which come from the world do not have strings attached, and they almost always do. What a Mighty God we serve!

"Loved with Everlasting Love,
"Led by Grace that Love to know;
"Spirit, Breathing from above,
"You have taught it is so!"

"Oh, this Full and Perfect Peace!
"Oh, this transport all Divine!
"In a Love which cannot cease,
"I am His, and He is mine."

"Heaven above is softer blue,
"Earth around is sweeter green,
"Something lives in every hue,
"Christless eyes have never seen."

"Birds with gladder songs overflow,
"Flowers with deeper beauties shine,
"Since I know, as now I know,
"I am His, and He is mine."

"Things that once were wild alarms,
"Cannot disturb my rest,

"Closed in Everlasting Arms,
"Pillowed on the Loving Breast."

"Oh, to lie forever here,
"Doubt and care and self resign,
"While He Whispers in my ear,
"I am His, and He is mine."

"His forever, only His;
"Who the Lord and me shall part?
"Ah, with what a rest of bliss,
"Christ can fill the loving heart!"

"Heaven and Earth may fade and flee,
"Firstborn light and bloom decline;
"But while God and I shall be,
"I am His, and He is mine."

ABRAHAM

CHAPTER

—————

11

Abraham And Fear

ABRAHAM AND FEAR

"After these things the Word of the LORD came unto Abram in a Vision" (Gen. 15:1).

Without a doubt, Genesis, Chapter 15, is one of the single most important Chapters in the entirety of the Word of God. We will find that the Lord appeared to Abraham in a Vision. The way that God approached Abraham presents one of four ways in which God spoke to individuals in Old Testament Times (Num. 12:6-8):

1. He spoke in Visions (Amos 7:1).

2. He spoke in Dreams (Gen. 41:1; Dan. 2:1).

3. He revealed Himself by speaking directly to the Prophets *"mouth to mouth"* (Dan. 12:8).

4. He spoke through His Word (Mat. 4:4). The time of the Gospels was still under Old Testament authority simply because the New Covenant had not yet been given.

How long it was after the events of Chapter 14 that Abraham had this Vision, we aren't told.

The contents of this Vision will include many things; however, the greatest part will be the Revelation of *"Justification by Faith,"* which we will address in the next Chapter of this Book. While this Revelation would continue to expand the balance of Abraham's life, it was here that the foundation was laid. Consequently, it would affect the entirety of the human race and, above all, those who would make Jesus Christ their Lord and their Saviour.

As it regards *"Justification by Faith,"* a great Foundation had already been laid. It is all found in the Altar. In fact, Abraham is known as the *"Altar Builder."* The Vision given here to the Patriarch gives him a much more expanded knowledge of what the Altar was all about.

"After these things the Word of the LORD came unto Abram in a Vision, saying, Fear not, Abram: I am your shield, and your exceeding great reward" (Gen. 15:1).

The short phrase, *"Saying, Fear not, Abram,"* proclaims the fact that fear had definitely been present, and to such an extent that the Lord would have to reinforce His Promises to the Patriarch.

From previous Manifestations, Abraham knew that a child was to be born to him. For all of these Promises to be carried out, it was absolutely necessary that this child, in fact, a little boy, be born. Due to the recent conflict with the four kings, Abraham had made powerful enemies. Most probably, the threats of death to the Patriarch had come to his ears. In that climate, human life was cheap. Even though he had defeated these kings in battle, it was still within their power to hire assassins to take the life of the Patriarch by stealth. What they had failed to do in battle, they may well have threatened to do in another manner.

The humiliation of their defeat must have been great, especially considering that they had been defeated by this stranger and his soldier-herdsmen.

Whatever the reason for the fear, it was not merely that the Lord had appeared to him in the Vision, but rather went far deeper than that. Even though the Appearance of the Lord is always a momentous occasion, still, the relationship between Abraham and Jehovah was such that the Appearance of the Lord would have evoked no fear, at least in this capacity.

Many might be quick to condemn the Patriarch, wondering why he would fear, considering that he had just experienced a tremendous victory.

The answer to that is not as difficult as it at first seems. Great victories in the Lord are often followed by an attack on our Faith. Jealous of the defeat recently suffered, the Evil One will renew his efforts by crowding the mind with all types of thoughts. If he cannot stop the victory, he will try to demean the victory, and fear is usually the result.

A PERSONAL EXAMPLE

What I'm about to say is small potatoes by comparison to that which Abraham experienced; however, the principle is the same.

In November, 2001, it had come to our attention that a powerful radio station in east Texas might be possible to obtain. It had a wide coverage, reaching nearly one and one-half million people.

In 1998, the Lord gave me a Vision regarding radio and what I must do regarding this particular medium. We set out to do what He had told us to do, and the success was immediate. I had been seeking the Lord for several months as it regarded coverage in the major cities, wondering how such could be done, especially considering the price of powerful FM stations. Now, here was a station that seemed to be within our reach.

I immediately went to prayer, asking the Lord what we should do. In a few minutes' time, the Lord told me how much money to offer the people and on what terms it would be offered. It was so simple that, in fact, it seemed to be too simple.

I had my associate, David Whitelaw, contact the necessary parties, and we made arrangements to go and speak with them the very next day. I took three of my associates with me.

THE OFFER

We met the broker and one of the principle owners at a designated place and discussed the situation for a short period of time.

I then asked the two men to step out of the room while I consulted with my associates. I related to them what I believed the Lord had told me to do. They immediately gave their approval. The two men were asked to come back into the room. On a piece of paper, I outlined to them what I would pay for the station and the terms that I would like to have.

They looked at my figures for a few minutes and then tried to push the price higher, but finally accepted my offer. Now, the point of this illustration:

After we shook hands on the deal, fear gripped my heart for the next several hours, seemingly, in a hundred different ways. How could we pay for it? I knew the Lord had told me to do this thing, but I also knew that I had to raise the money by going before our audience over radio and asking for their help. Would they respond favorably?

The truth is, we didn't have a single dollar on that particular day.

Now, why should I fear when the situation had worked out exactly as the Lord had told me it would work out?

Incidentally, the radio audience responded very favorably to my purchase of this station, supplying the funds for the down-payment, and doing so in a short period of time.

The reason for the fear was, as previously stated, Satan, not being able to stop the victory, would now try to demean the victory.

SHIELD

The phrase, *"I am your shield,"* proclaims the Lord informing the Patriarch that irrespective of the threats of these defeated kings, or anyone else for that matter, the Lord would be a Shield. In that case, there was nothing on Earth, in Heaven, or under the Earth that could hurt Abraham. To be frank, if the Lord has told someone that certain things are going to happen and that this certain person will be included in those things, to be sure, the Lord is a Shield for that individual.

If it is to be noticed, the Lord didn't merely say that He would provide a shield, but rather, *"I am your shield."* In fact, it was there all the time, not just when he was fighting those five kings. There is no higher power than such a word coming from *"El Elyon, Possessor of Heaven and Earth."*

Of course, people can rebel against the Lord and demand to have their own way, which can cause the shield to be removed, but unless that happens, the *"Shield"* remains.

REWARD

The phrase, *"And your exceeding great reward,"* in effect, was telling Abraham that the Lord was his Reward and not those things which the Lord had promised, as exceptional as they might have been.

As Believers, we have a tendency to get our eyes on the reward instead of the Rewarder. In fact, that's what Abraham was doing, as well, and actually, it is very easy to do.

When we do this, we see nothing but problems and difficulties exactly as Abraham saw nothing but problems and difficulties. If we keep our eyes on the Lord, understanding that He Alone is our Reward, then the other things take care of themselves because we know it's the Lord doing the doing and not man. Eyes on the reward, and the reward only, tend to shift faith from God to ourselves, which always brings problems.

In October, 1991, the Lord spoke to my heart, telling me to begin two prayer meetings each day. After these prayer meetings began, which I personally continue even unto this hour, the Lord spoke to my heart saying, *"Seek Me not so much for what I can do, but rather for Who I am."* In essence, that's the same thing that the Lord told Abraham.

WHAT WILL YOU GIVE ME?

"And Abram said, LORD God, what will You give me, seeing I go childless, and the steward of my house is this Eliezer of Damascus?" (Gen. 15:2)

As stated, Abraham knows that the great statement made to him by the Lord concerns him having a child, a little boy. He remembers very vividly the Promise made to him by the Lord some years earlier when the Lord appeared unto him and said, *". . . Unto your seed will I give this land . . ."* (Gen. 12:7). So, in effect, he is asking, *"How can I have all of these things, seeing I go childless?"* He wonders, *"Can this Eliezer of Damascus, my servant, be my heir?"*

Sarah is now well past 65 years of age, probably about 70. Considering her age, especially that she had been barren all of her life, how could this thing be?

As always, Abraham was trying to figure the thing out. How could it be done? How was it all possible?

With God, questions are useless! Even though Faith is tempted to ask questions, it should not do so. If God has said it, irrespective as to how impossible it might look, He will bring it to pass. He is able to do all things!

A SERVANT

"And Abram said, Behold, to me You have given no seed: and, lo, one born in my house is my heir" (Gen. 15:3).

Abraham holds a conversation with the Lord, pointing out the fact that he has heard the Promise given to him concerning *"his seed,"* but, as of yet, he has no seed, i.e., *"no son."* Also, as it stands at the present, *"The son of my house, not born of me, is, as of now, my heir. Eliezer is his name."*

So now, in this perplexing situation, even as we shall see in the next Verse, the Lord will expand this Revelation to the Patriarch.

THE HEIR

"And, behold, the Word of the LORD came unto him, saying, This shall not be your heir; but he who shall come forth out of your own bowels shall be your heir" (Gen. 15:4).

Now, as stated, the Revelation is expanded. The Lord tells Abraham that, in fact, he will have a son, and he shall be the father of that son. It will not be someone adopted, etc.

However, the Lord doesn't include Sarah in the mix at this time, actually saying nothing about her. That will come later. That's the way Revelation generally is.

The Lord gives us bits and pieces, so to speak, and does it in this manner for a particular reason. He's teaching us trust and Faith even as He reveals His Way and Direction to us.

From this we learn that, most of the time, we aren't quite as strong in Faith as we think we are. So, the Ways and Manners of the Lord are designed with several purposes in mind, all for our good.

"She only touched the hem of His Garment,
"As to His Side she stole,
"Amid the crowd that gathered around Him,
"And straight way she was whole."

"She came in fear and trembling before Him,
"She knew her Lord had come;
"She felt that from Him virtue had healed her,
"The mighty deed was done."

"He turned with 'daughter, be of good comfort,
"'Your Faith has made you whole,'
"And peace that passes all understanding,
"With gladness filled her soul."

ABRAHAM

CHAPTER

12

Abraham And
Justification By Faith

ABRAHAM AND JUSTIFICATION BY FAITH

THE STARS

"And He brought him forth abroad, and said, Look now toward Heaven, and tell (count) *the stars, if you be able to number them: and He said unto him, So shall your seed be"* (Gen. 15:5).

While Abraham is pondering the seeming impossibility of having even one child, the Lord takes him outside the tent, has him look up at the stars, and tells him, *"So shall your seed be."* So it was, and so it is!

God's Ways are always so much larger than our ways. In fact, as here illustrated, there is no comparison.

Whatever the Lord calls us to do, no matter how seemingly impossible it is at the outset, He will give us the Faith to believe for that which we should. It will not come immediately, and it will not come without incident or difficulty, but it will come.

A PERSONAL EXPERIENCE

When we began the SONLIFE BROADCASTING NETWORK, and I speak of television, I did not see how in the world that it could be done, but I knew the Lord had said to do it. As we set out to carry out what the Lord had commanded, the pieces began to fall into place. The Lord began to work Miracle after Miracle. As I dictate these notes on June 4, 2012, we are now going into slightly over one-half of the homes in the United States and some 14 million homes in the United Kingdom (England, Northern Ireland, Scotland, and Wales). As well, we are on satellites all over the world. The Lord has told us to place the programming, I speak of the MESSAGE OF THE CROSS, in every city in the world that will accept it,

and that's what we have set out to do. I have watched
the Lord work Miracle after Miracle. I've watched Him
bring the necessary people to this Ministry. I have
watched Him do what others said could not be done.
He is a God of Might and Miracles, and He only waits
for men and women to believe Him. So it was, and
so it is!

FAITH

*"And he believed in the LORD; and He counted it to
him for Righteousness"* (Gen. 15:6).

This Sixth Verse is one of the single most important Scriptures in the entirety of the Word of God. In
this simple term, we find the meaning of Justification
by Faith. Abraham was Saved by Grace through
Faith, not by his good works. There is no other way of
Salvation anywhere in the Bible (Eph. 2:8-10).

God demands Righteousness; however, it is the
Righteousness afforded strictly by Christ and Christ
Alone. Everything else is self-righteousness and totally
unacceptable to God.

Paul bases the central article of our Christian
Faith upon Genesis 15:6, which both the world and
the Devil hate, namely, that Faith alone justifies and
saves (Rom. 3:28).

It was to Paul that the meaning of the New Covenant
was given, which, in effect, is the meaning of the Cross.
The great Apostle framed the entirety of his teaching
around Genesis 15:6. In fact, he quoted the exact statement as made about the great Patriarch. He said:

*". . . Abraham believed God, and it was counted unto
him for Righteousness"* (Rom. 4:3).

To answer the question as to what Abraham
believed, we must point to the Cross. He believed that
God would send forth a Redeemer into the world, and
that the seed that he (Abraham) would bring forth

would have something to do with the coming of the Redeemer. He also believed that this coming Redeemer would give His Life in order to redeem the fallen sons of Adam's lost race, hence, the constant demands by God that Abraham build Altars.

Abraham would not have known anything about the Cross, just the Death of the One Who was coming. It remained for Moses to give that Revelation by the serpent on the pole (Num., Chpt. 21; Jn. 3:14-15).

Also, as Jesus spoke to Israel, He said:

"Your father Abraham rejoiced to see My Day: and he saw it, and was glad" (Jn. 8:56).

The short phrase, *"My Day,"* refers to Who Jesus was and what Jesus did. He was the Son of the Living God, God manifest in the Flesh. As such, He went to the Cross and offered Himself as a Perfect Sacrifice, which atoned for all sin, past, present, and future, at least for all who would believe (Jn. 3:16). That's what He did. Jesus Christ is the New Covenant, and the Cross of Christ is the meaning of that New Covenant, the meaning of which was given to the Apostle Paul.

The word, *"Believed,"* as used regarding Abraham, simply means to have Faith, but what does that mean?

THE OBJECT OF OUR FAITH

The Cross of Christ must ever be the Object of our Faith. This pertains to what Jesus did on our behalf and actually did as our Substitute. At the Cross, He satisfied the demands of the broken Law and did so by pouring out His Life's Blood, thereby, giving His Life (Eph. 2:13-18). Therefore, when the believing sinner evidences Faith in Christ and what Christ did at the Cross, a perfect, pure Righteousness, the Righteousness of God, is instantly imputed to the believing sinner. In fact, God will impart such Righteousness on no other basis than Faith in the Finished Work of Christ.

Christianity is very simple. It's not complicated at all. If it is complicated, it is because we have made it so. In order to be Saved, the Scripture simply says, *"Believe on the Lord Jesus Christ, and you shall be Saved, and your house"* (Acts 16:31), or *"Whosoever calls on the Name of the Lord shall be Saved"* (Rom. 10:13). Nothing could be simpler than that.

THE CHRISTIAN AND VICTORY

What I've said thus far is readily believed and understood by any true Christian. However, as it regards our everyday walk before God, that is, the *"living"* of this Christian experience, this is where most Christians go off track. They automatically relegate that which Abraham said about believing God, and how that God imputed it to him for Righteousness, to the initial, Born-Again experience. Most don't think of it at all as it regards our daily walk before God. However, this statement made about Abraham, and that which Paul used as the foundation of his great Gospel of Salvation by Grace, is just as apropos for the Believer as it is for the sinner coming to Christ, but most Christians don't know that. So, they cast about, trying to build their own victory, and always conclude by building a house on sand. It looks good for awhile, in fact, just as good as the real thing. However, once the adverse weather begins to come, and, sooner or later, it shall come, then the true story is told, and the house is lost.

THE CROSS

The truth is, the Cross is just as important to the Believer's ongoing victory as it is for the sinner being Saved. This is proven to us in Romans, Chapter 6.

Paul begins that Chapter by saying, *"What shall we say then? Shall we continue in (the) sin, that Grace may abound?"*

He answered by saying, *"God forbid. How shall we, who are dead to (the) sin, live any longer therein?"* (Rom. 6:1-2).

Paul is dealing here with the sin question, actually, the sin nature, as it pertains to Christians. In other words, he is about to tell us how to live a victorious, overcoming Christian life. So, what does he say in regards to that?

GOD'S PRESCRIBED ORDER OF VICTORY

Beginning with Verse 3 of the Sixth Chapter of Romans, Paul immediately goes into a dissertation on the Cross of Christ. He said:

"Do you not know, that so many of us as were baptized into Jesus Christ were baptized into His Death?" (Rom. 6:3).

Most Christians brush past this Scripture simply because they misunderstand the word, *"Baptize,"* thinking it means Water Baptism. It doesn't! They conclude that, inasmuch as they have been baptized in water, they do not need to dwell here for any length of time.

The truth is, Romans, Chapter 6, is one of the most important Chapters in the entirety of the Bible. One can say without it being an exaggeration, *"As it regards living for God and living a victorious life, Romans, Chapter 6, is the single most important Chapter in the entirety of the Bible."* In fact, every Chapter before this leads to Romans, Chapter 6, while every Chapter after this pushes back towards Romans, Chapter 6.

THE CRUCIFIXION OF CHRIST AND
NOT WATER BAPTISM

As stated, Paul is not speaking here of Water Baptism, but rather the Death of Christ on the Cross and how that we were baptized into His Death, which took place upon our evidencing Faith in Christ when we were Born- Again. Now, of course, the reader must understand that we're speaking here of something spiritual and not physical. The idea is this:

The moment you as a believing sinner expressed Faith in Christ, even though, at that time, you did not know too very much about Christ, in the Mind of God, you were literally placed in Christ as He died on the Cross. He died as our Substitute, and our Faith in Him places us in His Actual Crucifixion.

The Apostle then said:

"Therefore we are buried with Him by baptism into death: that like as Christ was raised up from the dead by the Glory of the Father, even so we also should walk in Newness of Life" (Rom. 6:4).

We not only were baptized into the Death of Christ when we evidenced Faith, but when Christ was buried, we, as well, were buried with Him. This means that the old you, the sinful you, the you that you would like to forget, with all of its filth, sin, and evil passions, were buried with Christ, meaning that the old you died.

You were then raised with Christ from the dead (from spiritual death), and you now *"walk in Newness of Life."* That's what your Faith gets you.

The Apostle then said:

"For if we have been planted together in the likeness of His Death, we shall be also in the likeness of His Resurrection" (Rom. 6:5).

This Passage plainly tells us that we cannot be in the likeness of His Resurrection until we first of all understand that we have been *"planted together in the likeness of His Death."* Resurrection Life is predicated on Faith in the *"likeness of His Death,"* i.e., *"the Cross."* In other words, we died with Him and came forth a new man.

BAPTISM

The word, *"Baptism,"* as used in the Bible, can be used literally or figuratively. Literally, it refers to being baptized in water. Figuratively, it is used as a metaphor. Let me give you Scripture:

"I indeed baptize you with water unto Repentance: but there comes One after me Who is mightier than I, Who shall baptize you with the Holy Spirit and with fire" (Mat. 3:11). In the first part of this Verse, John the Baptist uses the word, *"Baptize,"* in a literal sense. He is speaking of Water Baptism. In the latter part of the Verse, he uses the word, *"Baptize,"* in a figurative sense. That's what Paul is doing in the Sixth Chapter of Romans.

FAITH

Now, as a Christian, and determined to live a victorious life, the way we do that is to understand that everything we have from God comes to us entirely through the Cross. As stated, Paul explained that to us in Verses 3, 4, and 5 of Romans, Chapter 6. Understanding that, *"We are to reckon ourselves to be dead indeed unto sin, but alive unto God through Jesus Christ our Lord"* (Rom. 6:11).

We are to understand that Jesus Christ addressed every single problem at the Cross, which man incurred at the Fall. We are to believe that and, thereby, to reckon ourselves to be dead unto the old life. In other words, the old life has no more control over us.

As we keep our Faith in the Cross, understanding what Jesus has done for us, and that our victory is always in the Cross, the Holy Spirit through Paul gave us the guarantee that *"sin shall not have dominion over you: for we are no longer under the Law, but under Grace"* (Rom. 6:14).

However, if we shift our faith from the Cross to other things, to be sure, sin will once again begin to have dominion over us, which means that the sin nature will then begin to rule us.

Let's look at the sin nature in a little more detail:

THE SIN NATURE

Some 17 times in the Sixth Chapter of Romans, the Apostle Paul refers to *"sin."* Fourteen of those 17 times, he is directly referring to the sin nature. Two of the remaining three times actually means the sin nature even though it is only inferred. In the original Greek language, before the word, *"Sin,"* it carries what is referred to as *"the definite article."* In other words, using the First Verse as an example, Paul actually wrote, *"What shall we say then? Shall we continue in the sin. . . ."* This means that he is not referring to particular acts of sin, but rather the principle of sin, i.e., *"the sin nature."*

In fact, every Believer has three natures. He has:

1. Human nature: Christ had a human nature as well.

2. Sin nature: every human being has a sin nature as a result of Adam's fall. Jesus didn't have a sin nature because He was not born by natural procreation. In other words, He was not the product of Joseph's sperm or Mary's egg. He was actually conceived in Mary's womb as a result of a decree given by the Holy Spirit (Lk. 1:35).

3. Divine Nature: every Believer has the Divine Nature, and it is the most powerful nature of all (II Pet. 1:4). The Divine Nature comes into the Believer at the moment of Salvation, i.e., *"Born-Again."*

WHAT EXACTLY IS THE SIN NATURE?

The sin nature is what happened to Adam and Eve immediately after the Fall. They fell from a position of total God-consciousness way down to the far, far, lower level of total sin-consciousness. In other words, now, after the Fall, their every action and thought is labeled by God as sin. Their very nature becomes that of sin in totality. If you as a Believer will look back at your own life before Conversion, you will have to admit the same thing.

However, once the believing sinner comes to Christ, isn't the sin nature then removed?

No, it isn't! It is, in fact, made dormant, meaning that it's of no problem now whatsoever. However, it can have a resurrection very easily. Let me explain.

When the new Convert gives his heart to Christ, all of a sudden, he hates sin in every capacity. He thinks to himself that he will never sin again, but he finds to his dismay that, in fact, not very long after Conversion, he fails the Lord in some way.

In the doing of this, it scares him, and he resolves that it will never happen again. However, instead of placing his Faith exclusively in Christ and the Cross, he resorts to other means. The other means can be anything from A to Z, anything except the Cross. When he does this, this greatly hinders the Holy Spirit. Then, the sin nature begins to be revived and starts to rule the Believer, with this situation being as bad, or even worse, than it was before Conversion. He then resorts to a never-ending vortex of trying one method after the other to have victory, all to no avail. There is no victory over sin outside of the Cross of Christ.

The sad truth is, the far, far, greater majority of Believers in the world today, and I speak of those who truly love the Lord, are, in fact, being ruled by the sin nature. They don't want this, and they've tried everything to get victory over it. However, the problem is not only not better, it rather is worse, and getting worse as time goes on. That's exactly what will happen to the Believer if he makes something other than the Cross of Christ the object of his faith.

SALVATION AND SANCTIFICATION

Most Believers have an understanding of the Cross of Christ as it regards Salvation. The greatest statement in the world is *"Jesus died for me"*; however, that is where it stops with most Believers. When it comes to our Sanctification, how we live for God, how we grow in Grace and the Knowledge of the Lord, and how we have victory over the world, the flesh, and the Devil, not one Christian out of 10,000 understands what Paul taught concerning this situation.

Please understand, ninety-nine percent of the Bible is given over to telling us how to live for God. The other one percent relates to sinners being Saved. In fact, ninety-nine percent of Paul's writings, and he is the one to whom the meaning of the New Covenant was given, is given over to telling us how to live for God. The truth is, it is very simple and very easy to be Saved; however, living for God, and doing so victoriously, is something else altogether.

The sin nature is addressed by the modern church in several different ways. The first one is:

IGNORANCE

I think I can say without any fear of exaggeration that most Christians are totally ignorant of the sin nature. This, which can cause them more problems than they could ever begin to think or realize, is actually, for the most part, an unknown quantity in their lives. This is tragic, but it is true.

Whatever we learn about the Bible, for the most part, has to be taught from behind our pulpits. Regrettably, with most preachers not understanding the sin nature, almost nothing is said about this subject when, in reality, this is one of the most important aspects of the Christian life. In fact, this is why Paul spent so much time on this particular subject.

Using myself as an example, I cannot remember hearing one single message on the sin nature in all the years of my coming up in Church. As well, even though I have been a voracious reader all of my life, I don't recall ever reading one single message on the sin nature. This fact proved to be very hurtful to this Evangelist as it does to all. Sadly, the modern church is totally ignorant as it regards the sin nature.

DENIAL

Then we have a great segment of the church which denies that there is a sin nature. While they might admit that such existed before Conversion, they claim it was taken away at Conversion.

Once again, I counter with a question: *"If we have no sin nature as Believers, why did the Holy Spirit through Paul spend so much time on the subject?"* To use just one Scripture of many, listen to what he said:

"Let not (the) sin therefore reign in your mortal body, that you should obey it in the lusts thereof" (Rom. 6:12).

Paul is not speaking here of acts of sin, but rather the sin nature simply because he uses the definite article, *"The,"* in front of the word, *"Sin,"* making it read, *"The sin."* He's speaking of the sin principle or the nature of sin, that which took place with the fall of Adam. In other words, after the Fall, it became the very nature of mankind to sin.

It must be understood that when Paul wrote the Sixth Chapter of Romans, he was writing to Believers. So, if the sin nature does not exist in the life of the Believer, then what is Paul talking about?

The truth is, even as Paul deals with the subject over and over, the sin nature definitely does exist in the Believer. Momentarily, I will address the manner in which it is to be handled by the Believer.

LICENSE

The third way in which many Believers address the sin nature is the *"sin a little bit everyday"* syndrome. In other words, they admit that they have a sin nature, but because they have a sin nature, they are not really responsible, they say, for the many failures, which they have constantly.

They claim that no matter how much sin abounds, Grace abounds much more (Rom. 5:20).

It is certainly true that where sin abounded, Grace did much more abound; however, that in no way gives us a license to sin, but rather the liberty to live a Holy Life.

Paul's answer to that is:

"God forbid. How shall we, who are dead to sin, live any longer therein?" (Rom. 6:2). The Grace of God gives us liberty, but it definitely does not give us license. To be frank, license is the sin of antinomianism.

In the Greek, *"anti"* means, *"To be opposed."* The word, *"Nomos,"* means, *"Law."* So, the meaning of the word is that Christians who think this way, and I speak of turning Grace into license, are opposed to any law. In other words, they are lawless, which, of course, is unbiblical.

STRUGGLE

Not knowing how to address the sin nature or possibly not even knowing what it is, most Christians, especially those who fall into the first two categories, struggle against this monster. This means that their Christian experience is primarily one of *"sinning and repenting."* In fact, the harder the person struggles against this thing, the worse the situation becomes, which leaves the person confused.

Concerning this, Paul said of himself before he understood the Message of the Cross, *"For that which I do I allow not"* (Rom. 7:15). The word, *"Allow,"* should have been translated, *"Understand."* What he really said is:

"For that which I do I understand not." As stated, this characterizes most Christians. They struggle and fight, but not only do they not win this conflict, in fact, the situation just continues to get worse, which leaves the Believer in a quandary. What is wrong? Considering that they are trying so hard, why is it that they are not succeeding?

Let the reader understand that if the sin nature is not approached correctly, and by that, we speak of being Scriptural, the Believer is not going to come out successful. It doesn't matter what he does, to what church he belongs, how much he quotes Scriptures over and over, how much he prays or fasts, etc. While all of these things are very good in their own way, none will bring victory to the Child of God. Paul plainly addressed this by saying:

"I do not frustrate the Grace of God: for if Righteousness come by the Law, then Christ is dead in vain" (Gal. 2:21).

If you as a Believer can make yourself righteous by your struggle, which actually falls out to a law of some nature, then Christ came down to this world and died on a Cross in vain. In other words, He wasted His Time.

Well, of course, we know that He didn't waste His Time, so what is the true answer to this dilemma?

GRACE

Paul told us the answer in many and varied ways; however, this one Passage, I think, will explain it properly. The Apostle said:

"I am crucified with Christ: nevertheless I live; yet not I, but Christ lives in me: and the life which I now live

in the flesh I live by the Faith of the Son of God, Who loved me, and gave Himself for me" (Gal. 2:20).

Paul takes us back to Romans 6:3-5. He tells us that the secret of our victorious life is that we were *"crucified with Christ."* This means that everything we receive from the Lord comes to us through the Cross; consequently, as a Believer, the Object of our Faith must ever be the Cross and not other things.

Regrettably, as it regards victory in our living an overcoming life, the Faith of most Christians is anchored squarely in things other than the Cross. I speak of *"good works,"* belonging to a certain church, memorizing certain Scriptures and quoting them over and over, fasting so many days, etc. In fact, when it comes to devising ways to live this Christian life, there are about as many different ways as there are Christians. However, none of them will work, with the exception of the Grace of God.

GOD'S WAY

As a Believer, you are to simply place your Faith in Christ and what Christ did for us at the Cross. You are to keep your Faith anchored in the Cross and even renew that anchored Faith on a daily basis (Lk. 9:23). Then you will find the Holy Spirit grandly working within your life, thereby, giving you daily victory. This is God's Prescribed Order of Victory for the Saint. There is no other! (Rom. 8:1-13).

If we try to do other things, whatever they might be and however right they may be in their own way, all we succeed in doing is to *"frustrate the Grace of God."* In fact, our efforts in any direction other than the Cross are a gross insult to Christ, as ought to be obvious (Gal. 2:21).

Paul emphatically states that we can't do this thing without Christ and our Faith in what He did for us at the Cross. If we think we can, we're only fooling ourselves. Now read the following very carefully:

While the *"sin nature"* is definitely not dead in the heart and life of the Believer, the truth is, we are *"dead to the sin nature,"* or at least we are supposed to be (Rom. 6:7-8, 11). We are dead to the sin nature by the fact that we were crucified with Christ, buried with Him, and then raised with Him in Newness of Life (Rom. 6:3-5). The secret is that we stay dead. As long as we do, we'll have no problem with the sin nature.

How do we stay dead to the sin nature?

We stay dead by simply continuing to evidence Faith in Christ and what He has done for us at the Cross. It all comes through the Cross. I'm sure the reader understands that we aren't speaking of the wooden beam on which Jesus died, but rather what He there accomplished.

When our Faith is properly placed and when our Faith is properly maintained, the Holy Spirit gloriously and grandly works for us. Please look at the following very carefully:

VICTORY

• Jesus Christ is the Source of all things that we receive from God (Jn. 1:1, 14, 29; 14:6; Col. 2:10-15).

• With Jesus as the Source, the Cross is the Means by which all of these wonderful things are given to us (Rom. 6:1-14).

• With Jesus as the Source and the Cross as the Means, the Object of our Faith must always be Christ and what He has done for us at the Cross. Until the Believer does that, he's not really having faith in the Word of God because the Word of God is the Story of *"Jesus Christ and Him Crucified"* (I Cor. 1:17, 18, 23; 2:2).

• With Jesus as our Source, the Cross as our Means, and the Cross being the Object of our Faith, then the Holy Spirit, Who works exclusively within the parameters, so to speak, of the Finished Work of Christ, will grandly begin to work in our favor, doing for us what we cannot do for ourselves (Rom. 8:1-13; Eph. 2:13-18).

THE HOLY SPIRIT

Paul also said:

"For the Law *(a Law devised by the Godhead in eternity past)* **of the Spirit** *(Holy Spirit)* **of Life** *(all life comes from Christ but through the Holy Spirit)* **in Christ Jesus** *(what He did for us at the Cross)* **has made me free from the Law of Sin and Death"** **(Rom. 8:2).**

This one Passage plainly tells us that the Holy Spirit works according to a particular Prescribed Order; and what is that Order?

In fact, it is so much an Order that it is referred to as, *"The Law."* Now, the Believer certainly should understand that Paul is not speaking here of the Law of Moses, but rather, as we have stated, a Law devised by the Godhead sometime in eternity past. What is that Law?

WHAT IS THE LAW OF THE SPIRIT
OF LIFE IN CHRIST JESUS?

It is the Work that Christ carried out at the Cross and is referred to as *"in Christ Jesus."* That means that it is all in Him, and more particularly, in what He did for us at the Cross.

This means that our Faith, which is so very, very important, must ever be anchored in Christ and the Cross. That's why Paul said, *"But we preach Christ Crucified"* (I Cor. 1:23).

If it is to be noticed, he didn't merely say, *"We preach Christ,"* but rather, *"We preach Christ Crucified."*

CHRIST CRUCIFIED

One of the great problems with the modern church is that it preaches Christ, but it puts little emphasis on His Finished Work, which pertains to the Cross. Let the reader understand that it is only *"Christ Crucified"* which can set the captive free. Everything else falls into the realm of failure.

Christ, as God, as necessary as that was, never delivered anyone. It is only *"Christ Crucified"* which effects Deliverance.

That's why the Apostle also said to the Corinthians:

"For I determined not to know anything among you, save Jesus Christ, and Him Crucified" (I Cor. 2:2).

Understanding that and functioning from that basis of Faith, the Holy Spirit now has great latitude to work in our lives. He is God; consequently, He can do anything.

VICTORY?

Unfortunately, most Pentecostals (and I am Pentecostal) think that merely being baptized with the Holy Spirit and speaking with other Tongues is all they need. The tragedy is, there are millions who fall into that category, and while their experience is definitely real, they are still living lives of spiritual failure. Once again, we come back to the synopsis of the struggle, etc.

No, just because one is baptized with the Holy Spirit, it doesn't guarantee one victory in any capacity. The potential is there, but unless we function according to God's Prescribed Order, the Spirit-filled Believer will not really walk in any greater victory than the one who is not Spirit-filled.

God's Prescribed Order means we understand that everything comes to us through Christ and what he did at the Cross, and we ever make that the Object of our Faith. If we walk and function according to God's Prescribed Order, then the Holy Spirit, Who works exclusively within the parameters of the Finished Work of Christ, will do mighty things for us, with us, and within us. Listen again to Paul:

QUICKEN YOUR MORTAL BODY

"But if the Spirit (Holy Spirit) of Him (God the Father) Who raised up Jesus from the dead dwell in you, He (God the Father) Who raised up Christ from the dead shall also quicken your mortal bodies by His Spirit (Holy Spirit) Who dwells in you" (Rom. 8:11; I Cor. 3:16).

Most Christians skim past this Verse, thinking that Paul is speaking of the coming Resurrection. He isn't!

He is telling us that the same Holy Spirit, Who raised Jesus from the dead, lives within us. That means the same Power He used to bring Christ from the dead is available to us. When we think about that for a moment, we realize that we're thinking about Almighty Power that is to such an extent that it defies description.

However, that Power is available to us only if our Faith is properly placed, and I continue to speak of Christ and His Cross. Otherwise, although the Holy Spirit will definitely remain in the heart and life of the Believer, what He can do will be greatly curtailed.

No Believer wants that. We all want to walk in victory, and to be sure, God has a Prescribed Order. That Order is:

- Jesus Christ;
- The Cross;
- The Cross of Christ as the Object of our Faith;
- The Holy Spirit will then work mightily within us.

All of this, and much which I have not addressed, is bound up in the statement made of Abraham, *"And he believed in the Lord; and He (God) counted it to him for Righteousness."*

RIGHTEOUSNESS

The phrase, *"And He counted it to him for Righteousness,"* presents the place and position which God demands. This is where the conflict begins.

The only type of Righteousness which God will accept is a perfect, unspotted, unsullied Righteousness, which He Alone can provide. In other words, the type of Righteousness which God demands is absolutely impossible as it regards humanity. The only thing we can produce in this realm is self-righteousness, which is brought about by our attempting to function outside of God's Prescribed Order. Tragically, this is where most of the church actually is — self-righteousness.

JUSTIFICATION BY FAITH

The Righteousness which God demands can be found only by the believing sinner expressing Faith in Christ and what Christ has done for him at the Cross. That being done, the Lord instantly imputes to the believing sinner a perfect, unspotted, unsullied Righteousness. Once again, it is referred to as *"Justification by Faith."* This means that the individual is now justified, which means, *"To be declared just by God."* It is done strictly by the individual evidencing Faith. As repeatedly stated, this can only come about through Christ and what Christ did for us at the Cross, and our Faith in that Finished Work. If we try to obtain this Righteousness in any other manner, it is always, and without exception, a manner which God will never accept.

Once the believing sinner is made completely righteous by God according to his Faith in Christ, it is to be understood that we maintain this Righteousness by continuing to express Faith in Christ and what He has done for us at the Cross.

MAINTAINING RIGHTEOUSNESS

Most true Christians would acquiesce completely to the first part of my statement about the believing sinner trusting Christ and, thereby, being imputed a perfect Righteousness. Unfortunately, after the initial Born-Again experience, many Christians try to maintain their Righteousness by their own good works, or whatever methods they or someone else come up with. That's where the problem ensues.

In the manner that we obtain Righteousness, in that same manner we maintain Righteousness. That's why Paul kept taking us to Christ and the Cross. That's why he stated, *"I am crucified with Christ"* (Gal. 2:20). Sadly and regrettably, millions of Christians refuse to believe that which the Apostle taught. Just as the Judaizers of Paul's day, the modern brand continues to follow the same course of attempting to add some type of law of their own devising to that which Christ has sufficiently done. As always, such efforts only lead to disaster (Gal. 2:21).

CHRISTIAN DISCIPLINES

Sometime back, we had two guest preachers on our daily radio program, *"A Study in the Word."* We were discussing this very thing, and I speak of our living a victorious, overcoming life.

At a given point in the teaching, the younger of the two preachers spoke up and said, *"Whenever I have a problem of any nature,"* and he was speaking of sin, *"I fast three days, and that takes care of the problem."*

While fasting definitely is Scriptural and definitely will be a blessing to any Believer, the truth is, if *"fasting"* is the answer to our sin problem, whatever that problem might be, then once again I say with Paul, *"Jesus died in vain."* All He needed to have done was to teach us how to fast, etc., and the problem would be solved. Unfortunately, it's not that simple.

I diplomatically remonstrated to him that which I have just said in the above statement about Jesus having to die on the Cross. He quickly retorted, and with a touch of anger, *"Well, it works for me!"*

The tragedy is, when we put our faith in things other than the Cross, we become blinded to a certain degree. Didn't he stop to think that he was having to repeat this scenario over and over?

OVERCOMING SIN

While all Believers should fast as the Lord leads them, it must be for the right reason, which pertains to Christ coming back, etc. (Mat. 9:15). However, to try to use fasting, or any other Christian discipline, in the fashion of trying to overcome sin will always lead to defeat. Once again we come back to the simple thought that if these things could defeat sin within our lives, then why did Jesus have to come down here and die on a Cross?

The truth is, sin is of such magnitude and such power that it is only the Cross that could address this monster, which Jesus there did (Col. 2:10-15).

So, why did the brother get somewhat testy? Unfortunately, he's not alone in that attitude.

SELF-RIGHTEOUSNESS

The major reason that the Cross of Christ is an offense to many is because it lays bare the schemes, efforts, works, etc., of man. It exposes all of this and shows it to be totally worthless. That doesn't sit well with most.

Any effort other than the Cross of Christ always, and without exception, leads to self-righteousness. To be sure, self-righteousness is one of the worst sins that could ever attach itself to anyone. It was self-righteousness that nailed Christ to a Cross, and it's self-righteousness which keeps untold millions out of Heaven and makes life miserable for most Christians.

I realize one of the statements I just made comes as a shock; however, it happens to be true.

If we attempt to bring about Righteousness within our lives by any method other than Faith in Christ and what He did for us at the Cross, every time, without exception, that direction will lead to self-righteousness. Unfortunately, and I say this with no joy, the modern church is, I believe, the most self-righteous church since the Reformation.

Whenever Believers try to obtain something by their own means and efforts, then the praise and the glory go to the individual. When it's done by the Means of the Cross, the Glory goes to the Lord Jesus Christ. That's the reason that Paul said:

"But God forbid that I should glory (boast), save in the Cross of our Lord Jesus Christ, by Whom the world is crucified unto me, and I unto the world" (Gal. 6:14).

The great Apostle also said, *"Where is boasting then? It is excluded. By what Law? of works? No: but by the Law of Faith"* (Rom. 3:27).

Outside of the Cross, we have absolutely nothing to boast about.

The young preacher didn't want to give up his dependence on fasting because he had put a lot into that effort. We do not enjoy giving up our own particular efforts either. It's a struggle with the flesh when we are told that we must depend solely upon Christ and the Cross.

When one preacher was told the other day that his Faith must rest exclusively in the Cross, he remonstrated, *"Well, I guess that's alright for some people but not for all."*

Now, isn't that a ridiculous statement?

How could it be right for some and not for all?

No, the Cross is God's Way for all. There is no other way.

"There is healing at the fountain,
"Come, behold the crimson tide,
"Flowing down from Calvary's mountain,
"Where the Prince of Glory died."

"There is healing at the fountain,
"Come and find it, weary soul,
"There your sins may all be covered;
"Jesus waits to make you whole."

"There is healing at the fountain,
"Look to Jesus now and live,
"At the Cross lay down your burden,
"All your wanderings He'll forgive."

"There is healing at the fountain,
"Precious fountain filled with Blood,
"Come, O come, the Saviour calls you;
"Come and plunge beneath its flood."

ABRAHAM

CHAPTER

13

Abraham And
The Revelation

ABRAHAM AND THE REVELATION

REAFFIRMING THE REVELATION

"And He said unto him, I am the LORD Who brought you out of Ur of the Chaldees, to give you this land to inherit it" (Gen. 15:7).

After Abraham proclaimed the statement of Faith given to us in Verse 6, and it was *"counted to him for Righteousness,"* the Lord now reaffirms, and greater yet, expands the Revelation. In this Seventh Verse, He, in effect, says three things:

1. The Lord reaffirms Himself to Abraham as the *"Covenant God"* by using the Name, *"LORD."* In other words, He is saying that whatever He has said, it most definitely will come to pass, and Abraham believes that.

2. When He speaks of bringing Abraham out of *"Ur of the Chaldees,"* He is, in effect, referring to the fact that He has delivered the Patriarch from idolatry and all the evil of that former lifestyle. There must be a separation from that to the Lord, and only God can bring about such a separation. It involves much more than a geographical change, rather a spiritual Miracle. This Abraham experienced.

3. He has promised this land of Palestine, which would later be renamed Israel, to Abraham. All of this speaks volumes.

Even though Abraham would not personally own any of it, at least during his earthly sojourn, the fact is, his seed would own every part of it, with him personally owning it, so to speak, at the Second Coming.

If it is to be noticed, the Lord said He would *"inherit"* it, which means that it actually belongs to God, Who will give it to the Patriarch. However, even then, and we continue to speak of the coming Kingdom Age, it will still be symbolic. The land of Israel actually belongs to God (Ezek. 38:16; Hos. 9:3; Joel 1:6; 2:18; 3:2).

THE QUESTION

"And he said, LORD God, whereby shall I know that I shall inherit it?" (Gen. 15:8)

As stated, in this Vision, Abraham asks the Lord two questions. They are:

1. *"What will You give me?"*

Christ Alone is the Answer to this question.

Directly upon the sinner believing God's Testimony about His Beloved Son, he is not only declared righteous, but he is made a son and an heir. *"Sonship"* is introduction into the family; *"heirship"* is entrance into the Kingdom, hence, the second question:

2. *"Whereby shall I know that I shall inherit it?"*

Abraham is then shown the suffering that he must encounter, which all heirs of the Kingdom must know. The Apostle says, *"If we suffer with Him, we shall also reign with Him"* (Rom. 8:17).

THE FIVE SACRIFICES

"And He said unto him, Take Me an heifer of three years old, and a she goat of three years old, and a ram of three years old, and a turtledove, and a young pigeon" (Gen. 15:9).

The Lord now has Abraham to offer up five living creatures, which will set out the fullness of the great Sacrifice of Calvary.

Five is the number of Grace. The Covenant which God was making with Abraham was, in a sense, unconditional simply because God was the One and Only Contracting Party (Gal. 3:20). However, His Foundation is Grace as the entirety of the Foundation of God is Grace.

That the heifer, goat, and ram were to be three years old signifies the earthly Ministry of the Son of God.

- The *"heifer"* symbolized His Priestly Office.
- The *"she-goat"* symbolized His Prophetic Office.

- The *"ram"* symbolized His Kingly Office. Jesus was Priest, Prophet, and King.
- The *"turtledove"* symbolized His being led and guided strictly by the Holy Spirit.
- The *"young pigeon"* symbolized Him obeying the Spirit in every capacity.

THE EFFECTS OF SIN

"And he took unto him all these, and divided them in the midst, and laid each piece one against another: but the birds divided he not" (Gen. 15:10).

The heifer, goat, and ram were literally split open, in effect, totally divided, with one side of the carcass placed on the right and the other on the left. Probably, one bird was placed on one side with the other on the other side, for no mention is made of their small carcasses being split.

The carcasses being treated in this manner show the terrible effects of sin. It is far more than a mere surface problem, but rather reaching to the very vitals of each and every individual. Consequently, when Jesus would die on the Cross, He would suffer the full penalty of sin, which was death. That and that alone would God accept as full payment for the penalty of sin.

One need only take a look at these sacrifices and their mutilation to recognize the terrible futility of man attempting to address the sin problem any other way than by the Cross of Calvary. To be sure, it was addressed at Calvary in all of its totality, depth, destruction, and depravity. Nothing was left unanswered. In reply to this, Paul said:

THE WORK OF CHRIST ON THE CROSS

"In Whom *(Christ)* **also you are circumcised with the Circumcision made without hands**

(the circumcision of the heart), **in putting off the body of the sins of the flesh by the Circumcision of Christ** *(the Crucifixion of Christ).*

"Buried with Him in Baptism *(referring to His Death and Burial, not Water Baptism),* **wherein also you are risen with *Him*** *(in Newness of Life)* **through the Faith of the Operation of God, Who has raised Him from the dead.** *(This is what Paul also said in Romans 6:3-5; 8:11.)*

"And you, being dead in your sins and the uncircumcision of your flesh, has He quickened together with Him, having forgiven you all trespasses;

"Blotting out the handwriting of Ordinances that was against us, which was contrary to us *(the Mosaic Law),* **and took it out of the way, nailing it to His Cross** *(meaning that He satisfied at the Cross all the demands of Heavenly Justice)***;**

"*And* having spoiled principalities and powers *(powerful fallen Angels),* **He made a show of them openly, triumphing over them in it** *(meaning that inasmuch as all sin is atoned, past, present, and future, Satan has lost his legal claim upon man, which is sin. Thereby, every demon spirit and fallen Angel, along with Satan, was totally and completely defeated at the Cross)***" (Col. 2:11-15).**

DEMON SPIRITS

"And when the fowls came down upon the carcasses, Abram drove them away" (Gen. 15:11).

Satan hates the Cross, represented by the carcasses, as he hates nothing else, as should be obvious. This is where he was totally and completely defeated.

The defeat which he suffered was total and complete, so total, in fact, that he has no more valid claim on the Child of God.

Jesus atoned for sin at the Cross, and that speaks of sin in every capacity, whether past, present, or future. Sin is Satan's claim on humanity, but with all sin atoned, the Evil One now has no more claim whatsoever (Jn. 1:29).

Some Christians seem to think that Jesus fought Satan in some type of physical combat. Nothing like that ever happened! In fact, Satan wants no part of Christ in any capacity.

SIN

The conflict between Righteousness and unrighteousness has always been in the realm of sin. The fact of sin gives Satan certain legal rights, and to be sure, he has exercised those legal rights in every capacity. Sin is a breaking of the Law of God. When this is done, man finds himself on the side of unrighteousness. Actually, he is born into unrighteousness as a result of original sin, which came about as a result of Adam's fall. The entirety of the nature of man is completely ruined by the fact of the sin nature.

That's why John the Baptist, in his introduction of Christ, said, *"Behold the Lamb of God, which takes away the sin of the world"* (Jn. 1:29).

If it is to be noticed, he didn't say, *"Sins of the world,"* but rather, *"Sin of the world."* In other words, Jesus addressed the sin question, or the principle of sin, which refers to the very cause of sin, at the Cross. That *"cause"* is Satan, transferred to the fall of man from total God-consciousness, which existed before the Fall, to the far lower level of total self-consciousness, which took place immediately after the Fall and continues unto this hour.

At the Fall, man was totally separated from God and pronounced, *"Spiritually dead."* Paul said:

"And you *has He quickened* *(made alive),* **who were dead in trespasses and sins** *(total depravity due to the Fall and original sin);*

"Wherein in time past you walked according to the course of this world *(refers to the fact that the unredeemed order their behavior and regulate their lives within this sphere of trespasses and sins),* **according to the prince of the power of the air** *(pertains to the fact that Satan heads up the system of this world),* **the spirit that now works in the children of disobedience** *(the spirit of Satan, which fills all unbelievers, thereby, working disobedience)"* **(Eph. 2:1-2).**

We must quickly state, *"Dead is dead."* It means that man is dead to everything that pertains to God. He is now totally in the domain of Satan, who *"steals, kills, and destroys"* (Jn. 10:10). For this problem to be properly addressed, God would have to become man and die on a Cross, which was actually planned from before the foundation of the world (I Pet. 1:18-20).

So, it is easy to see how that Satan hates the Cross as he hates nothing else. It was there that his hold on humanity was broken.

Even though demon spirits continue to attempt to attack the Child of God in every way, as Abraham drove away the fowls, we as Believers, using the Name of Jesus, can drive away the powers of darkness also (Mk. 16:17-18).

DARKNESS

"And when the sun was going down, a deep sleep fell upon Abram; and, lo, an horror of great darkness fell upon him" (Gen. 15:12).

Williams says:

"The great horror that descended upon Abraham foretold the suffering of the heirs of Promise."[1] This pertained to Israel, which we will address to a greater degree momentarily, but, as well, it pertains to all Believers.

More particularly, it pertains to *"the offense of the Cross"* (Gal. 5:11). It involves persecution, and strangely enough, the far greater persecution comes from the church and not the world.

While the world, as well, is opposed to the Cross, not really understanding it, its opposition is limited mostly to a simple but deadly rejection of Christ.

However, when it comes to the church, its opposition is much different. It seeks to devise a way other than the Cross but, as well, seeks to eliminate all who place their Faith and Trust in the Cross. The murder of Abel by his brother, Cain, is an example (Gen., Chpt. 4).

Even now, as it has always been, if the Preacher says that he is going to preach the Cross and, thereby, look to the Cross for all victory, the far greater majority of the time, if not always, he will ultimately be ostracized by most other preachers. The reason is this:

THE TOTALITY OF THE CROSS

The Cross of Christ addresses every capacity of the Biblical experience of Salvation. It leaves out nothing.

It demands that the Believer adhere strictly to the Government of God, which, within itself, crosses the grain of most religious denominations. The Government of the Cross demands that total and complete allegiance be given to that which Christ has done for us by placing trust and Faith in nothing else.

Most religious denominations demand allegiance solely to that particular denomination, which, in a sense, demands total control. The Government of the

Cross will not allow allegiance to be placed elsewhere. Love, yes! Allegiance, no!

In Paul's day, some in the church were attempting to force the Law, i.e., *"physical circumcision,"* upon Believers. In other words, they were claiming that without adhering to the Law, one could not truly be saved (Acts 15:1). Even though the Apostles in Jerusalem opposed this erroneous doctrine, the evidence from Paul's writings is that it didn't die. That's why Paul said, ". . . for *if Righteousness come by the Law, then Christ is dead in vain"* (Gal. 2:21).

THE NEW TYPE OF LAW

In fact, as it was Law then, it is law now but in a different way. While the Law of Moses is now coming back into vogue, the church has also created another type of law. I speak of humanistic psychology. Not knowing the Way of the Cross, or else, registering rank unbelief as it regards the Cross, many have turned to this nefarious system of humanistic psychology. It was birthed in the hearts of unbelievers and was actually birthed by Satan himself. The world, not believing in Christ and His Cross, has to have another solution. In reality, it is no solution at all, but yet, building an entire system around this fabrication, it is held up as the answer to man's problems. As stated, one can understand the world going in that direction because they have nothing else. However, it is quite another matter to see the church following suit; but follow suit it has!

A REJECTION OF THE CROSS

In the two major Pentecostal denominations, the Assemblies of God and the Church of God, if a Preacher has a problem of any nature, he must undergo several months of psychological counseling before he can be reinstated in good standing with either one of these denominations. This, in effect, registers a vote of no confidence as it regards the Cross. Sadly, if the truth be known, almost all of these particular denominations have totally and completely departed from the Cross and, in effect, have rejected the Cross. Concerning this very thing, Jesus said:

"The Kingdom of Heaven is like unto leaven, which a woman took, and hid in three measures of meal, till the whole was leavened" (Mat. 13:33).

The *"Kingdom of Heaven"* could be translated, *"The Kingdom from Heaven."* It is the True Gospel, which can be summed up in the word, *"Jesus Christ and Him Crucified"* (Jn. 3:16; I Cor. 1:23; 2:2).

The *"leaven"* speaks of false doctrine, with the word, *"Woman,"* used here in an evil sense.

The *"meal"* represents the Word of God but with *"leaven"* (false doctrine) inserted *"till the whole is leavened."*

In this shortest of the parables as given by Christ, He, in effect, tells us that in the last days, the entirety of the church world will be totally and completely leavened, i.e., *"corrupted."* Regrettably and sadly, for all practical purposes, that has come to pass.

THE CHURCH

The church, even as Israel of old, is fastly being divided into two segments, so to speak. I speak of the true Church and the apostate church. In effect, it has always been this way, even beginning with Cain and Abel as recorded in Genesis, Chapter 4. However, it is more important now, I think, and even more distinct now simply because the Church is nearing the very end of its particular dispensation. The Rapture is about to take place (I Thess. 4:13-18). In fact, were it not for the Rapture of the Church, the Church, as a viable, Scriptural entity, would become extinct. In other words, as the Second Coming of the Lord will save the world from total destruction, likewise, the Rapture will save the Church from total extinction.

The dividing line between the true Church and the apostate church is the Cross of Christ. In effect, it has always been that way but serves in this capacity now in a greater way than ever before. This means that denominations, or anything else one might think, aren't the dividing line, but rather the Cross of Christ. In other words, as one views the Cross, so one states his position. If the Cross is opposed, one has to be placed in the position of being *"an enemy of the Cross"* (Phil. 3:18-19). He is, therefore, part of the apostate church. To place one's Faith, confidence, and trust solely in Christ and what He has done for us at the Cross places one into the true Body of Christ (I Cor. 2:2; Gal. 6:14; Col. 2:14-15).

SONSHIP AND HEIRSHIP

Directly upon the sinner believing God's Testimony about His Beloved Son, he is not only declared righteous, but he is made a *"son"* and an *"heir"* (Rom. 8:14-17).

As we have previously stated, *"sonship"* is introduction into the family; *"heirship"* into the Kingdom.

The believing sinner is made a *"son"* by his trust and Faith in Christ and what Christ has done for us at the Cross. With Faith thereby evidenced, the Lord imputes a perfect Righteousness to the believing sinner. In fact, this is what Genesis 15:6 actually means. If one understands that particular Verse, then one understands the entirety of the Bible. If one misunderstands that Verse, then one misunderstands the Word of God.

As it regards the Word of God and the Plan of Salvation, all of which was shown to Abraham as it regards Justification by Faith, this is where the great controversy lies. This is where Satan fights his hardest, and this is the core of all false doctrine. If we miss it in our faith, then we've missed it completely.

BELIEVED WHAT GOD HAD SAID

When Genesis 15:6 says that Abraham believed God, it doesn't mean that he merely believed in God but, in effect, believed what God had said. This pertained to a Redeemer coming into the world, Who would redeem fallen humanity. Because Abraham believed in this One Who was to come, God counted it to him for Righteousness, which, in effect, made Abraham totally and completely righteous. It was and is imputed Righteousness and was the Foundation of all Salvation as it regards every person who has ever come to Christ. That's why Paul referred to Abraham as the *"father of us all"* (Rom. 4:16).

There are two keys to Redemption, so to speak. They are *"Faith"* and *"Righteousness."* God demands Righteousness, and the only way that Righteousness can be obtained is by Faith in Christ and His Cross (Jn. 3:16; Rom. 10:9-10, 13).

Paul also said:

"Therefore being justified by Faith, we have peace with God through our Lord Jesus Christ" (Rom. 5:1).

That settles the *"sonship."*

What is Righteousness?

It is simply that which is right; however, it is God's Definition of what is right and not man's.

BY THE CROSS AND ONLY BY THE CROSS

"Sonship" and *"heirship"* are inseparably connected in the thoughts of God. Sonship is the proper basis

of everything, and, moreover, it is the result of God's Sovereign Council and Operation as we read in James, *"Of His Own Will begat He us."*

As it regards *"heirship,"* we enter into that position immediately after entering into *"sonship."* We do so in exactly the same way as we did by entering into sonship, and I speak of our Faith totally and completely in the Cross of Christ. The great mistake of the church is to accept *"proper sonship"* but then try to attain *"heirship"* in all the wrong ways. It all comes by the Cross and by nothing except the Cross. As we came to Christ, by that same manner, we maintain Christ, and Christ maintains us. The Believer must understand that it is through the Cross that we receive all things from the Lord, and we can receive nothing except by that method. As long as the Believer keeps his Faith in the Cross of Christ, the *"heirship"* will take care of itself. It is only when we go off on tangents that we miss what Christ has done for us.

FOUR HUNDRED YEARS

"And He said unto Abram, Know of a surety that your seed shall be a stranger in a land that is not theirs, and shall serve them; and they shall afflict them four hundred years" (Gen. 15:13).

The 400 years pertains to the time from the weaning of Isaac to the Deliverance of the Children of Israel from Egyptian bondage.

From Abraham's arrival in Canaan to the birth of Isaac was 25 years (Gen. 12:4; 17:1, 12); he was probably weaned at about five years old. This would total 400 years. Isaac was 60 years old at the birth of Jacob (Gen. 25:26); Jacob was 130 at his going down to Egypt. These three numbers make 215 years. As well, Jacob and his children dwelt in Egypt for the same period of 215 years, making a total of 430 years (Ex. 12:40), which would be from the time of Abraham's arrival in Canaan.

The Promises of God at times take awhile before fulfillment, but, that being the case, even as here, the Lord in one way or the other will relate this fact.

The Lord couldn't give the entirety of the land to Abraham at that present time. How could he hold it with only a few individuals? The Lord would have to raise up a people, which would take time to do so, in this case, about 400 years. As well, there were other particulars which had to be considered, even as we will see in the Sixteenth Verse.

EGYPT

"And also that nation, whom they shall serve, will I judge: and afterward they shall come out with great substance" (Gen. 15:14).

That particular nation would be Egypt even though at this time the Lord does not divulge that information. However, in this short Verse, he proclaims what will happen to Israel at that time.

By this time, and I speak of the last years in Egypt, the Israelites had become a mighty people, although slaves. As slaves, they were now serving Egypt exactly as the Lord said they would. However, He also promises to judge Egypt, which He definitely did.

What He said was fulfilled in totality. *"They came out with great substance."*

ABRAHAM

"And you shall go to your fathers in peace; you shall be buried in a good old age" (Gen. 15:15).

Once again, quite a number of things are said here with very few words:

- We learn here that Abraham would not see all of this fulfilled but would, in fact, die before this particular time.
- This statement is a proof of the survival of departed spirits in a state of conscious existence after death.
- When the Patriarch would die, which would be at a ripe old age, he would go in *"peace,"* proclaiming the fact that what God had called him to do, he will have done.

So, in effect, what the Lord is telling Abraham is the same thing He had previously said concerning the birth of a son. This Miracle child would come forth.

THE FOURTH GENERATION

"But in the fourth generation they shall come hither again: for the iniquity of the Amorites is not yet full" (Gen. 15:16).

From this statement concerning the *"fourth generation,"* the Lord, it seems, would not begin the countdown until the sons of Jacob were born. Consequently, the first generation began with Levi, with the second being Kohath, the third being Amram, and the *"fourth generation"* being Moses. Thus was fulfilled what the Lord had spoken. Even then, there was another situation at hand concerning the Amorites.

They seemed to be the most powerful people of the central hill country of Canaan where Abraham lived at this particular time. That being the case, all the other tribes of Canaan would fall under their umbrella.

The simple statement, *"For the iniquity of the Amorites is not yet full,"* proclaims much to us. As the Book of Job teaches, Job's friends were wrong when they thought that God immediately brings Judgment on sinners. In fact, He is Patient and Longsuffering. However, He is also just, and the Judgment will eventually come if there is no repentance.

Discoveries at the ancient Ugarit, north of Tyre and Sidon, have revealed that the Canaanite religion promoted child sacrifice, idolatry, and prostitution, all in the name of religion, with all kinds of occultic and immoral practices. In fact, after working for years in the Middle East, one archeologist stated that God, Who gave instructions for entire tribes to be wiped out, did future generations an untold service.

The mental aberrations brought on by these evil practices, along with physical disabilities, as well, continue to be rampant in many nations of the world and are definitely present in all nations.

So, we find from this that God did not destroy these particular tribes, whomever they may have been, until the cup of their iniquity was so full that He had no choice.

THE CUP OF INIQUITY

We have to ask ourselves the question, what nations at present are looking at a *"full cup"*? How far down the road has the United States gone? Let the reader understand that this holds true not only for nations but, as well, for individuals.

God's Nature is to bless. He does not delight in Judgment; however, He cannot bless sin, as should be obvious. If the sin gets bad enough, which it always does unless it's washed away by the Blood of Christ, ultimately, Judgment will have to come. The Cross alone can deal with sin, but yet, that simple truth seems to be beyond most in the modern church. They keep trying to address this evil, this destructive power, and this erroneous direction by humanistic methods, which, at best, are only cheap, surface Band-Aids. Faith in what Christ did at the Cross will totally eliminate sin. John beautifully said:

"The Blood of Jesus Christ God's Son cleanses us from all sin" (I Jn. 1:7).

THE DARKNESS

"And it came to pass, that, when the sun went down, and it was dark, behold a smoking furnace, and a burning lamp that passed between those pieces" (Gen. 15:17).

• The darkness represents the state of this world now filled with sin.

• The *"smoking furnace"* proclaims the furnace of affliction that Israel will have to pass through and, in fact, every Believer.

• The *"burning lamp"* proclaims the Word of God.

• The *"pieces"* speak of the sacrifices and portray the Cross.

The darkness here is meant to proclaim the condition of this present world as it regards sin. The conflict is between Light and darkness, and we speak of that in the spiritual sense. That's the reason that Isaiah prophesied of the coming Christ:

"The people who walked in darkness have seen a great light: they who dwell in the land of the shadow of death, upon them has the light shined" (Isa. 9:2).

THE SMOKING FURNACE

The phrase, *"Behold a smoking furnace,"* refers to the trial and test through which Israel, as well as all Believers, would have to go. Isaiah again said:

"Behold, I have refined you, but not with silver; I have chosen you in the furnace of affliction" (Isa. 48:10).

Some in the modern gospel have attempted to escape this particular *"furnace."* However, the manner in which the Lord gave this to Abraham, and considering that he is the father of us all, proclaims to us the fact that no true Christian can escape this *"furnace of affliction."* It must come and, in fact, will come simply because it is necessary. Why is it necessary?

The problem of *"self"* is a never-ending problem. Unfortunately, self cannot be properly placed, which is in Christ, unless it comes by the route mentioned here. The fire is necessary in order to burn out the dross.

A PERSONAL ILLUSTRATION

When I was a young man, I worked for a short period of time for a plumber. He taught me how to melt lead, which was poured between the joints of pipes, etc.

He had a small pot that had a gas burner attached under it, which would heat it red hot. The bars of lead would be placed in the pot and would be melted. All the impurities would float to the top, with extreme heat being the only way that the separation could be brought about. The impurities would then be siphoned off and pure lead poured between the joints, which then would not leak. Unfortunately, it is the same with Believers.

We may think there are no impurities. However, whenever the proper heat is applied, i.e., *"the furnace of affliction,"* we then find to our dismay that many impurities remain, which can now be removed. It is the Holy Spirit Who authors and engineers all of this. In fact, John the Baptist said the following about himself and Christ:

"I indeed baptize you with water unto Repentance: but He Who comes after me is mightier than I, Whose Shoes I am not worthy to bear: He shall baptize you with the Holy Spirit, and with fire:

"Whose fan is in His Hand, and He will thoroughly purge His Floor, and gather His Wheat into the garner; but He will burn up the chaff with unquenchable fire" (Mat. 3:11-12).

The *"unquenchable fire,"* as it regards the Holy Spirit and Believers, pertains to the *"furnace of affliction."*

THE BURNING LAMP

The phrase, *"And a burning lamp,"* has to do with the Word of God. The Psalmist said:

"Your Word is a Lamp unto my feet, and a Light unto my path" (Ps. 119:105). Every answer needed in this journey of life is found in the Word of God.

Satan is making his greatest attack presently against the Word of God, actually, greater than ever. However, he's doing it a little bit differently than the means in which he did it in the past.

Instead of denying the Word, which he has done for centuries, he is now causing the nations of the world to be flooded with books that are claimed to be Bibles but are not Bibles at all. I speak of those such as the *"Message Bible,"* etc. At best, these books can be labeled merely as religious books, but certainly not the Bible. I might quickly add:

If you do not have a word for word translation of the Bible, such as a *"King James,"* then whatever it is that you do have is really not a Bible. As stated, the Evil One is flooding the land with these paraphrases, etc.

Admittedly, translation is not easy at all; however, I believe the King James has come as close to the original as any Bible that's ever been printed. In fact, after a fashion, it is used as the foundation for the translation of Bibles into other languages. While that wouldn't hold true for all translations, and I speak of foreign languages, it does, I think, for most.

For instance, when we translated THE EXPOSITOR'S STUDY BIBLE into Spanish, we used, as should be obvious, THE EXPOSITOR'S. Of course, THE EXPOSITOR'S is King James. Jim Woolsey, who did the translation, plus those with him, actually worked on it for some five years. He also translated it into Portuguese and Russian. However, he did not do the actual Russian translation, that being done by a dear brother in Belorussia.

The Word of God is the single most important thing on the face of the Earth and, in fact, ever has been. That being the case, two things should be readily observed at all times:

1. We had better make certain that what we have is a proper translation.

2. We should make the Bible a lifelong study, thereby, understanding its worth and value.

THE SACRIFICE

The phrase, *"That passed between the pieces,"* concerns the sacrifice. The idea is, we can make it through the darkness only as the *"burning lamp"* goes before us, i.e., *"the Word of God."* It is superintended by the Holy Spirit, but all is based upon the Sacrifice of Christ. The Word of God will always portray the Story of the Cross, and the Holy Spirit will always lead us to the Cross (Rom. 8:1-13).

If we try to get through this world any other way, the *"burning lamp"* simply will not function because we have left the safety and protection of the Sacrifice of Christ. Let the reader remember that the safe path is only *"between those pieces."*

THE PROMISE

"In the same day the LORD made a Covenant with Abram, saying, Unto your seed have I given this land, from the river of Egypt unto the great river, the river Euphrates" (Gen. 15:18).

THE PROMISES OF GOD

The Promises of God are so sure that they can be spoken of in the past tense here even though they have not yet been realized.

The area promised to Abraham and his seed, which extended from *"the river of Egypt unto . . . the river Euphrates,"* came closer to being fulfilled under David than at any time in the history of Israel. It will be fulfilled in totality in the coming Millennial Reign, i.e., *"Kingdom Age."*

THE COVENANT

The *"Covenant"* of which the Lord mentions here is unique in that it is different. Most covenants, as would be obvious, are between two or more people, but here, God covenants to do the whole work. He would begin it. He would finish it. All Abraham had to do was accept it by Faith. In fact, he actually could not help God fulfill it. In truth, he would not even live to see it fulfilled, but it definitely would be fulfilled.

Normally, in the making of a covenant in those particular times, an animal would be killed and divided exactly as the heifer, she goat, and ram were divided, with the two individuals walking between the pieces. By doing this, each would solemnly promise to do his part, in effect, saying that if he did not, the other could cut him the way the sacrifices were cut.

However, in this Covenant, it was only God Who passed between the pieces and did so by a symbol of fire. As stated, all Abraham did, and, in fact, all he could do was evidence Faith in this which God had promised.

In reality, that is all that God requires of us today under the New Covenant, of which this the Lord showed Abraham was a Type.

THE RIVER OF EGYPT AND
THE RIVER EUPHRATES

The Covenant at that particular time consisted of the land of Canaan, which the Lord would give to the seed of Abraham, with its borders being the river of Egypt on the south and the river Euphrates up north.

"River" in both cases is the word for a river or canal with water in it all the year round. Some take the river of Egypt to be the insignificant *"Wadi el-Arish"* in northeastern Sinai; however, the Hebrew word for the Wadi is different. The promised southern border is rather a branch of the Nile River in its delta. This promise was nearly fulfilled in Solomon's time (I Ki. 8:65) but will have its complete fulfillment in the Millennium. However, the Rule of Christ will extend over the entirety of the Earth, and, in fact, He will rule from this land of Israel during the time of the Millennium.

The actual area promised by God to Abraham goes all the way to Egypt, which, of course, includes the Sinai, the Arab Peninsula, much of modern Iraq, all of Syria, and all of Lebanon.

During the times of David and Solomon, Israel made no attempt to take the Arab Peninsula simply because it was nothing but desert. Although it was rich in oil, that particular commodity at that time meant nothing. Of course, God knew what the future would hold and what the future would need. Consequently, during the coming Millennium, Israel will control most of the oil of the world because she will then control the entirety of the Arab Peninsula plus most of modern Iraq.

TEN

"The Kenites, and the Kenizzites, and the Kadmonites,
"And the Hittites, and the Perizzites, and the Rephaims,
"And the Amorites, and the Canaanites, and the Girgashites, and the Jebusites" (Gen. 15:19-21).

Ten nations are listed here, so to speak. Ten is the number of completeness in the Bible and indicates that the entirety of this land, which would also include other tribes, would be given to Abraham's descendants.

Up to this day in Abraham's life, God would say to him, *"I will give you this land."* However, from the hour of this blood-sealed Covenant, He says, *"I have given you this land,"* for Promises based upon the Precious Blood of Christ are so absolutely sure that Faith can claim them as already possessed. Hence, the Believer in the Lord Jesus Christ is neither ashamed nor afraid to say, *"I am Saved."*

Up to the close of this Chapter, attention is directed to God's Plans with respect to the Blessing of man. From this Chapter on, God's Ways in carrying out those Plans are recorded.

"Praise Him! Praise Him!
"Jesus, our Blessed Redeemer!
"Sing, O Earth,
"His Wonderful Love proclaim,
"Hail Him! Hail Him!
"Highest Archangels in Glory,
"Strength and honor give to His Holy Name!"

"Like a shepherd Jesus will guard His Children,
"In His Arms He carries them all day long:
"Praise Him! Praise Him!
"Jesus our Blessed Redeemer!
"For our sins He suffered and bled and died;
"He's our Rock,
"Our hope of eternal Salvation,
"Hail Him! Hail Him!
"Jesus the Crucified."

"Sound His Praises,
"Jesus Who bore our sorrows.
"Love unbounded, wonderful, deep, and strong:

"Praise Him! Praise Him!
"Jesus, our Blessed Redeemer!
"Heavenly portals loud with hosannas ring!
"Jesus, Saviour, reigns forever and ever,
"Crown Him! Crown Him!
"Prophet and Priest and King!"

"Christ is coming,
"Over the world victorious,
"Power and Glory,
"Unto the Lord belong."

ABRAHAM

CHAPTER

14

Abraham And Hagar

ABRAHAM AND HAGAR

"Now Sarai Abram's wife bore him no children: and she had an handmaid, an Egyptian, whose name was Hagar" (Gen. 16:1).

This Chapter begins with a terrible sin about to be committed by Abraham and Sarah. In some way, sin is always a lack of faith. The *"conception"* was a work of the flesh and, therefore, unacceptable to God.

For the Promise of God to be fulfilled, a child would have to be born through whom, ultimately, the Messiah, the Redeemer of the world, would come. The idea is: God would have to become Man in order to redeem man.

Paul said:

"For if by one man's offense (the fall of Adam) death reigned by one; much more they which receive abundance of Grace and of the Gift of Righteousness shall reign in life by One, Jesus Christ" (Rom. 5:17).

He then said:

"And so it is written, The first man Adam was made a living soul; the Last Adam (the Lord Jesus Christ) was made a quickening Spirit (One Who makes alive)" (I Cor. 15:45).

The child that Abraham and Sarah must have had to do with the Incarnation, God becoming Man, and there was nothing more important than that. In fact, this is what this is all about.

THE PATH OF FAITH

Concerning this dark episode in the story of Abraham, Williams says:

"Chapter 15 sets out the faithfulness of God, Chapter 16 the faithlessness of Abraham. The Covenant that secured to Abraham riches far exceeding the wealth of Sodom was the more amazing because it necessitated

the death of Him (Christ) Who made it! Such was the faithful love to which Abraham responded with unbelief and impatience. The Apostle says you have need of patience that you may inherit the Promises, the 'flesh' can neither believe nor wait for a Divine Promise.

"The path of Faith is full of dignity, the path of unbelief full of degradation. Abraham, finding that God has failed to give him a son, and tired of waiting, no longer sets his hope upon God, but upon an Egyptian slave girl. The natural heart will trust anything rather than God. Abraham thinks that he can, by his clever plan, hasten and bring to pass the Divine Promise. The result is misery. He succeeds in his plan, Ishmael is born; but better were it for Abraham and the world had he never been born! It is disastrous when the self-willed plans of the Christian succeed."[1]

SARAH

"And Sarai said unto Abram, Behold now, the LORD has restrained me from bearing: I pray you, go in unto my maid; it may be that I may obtain children by her. And Abram hearkened to the voice of Sarai" (Gen. 16:2).

Sarah saying, *"The LORD has restrained me from bearing,"* proclaims the usual impatience of unbelief. Abraham should have treated it accordingly and waited patiently on the Lord for the accomplishment of His Gracious Promise. However, we have a problem here, and the problem is the flesh.

The poor heart prefers anything to the attitude of waiting. Concerning this, Mackintosh said, *"It will turn to any expedient, any scheme, and resource, rather than be kept in that posture. It is one thing to believe a promise at the first, and quite another thing to wait quietly for the accomplishment thereof."*[2]

How different it would have been had Sarah said, *"Nature has failed me, but God is my Resource."*

And yet, it is very easy to look at these Bible greats and point out their weaknesses and failures. However, if we had been placed in the same situation with the same set of circumstances, would we have done any better or even as well?

GOD'S INSTRUMENT

We receive the Revelation; however, most of the time, the Lord gives very little information concerning His Leading. He expects us to ardently seek His Face as it regards direction. To be sure, He has planned everything, even down to the minute details, but, most of the time, we don't know the details.

All of this is meant to teach us trust and Faith. It, as well, is meant to teach us patience.

Hagar was *"not"* God's Instrument for the accomplishment of His Promise to Abraham. God had promised a son, but He had not said that this son should be Hagar's. To be sure, their foray into that direction would only seek to multiply their sorrow.

To be sure again, Abraham's mission was of such magnitude that we are still suffering the results of that ill-fated direction. In fact, the horror of September 11, 2001, is a direct result of Abraham's lack of faith, i.e., *"sin."*

TEN YEARS IN THE LAND OF CANAAN

"And Sarai Abram's wife took Hagar her maid the Egyptian, after Abram had dwelt ten years in the land of Canaan, and gave her to her husband Abram to be his wife" (Gen. 16:3).

Let the reader understand: as it regards the morality of this act, we find that marriage with one wife was the original Law (Gen. 2:24), and that when polygamy (several wives) was introduced, it was coupled by the inspired narrator with violence and license (Gen. 4:19). Monogamy (one wife) was the rule, as we see in the households of Noah, Terah, Isaac, and others; but many, like Esau and Jacob, allowed themselves a greater latitude. In so doing, their conduct fell below the level of Biblical morality. Everyone's actions are strongly influenced by the general views of the people among whom they live. In Abraham's case, it must be said in his defense that with so much depending on his having offspring, he took no steps to obtain another wife but remained content with a barren Sarah. When he did take Hagar, it was at his wife's request and for a reason which seemed to them adequate and even sacred.

THE CULTURE

It must also be remembered that during those times, if a wife could not have a child, it was somewhat normal for a surrogate to be brought in. The baby then born to the surrogate would be looked at as the baby of the actual wife of the man involved, whomever he may have been. Still, even though that was then the culture, that did not at all make it right in the Eyes of God.

Abraham and Sarah had now been some 10 years in Canaan. Even as we have previously stated, 10 being the number of completion, is it possible that at this time God had planned to bring forth Isaac? Perhaps it would be better to ask the question in another way:

How much do our failures of faith hinder in our lives that which God desires to do? Worse still, how much does it delay us with what He desires to do?

Of course, only God can answer that; however, I think we must come to the conclusion that failure certainly doesn't help. If it doesn't help, then it definitely must hurt in some way despite the fact that God is

Gracious and Merciful! Beside the harm that the birth of Ishmael caused, I have to believe that the possibility at least existed that this excursion into unbelief also caused a delay.

A PERSONAL EXAMPLE

If I remember the time, it was somewhere close to the year 2000. Listening to a radio program, I heard the Preacher make the statement, *"Before Isaac could be born, Abraham and Sarah had to deal with their sin."*

When the dear brother made the statement, the Spirit of the Lord came all over me. I sat there in the car and continued to listen, with tears rolling down my face, knowing that I had just heard something that was very important.

I don't remember exactly what the Preacher said thereafter, that is, if he even answered his own question. I just remember that of which I have related and especially the Moving and Operation of the Holy Spirit on me at that time. I knew the Lord had spoken, but I didn't understand what it meant. What was Abraham and Sarah's sin? Was it this Hagar? Was it their foray into Egypt?

As I sought the Lord about the situation, asking the same questions, I knew in my spirit that wasn't it. After I learned what it was, I learned that these things mentioned were really only the symptoms of the real problem. That's the problem with the modern church. All of us have been guilty of dealing with the symptoms instead of the real problem.

THE FLESH

Several weeks, or possibly several months, later, after finishing our daily radio program that morning, I arose from the chair and turned to walk out the door.

All of a sudden, the Presence of God came over me, and the Lord spoke to my heart what the sin of Abraham and Sarah actually was.

Their sin was trying to bring forth by the means of the flesh that which could only be done by the Power of the Holy Spirit.

The flesh pertains to that which is indicative to a human; in other words, our ability, education, intellect, knowledge, personal power, self-will, willpower, etc. While these things, within themselves, aren't necessarily wrong, the fact is, due to the Fall, man is simply unable to live for God by the means of the flesh. That's exactly what Abraham and Sarah were attempting to do. They were trying to bring to fruition the Promise of God by the means of the flesh, which is impossible. That's the greatest problem in the modern church. It keeps trying to do what only God can do.

THE CROSS

It should be understood, as well, unless the Believer understands the Cross of Christ not only relative to Salvation but, as well, relative to Sanctification, in other words, how we live for God, he will never be able to operate by the Power of the Holy Spirit but will continue functioning in the flesh. The Believer must understand that the Cross of Christ is the Means by which all things are given unto us by the Lord. This means that the Cross of Christ must ever be the Object of our Faith. Only then will the Holy Spirit, Who works exclusively within the parameters, so to speak, of the Finished Work of Christ, begin to work within our hearts and lives. Please understand; the Holy Spirit is God. This means that He can do anything. However, the Believer should understand that the Holy Spirit works exclusively within the parameters of the Cross of Christ.

That's what gave Him and gives Him the legal means to do all that He does within our hearts and lives. Before the Cross, He was greatly limited as to what He could do simply because the sin debt still remained on all of humanity, even the Old Testament greats. The reason is simple, *"The blood of bulls and goats could not take away sins"* (Heb. 10:4). If one desires to function in the Spirit, one must understand the Cross of Christ, otherwise, they will function in the realm of the flesh.

DESPISED!

"And he went in unto Hagar, and she conceived: and when she saw that she had conceived, her mistress was despised in her eyes" (Gen. 16:4).

Hagar now becomes pregnant. With the accolades which came her way, she begins to treat Sarah in a haughty manner. Having no grace or faith, she, as well, has no regard for Sarah and, thereby, oversteps her position. In other words, she looks down on Sarah with contempt. This could probably be said to be the inevitable result. Even though Hagar was a part of the family of Abraham in some distant way, even though a servant, still, there is no record that she really knew the Lord. She was so very close, but yet, so very far away.

THE BLAME

"And Sarai said unto Abram, My wrong be upon you: I have given my maid into your bosom; and when she saw that she had conceived, I was despised in her eyes: the LORD judge between me and you" (Gen. 16:5).

Concerning all of this, Williams says:

"The Epistle to the Galatians declares that Sarah and Hagar represent the two principles of Law and Grace. Hagar represents Salvation by works; Sarah, Salvation by Faith. These principles are opposed to

*one another. Ishmael is born as a result of man's plan-
ning and energy. Isaac is born as the result of God's
planning and energy. In the birth of Ishmael, God had
nothing to do with it, and as regards the birth of Isaac
man was dead. So it is today, Salvation by works
entirely depends on man's capacity to produce them;
Salvation by Faith upon God's ability to perform them.*

*"Under a Covenant of works, God stands still in order
to see what man can do. Under the Covenant of Grace,
man stands still to see what God has done. The two
Covenants are opposed; it must be either Hagar or
Sarah. If Hagar, God has nothing to do with it; if Sarah,
man has nothing to do with it."[3]*

SARAH AND HAGAR

*"But Abram said unto Sarai, Behold, your maid is in
your hand; do to her as it pleases you. And when Sarai
dealt hardly with her, she fled from her face"* (Gen. 16:6).

While the Scripture doesn't say exactly what Sarah
did, whatever it was, it must have been severe. It is
believed by some expositors that she actually had one
of the servants to administer corporal punishment to
her in the form of a whipping. Whatever it was, it was
so severe that Hagar fled the premises.

As we here see, when the *"flesh"* is put forth, the situation does not improve but steadily gets worse. In fact,
as we will later see, the situation finally became so bad
that Ishmael, at the behest of his mother Hagar, was trying to kill Isaac and make it seem like an accident.

THE ANGEL OF THE LORD

*"And the Angel of the LORD found her by a fountain
of water in the wilderness, by the fountain in the way
to Shur"* (Gen. 16:7).

Every evidence is that the *"Angel of the LORD"* mentioned here is none other than a preincarnate appearance of the Lord Jesus Christ.

Upon meeting Hagar, the Lord promises to bless her, tells her He has seen her affliction, and comforts her.

Regrettably, later on, as we have just stated, she despised this Grace and sought to murder the divinely given child, which would later come, who would be Isaac.

She calls the name of the well where she met Jesus the Lord, *"The well of living after seeing,"* for she said, *"Do I live after seeing God?"* She did live but not as the other woman whom Jesus met at Jacob's well. These wells and these women are contrasted here.

Did Hagar know to whom she was actually speaking? It is very doubtful that she did.

QUESTIONS

"And He said, Hagar, Sarai's maid, from where do you come? and where will you go? And she said, I flee from the face of my mistress Sarai" (Gen. 16:8).

As we shall see, the Lord will not recognize her marriage to the Patriarch (Gen. 16:3). The Lord will remind her of her original position as a bondwoman, from which liberty was not to be obtained by running away, but rather by submission.

As we found with Lot, we find here, as well, even with a servant girl, even one who did not necessarily believe the Covenant. Inasmuch as she was in the household of Abraham, she would receive special attention by the Lord. In fact, He would save her life inasmuch as had she continued on her journey, she would, no doubt, have perished in the wilderness.

This shows us the protection afforded by God's People. In other words, the only *"salt"* and *"Light"* in this world presently, and, in fact, always have been, are those who truly know the Lord and, thereby, truly serve Him. Everything else is darkness.

SUBMISSION

"And the Angel of the LORD said unto her, Return to your mistress, and submit yourself under her hands" (Gen. 16:9).

The Lord demands that Hagar place herself back under her mistress, who was Sarah, and submit herself unto her hands. He promised that the seed of Hagar would be great for multitude, but it says nothing about Faith.

In the case before us in this Chapter, it is evident that Hagar was not God's Instrument for the accomplishment of His Promise to Abraham. He had promised a son, no doubt, but He had not said that this son should be Hagar's. In point of fact, we find from the narrative that both Abraham and Sarah *"multiplied their sorrow"* by having resorted to Hagar. Sarah's dignity was trampled down by the Egyptian bondwoman, and she found herself in the place of weakness and contempt.

The only true place of dignity and power is the place of weakness and dependence. There is no one so entirely independent of all around as the man who is really walking by Faith and waiting only upon God. However, the moment a Child of God makes himself or herself a debtor to nature or to the world, he loses his dignity and will speedily be made to feel his loss. It is no easy task to estimate the loss sustained by diverging in the smallest measure from the path of Faith. Now, Sarah feels that loss.

THE BONDWOMAN

However, *"the bondwoman"* cannot be eliminated by hard treatment. When we make mistakes, as Sarah did, and find ourselves called upon to encounter the results thereof, we cannot counteract these results by carrying ourselves with a high hand. We frequently try this method, but we are sure to make matters worse thereby.

If we have done wrong, we should humble ourselves, confess the wrong, and wait on God for Deliverance, but Sarah didn't do that. So, far from waiting on God for Deliverance, she seeks to deliver herself in her own way. However, it will always be found that every effort we make to rectify our errors previous to the full confession thereof only tends to render our path more difficult. Thus, Hagar had to return and give birth to her son, the son which proved to be not the child of promise at all but a very great trial to Abraham and his house, as we shall see.

Grace forgives the sin and restores the soul, but that which is sown must be reaped. Abraham and Sarah had to endure the presence of the bondwoman and her son for a number of years and then seek the separation brought about in God's Way.

There is a peculiar Blessedness in leaving ourselves in God's Hands. Had Abraham and Sarah done so on the present occasion, they would never have been troubled with the presence of the bondwoman and her son. However, having made themselves debtors to nature, they had to endure the consequences, and so do we!

DID HAGAR TRULY SUBMIT?

The Lord told Hagar to go back and to submit herself totally and fully to Sarah. While she did this somewhat, she did not fully obey. As we shall see, she submitted outwardly but never really submitted from her heart. As we have previously stated, even though Hagar was in the Church, so to speak, she was not of the Church, as is obvious. This typifies so many millions in the world of religion at this particular time.

THE FLESH

"And the Angel of the LORD said unto her, I will multiply your seed exceedingly, that it shall not be numbered for multitude" (Gen. 16:10).

As previously stated, looking at Hagar is like looking at so many in the modern church. She is in the Church, i.e., *"the Covenant,"* but is actually never really a part of it. She never recognized Isaac as the Promised Seed and, in fact, actually plotted the murder of Isaac (Gal. 4:29). So, she represents all who would seek to obtain the Promise *"after the flesh,"* which refers to doing so by means other than by the Cross (Gal. 4:23-25).

In the natural, the Arab people, descendants of Ishmael, are approximately 100 million plus regarding population. In the spiritual sense, the church is filled with *"workers of the flesh,"* so much so, in fact, that it cannot be *"numbered for multitude."*

Isaac represents the Cross while Ishmael represents the flesh. These two directions are ever before the Church. One or the other must be chosen, and whichever one is chosen, the other one must be cast out. Regrettably and sadly, the far greater majority of the modern church has cast out the Cross in favor of the flesh. The true way is to cast out the bondwoman and her son and, in fact, if the *"Promise"* is to be attained (all that Jesus did for us at the Cross), they must be cast out (Gal. 4:30).

ISHMAEL

"And the Angel of the LORD said unto her, Behold, you are with child, and you shall bear a son, and shall

call his name Ishmael; because the LORD has heard your affliction" (Gen. 16:11).

The fault of her situation did not belong with Hagar, but rather with Abraham and Sarah. However, she ultimately forfeited what the Lord could have done for her by opposing His Plan, which was Isaac.

The Lord does not condone mistreatment, irrespective as to who does it or to whom it is done. While Hagar definitely had not treated Sarah right after it was found that she had conceived, still, this gave Sarah no right to mistreat this servant girl. As Believers, we do not return kind for kind regarding evil.

The Lord tells Hagar to name the son that will be born to her *"Ishmael."* The name means, *"God hears,"* but it really has nothing to do with Ishmael, but rather the plight of Hagar.

PERSONALITY

"And he will be a wild man; his hand will be against every man, and every man's hand against him; and he shall dwell in the presence of all his brethren" (Gen. 16:12).

These predictions describe the Arab people perfectly. They cannot get along with anyone in the world, and they cannot even get along among themselves.

At the present time, they have tried to unite regarding the destruction of Israel. However, despite the fact that they are about 25 times larger than Israel regarding population and land mass, they have failed to make any inroads in regards to this effort. The reason is mostly because they cannot agree among themselves. Ishmael opposed the Cross in his efforts to kill Isaac, and his descendants have continued in the same vain. So, he dwells in the presence of all his brethren (Israel) but does not subdue them and, in fact, never will subdue them.

THE LORD

"And she called the Name of the LORD Who spoke unto her, Your God sees me: for she said, Have I also here looked after Him Who sees me?" (Gen. 16:13)

Hagar eventually recognized that the Angel was, in fact, the Lord, actually the God of Abraham.

Hagar gave the name *"El Roi"* to the Lord, which means, *"You are a God Who permits Himself to be seen."* She then exclaims, *"Do not I still see after seeing?"* According to Ellicott, her meaning is this:

"Do I not see, therefore am alive, and not even blinded, nor bereft of sense and reason, though I have seen God."[4]

All of this tells us that the Lord made a visible appearance unto Hagar.

As is obvious, she truly had a wonderful Revelation, but sadly and regrettably, her self-will overrode her Faith. She wanted her son Ishmael to be the heir of Promise, mostly for the material goods, but that was not to be. As we shall see, she would even go so far as to try to kill Isaac, and all who reject the Cross follow in her footsteps.

THE WELL

"Wherefore the well was called Beer-lahai-roi; behold, it is between Kadesh and Bered" (Gen. 16:14).

"Beer-lahai-roi" means, *"Well of the Living-Seeing God."* It was the well where God had been seen, and the beholder still lives. It was a place later frequented often by Isaac (Gen. 25:11).

ISHMAEL

"And Hagar bore Abram a son: and Abram called his son's name, which Hagar bore, Ishmael" (Gen. 16:15).

Without a doubt, Hagar related to Abraham all that had happened. She then placed herself under the authority of Sarah, and Abraham was careful to name the boy what the Lord had said — *"Ishmael."*

Here we are now introduced to the beginning, one might say, of the Muslim religion. Of course, this religion would not come into being for another approximate 4,000 years, but it has been, and is, the blight of the world. It is the greatest enemy of Israel and America, hating us with a murderous passion. Of course, when Abraham looked down into this baby's face right after it was born, he could hardly grasp or understand what it all meant. Ishmael was a work of the flesh, and works of the flesh always cause tremendous problems.

EIGHTY-SIX YEARS OLD

"And Abram was four score and six years old, when Hagar bore Ishmael to Abram" (Gen. 16:16).

Abraham would have to wait some 13 more years before the Promise would begin to be fulfilled, and actually some 14 years before Isaac would be born.

As previously stated, I have to wonder if this lapse of faith did not prolong the waiting period for the Promise to be realized. I would not venture to say that such is always the case; however, I do believe that a lapse of faith does definitely have a negative effect. I cannot really see how it could be otherwise. I think I can say without any fear of exaggeration or contradiction that every sin in some way can be traced back to a lapse of faith. Of course, we're speaking of Believers.

Perhaps one could better explain this situation by saying that it's not so much a lapse of faith as it is the Object of Faith being changed. The faith of Abraham and Sarah was switched from God and His Promise to themselves and the Egyptian girl.

THE GALATIANS

The Holy Spirit through the Apostle Paul uses this scenario in the Epistle to the Galatians to teach us a tremendous truth.

The error into which the Galatians, or at least some of them, were being drawn was that of adding something to what Christ had already accomplished for them by the Cross. The Gospel, which Paul had preached to them, was the simple presentation of God's Absolute, All-encompassing, and unconditional Grace. *"Jesus Christ had been evidently set forth, crucified among them"* (Gal. 3:1). A Crucified Christ settled everything in reference both to God's Claims and man's necessities.

However, false teachers came in, telling the Galatians that unless they were circumcised, they couldn't be saved. They were attempting to add *"Law"* to *"Grace."*

Paul countered by telling them that if they attempted to add something to the Cross, *"Christ is become of no effect unto you"* (Gal. 5:4).

The moment anyone attempts to add something to Faith, he has nullified the Grace of God and, thereby, has subverted Christianity. In other words, it is the Cross of Christ, or it is nothing!

GRACE

The True Message of Christianity, at least as the Bible teaches it, is that God comes down to me, just as I am, a lost, guilty, and self-destroyed sinner. His coming, moreover, is with a full Remission of all my sins, and then a full Salvation is given to me. It is all perfectly brought about by Jesus having died on the Cross and my Faith in that Finished Work (Jn. 3:3, 16; Rom. 5:1-2; I Cor. 1:17-18, 23; 2:2, 5; Col. 2:10-15; I Pet. 1:18-20).

Understanding this, Paul does not hesitate to say to the Galatians, *"Christ is become of no effect unto you, whosoever of you are ('seek to be') justified by the Law; you are fallen from Grace"* (Gal. 5:4).

If it is of Grace, it must be all of Grace. It cannot be half Grace and half Law. The two Covenants, one of works and one of Faith, are perfectly distinct. To make it clearer, it cannot be half Sarah and half Hagar; it must be either the one or the other. If it is Hagar, God has nothing to do with it, it being all of man. If it is Sarah, man has nothing to do with it, it being all of God.

The Law addresses man, tests him, sees what he is really worth, proves him a ruin, and puts him under the curse. It not only puts him under it, but it keeps him there, so long as he is occupied with it, as long as he is alive.

However, once the believing sinner accepts Christ, he is actually baptized into the Death of Christ, is buried with Christ, and is raised with Christ in Newness of Life. Consequently, what the sinner once was, he no longer is. He is dead, at least as far as the *"old man"* is concerned. Paul said:

THE RIGHTEOUSNESS OF GOD

"Knowing this, that our old man is crucified with Him, that the body of sin might be destroyed (its guilt and its power), that henceforth we should not serve sin.

"For he who is dead is freed from sin" (Rom. 6:6-7).

I'm certain that the reader understands that Paul is not speaking here of one dying physically, but rather dying in Christ, which happens when one accepts Christ. That's why we are referred to as a *"new Creation"* (II Cor. 5:17). The Lord cannot accept anything else. He can only accept perfection, which alone is found in Christ. Our Faith in Christ and what Christ has done for us at the Cross guarantees us a perfect, imputed Righteousness, i.e., *"the Righteousness of God."*

There is no way that man can attain to such Righteousness by his own machinations and religiosity. Whenever he attempts to do so by adding his own rules and regulations, or whatever he may submit, the only thing such tends to do is to insult Christ. It, in effect, says that Christ did not finish the Work at the Cross, and something needs to be added.

Of course, God cannot tolerate such thinking and cannot tolerate such action. It is all of Christ, or it is nothing!

ISHMAEL

That's the reason that Ishmael, spiritually speaking, must go. Isaac and Ishmael cannot remain in the same place. The former is a child of Promise while the latter is a work of the flesh. This is what the Believer faces in his living for God.

He can either resort to his own efforts or the efforts of others, thereby, accepting Ishmael, or he can rely totally on Christ and what Christ has done at the Cross, thereby, relying on Isaac, so to speak. However, let the reader understand the following, that is, if he accepts Ishmael:

Paul said:

"Nevertheless what says the Scripture? Cast out the bondwoman and her son: for the son of the bondwoman shall not be heir with the son of the freewoman" (Gal. 4:30).

If we attempt to keep *"Ishmael"* in any capacity, that is, to depend upon the flesh or our works, which means to reject the Cross, all we succeed in doing is to *"frustrate the Grace of God"* (Gal. 2:21). That is a frightful place for any Christian. We forfeit the inheritance, for only Faith in Christ and the Cross can inherit the Blessing.

RELUCTANCE TO ACCEPT THE CROSS!

The Cross of Christ is the greatest cause of contention in the church. Most will deny that because the Cross is seldom mentioned. However, whenever anything is placed before the Christian as necessary, which is an addition to the Cross, the Cross has just become the focal point of contention, whether addressed or not.

Considering that the Cross is so prominent throughout the entirety of the Bible, so prominent, in fact, that it's impossible to escape its center of gravity, why should it raise a question?

Let the reader peruse the following statements very carefully because they are so very, very important:

No human being denies the Cross from a position of theology but always from a position of morality. What do we mean by that?

The Message of Christ, that He came to this world and died to save sinners, is about as simple as anything could ever be (I Tim. 1:15). Consequently, no individual can claim that he has rejected the Cross simply because he cannot understand the Cross. If it is rejected, it will always be from a position of morality. In other words, whether we're speaking of a Believer or an unbeliever, the cause is always unbelief, pride, self-will, etc. As we've stated, Believers do not give up their Ishmaels easily. It is always a struggle because Ishmael is always a fruit, and a fair fruit at that, of our own efforts. As a result of it being such, men do not part such company very quickly or very easily.

THE OFFENSE OF THE CROSS

Paul said:

"And I, brethren, if I yet preach Circumcision, why do I yet suffer persecution? then is the offense of the Cross ceased" (Gal. 5:11).

In Paul's day, circumcision, which was a part of the old Mosaic Law, was the big thing. Many Christian Jews were saying that Gentiles had to be *"circumcised after the manner of Moses,"* that is, if they were to be Saved (Acts 15:1). So, they were adding circumcision to Grace, which, of course, cannot be done.

Presently, circumcision is not the problem, but rather other things. However, it doesn't really matter what we attempt to substitute for the Cross or else add to the Cross; the end result is the same. In such a case, *"Christ shall profit you nothing"* (Gal. 5:2).

Why is it that these other things, whatever they might be, carry no offense, and the Cross does?

THE REASON FOR THE OFFENSE
OF THE CROSS

Among other things, the Cross proclaims the fact of how sinful and wicked that man is. He is so sinful and wicked, in fact, that God would have to become Man and die on a cruel Cross, shed His Life's Blood, in effect, offering Himself for Sacrifice, in order that man might be Saved. Man doesn't want to admit that he's that bad. He likes to think that while he might have a problem of sorts, still, he can save himself in some way. So, he keeps trying, and he keeps trying, and he keeps trying, all to no avail. However, despite the fact that the guilt doesn't leave, because his own efforts never bring about a Born-Again experience, he tries to cover up the emptiness of his soul by claiming that which he really doesn't have.

Far too often, the Believer who has rejected the Cross, or else doesn't understand the Cross, will also try to cover up his lack of victorious living by loudly claiming, even as the unbeliever, that which he, as well, doesn't have.

THE FAÇADE

The modern church is literally built, at least for all practical purposes, on methods devised by man, which actually will not work. It's another *"Ishmael."*

However, instead of tearing down the façade, because that's what it is, the façade is strengthened. In other words, we groom and we dress up Ishmael.

Outside of the Cross, there are probably as many methods of so-called victory as there are people.

I received a letter just the other day from a preacher who was touting the following:

He was invited to a *"seminar"* with only preachers and their wives present, at least that's what his letter seemed to imply, with all being in desperate need of victory.

The method proposed at this seminar was that each preacher and his wife, that is, if she was with him, should take a piece of paper and write on that paper all of their faults, sins, etc. They were then to pair off with a stranger, men with men and women with women, and then read their list of faults and failures out loud to each other.

After this was done, they were to rip up the pieces of paper on which their faults and failures had been listed and throw it all on the floor. This was to somehow symbolize their weaknesses and faults being destroyed. They were then to trample the pieces underfoot, and, somehow, all of this was to give them victory, at least, according to the pastor of a large church who was sponsoring the seminar. Several hundreds of preachers believed this stupidity and attended and did what they were told to do.

The sadness is, all of these preachers were supposed to be Spirit-filled.

This is just another ridiculous method (and ridiculous it is) of substituting something else in place of the Cross. Not a shred of such foolishness is found in the Bible, but yet, it was being touted as a great spiritual breakthrough.

The non-Pentecostal world has attempted to preach the Cross without the Holy Spirit. Now, for all practical purposes, they are preaching neither one. The Pentecostal world has attempted to preach the Holy Spirit without the Cross and has degenerated into fanaticism, of which I've just given an example. If the church doesn't return to the Cross, which must always be the Foundation of all that we believe and preach, the situation will only grow worse.

> *"There is a Name I love to hear,*
> *"I love to sing its worth;*
> *"It sounds like music in my ear,*
> *"The sweetest Name on Earth."*

> *"It tells me of a Saviour's love,*
> *"Who died to set me free;*
> *"It tells me of His Precious Blood,*
> *"The sinner's perfect plea."*

> *"It tells me what my Father has,*
> *"In store for every day,*
> *"And, tho' I tread a darksome path,*
> *"Yields sunshine all the way."*

> *"It tells of One Whose Loving Heart,*
> *"Can feel my deepest woe,*
> *"Who in each sorrow bears a part,*
> *"That none can bear below."*

ABRAHAM

CHAPTER

15

Abraham And
The Promise Of God

ABRAHAM AND THE PROMISE OF GOD

EL-SHADDAI

"And when Abram was ninety years old and nine, the LORD appeared to Abram, and said unto him, I am the Almighty God; walk before Me, and be thou perfect" (Gen. 17:1).

It had probably been about 13 years since the Lord had last spoken with Abraham. During this time, he probably continued to think that Ishmael was the Promised Seed. That is indicated in Verse 18. However, now he will know differently.

The last personal Revelation that Abraham received from the Lord, regarding the Name of the Lord, concerned the meeting with Melchizedek. Even then, the Revelation was given by Melchizedek to Abraham, with the Lord referred to as *"El Elyon,"* which means, *"Most High God, Possessor of Heaven and Earth."* As well, through Hagar, he had learned of God as *"El Roi,"* which means, *"You are a God Who permits Himself to be seen."* Now, he will be given the Revelation of *"Almighty God,"* which in the Hebrew is, *"El Shaddai."* It means, *"Strong so as to overpower."* Keil says of this name, *"As possessing the power to realize His Promises, even when the order of nature presented no prospect of their fulfillment, and the powers of nature were insufficient to secure it."*[1]

In the various names of God given in the Bible, we learn of His Nature and His Characteristics. These names define Who He is and, as well, What He is.

ALMIGHTY

Concerning this time, Williams says:

"Thirteen years of silence on the part of God follow upon Abraham's folly in the matter of Ishmael;

but man's foolish planning cannot undo God's eternal counsels. The time is fulfilled and the child of Promise must be born.

"But Faith must be energized if Isaac is to be begotten; and accordingly there is a new and abrupt Revelation made of Jehovah to Abraham's soul as 'El-Shaddai.' This is the first occurrence of this great Divine title. It assured Abraham that what God had promised, He was Almighty to perform. The first occurrence of this title in the New Testament (II Cor. 6:18) expresses the same truth. Throughout the Chapter therefore, man is dead and God is the Actor; and it was not so much what God was for Abraham, but what He was Himself — not 'I am your shield,' but 'I am El-Shaddai.'"²

THE WALK OF THE PATRIARCH

Concerning Abraham's life and living, it is very evident that he had not been walking before Almighty God as he should have walked when he adopted Sarah's suggestion in reference to Hagar. It is Faith alone that can enable a man to walk before God as he should walk. Above all, it is Faith with its Object being the Cross, which it must ever be, or else, it is faith which God will not recognize. The Holy Spirit superintends Faith with the Cross as its Object, but He will not superintend faith in anything else (Rom. 8:1-2, 11).

With the words, *"I am the Almighty God; walk before Me, and be thou perfect,"* the Lord was telling Abraham two things:

1. He must be perfect in his Faith. It must not waver, as it had done regarding the situation with Hagar, but must rest in Almighty God.

2. There is no way that one's *"walk"* can be as it ought to be without the Power of Almighty God. It is simply impossible otherwise!

THE HOLY SPIRIT

As Believers, we presently have the Power of the Holy Spirit, Who is Almighty God, and Who will help us, even as He is meant to do. To be sure, without Him, the task simply cannot be performed.

Unfortunately, most modern Christians do not understand the Way and the Means by which the Holy Spirit works. They take Him for granted, or else, they know next to nothing about Him, looking at Him as someone or something mysterious. The truth is, He desires to lead us, guide us, empower us, and make us what we ought to be. This is all done by development of the Fruit of the Spirit and, above all, to glorify Christ within our lives. For us to have His Help on a constant basis, we must *"walk after the Spirit."* To not walk after the Spirit is to *"walk after the flesh,"* which automatically brings failure (Rom. 8:1).

As it regards the New Covenant, the modern Christian has a much better Covenant by comparison to the Covenant under which Abraham functioned. Relative to a work before the Cross, our New Covenant is much better because it's based on a Work already done by Christ on the Cross. Before the Cross, it was only promised.

The Covenants before the Cross were based on animal blood, which was woefully insufficient. The New Covenant is based on the Blood of our Lord and Saviour, Jesus Christ. Whereas the blood of animals could not take away sins, the Blood of Christ definitely can take away sin and all its effects (Heb. 10:4). So, since the Cross, so to speak, we now have a much better Contract (Jn. 1:29).

HOW DOES ONE WALK AFTER THE SPIRIT?

To give the answer, before we deal with the particulars, walking after the Spirit simply means that the

Believer places his Faith exclusively in the Cross of Christ, understands what Jesus did for him there, and, thereby, places his Faith in nothing else (Rom. 8:1-2, 11).

"Walking after the flesh," is placing ones faith in anything, irrespective as to what it might be, other than the Cross of Christ.

Most Christians don't have the slightest idea as to what *"walking after the Spirit"* or *"walking after the flesh"* actually is. Were they to give an answer, at least as it regards *"walking after the Spirit,"* they would think it refers to doing spiritual things. It doesn't!

By *"spiritual things,"* I'm speaking of faithfulness to church, giving money for the Work of the Lord, fasting, having a regular prayer time each day, reading one's Bible, witnessing to souls, etc. These things are what we refer to as *"Christian disciplines"* and are what every good Christian will always do. To be sure, those things are deeply spiritual and will prove to be a great blessing to any and all Believers in the carrying out of these particulars. However, the doing of those things is not *"walking after the Spirit."*

THE LAW OF THE SPIRIT OF LIFE
IN CHRIST JESUS

In effect, Paul tells us what it is in Romans 8:2. He said:

"For the Law (a Law devised by the Godhead in eternity past) of the Spirit (Holy Spirit) of Life (all life comes from Christ but through the Spirit) in Christ Jesus (this Law is made up of what Christ did at the Cross on our behalf) has made me free from the Law of Sin and Death." When we place our Faith in Christ and what Christ has done for us at the Cross, such constitutes *"walking after the Spirit."* We must keep our Faith in Christ and the Cross on a constant basis, in effect, never divorcing Christ from His Cross. This

refers to the fact that we know and understand that everything we receive from God comes to us by and through Christ and what He did at the Cross. Such constitutes a perfect walk. Without our faith properly placed, our *"walk"* (manner of life) will be erratic, to say the least. We can walk before the Lord, even as God demanded of Abraham, and do so correctly if we follow God's Prescribed Order, which is the Cross of Christ (Rom. 6:3-5).

COVENANT

"And I will make My Covenant between Me and you, and will multiply you exceedingly" (Gen. 17:2).

Concerning this *"Covenant,"* one could say that it is an extension of the Covenant already given to the Patriarch in Genesis, Chapter 15. Because it goes into much greater detail, one might even place it in the position of an enlarged Covenant.

In Covenants made by the Lord, we find that the Lord doesn't leave anything undone. He will perfectly settle everything on behalf of those who simply put their trust in Him, and that refers to what Christ has done for us at the Cross. When Unerring Wisdom, Omnipotent Power, and Infinite Love combine, the confiding heart may enjoy unruffled repose. Unless we can find some circumstance too big or too little for *"The Almighty God,"* we have no proper base on which to found a single anxious thought. Now, that is an amazing statement, but it happens to be true. There should be no room for worry, anxiety, or fear in the heart and life of any Believer, who has placed his Faith totally and completely in Christ and what Christ has done for us at the Cross.

This is an amazing truth and one eminently calcu-lated to put all who believe it into the blessed position in which we find Abraham in this Chapter. When God had, in effect, said to him, *"Leave all to Me, and I will settle it for you, beyond your utmost desires and expectations: the seed and the inheritance, and everything pertaining thereto, will be fully and everlastingly settled, according to the Covenant of the Almighty God."*

FAITH

All of this hinges on Faith, and more particularly, it hinges on Faith properly placed. Faith properly placed always and without exception refers to the Cross of Christ. We should certainly place our Faith in the Word of God; however, if we attempt to place our Faith in the Word of God without first anchoring it in the Cross, we will find that we will misinterpret the Word. The Word of God is, in effect, the Story of Christ and His Cross. This is the tenor and timbre of the Bible from Genesis 1:1 through Revelation 22:21.

The Living Word came to this world (Jn. 1:1), *"That Word was made flesh, and dwelt among us"* (Jn. 1:14).

He did this for a particular reason, and John tells us what that reason was.

When John the Baptist introduced Jesus, he said, *"Behold the Lamb of God, Who takes away the sin of the world"* (Jn. 1:29).

In effect, these two Passages I have just given give us the Story of the Bible.

I made the statement last night in preaching at Family Worship Center, *"If one understands Genesis 15:6, then one understands the entirety of the Bible. If that one Scripture is misunderstood, then basically the entirety of the Word of God, in some way, is misunderstood."*

I do not think that any Believer can properly understand the Bible unless he first understands the Cross. Once he begins to properly understand the Cross, then the entirety of the Word of God will begin to come into focus. This is true Faith and the only way that Faith can be properly expressed and anchored in the Word of God. In fact, even as Jesus and His Cross must never be separated, the Word and the Cross must, as well, not be separated for the simple reason that the Story of the Word is the Cross (Jn. 1:1-3).

THE BLESSING

"And will multiply you exceedingly," could be translated, *"And will bless you exceedingly."*

Blessing from God always falls out to increase, with increase explained in the realm of multiplication. It means that the Lord doesn't merely add to, but rather that He multiplies. There is a vast difference!

Abraham is concerned about one particular seed. He can't see how in the world it can be brought to pass, considering his age and the age of Sarah, especially since she has been barren all of her life. Now God tells him that not only will the seed be forthcoming, but He is going to multiply that seed exceedingly, which He most definitely did.

Concerning the Power of God, Paul said:

"Now unto Him Who is able to do exceeding abundantly above all that we ask or think, according to the power that works in us" (Eph. 3:20). That's the kind of God that we serve and, if our Faith is properly placed, the reason we need have no occasion for worry, fear, or anxiety.

THE RESPONSE

"And Abram fell on his face: and God talked with him, saying" (Gen. 17:3).

The Power of God was, no doubt, expressed here

in a tremendous way. So, Abraham falling on his face was either because he simply couldn't stand due to the Power, or else, he fell on his face in Reverence to God. More than likely, both circumstances came into play here. He could not continue to stand because of the Power, and his desire, as well, was to prostrate himself before the Lord, which would be a sign of total dependence on the Lord.

THE NAMES OF GOD

In these three Verses, the Lord reveals Himself by three different Names.

1. The Name, *"Lord,"* in Verse 1 means, *"Jehovah."*

2. In the latter part of Verse 1, the Lord refers to Himself as *"The Almighty God,"* Who, in effect, is *"El-Shaddai,"* the *"All-powerful One."*

3. In Verse 3, He refers to Himself as *"Elohim,"* which refers to Him being Creator.

The *"Perfection"* demanded in Verse 1 means, *"Guileless."*

In effect, the Lord is saying, *"Leave all to Me, let Me plan for you. I am Almighty. No longer scheme to beget an Ishmael, but trust Me to give you an Isaac."* In effect, one might say that this is the meaning of the word, *"Perfect,"* in Verse 1. It does not mean that Abraham was sinlessly perfect, for he wasn't, and neither is there any other individual either.

A FATHER OF MANY NATIONS

"As for Me, behold, My Covenant is with you, and you shall be a father of many nations" (Gen. 17:4).

From the one seed, i.e., *"child,"* which Abraham was worried about, the Lord takes him to the position of *"father of many nations."* In effect, He is saying to the

Patriarch, *"I am Almighty God, and I can do anything."*

Ellicott says that this Fourth Verse is translated poorly. He goes on to say, *"Literally the word, 'of many nations,' signifies a confused noise like the din of a populous city. Abraham was to be the father of a 'thronging crowd of nations.'"*[3]

ABRAHAM

"Neither shall your name any more be called Abram, but your name shall be Abraham; for a father of many nations have I made you" (Gen. 17:5).

"Abram" means, *"Exalted father,"* while *"Abraham"* means, *"Father of the multitudes."*

The *"multitudes"* of which are spoken here concern all who have come to Christ. Nations and kings actually came from Abraham, in fact, the entirety of the Arab world, now numbering approximately 100 million or more, along with the Jews, presently numbering approximately 20 to 25 million. If all are counted in the world, all of these would be other than the Body of Christ.

The True Seed, Who came from Abraham, is Christ (Gal. 3:16). Consequently, all who are of Faith are blessed with faithful Abraham, being partakers of the same Covenant Blessings secured by the same oath and promise.

All that the Christian world enjoys, or ever will enjoy, is indebted to Abraham and his Seed. A high honor this is, to be the father of the faithful, the stock from which the Messiah should spring, and on which the Church of the Living God should grow.

This honor Esau despised when he sold his birthright, and here lay the profaneness of that act, which involved a contempt of the most sacred of all objects, the Messiah and His Everlasting Kingdom.

FRUITFUL

"And I will make you exceeding fruitful, and I will make nations of you, and kings shall come out of you" (Gen. 17:6).

Without a doubt, the two greatest kings to come from Abraham would be David and Solomon. But yet, the greatest of all, and Who cannot be classed among mere men, is the Lord Jesus Christ, the King of kings and the Lord of lords. Actually, Christ is referred to as *"the Son of David, the Son of Abraham"* (Mat. 1:1).

> *"It may be at morn, when the day is awaking,*
> *"When sunlight through darkness shadow is breaking,*
> *"That Jesus will come in the fullness of Glory,*
> *"To receive from the world His Own."*

> *"It may be at midday, it may be at twilight,*
> *"It may be, perchance, that the blackness of midnight,*
> *"Will burst into light in the blaze of His Glory,*
> *"When Jesus receives His Own."*

> *"O, joy! O, delight! Should we go without dying,*
> *"No sickness, no sadness, no dread and no crying,*
> *"Caught up through the clouds with our Lord into Glory,*
> *"When Jesus receives His Own."*

ABRAHAM

CHAPTER

16

Abraham And
The Covenant

ABRAHAM AND THE COVENANT

"And I will establish My Covenant between Me and you and your seed after you in their generations for an Everlasting Covenant, to be a God unto you, and to your seed after you" (Gen. 17:7).

This Covenant made with Abraham is totally different than the Covenant made with Moses, with the latter being temporary. The Covenant with the Patriarch is everlasting simply because even though it involves many things, its end result is Justification by Faith. In fact, its conclusion will be the New Covenant, Which and Who is Jesus Christ, the meaning of which is the Cross of Christ and, as well, is referred to as, *"The Everlasting Covenant"* (Heb. 13:20).

CANAAN

"And I will give unto you, and to your seed after you, the land wherein you are a stranger, all the land of Canaan, for an everlasting possession; and I will be their God" (Gen. 17:8).

Both the Jewish and Arab worlds point to Abraham as their father, and rightly so. The difference is the Seed. The Arabs, who are mostly Muslim, claim Ishmael is the true seed while the Jews claim Isaac to be the true seed, the latter of which corresponds with the Word of God. Because of this contention, probably one could say that the *"land of Canaan"* has been the world's chief trouble spot. This conflict between the Muslims and the Jews, especially as it regards the land of Canaan, has raged, more or less, for some 1,400 years. To be frank, the greatest contention is just ahead, as it regards the coming Antichrist, etc.

THE KEEPING OF THE COVENANT

"And God said unto Abraham, You shall keep My Covenant therefore, you, and your seed after you in their generations" (Gen. 17:9).

This could well be called a *"Covenant of Grace"* and, as such, is everlasting. It is *"from"* everlasting in the counsels of it and *"to"* everlasting in the consequences of it.

On becoming a Nation some 500 years later, Israel recognized the great Covenant as given to Abraham. However, instead of making it the Foundation Covenant, they placed the Law or Covenant of Moses in the first place and made the Abrahamic Covenant second place, that is, if given any place at all. This means that they inverted it; consequently, they destroyed themselves. Law must never precede Grace. If so, Grace is abrogated.

THE MODERN CHURCH

Regrettably, for all practical purposes, the church is doing the same identical thing. Abraham is our father, but, in a sense, the modern church has made Moses their father. While it's done in a subtle way and, thereby, not recognizable to all, the fact is, if we look to man-devised law instead of the Cross, we have abrogated this beautiful and wonderful Abrahamic Covenant exactly as did Israel. Both, and I speak of the Covenant of Grace and the Covenant of Law, cannot exist side by side. One or the other must go. Jesus has totally and perfectly kept the Mosaic Covenant. He is the only One Who has done this and, in fact, He did it all on our behalf. We are meant to function only in the Covenant of Grace, which, in effect, is the Abrahamic Covenant (Rom. 4:16), of which Jesus is the result. Regrettably, the Covenant of Law seems to be far more enticing!

CIRCUMCISION

"This is My Covenant, which you shall keep, between Me and you and your seed after you; Every man child among you shall be circumcised" (Gen. 17:10).

The Rite of Circumcision is now introduced. Every male member of the household of Faith must bear in his body the seal of that Covenant, which is circumcision. There must be no exception.

We are taught in Romans, Chapter 4, that circumcision was *"a seal of the Righteousness of Faith. Abraham believed God, and it was counted unto him for Righteousness"* (Rom. 4:3).

Since the Cross, the seal with which the Believer is now sealed is not a mark in the flesh but *"that Holy Spirit of Promise, whereby he is sealed, unto the day of Redemption."* This is founded upon our everlasting connection with Christ and our perfect identification with Him in Death and Resurrection.

PAUL
Paul said:

"And you are complete in Him *(the satisfaction of every spiritual want is found in Christ, made possible by the Cross)*, **which is the Head of all principality and power** *(His Headship extends not only over the Church, which voluntarily serves Him, but over all forces that are opposed to Him as well [Phil. 2:10-11])*:
"In Whom also you are circumcised with the Circumcision made without hands *(that which is brought about by the Cross [Rom. 6:3-5])*, **in putting off the body of the sins of the flesh by the Circumcision of Christ** *(refers to the old carnal nature that is defeated by the Believer*

*placing his Faith totally in the Cross, which gives the Holy Spirit latitude to work)***:**

OUR POSITION IN CHRIST

"**Buried with Him in Baptism** *(does not refer to Water Baptism, but rather to the Believer baptized into the Death of Christ, which refers to the Crucifixion and Christ as our Substitute [Rom. 6:3-4])*, **wherein also you are risen with *Him* through the Faith of the Operation of God, Who has raised Him from the dead.** *(This does not refer to our future physical Resurrection, but to that Spiritual Resurrection from a sinful state into Divine Life. We died with Him, we are buried with Him, and we rose with Him [Rom. 6:3-5], and herein lies the secret of all Spiritual Victory)*" **(Col. 2:10-12).**

This Passage, as given by Paul, proclaims to us the true idea of what circumcision was meant to typify. Every Believer belongs to *"the Circumcision"* by virtue of his living association with Him Who, by His Cross, has forever abolished everything that stood in the way of a perfect Justification. One might say that there is not a speck of sin or a principle of sin in the nature of God's People for which Christ was not judged on the Cross. We are now looked upon as having died with Christ, lain in the grave with Christ, and then raised with Christ. We are perfectly accepted in Him with all of our sins, iniquities, transgressions, and enmity having been entirely put away by the Cross (Rom. 6:3-5).

CHRIST

Circumcision, in a sense, is a type of the Cross. Blood is shed and separation is made. This speaks of the shed Blood of Christ, which separates us from our sins, and, in fact, is the only thing which will separate us from our sins.

So, Christ fulfilled this *"Rite of Circumcision"* by what He did on the Cross. As well, He fulfilled all of the Law in totality.

Unfortunately, during the time of Paul, some of the Christian Jews were attempting to demand circumcision of all Gentile converts, all boys and all men.

Knowing that Jesus had fulfilled this particular physical act by what He did at the Cross, which now made the physical act meaningless, he addresses this subject by saying:

"Behold, I Paul say unto you, that if you be circumcised, Christ shall profit you nothing" (Gal. 5:2).

This doesn't mean at all that Paul was opposed to the physical act of circumcision, but he was deadly opposed to this act if it was claimed that it was necessary in order for a person to be Saved. Either what Christ did at the Cross was totally sufficient, or it was not sufficient at all.

Inasmuch as what Christ did was definitely sufficient, then neither circumcision nor any other physical act or rite was necessary. It is Faith alone that counts, and it must be Faith in Christ and the Cross (I Cor. 1:17, 18, 23; 2:2). The idea is, even as previously stated, it is impossible to have both *"Grace"* and *"law"* as the Object of one's Faith.

So, the Apostle is saying that if any man or boy submits to the physical act of circumcision, thinking that it adds spiritual profit, *"Christ shall profit you nothing."* Regrettably, that is where much of the modern church is presently. Trusting in law of one type or the other, *"Christ profits them nothing."* As stated repeatedly, one cannot have both the Cross and law. One or the other must go!

A TOKEN OF THE COVENANT

"And you shall circumcise the flesh of your foreskin; and it shall be a token of the Covenant between Me and you" (Gen. 17:11).

According to the Pulpit Commentary, circumcision says several things:

• It was a sign of the Faith that Christ should be descended from Abraham.

• Circumcision was to be a symbolic representation of the putting away of the filth of the flesh and of sin in general.

• It was to distinguish the seed of Abraham from the Gentiles.

• It was to perpetuate the memory of Jehovah's Covenant.

• It was to foster in the Nation the hope of the Messiah.

• It was to remind them of the duty of cultivating moral purity (Deut. 10:16).

• It was to preach to them the Gospel of a Righteousness by Faith (Rom. 4:11).

• It was to suggest the idea of a Holy or a Spiritual Seed of Abraham (Rom. 2:29).

• It was to foreshadow the Christian Rite of Water Baptism (Mat. 3:11).[1]

"And he who is eight days old shall be circumcised among you, every man child in your generations, he who is born in the house, or, bought with money of any stranger, which is not of your seed.

"He who is born in your house, and he who is bought with your money, must needs be circumcised: and My Covenant shall be in your flesh for an Everlasting Covenant" (Gen. 17:12-13).

This Covenant is everlasting, but only in Christ. As the Holy Spirit related through Paul, the time came that

Christ finished His Work on the Cross. Consequently, physical circumcision, as well as any other ordinance or rite, must be laid aside, that is, if it is thought of as pertaining to Salvation. Either the Work of Christ was total and complete, or else, it wasn't. If it was total and complete, then nothing else was needed. To be sure, it definitely was total and complete and definitely was in every respect.

THE BROKEN COVENANT

"And the uncircumcised man child whose flesh of his foreskin is not circumcised, that soul shall be cut off from his people; he has broken My Covenant" (Gen. 17:14).

This simply means that if any Israelite, whether child or adult, refused to follow this Commandment of Circumcision, he would forfeit his standing in the congregation and, in effect, would cease to be a part of the Covenant, which means that he was lost.

The same can be said presently for those who disavow the Work of the Cross. That being the case, that individual is lost, irrespective of all other religious activity. In fact, the entirety of the Book of Hebrews was written for this very purpose.

Particular Christian Jews had grown discouraged, turned their backs on Christ, and had gone back into Judaism, i.e., *"Temple worship,"* etc. To do this, they had to disavow Christ and the Cross. With this being done, they would be eternally lost if they remained in this position.

As important as was circumcision to the Abrahamic Covenant and even to the Mosaic Covenant, as important is the Cross to the modern Believer. When I speak of the Cross, I'm not speaking of a wooden beam. I'm speaking of the great Work which Christ carried out on that gibbet, all for you and me. However, there was a great difference in regards to circumcision and the Cross.

THE DIFFERENCE BETWEEN
THE CROSS AND CIRCUMCISION

As it regards the ancient Rite of Circumcision, a Jewish man could easily come to the place that he believed the act of circumcision itself constituted Salvation, even as did millions of Jews. Of course, that was basely incorrect. The physical circumcision afforded no salvation, even as Water Baptism affords no salvation. Only Faith in what circumcision represented and Faith now in what Water Baptism represents, namely Christ, brought and now brings about Saving Grace.

It is not possible, however, for one to place his Faith in Christ and the Cross as a mere form. In fact, the Cross is the only guarantee given in the Bible against mere form (I Cor. 1:17-18, 23; Col. 2:10-15).

SARAH

"And God said unto Abraham, As for Sarai your wife, you shall not call her name Sarai, but Sarah shall her name be" (Gen. 17:15).

The name, *"Sarai,"* means, *"My princess,"* referring to the fact that she was Abraham's princess alone.

"Sarah" simply means, *"Princess."* The idea is: whereas she was formerly Abraham's princess only, she will now be recognized as a princess generally, in fact, as the *"mother of the Church."* Actually, she is now to be a *"princess to the Lord."*

If it is to be noticed, the letter, *"H,"* is taken from the name, *"Je-Hova-h,"* as in the change of Abram into Abraham, with the name Sarai being changed to Sarah.

The very fact of the changing of the name of Sarah spoke volumes to Abraham or, at least, certainly should have. Formerly she belonged only to him, but now, in essence, she will belong to the entirety of the world. The very change of her name proclaimed the fact that she was now to be a great part of the Covenant.

THE SEED OF THE WOMAN

As well, the change to a Hebrew form of the name, which the new name, *"Sarah,"* proclaims, shows a complete break with the past. She would never return to her birthplace, for she was to focus her life on the Promise of God.

As well, the change of her name proclaims a giant step taken towards the fulfillment of the *"Seed of the woman"* bruising the head of Satan. All of this portrays the fact that God has so much more for us than our own pitiful efforts can provide. That's the reason that Salvation must be all of God and none at all of man.

THE COVENANT

"And I will bless her, and give you a son also of her: yes, I will bless her, and she shall be a mother of nations; kings of people shall be of her" (Gen. 17:16).

This is the first time in all of God's Dealings with Abraham that He had mentioned the fact that the promised son would be of Sarah, as one might say, *"Sarah's own son."* In effect, regarding Sarah, the Promise was very similar to that regarding Abraham, at least as it pertains to entire nations proceeding from her.

The word, *"Bless,"* refers to all the things that God can do. This means that He can do all things, but more particularly, it refers to the culmination of all Blessing, Who is the Lord Jesus Christ.

The Covenant of Circumcision was to be enforced until the Messiah would come. Inasmuch as this rite was carried out on the male member and not on women, for they were exempt, shows us several things.

It shows us that man was responsible for the Fall inasmuch as the seed of procreation is in him. As well, the foreskin of the male member being removed by circumcision was to be a reminder to the people of Israel of original sin, which is hereditary, one might say, and remains in us till we die. Even though Eve was tempted and actually fell first, due to the fact that the seed was alone in the man and not in the woman, we find that God held man responsible much more than women. Thus, God foreshadowed in the Circumcision Rite the whole theology of Redemption, namely both sin and Grace.

It reminded the Jews of the fact that all men by nature are children of wrath on account of hereditary sin (Eph. 2:1-3). It also reminded them of Grace, for it indicated the Birth of Christ from a virgin. He was to abrogate circumcision and save all men from sin and death. He would do so by His Own Death.

LAUGHTER

"Then Abraham fell upon his face, and laughed, and said in his heart, Shall a child be born unto him who is an hundred years old? and shall Sarah, who is ninety years old, bear?" (Gen. 17:17).

Concerning that which is recorded in this Verse, Ellicott says, *"The Jewish interpreters regard Abraham's laugh as one of joy, and Sarah's as one of unbelief" (Gen. 18:12).*[2] Actually, that seems to be the case, and our Lord confirmed the view that joy was utmost in Abraham's heart as it regards these things (Jn. 8:56).

These questions asked by Abraham were not questions of unbelief or derision. They were really an exclamation of holy wonder. What reason declared impossible was possible to Faith. Paul said of him, *"He considered not the deadness of Sarah's womb"* (Rom. 4:19).

When we read these illustrations, it should make us ashamed of ourselves. If Abraham felt such joy and expressed it accordingly as it regarded a Promise, for that's all he had then, how much more should we rejoice presently when, in fact, the Promise has totally and completely been realized in the Lord Jesus Christ?

This Salvation is that which can be felt. It is that which is experienced not only in conduct but also in joy, which fills the soul to overflowing and invigorates the spirit. I am persuaded that most stress, worry, anxiety, fear, and all of their attendant woes can be throttled completely by Believers exhibiting expressions of Faith, for that is exactly what Abraham did. So, what am I saying?

FAITH REJOICES

I'm saying that Faith rejoices, and that Faith always rejoices. When we realize what Jesus has done for us at the Cross, that His Work is not merely a Promised Work but a Finished Work, then we must shout for joy. How can we do less, considering this great Salvation that fills our hearts? If Abraham laughed in wonder and exclamation, which, in essence, was a laugh of victory, how can we as Believers presently do less?!

I feel that these Passages completely abrogate a cold, lifeless, even one might say, a cold storage faith. A faith that never rejoices, never marvels, and never exclaims with joy, I seriously doubt to actually be Faith. If it's true Faith, which refers to Christ and what Christ has done for us at the Cross, then there must be a joy which accompanies such Faith. It must be that which occasions us to marvel constantly, even as did Abraham.

Again I emphasize the fact that he had only the Promise while we now have the Possession.

"Jesus may come today,
"Glad Day! Glad Day!
"And I would see my friend:
"Dangers and troubles would end,
"If Jesus should come today."

"I may go home today,
"Glad Day! Glad Day!
"Seems I hear their song:
"Hail to the radiant throng!
"If I should go home today."

"Why should I anxious be?
"Glad Day! Glad Day!
"Lights appear on the shore,
"Storms will affright nevermore,
"For He is at hand today."

"Faithful I'll be today,
"Glad Day! Glad Day!
"And I will freely tell,
"Why I should love Him so well,
"For He is my all today."

ABRAHAM

CHAPTER

17

Abraham And Ishmael

ABRAHAM AND ISHMAEL

"And Abraham said unto God, O that Ishmael might live before You!" (Gen. 17:18)

As it regards Ishmael, the prayer that Abraham prays was not that he would be the child of Promise, but that he might receive some measure of Divine Blessing, though he was to be set aside in favor of the unseen child now promised.

As should be obvious, Ishmael was very dear to Abraham, but as we shall see, he would not prove to be worthy of that trust and love. In fact, as we shall also see, at a point in time, he would try to kill Isaac.

Actually, Ishmael and his mother, Hagar, had no regard for the birthright as it pertains to spiritual things; they only wanted the material things. Unfortunately, that is so like many in the modern church. They are more interested in the *"here and now"* than they are in the *"there and then."*

THE COVENANT

"And God said, Sarah your wife shall bear you a son indeed; and you shall call his name Isaac: and I will establish My Covenant with him for an Everlasting Covenant, and with his seed after him" (Gen. 17:19).

Concerning this Everlasting Covenant, Williams says:

"The great subject of Chapter 17 of this great Book of Genesis, is the expansion of the Covenant already revealed in Chapters 12 and 14. The new features introduced are the purposes of God as it regards Israel and the Gentiles, pertaining to Salvation. Both of the countless multitudes of redeemed men spring from Abraham as the first vessel of promise and the root of all who should after him believe unto life everlasting.

"At the same time this Chapter sets out the two principles upon which these Divine purposes are founded. These principles are 'death' and 'Grace.' The sign of circumcision expressed the One, the Divine Promise the other.

"Man must have the sentence of death written upon his flesh, which circumcision did, and Grace brings to this dead man life and ever-enduring riches. The sign of circumcision, therefore, declared man to be absolutely without moral value, and justly, as a sinner, sentenced to death. Grace, which comes in the Covenant, takes up Abraham who was by nature an idolater, declares him to be a righteous man because he believed the Testimony of God, and makes him the root out of which Israel and the redeemed nations should proceed."[1]

So, we have circumcision, which points to man's sin, and the Covenant, which points to Christ, Who will lift man out of his sin, and will do so by the Cross. For the Covenant must of necessity include the Cross, even as Genesis 3:15 proclaims.

THE EVERLASTING COVENANT

As we have previously stated, this Covenant, which God established with Abraham, pointed to Christ and what Christ would do to redeem humanity; therefore, it could be called an *"Everlasting Covenant"* (Heb. 13:20).

This *"Everlasting Covenant"* is to be established with Isaac and not with Ishmael.

The world of Islam claims the very opposite, that Ishmael was the promised seed and, therefore, the heir of the Covenant. As well, they claim that Christ is not the fulfillment of the Promise, but rather Muhammad.

Of course, only a cursory examination of the Koran will prove the fallacy of such claims. In attempting to relate to Bible illustrations, Muhammad puts people in the wrong generations, which are glaring mistakes.

They also are glaring evidence that what he proposed to be Divine is, in fact, not inspired at all, but rather the prattle of an unregenerate man. The Holy Spirit doesn't make mistakes; and Muhammad's futile attempts to rewrite history proclaim the utter foolishness of the claims of inspiration regarding the Koran.

At the present time (2012) in America's so-called fight against terrorism, our diplomats are demanding that Israel come to an agreement with the Palestinians.

ISRAEL

The irony of all this is that it doesn't take a seasoned diplomat to instantly recognize the futility of such an effort. How can agreements be made with people who respect agreements not at all? As well, how can agreements be made with those who have sworn your destruction? To be sure, the Palestinians aren't attempting to have a *"piece"* of Israel which they may call their homeland, but rather they want every Jew dead and the entirety of the land of Israel to be claimed as their own. So, again I ask the question, *"How can agreements be made with a mindset of that nature?"*

No, even as the Word of God broadly proclaims, the Covenant is with Isaac and not with Ishmael. This means that the land of Israel belongs to the Jews and to no one else. In fact, it belongs to God. This means that even Israel doesn't have the right to give great portions of it to the Palestinians, or anyone else for that matter.

To be frank, the Country of Jordan, which is several times larger than Israel, has plenty of room for the Palestinians. In fact, the Country of Jordan was originally carved out by the British to be a homeland for the Palestinians. However, the problem is spiritual and not material, which means that it's not really the land area in question, but rather the Word of God.

THE BLESSING OF ISHMAEL

"And as for Ishmael, I have heard you: Behold, I have blessed him, and will make him fruitful, and will multiply him exceedingly; twelve princes shall he beget, and I will make him a great nation" (Gen. 17:20).

The Lord, of course, kept this Promise as it regards Ishmael (Gen. 25:13-16). He has multiplied exceedingly, and the Blessing comes down even unto this hour.

However, the Blessing pronounced here is certainly not because of Ishmael but because of Abraham and Abraham alone. The Blessing should have caused the Arabs to serve God as it regards the Bible, but most of them have completely gone astray, following the Koran, which is a web of deceit, and will lead all of its followers to eternal perdition.

THE COVENANT AND ISAAC

"But My Covenant will I establish with Isaac, which Sarah shall bear unto you at this set time in the next year" (Gen. 17:21).

In this one Verse, the Lord says several things:

• For the third time in this dialogue with Abraham, the Lord promises that Sarah would bear a son, and that despite her age.

• Furthermore, this child would be born within the next year.

• Even though He would bless Ishmael, it was with Isaac that the Covenant would be established.

COMMUNION

"And He (God) left off talking with him, and God went up from Abraham" (Gen. 17:22).

Communion with God is the most profitable exercise there is. Paul taught us this in his Epistle to the

Ephesians. He said:

"Now unto Him Who is able to do exceeding abundantly above all that we ask or think, according to the Power that works in us,

"Unto Him be Glory in the Church by Christ Jesus throughout all ages, world without end. Amen" (Eph. 3:20-21).

It has been said that God's Proper Name is the *"Hearer of Prayers."* However, the problem, most of the time, is that we do not know what we ask (Mat. 20:22). Martin Luther said concerning this:

"Our hearts are too weak to understand the great things which God desires to give us. We worry about the time, place, and means for God to help us. We make our goals too narrow and small, for we must always wrestle with unbelief in our hearts."

He went on to say, *"We poor weak persons can never really understand the exceeding Grace and Mercy of God. We have a God Who wants to give us far more than we ask or think. Therefore since we do not know how and what to ask, the Holy Spirit intercedes for us with groaning which cannot be uttered (Rom. 8:6)."*

And then he said, *"I write this in order that no-one may despair on account of his unworthiness, or also on account of the high majesty of God Whom we address in our prayers. Nothing is too great for Him for which we pray, even if we ourselves do not understand the things for which we ask. Abraham received far more than he requested, and in this he left us an example that we should not discontinue our pleadings before the Lord, but surely believe that they will never be without fruit or benefit. God regards the heart and knows the groanings in us which we cannot utter, indeed, which even we ourselves cannot understand, for we are like the little children who stammer their prayers before meals."*

PERSONAL COMMUNION

Personally, there are many things we are attempting to do for the Lord, even as He directs us. THE SONLIFE BROADCASTING NETWORK is but one example. I believe the Lord has instructed us to put THE MESSAGE OF THE CROSS in every city in the world that will open its door to us. Consequently, I believe we are going to see a Moving and Operation of the Holy Spirit as we have never previously known.

In all of this, we are learning that the most important thing of all is the working of the Holy Spirit within us. In the last few years, I've learned several things, but I think the two most important are:

1. We must be totally and completely led by the Spirit in everything we do, even the small things. He is God, and He has the capacity to do whatever needs to be done. Unfortunately, far too often, we only consult Him as it regards very serious matters, somehow thinking we have the ability to handle everything else. The truth is, we really don't have the ability to handle anything. We need His Help in all matters and in all things.

2. There must be a Moving and Operation of the Spirit within our lives at all times. This refers to prayer and ministry, for He Alone can move and flow through us in order to bless the hurting hearts of others. All of this comes by the Means of the Cross.

When I was but a boy, my grandmother taught me the tremendous value of prayer. To be frank, it has been my mainstay through the many years, but in the last few years, has taken on a completely new dimension.

A TIME OF DESPERATION

In 1991, at a time of great crisis in my life and Ministry, I determined to seek the Lord to whatever extent it took in order to find the answer to my dilemma. As someone has well said, oftentimes, if not most of the time, desperation precedes Revelation. I know it did in my case. In fact, my petition was the same as the cry uttered by Paul nearly 2,000 years ago, *"O wretched man that I am! Who shall deliver me from the body of this death?"* (Rom. 7:24).

The Lord was some six years in answering that prayer, even as I sought His Face with tears on a daily basis. However, in 1997, the great Revelation of the Cross began to come to me. I say, *"Began,"* simply because the Revelation has continued to expand unto this hour.

In fact, what the Lord gave me was nothing new, actually that which the Lord had long since given to the Apostle Paul, and the great Apostle had given it to us in his Epistles. However, this Revelation cannot be understood except the Holy Spirit reveals it to us. To be sure, He definitely will do that with anyone who will earnestly seek the Face of the Lord and earnestly desire that which He has for us. Our problem is *"self."* It looms so large and hinders so greatly that the Holy Spirit cannot give us that which He desires.

SELF

Self is not something new; it is the problem that every single Believer has faced, even the Bible Greats. We will see this even to a greater extent when we come to Genesis, Chapter 21, where God demanded of Abraham that he part with Ishmael, which is a type of self-will.

Since the Revelation of the Cross, prayer has taken on a completely new dimension. I now know the correct Object of Faith, which is a knowledge of unsurpassed value. That correct Object is the Cross of Christ. Of course, I'm not speaking of the wooden beam on which Jesus died, but rather what He there accomplished. When Faith is properly placed, and when it is properly maintained in that event, the Holy Spirit will then do great and mighty things within our hearts and lives. To be sure, *"self"* cannot be properly conquered, and I speak of it being placed *"in Christ,"* until we properly understand the Cross. In fact, without a proper understanding of the Cross, one cannot really understand the Bible as a whole as one should, and one certainly cannot be led by the Spirit as one should. Everything hinges on the Sacrifice of Christ (Eph. 2:13-18).

OBEDIENCE

"And Abraham took Ishmael his son, and all who were born in his house, and all who were bought with his money, every male among the men of Abraham's house; and circumcised the flesh of their foreskin in the selfsame day, as God had said unto him" (Gen. 17:23).

The short phrase, *"As God had said unto Him,"* regarding circumcision, presents Abraham obeying the Lord minutely and immediately.

Even though every male in Abraham's house, young or old, was circumcised, which means, in a sense, that they became a part of the Covenant, did it also mean that they all were Saved?

Salvation is never by *"rites,"* *"rituals,"* *"ordinances,"* or *"ceremonies."* Without exception and for all time, Salvation has always been Faith in Christ and never in the symbols, which are supposed to represent that Faith.

How many of these people were truly Saved, only the Lord knows. I think we can say without any fear of contradiction that most definitely Hagar and Ishmael were not saved.

HAGAR AND ISHMAEL

About 2,000 years after Abraham, the Holy Spirit through Paul said of Ishmael and his mother, *"But as then he (Ishmael) who was born after the flesh persecuted him (Isaac) who was born after the Spirit, even so it is now.*

"Nevertheless what says the Scripture? Cast out the bondwoman and her son: for the son of the bond-woman shall not be heir with the son of the freewoman" (Gal. 4:29-30).

The word, *"Persecuted,"* in Verse 29 of Galatians, Chapter 4, carries the idea of murder. The Jewish Targums, which are Commentaries of a sort, say that when Ishmael was about 18 years old, he would send Isaac, who, at the time, was about four years old, running after arrows he (Ishmael) had shot. The idea was that he tried to hit him with one of the arrows, thereby, killing him, with it looking like an accident. Because of murder in the heart of his mother and himself, the Lord would dispel them from the home of Abraham, even as Chapter 21 proclaims.

No, the *"Rite"* of Circumcision, even though demanded and entered into, didn't automatically mean that the person was Saved. That was a matter of Faith, and we speak of Faith in Christ, even as it always has been a matter of Faith.

ABRAHAM

"And Abraham was ninety years old and nine, when he was circumcised in the flesh of his foreskin" (Gen. 17:24).

As we've already stated, the act of circumcision on the man's private member, which is his reproductive organ, proclaims the fact of original sin. Due to Adam's fall, as each baby is born into the world, each child is born in sin. Concerning this, David said, *"Behold, I was shaped in iniquity; and in sin did my mother conceive me"* (Ps. 51:5).

David wasn't meaning here that his mother had played the harlot, but rather that he, along with every other child that is born, with the exception of Christ, was conceived in original sin. So, the Rite of Circumcision proclaims that fact. As well, it also proclaims the fact of the Cross of Christ, in that blood is shed. The foreskin being cut loose proclaims a picture of the person being cut loose from sin upon the acceptance of Christ due to what Christ did at the Cross by the shedding of His Precious Blood (I Pet. 1:18-20).

ISHMAEL

"And Ishmael his son was thirteen years old, when he was circumcised in the flesh of his foreskin" (Gen. 17:25).

Even though the male member of Ishmael was circumcised, his heart wasn't. As well, untold millions of individuals have been baptized in water, which is a symbol of Regeneration, but, in fact, were not and are not saved. As we have stated, outward *"rites"* and *"ceremonies"* have never saved anyone.

In fact, virtually every Jew thereafter was circumcised, which numbered untold millions; however, many, if not most, Jews were eternally lost simply because they had no faith in Christ, but rather in outward ceremonies, etc.

ABRAHAM AND ISHMAEL

"In the selfsame day was Abraham circumcised, and Ishmael his son" (Gen. 17:26).

Two men were circumcised. By that *"rite,"* both men entered the Covenant; however, only one of the men, Abraham, was Saved.

How many millions presently think they're Saved simply because they belong to a particular church, or they engage in some type of religious activity? The truth is, they have never been Born-Again, which means there has never been a change within their hearts and lives. This means they have never evidenced Faith in Christ and what He has done for us at the Cross. They are religious but lost!

Nicodemus is an excellent case in point. He was a ruler of the Jews and most definitely had been circumcised, which means that he had entered the Covenant. As well, one could certainly say that he was a good man and, in fact, was a student of the Word of God. However, the truth is, Nicodemus was not actually saved.

When he approached Jesus about the Miracles that Christ had performed, Jesus, in essence, ignored what he said, and rather said to him, *"Verily, verily, I say unto you, Except a man be born again, he cannot see the Kingdom of God"* (Jn. 3:3).

Regrettably, even though Nicodemus was very religious, he did not really understand what Jesus meant.

When Nicodemus asked Him, *"How can these things be?"* Jesus answered and said unto him, *"Are you a Master of Israel, and know not these things?"* (Jn. 3:9-10)

TRUST IN CHRIST

In other words, Jesus was telling Nicodemus that if he was truly Saved, he would know what was being addressed concerning being *"Born-Again."*

Unfortunately, there are untold millions presently who claim Salvation, but all on the wrong basis; therefore, they aren't saved. I realize that's blunt, but it cannot be any other way.

One is Saved by trusting explicitly in Christ and what Christ has done for us at the Cross. In fact, it doesn't take much understanding as it regards this, only Faith and trust in the Lord. The moment this is truly done, and anyone can do that if he so desires, that person is then instantly Saved (Jn. 3:16; Rom. 10:9-10, 13). It has nothing to do with ceremonies, the joining of churches, or anything of that nature. As stated, it is all by Faith, and we refer to Faith in Christ and what He did for us in offering Himself as a Sacrifice on the Cross (Gal. 1:4).

SALVATION IS FOR ALL

"And all the men of his house, born in the house, and bought with money of the stranger, were circumcised with him" (Gen. 17:27).

This one Passage tells us that every single man in the house of Abraham was Saved, whether servants, slaves, or family, that is, if they believed. This tells us that all can be Saved, and there are no distinctions made by the Lord regarding humanity and the Salvation of all.

As well, mighty Abraham had to come the same identical way as the lowliest slave, whomever that might have been. There was no difference, and there were no exceptions.

How fortunate and blessed were these individuals, whomever they might have been, to be in the house of Abraham and, therefore, to be a party to the Covenant. Of course, they had to accept by Faith that which the Covenant represented, but the opportunity, at least, was before them. As stated again, how many truly accepted in their heart, only God knows, but the facts are, all were given the opportunity to do so, and a grand opportunity it was.

OPPORTUNITY

The sadness is, many people in the world, and, no doubt, we can say most, never really have that opportunity. Even, the so-called gospel, which is preached, too oftentimes is *"another gospel"* (II Cor. 11:4). This being the case, the person cannot be saved, even if he hears such a gospel.

The other day, I happened to listen to a preacher for a few minutes over television. He closed his message by stating that it was imperative that a person be baptized in water in order to be Saved. Inasmuch as this preacher was making Water Baptism the object of faith, whoever listened to him would not be able to find Christ.

THE CATHOLIC CHURCH

As another example, the Catholic church claims that Salvation is in the church. In other words, they claim that keeping the sacraments of the church ensures Salvation. Therefore, they have moved the Faith from its true place in Christ to the church, which means that all who belong to that system cannot be saved.

SEVENTH DAY ADVENTISTS

As well, if our Seventh Day Adventist friends make the keeping of the seventh day a requirement for Salvation, they have, as well, moved the center of gravity, so to speak, from Faith in Christ to something else.

THE CHURCH OF CHRIST

This particular denomination, even as the preacher above, claims that Water Baptism is necessary for Salvation. This means that Water Baptism is the object of their faith and not the Lord Jesus Christ. While Water Baptism is definitely important, the water carries no Salvation.

ONENESS PENTECOSTALS

These good people claim that to be Saved, one has to speak with other Tongues and be baptized in water according to a particular formula, which they have devised. This means that the object of Faith for these individuals is in something else other than Christ. While those other things may or may not be important, even as important as they might be, there is no Salvation in speaking in Tongues, in water, etc. Don't misunderstand, speaking with other Tongues is Scriptural. I personally speak with other Tongues virtually every day of my life. However, it did not save me and does not save me. Again, while Water Baptism is a representative or symbol of the Salvation experience, that's all that it is. It is a symbol of what has already taken place in the heart of the individual being baptized, or is supposed to have already taken place.

WORD OF FAITH

Our Word of Faith friends make the object of their faith particular Scriptures, which they have memorized and quoted over and over again. While memorizing the Word of God is a very fruitful exercise, which I exercise constantly, and quoting them by rote can be a blessing, as well, still, that is not the solution to man's problem. The Believer must make the Cross of Christ the Object of his Faith (Rom. 6:1-14; 8:1-11; I Cor. 1:17-18, 23; 2:2; Gal. 6:14; Col. 2:10-15).

One of the major problems of many churches is the equating of doing certain things, such as ceremonies, rites, or rituals, as being the same as Faith in Christ. It isn't, no matter how important it may be in its own right. One cannot engage in a ceremony and equate that with Faith in Christ. It never works that way.

JESUS CHRIST AND HIM CRUCIFIED

True Faith in Christ is the placing of one's total and complete confidence in Him and in nothing else. Christ plus other things, whatever those other things might be, abrogates Christ. It's either Christ totally and completely, plus nothing else, or it's Christ not at all.

Getting Saved is not difficult. In fact, Paul said, *"For whosoever shall call on the Name of the Lord shall be Saved"* (Rom. 10:13). However, that doesn't mean to call upon the church or one of its many ordinances. It means exactly what it says, to *"call upon the Name of the Lord."*

After we come to Christ, it is incumbent upon us to understand that all we receive from Christ and through Christ is received totally and completely by and through what He did at the Cross, and through no other instrument or means. As previously stated, when we say the Cross, we aren't speaking of a wooden beam, but rather what Jesus there did.

"Christ and Him Crucified" is to ever be the center of our gravity as we speak of Faith. Even though we are Christians, if it's in anything else, we will cause ourselves great difficulties (Gal. 2:20-21).

"Depth of Mercy! Can there be,
"Mercy still reserved for me?
"Can my God His Wrath forebear?
"Me, the chief of sinners spare?"

"I have long withstood His Grace,
"Long provoked Him to His Face,
"Would not hearken to His Call,
"Grieved Him by a thousand falls."

"Lord, incline me to repent;
"Let me now my fall lament,

"Deeply my revolt deplore,
"Weep, believe, and sin no more."

"Still for me the Saviour stands,
"Shows His Wounds, and spreads His Hands;
"God is Love, I know, I feel,
"Jesus weeps, and loves me still."

ABRAHAM

CHAPTER

18

Abraham And
The Visit From The Lord

ABRAHAM AND THE VISIT FROM THE LORD

"And the LORD appeared unto him in the plains of Mamre: and he sat in the tent door in the heat of the day" (Gen. 18:1).

Jewish tradition claims that this visit by the Lord to Abraham was on the third day after the Rite of Circumcision had been performed, and was for the purpose of healing him from the painful consequences of it. It was on this account, they think, that Abraham was resting at home instead of being with his herds in the field.

Of course, this is only an assumption, but the fact remains that the Lord did appear to the Patriarch, the consequences of which will be striking, to say the least.

At this particular time, two momentous events will transpire, the first being the announcement by the Lord of the conception by Sarah. In fact, I think one can say without fear of contradiction that this is one of the most momentous occasions in history. From this beginning will come the Jewish people. They will give the world the Word of God and, in effect, will serve as the Womb of the Messiah, which will bring the Redeemer into the world, which is what this is all about.

All of this must be done in this manner because Angels could not redeem humanity, and even God, as God, wouldn't redeem humanity in this fashion. God would have to become Man, and as the God-Man, Jesus Christ, would then redeem the lost sons of Adam's fallen race.

RIGHTEOUSNESS

Dominion had been given to Adam, which means that tremendous responsibility had been given to the first man (Gen. 1:26; Ps. 8; Rom. 5:12, 17-19; I Cor. 15:45-47).

As well, in all of the doings, and I continue to speak of the Plan of Redemption being carried out, God would have to do things according to His Personal Nature. When many people think of God, they think of Him in an entirely wrong manner. They think that if God is All-powerful, and, in fact, He definitely is, then He can do anything.

While it is certainly true that He definitely can do anything, the facts are, He will not do anything against His Nature. So, to bring Redemption into this world, God would have to prepare a people who would evidence Faith in Him, even as He would reveal Himself to them, because He is a God of Faith (Heb. 11:1-3).

The end result of all of God's Workings and Dealings with man is Righteousness; however, we have a problem here. Man thinks that he can perfect or concoct Righteousness by his own efforts, but, of course, that is impossible. The Righteousness that God accepts, which is the Righteousness of God and, in fact, the only Righteousness He will accept, could only be brought about in a particular way. As stated, God would have to become Man, which He did, keep the Law perfectly, all on our behalf (Gal. 4:4-5), and then die on a Cross. This alone could satisfy the demands of the broken Law.

When we speak of the Law, we're speaking of the Law of Moses, of which the moral aspects were centered in the Ten Commandments (Ex., Chpt. 20).

THE CROSS

Without the Cross, the Perfect Life of Christ would have availed us nothing. In fact, without the Cross, His Healings and Miracles, as stupendous as they were, would have availed nothing. Only the Cross could address the terrible problem of sin and all of its effects, which it did (Eph. 2:13-18; Col. 2:10-15).

The greatest shame of this modern age is, the modern church little knows or understands the tremendous significance of the Cross. To most, the Cross is just incidental in their lives and living for God. In fact, whatever credence that the modern church gives the Cross in any regard, which is very little indeed, is centered up in the initial Salvation experience. Thank God for that. However, the sadness is, not understanding at all the part the Cross plays in their ongoing Christian experience, most in the modern church try to *"live"* for the Lord in other ways. What do we mean by that?

GOD'S PRESCRIBED ORDER OF VICTORY

As Salvation is *"attained"* by Faith in Christ and what He has done for us at the Cross, likewise, it is *"maintained"* by continued, exclusive Faith in the Cross, which is the way that we grow in Grace and the Knowledge of the Lord. Having such little teaching in this regard, most Christians try to function outside of God's Prescribed Order, which is always catastrophic simply because the Holy Spirit will not function in this capacity. While He definitely will remain with us, He demands that we have Faith in Christ exclusively. This refers to what He did for us at the Cross, which will then guarantee His Function within our hearts and lives (Rom. 8:1-2, 11).

The Lord works exclusively on the premise of Faith; however, it is always to be Faith in Christ and what Christ has done for us at the Cross. This Cross must ever be the Object of our Faith. The whole gist of Salvation is Christ Himself, but more particularly, it is what He has done for us regarding His Sacrifice that makes it all possible.

CHRIST AND HIS CROSS

If we try to divorce Christ from the Cross, which most of the modern church does, we then have *"another*

Jesus," which is always of *"another spirit,"* which presents *"another Gospel"* (II Cor. 11:4).

The reader needs to peruse these words very carefully. We're speaking here of God's Prescribed Order for a victorious life. To be sure, He only has one order, and man has none and, in fact, will never have any. Therefore, the Appearance of the Lord to Abraham at this particular time would ultimately lead to these things that we have been addressing, which is the Salvation of humanity in every capacity.

THREE MEN

"And he lift up his eyes and looked, and, lo, three Men stood by Him: and when he saw them, he ran to meet them from the tent door, and bowed himself toward the ground" (Gen. 18:2).

The energy and intelligence of the Divine Life in Abraham's soul is seen in his conduct. He sits, not sleeps, in the heat of the day; he looks, and he recognizes his Divine Visitor, Who is accompanied by His Angelic Servants. He runs to meet them; he bows himself to the ground; he urges them to rest; he hastens into the tent; he presses Sarah to quickly make ready cakes upon the hearth; he, himself, runs into the herd and fetches a calf; he commands the servant to hasten to dress it; he, himself, as a servant, places the food before his guests; and, as a slave ready for further service, he stands while they eat.

All is activity, for not only is he active himself, but he makes everybody else active as well. Here is the great principle that can be a great teacher. Spiritual activity in the heart of one Servant of Christ stirs up activity in the hearts of other servants.

Several things should be said here about Abraham. They are:

• The word, *"Looked,"* implies an act of mental perception. In other words, he now knows that one of them is Jehovah.

• His *"bowing himself toward the ground"* implies *"worship."* It is more than a mere oriental expression.

• Abraham's heart was right with God; therefore, he was glad to see the Divine Visitor. Such could not be said of many modern Christians.

PETITION

"And said, My LORD, if now I have found favor in Your Sight, pass not away, I pray You, from Your Servant" (Gen. 18:3).

Proving that Abraham now knows Who One of the three actually is, he addresses Him as *"LORD,"* the same terminology that he used in Genesis 15:2.

The phrase, *"If now I have found favor in Your Sight,"* implies far more than a mere formal remark or question. Abraham had found favor in God's Sight but only by and through the Faith which Abraham exhibited. To be sure, it was Faith in Christ and what Christ would do to redeem us. Again I refer to the fact that Jesus spoke of Abraham seeing His Day and, therefore, being glad (Jn. 8:56).

Favor in God's Sight can be obtained in one manner and in one manner only, and that is by Faith. However, when we speak of Faith, we are speaking exclusively of Faith in Christ and His Cross. That, in fact, is having Faith in the Word because the Word of God is the Story from cover to cover of Jesus Christ and Him Crucified.

Who Jesus is and what Jesus has done, and again we refer to the Cross, is where all Faith should be anchored and maintained. This alone guarantees the Favor of God, and all else guarantees His Disfavor.

HOSPITALITY

"Let a little water, I pray You, be fetched, and wash Your Feet, and rest Yourselves under the tree" (Gen. 18:4).

Does Jehovah, or even Angels for that matter, need their feet washed? Do they grow tired and, therefore, require rest?

The answer, of course, is, *"No,"* to both questions. So, why did Abraham conduct himself in such fashion, knowing that One of these *"Men"* was Jehovah, and the other two were undoubtedly Angels?

I believe that the Holy Spirit must have moved upon Abraham, as it regards his conduct. If, in fact, that was the case, and it had to be, then we must also know that the Holy Spirit causes all things to be done for a purpose.

The washing of the feet, which, incidentally, was a common, Oriental practice, also contains a great spiritual meaning. As the Patriarch washed the feet of his Divine Guest and His Associates, such would proclaim the fact that all Believers would need their feet washed daily, as it involves our daily walk before God (Jn. 13:5). Of course, we speak of the spiritual sense, which would be typified by Christ washing the feet of the Disciples.

As well, the *"rest,"* which Abraham here mentioned, refers to the *"rest"* afforded all true Believers as their Faith is anchored solely in Christ. In fact, Jesus said, *"Come unto Me, all you who labor and are heavy laden, and I will give you rest"* (Mat. 11:28).

We know that the Lord does nothing but that it provides for us a lesson, which we are intended to learn.

THE BREAD

"And I will fetch a morsel of bread, which will comfort Your Hearts; after that You shall pass on: for therefore

are You come to Your Servant. And they said, So do, as you have said" (Gen. 18:5).

Bread is used at times as a symbol to portray the Gospel. Hence, Jesus would say of Himself, *"I am the Bread of Life: He who comes to Me shall never hunger; and he who believes on Me shall never thirst"* (Jn. 6:35).

Abraham giving bread to the Lord and his Angelic associates proclaims what the Lord will do for the whole of humanity and, above all, that He will actually be that Bread. This is the *"Bread"* which satisfies all hunger.

SARAH

"And Abraham hastened into the tent unto Sarah, and said, Make ready quickly three measures of fine meal, knead it, and make cakes upon the hearth" (Gen. 18:6).

The *"fine meal"* mentioned here should have been translated, *"Fine flour,"* for that's actually what it says in the Hebrew.

Flour was used in the Thank-Offering (Meat-Offering) and was meant to represent the Perfection of our Incarnate Lord (Lev. 2:1). So, even though Abraham little recognized the situation, it was all planned by the Holy Spirit.

While we can certainly pass off this incident as merely an action of hospitality, I think to do so would belittle the Action of the Holy Spirit. Of course, the true reason for the Visit of our Lord and the two Holy Visitors (Angels) was to announce the conception that Sarah would experience and, as well, the destruction of Sodom and Gomorrah, which also would affect Lot. All of these reasons are obvious, but, at the same time, we must come to the conclusion that everything done by the Lord is never without spiritual significance.

There is a lesson in every action, move, and word. While we must not take flights of fancy with that which is done, at the same time, we must not discount that which is done, but rather do our very best to ascertain what the Holy Spirit is saying to us and learn thereby.

THE TENDER CALF

"And Abraham ran unto the herd, and fetched a calf tender and good, and gave it unto a young man; and he hastened to dress it" (Gen. 18:7).

The young calf that was prepared was not a common article of consumption among orientals.

This shows that Abraham gave his very best on this particular day, even as he should have, which signifies that we are to do the same. As well, the Lord would also give His Very Best, even His Only Son, which would be necessary if we were to have Eternal Life (Jn. 3:16). As the calf would be killed, likewise would the Son of God. Also, as the calf would be eaten, Jesus Himself said:

"Verily, verily, I say unto you, Except you eat the Flesh of the Son of Man, and drink His Blood, you have no life in you.

"Whoso eats My flesh, and drinks My Blood, has Eternal Life; and I will raise him up at the last day.

"For My flesh is meat indeed, and My Blood is drink indeed.

"He who eats My Flesh, and drinks My Blood, dwells in Me, and I in him.

"As the Living Father has sent Me, and I live by the Father: so he who eats Me, even he shall live by Me.

"This is that Bread which came down from Heaven: not as your fathers did eat Manna, and are dead: he who eats of this Bread shall live forever" (Jn. 6:53-58).

WHAT DID JESUS MEAN BY THIS?

He would quickly answer by saying:
"It is the Spirit Who quickens; the flesh profits nothing:

the words that I speak unto you, they are Spirit, and they are Life" (Jn. 6:63).

To make the explanation brief: Jesus was simply speaking of the absolute necessity of mankind placing his Faith and trust in Christ and what Christ did for him at the Cross.

There are millions of people who claim to believe in Christ, but they ignore the Cross. This means they've only given a mental assent or acceptance to Christ, which is woefully insufficient.

The mention of His *"Flesh"* and *"Blood"* and humanity *"eating"* and *"drinking"* of same refers to nothing physical, but rather an act of Faith. Above all, it speaks of Faith in what Christ suffered for us, which, in effect, Jesus explained in John 7:63.

Jesus was speaking of when the believing sinner places his or her Faith exclusively in Christ and what Christ did for us at the Cross and maintains it there. In other words, His *"Flesh"* speaks of us becoming a literal part of His Crucifixion. His shed *"Blood"* refers to the price that He paid and the giving of His Life, which was done exclusively for us.

In this Sixth Chapter of John, the Lord proclaims to us the absolute necessity of the Cross. This is obvious by the statements that He made, which we have just quoted. Upon simple Faith evidenced by the believing sinner, and continued by the Believer per se, in the Mind of God, we literally eat the Flesh of Christ and drink His Blood. Of course, as previously stated, this is all spiritual and not at all physical.

Tragically, even though the Children of Israel should have understood, they understood not at all. All they had to do was look at the Priests of old and even continuing unto that very hour, who partook of a part of each and every sacrifice, except the Whole Burnt Offering. They physically ate of that sacrifice as it was cooked, which typified partaking of Christ in His Incarnation.

Actually, when the Israelite sinned and brought a lamb for it to be offered, he should have brought two. One should have been for a Sin-Offering and the second lamb for a Peace-Offering. While a small portion of the Peace-Offering was given to the Priests, the majority of the carcass of the little animal that had been roasted over the fire was to be eaten by the person who had brought it to begin with. If he so desired, he could call in friends and neighbors and have a feast. It meant that his trespass had been forgiven through the Sin-Offering, and now Peace with God had been restored, hence, eating of the Peace-Offering. Sadly, the religious leaders of Jesus' Day had so departed from the Word of God that, anymore, what they did was hardly recognizable at all as being a part of the Scriptures.

THEY DID EAT

"And he took butter, and milk, and the calf which he had dressed, and set it before Them; and he stood by Them under the tree, and They did eat" (Gen. 18:8).

As They did eat, likewise, Jesus told us that we must eat as well. I speak of the *"eating of Christ,"* which, in effect, speaks of us evidencing Faith in Him and what He has done for us at the Cross.

Untold millions have the food, so to speak, set before them but actually do not eat. Let it be known and understood that unless we *"eat,"* which, again, refers to evidencing Faith in Christ and His Cross, we do not really have Christ.

The world is full of religion. Sometime ago, one of the major magazines named Christ as one of the 10 most powerful men who has ever lived, etc.

While they may have thought they were being generous, the facts are, they were blaspheming. To even remotely think of comparing other men to Christ, at least as it regards significance, etc., is gross stupidity, to say the least! However, the problem is, they know *about* Christ but they really don't *know* Christ. If I remember correctly, He was named as the tenth most important man, meaning there were nine men before Him who, in the eyes of these individuals, they considered to be more important than Christ. How much more stupid can one get!

CHRIST IS GOD

Christ is God and to think of Him as anything else is to blaspheme.

As well, and is so important, we must recognize what He did to redeem humanity, which was to go to the Cross. As we've stated again and again, Christ and the Cross must never be divided, that is, according to His Finished Work. When we speak of the Cross, of course, we aren't speaking of the wooden beam on which Jesus died, but rather what our Lord there accomplished. As well, Jesus is not still on the Cross but, in fact, is presently at the Right Hand of the Father. His Work is complete. So, we are speaking of not separating Him from what He has done for us at the Cross. Every good thing comes from God the Father with Jesus Christ as the Source. The Cross is the Means by which all of these wonderful and good things are given unto us. The Cross has made it all possible; that's what we are trying to say.

To recognize Christ apart from the Cross is to fail to evidence proper Faith and, therefore, to *"eat Him."* As we've already stated, such plays out to *"another Jesus"* (II Cor. 11:4).

It is my feeling that John, Chapter 6, portrays the Offering Up of Christ on the Cross and our Faith in that Finished Work as being an absolute necessity. If we attempt to interpret these Passages in any other capacity, we do great violence to the Word of God and stand in jeopardy even of the Salvation of our souls.

WHERE IS SARAH YOUR WIFE?

"And They said unto him, Where is Sarah your wife? And he said, Behold, in the tent" (Gen. 18:9).

The question, *"Where is Sarah your wife?"* proclaims the Omniscience of the Lord. As there is no evidence that she had previously revealed herself, the Lord could have known her name only by the fact that He knows all things.

From the following conversation, it would seem that Abraham had not revealed to Sarah this which the Lord had told him some days, or perhaps some weeks, earlier, about her having a son (Gen. 17:16). If, in fact, he didn't tell her, which it seems he didn't, why not?

While there is no evidence that Abraham doubted the Lord, there is evidence that possibly he doubted himself. Had he heard correctly? Did the Lord really tell him this, or did he fabricate it in his own mind?

Sometimes we can want something so badly that we can imagine God telling us all types of things when, in reality, He hasn't.

As well, of all people, Abraham knew the impossibility of Sarah having a child, especially considering that she was now 90 years of age, and he was 100 (Gen. 17:17).

Irrespective of what Abraham thought, the Lord, it seems, desired at this time that Sarah would also know, and that the information would not be withheld from her. He knew she was listening, so He then tells Abraham what is shortly to come to pass.

A SON

"And He said, I will certainly return unto you according to the time of life; and, lo, Sarah your wife shall have a son. And Sarah heard it in the tent door, which was behind Him" (Gen. 18:10).

It is evident that this statement concerning *"returning . . . according to the time of life,"* denotes some fixed period. Jewish tradition says that it means, *"According to this time next year."*

The statement is emphatic, *"Sarah your wife shall have a son."*

As we've already stated, Sarah is now 90 years old and Abraham 100. Why did God wait this long?

God's Timing is just as important as His Actions. Among other things, and probably the most important, all hope of the flesh had to die before this Miracle could be brought about. This should be a great lesson for us all.

What do we mean by all hope of the flesh dying?

When Abraham and Sarah finally came to the place that they knew and understood that they could not bring about this great Promise of God by their own machinations, despite how hard they might try, then all hope of the flesh was gone. In other words, within themselves, they could not do this thing. So, when they finally ceased from their own actions, God then would perform a Work of the Spirit. Then and only then would Sarah conceive.

Incidentally, have you noticed how the Lord specifically stated, *"Sarah your wife"*? This tells us that the Lord was not pleased at all with the excursion to Hagar.

WHAT IS THE FLESH?

The *"flesh,"* as Paul often used the term in his Epistles, concerns that which is indicative to human beings. It speaks of our education, motivation, willpower, personal efforts, zeal, talent, etc. While these things within themselves aren't necessarily wrong, the idea is that no matter how proficient some of these things may be in the realm of our person, still, such is inadequate as it regards living for God. In other words, if we try to live for the Lord by that means, we will fail every time. In fact, if man could live for the Lord by this means, then Jesus died needlessly on the Cross of Calvary. Paul tells us why we are unable to live for God by this means. He said:

> **"And if Christ *be* in you** *(He is in you through the Power and Person of the Spirit [Gal. 2:20]),* **the body *is* dead because of sin** *(means that the physical body has been rendered helpless because of the Fall; consequently, the Believer trying to overcome by willpower presents a fruitless task)*; **but the Spirit *is* Life because of Righteousness** *(only the Holy Spirit can make us what we ought to be, which means we cannot do it ourselves; once again, He performs all that He does within the confines of the Finished Work of Christ)*" **(Rom. 8:10).**

To reemphasize, due to the Fall, the physical body is incapable of doing what needs to be done. This means we must have the Help of the Holy Spirit, and that help is given to us on the premise of the Lord Jesus Christ and what He did for us at the Cross of Calvary.

To say it another way, *"The 'flesh' denotes man's own efforts and ability."* If we try to live for the Lord by that means, we frustrate the Grace of God (Gal. 2:21). The Christian must learn that every single Work of the Lord carried out within our lives, irrespective as to what it might be, must, without exception, be carried out by the Holy Spirit. He does all of His Work predicated on one premise, and that is according to Who Christ is and what He has done for us in His Suffering (Rom. 8:1-11).

THE CROSS

So, as we have repeatedly stated, the Lord demands that we, as Believers, maintain Faith in Christ, with the understanding that everything Christ has done for us has been through the instrument of the Cross.

The sinner cannot be saved except through Faith in Christ and His Finished Work.

The Believer cannot live a victorious life except he maintains his Faith in Christ and what Christ has done for us at the Cross. It is not possible to overstate the Cross, especially considering that every single thing we receive from the Lord comes to us through that Sacrifice (I Cor. 1:17-18; 2:2; Eph. 2:13-18; Col. 2:10-15).

It seems that despite the fact that the Cross of Christ is now history, we continue to make the mistakes made by Abraham and Sarah. In one way or the other, we keep trying to do what only the Holy Spirit can do. The major reason that we have this problem is simply because we do not understand the Cross or its implications. We claim Faith in Christ; in fact, we constantly claim that our trust is in Christ. However, the Jesus in Whom we trust is by and large a fabricated Jesus or as Paul referred to the situation, *"Another Jesus"* (II Cor. 11:4).

The tragedy is, all of the time, we think we are properly trusting Christ, but the truth is, if we do not understand the Cross, it is impossible to fully under-stand and trust Christ.

IMPOSSIBLE!

"Now Abraham and Sarah were old and well stricken in age; and it ceased to be with Sarah after the manner of women" (Gen. 18:11).

At this particular juncture, the Holy Spirit is quick to emphasize the point that, in the natural, it was impossible for Sarah to conceive. As well, Abraham was also *"well stricken in age."*

As Believers, we must not look at the impossibilities, at least things which are impossible to us. We must look to God, with Whom nothing is impossible. Jesus plainly said concerning so-called impossibilities:

"With God all things are possible" (Mat. 19:26).

As well, we should understand that God is no respecter of persons, and He is the same yesterday, today, and forever.

However, that doesn't mean that God will give children to women who are 90 years old and their husbands who are 100. If it's God's Will for such to be, then it will be; however, God never functions against His Will and His Wisdom.

THE WILL OF GOD

The Will of God for our lives is of extreme importance, as all of us should understand. True Faith will never circumvent that Will, nor will it even desire anything that's not according to God's Will. People who think they can bring anything into being by using some little formula of Faith are in for a rude awakening. God will never allow His Word to be used against Himself. In fact, if man could do that, he would make himself God, and do so in short order. That's been the great problem with mankind from the beginning and continues to be the great problem in the church. Men twist and pervert the Word of God, attempting to make it their servant, when God will never allow such things. In fact, the Word of God and the Will of God go hand in hand, and all of it is tied to the Finished Work of Christ on the Cross.

UNBELIEF

"Therefore Sarah laughed within herself, saying, After I am waxed old shall I have pleasure, my lord being old also?" (Gen. 18:12).

Upon the announcement that Sarah would have a son, even at her advanced age, the Scripture says that Abraham laughed (Gen. 17:17). However, his laugh was the laughter of Faith while the laughter of Sarah was the laughter of unbelief. It is incredulous to her that she could have a child, her being 90 years old, or that Abraham could father a child, his being 100 years old. While her unbelief did not stop the process, it did solicit a mild rebuke from the Lord, even as we shall see.

There are always two ways of receiving God's Promises; the one of which secures, but the other of which imperils their fulfillment (Mk. 9:23; 11:23).

As we shall see, the Lord will seek to pull Sarah from unbelief to Faith, and He will do so in three different ways:

1. He will proclaim the fact that the thing promised is not beyond the Resources of Jehovah to accomplish.

2. He will do so, as well, by a further certification of the event, *"According to the time of life"* (Gen. 18:10).

3. He will also do so by an impressive display of miraculous Power, first, in searching Sarah's heart, and second, in arresting Sarah's conscience.

RESPONSE

"And the LORD said unto Abraham, Wherefore did Sarah laugh, saying, Shall I of a surety bear a child, which am old?" (Gen. 18:13).

We should note several things from this particular Passage.

As should be obvious, God knows all things. He knows the reaction of our spirit, and He knows the things which we say. So, we should be very careful what we say and what we do as it regards the Lord and His Work.

MIRACLES

"Is anything too hard for the LORD? At the time appointed I will return unto you, according to the time of life, and Sarah shall have a son" (Gen. 18:14).

In Verse 13, one of the Divine Visitors announces Himself as the *"LORD,"* which, in effect, proclaims this as a Preincarnate Appearance of Christ. He now remonstrates in Verse 14 that nothing is too hard for the Lord. The actual Hebrew rendering is:

"Is anything too wonderful for Jehovah?"

As it regards the phrase *"too hard"*, I think the way it is translated leaves a wrong impression. The truth is, as it regards Miracles, there is nothing even hard for the Lord. The idea as presented here in the English version seems to be that while God can do such a thing, it would be difficult. The actual rendering is that not only can He do whatever is necessary, but, as well, it's not even hard for Him to accomplish the task. In other words, He does whatever is needed with ease.

THE TIME APPOINTED

The words, *"Time appointed,"* tell us that God had long since appointed a time for Sarah to have a child. To be frank, it had been appointed even before Sarah was born (I Pet. 1:18-20).

As it regards the wills of individuals, we are not teaching predestination here; we are rather teaching the Foreknowledge of God. God being Omniscient, that is all-knowing, He has the capacity and, in fact, does know the past, the present, and the future. This doesn't mean that He predestines people to act in certain ways but, as stated, through Foreknowledge, He can know what they will do. For instance, He knew that Abraham and Sarah would accept Him as Lord and Saviour. He also knew that even though they would stumble in their efforts, they wouldn't stumble according to their Faith. In other words, despite the lapses as recorded here, they would always respond favorably to the Lord with Faith renewed. Therefore it had been appointed all along that Sarah would ultimately have a son, irrespective of circumstances, events, or her advanced age. What had been appointed, God was able to carry through.

Now, let me quickly say to the reader that the Lord has appointed certain things for you also. You must continue to believe and not allow yourself to be pulled aside by circumstances and hindrances. Despite the occasional setback, you must continue to believe. Remember, *"It is appointed,"* which means it's going to happen, that is, if it's the Will of God.

REBUKE

"Then Sarah denied, saying, I laughed not; for she was afraid. And He said, No; but you did laugh" (Gen. 18:15).

Unbelief will never stop at skepticism but will always degenerate into works of the flesh, such as *"lying."*

When confronted, Sarah denied that she had laughed. She now stands in the Presence of Jehovah, and the Scripture says, *"She was afraid."* No wonder!

Unbelief always tenders fear. We need never fear God in a negative way when we are functioning in Faith. It is always when we are functioning in unbelief that such fear is brought about.

The Lord gently rebuked her by simply saying, *"But you did laugh."*

The narrative ends there, at least as it regards Sarah; however, it is positive that the rebuke had its intended result. She was smitten in her conscience, knowing that she had doubted God and was now brought back to a place of Faith.

How many times does the Lord gently rebuke us? Our sin, even as that of Sarah, is far more serious than we realize; but in Grace, the Lord only sets us straight and doesn't bring Judgment on us. When we look at Sarah and evaluate her actions, we should do so with the thought in mind that we ourselves have been in the same position, possibly any number of times. However, as with Sarah, the Lord only gently rebuked us and, thereby, did not bring upon us the Judgment which we deserved.

"Some glorious morning sorrow will cease,
"Some glorious morning all will be peace;
"Heartaches all ended, school days all done,
"Heaven will open, Jesus will come."

"Sad hearts will gladden, all shall be bright,
"Goodbye forever to Earth's dark night;
"Changed in a moment, like Him to be,
"Oh glorious daybreak, Jesus I'll see."

"Oh, what a meeting, there in the skies,
"No tears nor crying shall dim our eyes;
"Loved ones united eternally,
"Oh, what a daybreak that morn will be."

ABRAHAM

CHAPTER

19

Abraham And Sodom

ABRAHAM AND SODOM

"And the men rose up from thence, and looked toward Sodom: and Abraham went with them to bring them on the way" (Gen. 18:16).

God, as well as the two Angels with Him, are referred to as *"men"* simply because they had taken on such an appearance.

They now look toward Sodom and will divulge to Abraham their intentions.

We note from this, as well, that the Lord monitors every country, city, and each individual in the world. While Sodom and Gomorrah were destroyed in a most unusual way, I have every confidence that the Lord has likewise destroyed many other cities down through the centuries. He may not have done so in the same way, but nevertheless, He could bring about their destruction in many and various ways. With some, He used the elements, while with others, He used war. Nevertheless, the reason for their destruction has always been *"sin,"* and sin to such a degree that their destruction was warranted.

THE WORK OF THE LORD

As well, the interest of the Lord in all things concerning this world is predicated more so on how it affects His Work in the world than anything else. Had Sodom and Gomorrah continued, no doubt, Satan would have used these twin cities to greatly subvert in the land of Canaan, which would have greatly hindered, if not stopped altogether, the advent of the Israelites into Canaan.

During the period of the Book of Acts, mighty Rome then ruled the world — the world of that day. However, as mighty as they were and as far reaching as were their effects, Rome is mentioned only as it impacts the Work of God.

It should go without saying that the Work of God is the singular most important thing in the world, at least as far as God is concerned. Therefore, He is very interested in anything that hinders that particular Work in an adverse way.

Sodom and Gomorrah are now the center of that attention.

ABRAHAM

"And the LORD said, Shall I hide from Abraham that thing which I do" (Gen. 18:17).

Concerning this, Matthew Henry said:

"The secret of the Lord is with them who fear Him. Whether He be pleased to show them what He intends to do or not, He will cause them to understand and to adore the justice and reasonableness of His Dispensations, and show them the Glory of His Works."[1]

BLESSING

"Seeing that Abraham shall surely become a great and mighty Nation, and all the nations of the Earth shall be blessed in him?" (Gen. 18:18).

It's one thing for man to say certain things, but quite something else when the Lord says certain things. Both predictions came through exactly as spoken by the Lord.

Abraham became a great and mighty Nation as it regards Israel. Secondly, *"All the nations of the Earth have been blessed in him,"* which refers to Christ. Christ came through the Jewish people and through His Sacrificial, Atoning Death on the Cross of Calvary. All the nations of the world have truly been blessed because Abraham is the father of us all as it regards the Born-Again experience (Rom. 4:16).

THE COMMAND

"For I know him, that he will command his children and his household after him, and they shall keep the Way of the LORD, to do justice and Judgment; that the LORD may bring upon Abraham that which He has spoken of him" (Gen. 18:19).

The actual Hebrew says, *"For I have known him in order that he may command his sons,"* etc.

The idea reaches out more so to the Knowledge of God instituted in Abraham than Abraham commanding his family, etc.

The idea is that Abraham should bring forth a Nation whose institutions were to be imbued with Divine Truth, whose Prophets were to be the means of revealing God's Will to man, and of whom, as concerning the flesh, the Messiah should come.

It was the unique and high purpose for which this Nation was to be called into being (Israel) that brought Abraham into so close a relation to Jehovah.

ISRAEL

Israel was the only Nation in the world which even remotely carried out the Commands of the Lord as it regards *"justice and Judgment."* They could do this because they had the Word of the Lord, which, in fact, no other nation in the world possessed at that time. This put Israel proverbial light years ahead of all other people. In fact, the Law of God given to Moses was the only fair and equitable Law that man ever knew. This is because it was instituted by Jehovah and not by man. While, of course, there were many laws in the world of that day, they were all devised by man. As such, they were fraught with injustice and a lack of Judgment on those who would seek to take peace from the Earth.

The old adage is true:

- Much Bible, much freedom;
- Little Bible, little freedom;
- No Bible, no freedom.

In a sense, Abraham (under God), more than any other man, has been responsible for every iota of freedom that's in the world today and every Blessing that has come upon humanity, irrespective as to whom the people might be. As well, if one wants to put one's finger on the reason for Abraham being the result of all of this, one would have to point toward his Faith. However, in understanding this, we might say that his Faith centered up in *"Jesus Christ and Him Crucified"* (Jn. 8:56).

SODOM AND GOMORRAH

"And the LORD said, Because the cry of Sodom and Gomorrah is great, and because their sin is very grievous" (Gen. 18:20).

Due to the efforts of Abraham, Sodom and Gomorrah had been rescued from the hands of a tyrant some 15 years before. By freeing them, this showed that God was willing to forgive their transgressions if they would repent; however, they seemed to little inquire after Abraham's God, if at all. So, there was no repentance; consequently, there could be no forgiveness.

The human heart is so altogether corrupt that it seems that seldom do God's Threats or His Mercies lead the wicked to Repentance.

There is evidence that at the beginning, the Sodomites were somewhat grateful to God for His Mercy extended to them. However, soon they forgot entirely the help that Abraham had given, and they blasphemed the Divine Message which he and Lot proclaimed.

At the same time, they were a proud people and believed themselves to be wise.

Martin Luther said:

"Wherever people are ungrateful to God and despise His Word, there is neither honor nor honesty among them, for these virtues, like good fruits, spring forth entirely from the seed of the Divine Word." When the Divine Word is no longer proclaimed, or it is erroneously interpreted, blasphemy and extreme wickedness are the end result.

As we go down into the Text, we shall see just how wicked Sodom and Gomorrah had become.

THE CRY

"The cry of Sodom and Gomorrah" was not the cry of the oppressed, as some have claimed. It was the cry of evil and wickedness, which came up into the Ears of God, and which He always sees. However, in this case, it had become so great that it could no longer be ignored. Their sins had become more and more wicked, which meant that it grieved the Heart of God.

Let the reader understand that God cannot abide sin in any capacity. A thrice-Holy God cannot condone sin. There is only one remedy for sin, and that is the Cross of Christ. The world may put forth its proposed cures for the situation, but it is all to no avail. Regrettably, the church all too often follows suit. In other words, the modern church little looks toward the Cross anymore, that is, if it ever did.

The answer to sin, which has been accepted by the world and, regrettably, most of the church, as well, is humanistic psychology. Is there any hope in these claims? Does it hold the answer for hurting humanity?

Perhaps the following illustration will be of some help:

HUMANISTIC PSYCHOLOGY

I happened to see a documentary the other day on the addiction of gambling. The principal in the documentary was a man who had an earned Ph.D. His field of study was psychological counseling. As one should know, a Ph.D. is the highest educational attainment to which one can ascribe. He specialized in counseling alcoholics and drug addicts.

In this state, he had no belief in God and, in fact, ridiculed the Bible and all for which God stands.

To make the story brief, he and his wife went with some friends to a gambling casino. He had little interest in going, but to please them, he went. He had promised himself he would only stay about 20 minutes.

He had never gambled in his life and determined to spend about 20 minutes at the slots and then go home. Two hours later, he was still there and in two or three days, he was completely hooked.

During the next two years, he went through the entirety of their savings, sold their home, sold his automobile, and borrowed every dollar that he could borrow, all in order to continue his gambling habit.

After a period of time, he realized he was in deep trouble and, at one point, planned to take his own life simply because he could not quit gambling, no matter how hard he tried.

A BANKRUPT PHILOSOPHY

As he parked his car under a tree out on a side road, he reached in the glove compartment to get a gun, which he thought was there, but it was gone. His wife had taken it a couple of days earlier, planning to sell it, which she actually did, in order to pay the light bill, so their lights would not be turned off. That's how bad the situation had become.

In his profession, this man had used all of the skills of humanistic psychology as it regarded psychological counseling for alcoholics and drug addicts. He now used these skills on himself, but to no avail. He tried every trick in the book, but the addiction yielded to none of his efforts.

He then realized that what he was promoting was a bankrupt philosophy. It had no power to set anyone free.

At this stage, he began to call on God, Whom he had once ridiculed. The Miracles at which he had once laughed, he now sought. As the Lord has met untold millions down through the centuries, he met this man, as well, at the point of his need.

He gave his heart and life to Jesus Christ, with the Lord then breaking the addiction of gambling, which only the Lord could do.

This is one of the most strident illustrations I've ever known as it regards the futility of humanistic psychology. And yet, the church, which ought to know better, has bought this lie and has done so in totality.

THE CROSS

As we have stated, the only cure for sin, and we mean the only cure, is the Cross of Christ. Any so-called preacher of the gospel who would recommend psychology is, in effect, placing a vote of no confidence in the Cross. One cannot have it both ways. One either believes in the Cross, or one believes in the world. One cannot believe in both at the same time.

To be frank, at least as it regards the church, unbelief is the great problem. Men claim to believe in Christ, but, in reality, they don't! Preachers claim to present Christ, but, many times, it is *"another Christ"* (II Cor. 11:4).

To put it in Biblical terms, the sin of the church in rejecting the Cross and accepting humanistic psychology, *"Is very grievous."*

JUDGMENT

"I will go down now, and see whether they have done altogether according to the cry of it, which is come unto Me; and if not, I will know" (Gen. 18:21).

All sin is inherently offensive in the Eyes of the Almighty, but some forms of wickedness are more presumptuously daring or more intrinsically loathsome than others. Of such sort were the sins of Sodom. Though God speaks of making investigation into the sins of Sodom, this was really unnecessary. The moral degeneracy of the inhabitants of these twin cities was one of the *"all things"* that are ever *"naked and manifest"* unto His Eyes. So, nothing can be hidden from God (II Chron. 16:9; Prov. 15:3; Amos 9:8).

The meaning of these phrases is that though the guilt of Sodom was great, God would not let loose His Vengeance until it should be seen to be perfectly just. Nothing would be done in haste, but all with judicial calmness.

TWO ANGELS

"And the Men turned their faces from thence, and went toward Sodom: but Abraham stood yet before the LORD" (Gen. 18:22).

The idea seems to be, the Lord remained here with Abraham while the two Angels with Him would go into Sodom, but they were going there for the purpose of rescuing Lot. They would then bring Judgment upon these cities.

Abraham's posture before the Lord refers to a petition he will lay out, all of which concerned Lot and his family. He would intercede on the part of his nephew.

THE RIGHTEOUS?

"And Abraham drew near, and said, Will You also destroy the Righteous with the wicked?" (Gen. 18:23).

I think the Text bears it out that while Abraham was definitely concerned about the entirety of the population of these cities, his greatest concern was about Lot. When he mentions the word, *"Righteous,"* he could only be thinking of Lot; however, the question posed by Abraham covers a broad waterfront. The answer is as follows:

No, the Lord will not destroy the Righteous with the wicked. While the Lord definitely oversees all, and that regards the unredeemed as well as the Redeemed, to be sure, the Redeemed are in a category all by themselves. The Scripture plainly says that we are *"bought with a price: therefore glorify God in your body, and in your spirit, which are God's"* (I Cor. 6:20). So, that means that the Lord monitors every action of the Child of God, and that nothing happens to Believers but that the Lord either causes it or allows it.

For instance, if God in His Foreknowledge knows that an airplane is going to crash, killing all on board, He will do one of two things as it regards Believers:

1. He will either stop the Believer from getting on the plane, which He can do with no difficulty, or else,

2. He will delay the *"accident"* because of the Believer. In other words, because of the Believer being on board, the plane won't go down, that is, unless the Believer is to be taken home to Glory at that time.

This is the reason that the presence of a Believer is of utmost benefit to all concerned, even the ungodliest.

Regrettably, most unredeemed don't know that and would ridicule such a statement if it came to their attention; however, it is nevertheless true.

FIFTY

"Peradventure there be fifty Righteous within the city: will You also destroy and not spare the place for the fifty Righteous who are therein?" (Gen. 18:24).

The 50 doesn't include the children. Even though they were destroyed in the Judgment, they were not eternally lost even though their parents were. This we conclude from Jonah 4:11, which tells us of little children who *"cannot discern between their right hand and their left hand."* So, I believe and teach that, irrespective of the state of the parents, every child below the age of accountability, who dies in that innocent state, is protected by the Lord and, in fact, goes to be with Him in Heaven. I don't believe there is a single baby or child below the age of accountability in Hell, nor will there ever be.

THE AGE OF ACCOUNTABILITY

What the age of accountability is will vary for the child. With some, it could be as young as five or six years old, and with others, it could be as much as nine or 10 years old. All that would depend on many things, and only the Lord would know the answer as it regards each child.

Abraham now begins to intercede for the city of Sodom, which would probably include all five cities of the plain, with four ultimately destroyed. He asked that if 50 Righteous were found in this city or cities, will the Lord spare the place?

Every Believer has the spiritual and Scriptural right to intercede on behalf of whatever it is that is thought to be needed. In fact, it was the Holy Spirit Who prompted Abraham to intercede, and it is the Holy Spirit Who prompts us likewise.

Many Believers have the mistaken idea that God is going to do whatever it is He desires to do, and there is nothing that can stop it. The truth is, the Lord has put great responsibility into the hands of all Believers. This means that if we fall down on the job, whatever it is that needs to be done simply will not be done.

For instance, if the church lets down as it regards Evangelism, untold millions in the world will be lost. In fact, God has already done His Part. He has given His Son, the Lord Jesus Christ, which makes all things possible. It's up to us now to tell others this Greatest Story of all.

RESPONSIBILITY

At this very moment, there are Sodoms hanging in the balance. If Saints somewhere in this world don't intercede, these cities will be lost, which could mean that untold thousands or even millions could die and go to Hell.

Even if the areas aren't spared, much good will still be done, even as it was done with Abraham's intercession. While Sodom and Gomorrah were not spared, Lot, in fact, was spared.

One of the major problems is that most Christians aren't living close enough to the Lord to even hear His Voice. The Holy Spirit attempts to move upon them, but all to no avail. What a tragedy!

THE JUDGE

"That be far from You to do after this manner, to slay the Righteous with the wicked: and that the Righteous

should be as the wicked, that be far from You: shall not the Judge of all the Earth do right?" (Gen. 18:25).

As stated, the Lord doesn't slay the Righteous with the wicked. In fact, the Righteous aren't like the wicked in any manner, the Precious Blood of Jesus having made the great difference.

Of all things, exactly as Abraham said, we can be totally confident that the Judge of the Earth shall do right. That Judge is the Lord!

He is the Judge of all the Earth; He always does right in everything He does and carries out. As well, He has the Power to guarantee whatever it is that needs to be done.

THE ANSWER

"And the LORD said, If I find in Sodom fifty Righteous within the city, then I will spare all the place for their sakes" (Gen. 18:26).

As previously stated, we learn from this that the Righteous are a tremendous boon and blessing to the entire area which they occupy. This means that the more Believers that are in any given place, the more the Blessings of God will be poured out on that place and destruction withheld.

Think of it! If only 10 Righteous had been found in Sodom, the city, possibly numbering 25,000 or more, would have been spared despite its wickedness.

The world doesn't understand this at all and, in fact, maligns and even curses the Child of God oftentimes. However, the truth is, every single blessing that the unredeemed receives, in whatever capacity, is received because of the righteous ones who are in their midst.

Now, this is not understood by the world and, in fact, never will be; however, it is nevertheless true. The Lord has spared untold numbers of people, as well as entire cities, because of the Righteous, as few as they may be.

HUMILITY

"And Abraham answered and said, Behold now, I have taken upon me to speak unto the LORD, which am but dust and ashes" (Gen. 18:27).

With Abraham referring to himself as *"but dust and ashes,"* we find here the humility of the great Patriarch. The Lord had come all the way from Heaven, and on this journey, He had visited Abraham. Despite that fact and despite the fact that, through the Patriarch, all the nations of the world would be blessed, Abraham thought of himself even as he should have done so.

It is very difficult for men and women to be singularly honored and blessed by the Lord and it not affect them in the realm of pride. Consequently, the Lord cannot bless many people for the obvious reasons.

As well, spiritual pride is the worst pride of all. Such exists simply because the individual has an improper view of the Cross. In fact, one cannot really know humility unless one knows and understands the Cross.

The knowledge of the Cross humbles anyone who understands it accordingly. The very fact of the Cross was the greatest act of humility the world has ever known. For God to become Man and to lay aside the expression of His Deity, and then to die upon a Cross, portrays humility as humility has never been portrayed. As well, for the Believer to know and understand this tremendous quality, which, incidentally, God commands, the Believer must, without fail, understand the Cross. That alone will bring the Believer to the place we ought to be concerning the opposite of spiritual pride.

FORTY FIVE

"Peradventure there shall lack five of the fifty Righteous: will You destroy all the city for lack of five? And He said, If I find there forty and five, I will not destroy it" (Gen. 18:28).

If it is to be noticed, Abraham frames his requests in an uncanny manner. He doesn't ask for the city to be spared if there are 45 Righteous, but rather if five of the fifty are lacking, throwing the emphasis on *"five,"* which, of course, plays out to 45, would the city be spared? Instead of putting the emphasis on the 45, he puts it on the five.

FORTY

"And he spoke unto Him yet again, and said, Peradventure there shall be forty found there. And He said, I will not do it for forty's sake" (Gen. 18:29).

Emboldened now with courage as well as Faith, he lowers the number to 40. Again, the Lord acquiesces to the lower number.

THIRTY

"And he said unto Him, O let not the LORD be angry, and I will speak: Peradventure there shall thirty be found there. And He said, I will not do it, if I find thirty there" (Gen. 18:30).

By his constant persistence, Abraham prays that he will not anger the Lord.

While Abraham would not have had the Knowledge of the Lord that we presently have, I think it can easily be said that the Lord delights in the Believer pressing, as it regards petitions and desires. While it should always be done with humility, which means that we know and understand that we deserve nothing good, the Believer should press through to the desired results.

If 30 Righteous could be found, the Lord would spare the city.

TWENTY

"And he said, Behold now, I have taken upon me to speak unto the LORD: Peradventure there shall be twenty found there. And He said, I will not destroy it for twenty's sake" (Gen. 18:31).

It is obvious that the Patriarch fears that, other than Lot, the number of Righteous in Sodom is virtually non-existent. He asks for 20, and the Lord acquiesces.

However, through foreknowledge, the Lord knew exactly how many Righteous were in the city and that Abraham's petition really would not do any good. So, why did He not inform him of this to begin with?

This we do know: everything the Lord does is always for our benefit. In other words, He has a prime reason for all things.

I think He allowed Abraham to continue in this vein in order that this narrative may teach us the practice of intercession and, as well, the position of relationship.

Abraham was the friend of God, and this illustration proclaims that fact. Due to the Cross, we presently carry a higher claim.

When I was a child, my grandmother taught me a very valuable lesson. She said to me, *"Jimmy, God is a Big God, so ask big."*

I've never forgotten that! Abraham asked big! While he did not succeed in his quest for Sodom to be spared, still, he did succeed in once again rescuing Lot.

TEN

"And he said, O let not the LORD be angry, and I will speak yet but this once: Peradventure ten shall be

found there. And He said, I will not destroy it for ten's sake" (Gen. 18:32).

What the population of the city of Sodom was at this time, we have no way of knowing. It was probably at least 25,000 and could have been as much as 100,000 strong, if not more. And yet, there were not even 10 righteous people in the city.

We should note in this that Abraham ceased asking before God ceased giving. Such is the power and the value of prayer!

THE LORD

"And the LORD went His Way, as soon as He had left communing with Abraham: and Abraham returned unto his place" (Gen. 18:33).

While the Lord now goes His Way, He doesn't do so until Abraham ceases his petitioning. As stated, Abraham ceased asking before God ceased giving. That's quite a statement and should be looked at very closely.

Howsomuch we miss simply because we do not take it to the Lord in prayer.

Why? There are two reasons:

1. In many cases, it's unconfessed sin in the person's life, and prayer immediately demands that such sin be repented of and forsaken. Many Christians simply don't want to forsake their sin.

2. There isn't much Faith on the part of most Believers. To have the necessary prayer life we ought to have, a great deal of Faith is required. However, I believe the greatest problem of prayerlessness is because of the following:

If the Believer doesn't properly understand the Cross, prayer will not be nearly as important to him as it could be. That is the condition of the modern church. There has been so little teaching and preaching on the

Cross in the last several decades that for all practical purposes, the modern church is all but Cross illiterate. Consequently, without the Cross as the central core of our Faith, the church is splintered in every direction.

A proper understanding of the Cross will give the Believer Faith simply because the Word of God is the Story of the Cross. When we properly understand the Cross, we are properly understanding the Word; therefore, Faith is generated!

"Thanks to God for my Redeemer,
"Thanks for all You did provide!
"Thanks for time now but a memory,
"Thanks for Jesus by my side!
"Thanks for pleasant, cheerful springtime,
"Thanks for summer, winter, fall;
"Thanks for tears by now forgotten,
"Thanks for peace within my soul!"

"Thanks for prayers that You have answered,
"Thanks for what You did deny,
"Thanks for storms that I have weathered,
"Thanks for all You do supply!
"Thanks for pain, and thanks for pleasure,
"Thanks for comfort and despair!
"Thanks for Grace that none can measure,
"Thanks for Love beyond compare!"

"Thanks for roses by the wayside,
"Thanks for thorns that stems contain!
"Thanks for homes and thanks for fireside,
"Thanks for hope, that sweet refrain!
"Thanks for joy and thanks for sorrow,
"Thanks for Heavenly Peace with Thee!
"Thanks for hope in the tomorrow,
"Thanks through all eternity."

ABRAHAM

CHAPTER

20

Abraham
And The Angels

ABRAHAM AND THE ANGELS

"And there came two Angels to Sodom at evening; and Lot sat in the gate of Sodom: and Lot seeing them rose up to meet them; and he bowed himself with his face toward the ground" (Gen. 19:1).

While Abraham was interceding with the Lord, the two Angels went into Sodom, and did so for the sole purpose of rescuing Lot. As these two Angels entered the city dressed like men and looking like men, little did the citizens of Sodom know the Power these men held in their possession. They had been sent on a mission. That mission was to rescue Lot, and this they would do.

Sometime back, Abraham, Lot's uncle, had saved the life of the king of Sodom. In fact, along with the king, he had saved the lives of Lot and all who had been taken captive. As well, he recovered the material goods that had been taken. At that time, Lot was probably elevated and because of this, he could possibly have even been the mayor of the city. However, that is only supposition.

How Lot knew these two men (Angels) when they came into the city, we aren't told. They definitely knew who he was, so they may well have introduced themselves in some fashion, which is probably what happened. It is even possible that they revealed their true identity to Lot inasmuch as he *"bowed himself with his face toward the ground."* As well, we will find that he will do everything in his power to protect them, even to the proposal of giving his two daughters to the mob.

THE INVITATION

"And he said, Behold now, my lords, turn in, I pray you, into your servant's house, and tarry all night, and

wash your feet, and you shall rise up early, and go on your ways. And they said, No; but we will abide in the street all night" (Gen. 19:2).

Other than the destruction of this place, we aren't told what else the Angels had in mind. As if they didn't already know, they would see firsthand the terrible wickedness of this place called, *"Sodom."*

There are two methods used by the Lord to draw Believers away from the attractions of the world. They are as follows:

1. He reveals to us the stability and eternal value of the *"things above."*

2. He shows us the temporal nature of the things of this world. Thus, if we fully realize the stability of Heaven, we will have no problem rejecting the delusive joys of Earth.

Looking at Lot as he *"sits in the gate,"* we see that he has *"gotten on in the world."* If we look at his situation from a worldly point of view, it seems that he had been successful.

BY FAITH?

Lot *"pitched his tent toward Sodom."* He then found his way into the city, and now we find him sitting at the gate — a prominent, influential post.

Concerning Abraham, the Scripture says, *"By Faith Abraham sojourned in the Land of Promise, as in a strange country, dwelling in tabernacles"* (Heb. 11:9). We read no such statement as it regards Lot. It could not be said, *"By Faith Lot sat in the gate of Sodom."* Actually, he gets no place at all among the Faith notables in Hebrews, Chapter 11.

It should be observed that there was a material difference between these two men, Abraham and Lot, even though they both started together on the same course.

The tragedy is, they reached a very different goal, at least so far as their public Testimony was concerned.

I think the Scripture is clear that Lot was Saved, yet it was *"so as by fire"* with his works being *"burned up."*

As it regards Abraham and Lot, the Lord remained to commune with the Patriarch while he merely sent His Two Angels to Sodom as it regards Lot.

In fact, as we have seen here, the Angels didn't even desire to enter into the house of Lot, but rather said, *"We will abide in the street all night."* What a rebuke!

CONDEMNATION

Even though they ultimately did go into his house, the answer of the Angels to Lot contains a most unqualified condemnation of his position in Sodom. The idea is, they would rather stay in the street all night than to enter under the roof of one in a wrong position. In fact, had it not been for Abraham, every evidence is that Lot would not have been spared at all. It was simply for Abraham's sake that Lot was allowed to escape. The Lord has no sympathy with a worldly mind, and such a mind it was that had led Lot to settle down amid the defilement of that guilty city. Faith never put him there; a spiritual mind never put him there; and *"his righteous soul"* never put him there. It was simply love for this present evil world that led him first to *"choose,"* then to *"pitch his tent toward,"* and finally to *"sit in the gate of Sodom."*

Now, look at what he chose! He chose a city that was doomed to destruction; a destruction so awful that none would be spared.

No doubt, Lot thought that he was doing well when he came to Sodom. When he was honored to be able to sit in the gate, which insinuates a place of authority and position, he was even more gratified. However, that which followed shows how entirely he erred. It also sounds in our personal ears a voice of deepest solemnity — a voice telling us to be aware how we yield to the incipient workings of a worldly spirit.

HOSPITALITY

"And he pressed upon them greatly; and they turned in unto him, and entered into his house; and he made them a feast, and did bake unleavened bread, and they did eat" (Gen. 19:3).

The idea seems to be that Lot would not take, *"No,"* for an answer, as it regards them coming into his house and partaking of his hospitality.

We do know that everything the Lord does, even through His Angels, is always with design and purpose. So, their reluctance to enter into his house may have been more of a test than anything else.

While Abraham's intercession was to be greatly heeded, still, Lot could not be spared on that alone. He had to have a personal relationship with the Lord, that is, if he was to be saved.

So, quite possibly, they refused his hospitality at the beginning just to see what he would do. Would he insist, or would he easily take, *"No,"* for an answer, showing little regard and concern?

To his credit, *"He pressed upon them greatly."* Only then did they *"turn in unto him, and enter into his house."* Only then did they partake with him in the feast that was prepared, which speaks of communion and carries a tremendous spiritual meaning.

Even though he was in sad shape spiritually, still, his righteous soul cried out to God, which became evident by his actions. This meant that they could now commune with him, which they did!

While his Faith was too weak to reject Sodom, it was too strong to reject the Angels, and thank God for that!

THE HOMOSEXUALS

"But before they lay down, the men of the city, even the men of Sodom, compassed the house round, both old and young, all the people from every quarter" (Gen. 19:4).

The homosexual lust of the men of Sodom, which was so great, seems to have possessed the entirety of the city. It was so great, in fact, that they would literally force the door in order to get to the two Angels, who they thought were mere men.

I think we can see from the account given just how deep into sin Sodom had deteriorated. It was past Redemption and past Saving. It was like a cancer that had to be surgically removed, which the Lord would now do.

Whether the sin of homosexuality is the worst sin there is or not, only the Lord knows. However, this we do know, Sodom and Gomorrah, plus two smaller ones at that time, are the only cities which have ever been destroyed in this fashion. While down through the centuries, the Lord has, no doubt, destroyed many, these are the only ones done in this manner and in this way. That being the case, we should understand that the sin of homosexuality is at least one of the worst sins known to man.

Homosexuals are not born this way, just as alcoholics, thieves, etc., are not born as such. While all people are born in original sin, which means that the seed of all sin is present in our hearts and lives, this does not mean that certain ones are predestined for certain particular lifestyles. So, how does one become a homosexual?

LIFESTYLES

Every human being is born in original sin, meaning that there is predilection in every human being toward something ungodly before one is Born-Again, that is, if he ever is. This means that some babies are born with a predilection toward stealing, or lying, or alcohol, or gambling, or jealousy, or homosexuality, etc. That doesn't mean that such a person is born an alcoholic, a gambler, a homosexual, etc. It means he only has a bent or predilection toward certain things that we have named, and many we haven't named. Of course, the answer, and the only answer, to all of this is to be Born-Again (Jn. 3:3).

Many boys are pushed over the edge, so to speak, when they are molested by homosexuals. The Scripture says:

"But every man is tempted, when he is drawn away of his own lust, and enticed" (James 1:14).

Without a doubt, evil spirits enter into this situation, as evil spirits enter into all sin.

Medical scientists are investigating the possibility of a particular gene being perverted or malformed, which could bring about a homosexual lifestyle, or other problems as well. However, if they, in fact, do find that this is the case, they will still only be treating the symptom and not the real cause.

The cause is the sin principle or sin nature, which came upon the human race as a result of the Fall in the Garden of Eden. It takes many forms and many directions, but it is that which is more powerful than man, and which drives him toward more and more evil.

DELIVERANCE

There is Deliverance in Jesus Christ from any and all bondages, irrespective as to how awful they might be. However, the manner in which Deliverance is brought about is through what Christ did at the Cross. As we've said repeatedly, to divorce Christ from the Cross is to make Christ ineffective.

Deliverance from sin is of greater magnitude than a mere display of Power, which the Lord readily has. Sin is an affront to God, and for sin to be properly handled, God's Nature and Justice must be totally and completely satisfied. He is the One Who has been offended, and He is the One Who must be satisfied.

The Cross alone satisfied Him, in that there, all sin, in its totality, was atoned. It was at the Cross that the *"body of sin was destroyed,"* which means to be made ineffective (Rom. 6:6). This means that the *"guilt"* of sin was removed, and the *"power"* of sin was broken. As stated, it was done at the Cross, and it is through the Cross that all victory comes, and through the Cross alone!

If it is to be noticed, Jesus did not say that He came to deliver people, even though He most definitely did do that, but rather that He came to *"preach Deliverance to the captives"* (Lk. 4:18). What did He mean by that?

PREACHING DELIVERANCE TO THE CAPTIVES

What I'm doing right here is preaching Deliverance to you. He also stated, *"You shall know the Truth, and the Truth shall make you free"* (Jn. 8:32).

The Truth is Jesus Christ and what He did for us at the Cross. That's why Paul said:

"I determined to know nothing among you, save Jesus Christ, and Him Crucified" (I Cor. 2:2).

That's why he also said:

"For the preaching of the Cross (which is actually the preaching of Deliverance) is to them who perish foolishness; but unto us who are Saved it is the Power of God" (I Cor. 1:18).

The homosexual can be delivered totally and completely; the alcoholic and drug addict can be delivered totally and completely; and the thief and the liar can be delivered totally and completely. In fact, irrespective as to what the bondage or vice might be, one can be totally and completely delivered. However, this can only be done by the Lord Jesus Christ, and the Means by which He does this is by and through what He did for us at the Cross. Paul continued to say:

"Who gave Himself for our sins, that He might deliver us from this present evil world, according to the Will of God and our Father" (Gal. 1:4).

JESUS DIED TO SAVE US FROM SIN

This means that the sinner, homosexuals included, must accept Christ as his Saviour. He must then place his Faith totally and completely in Christ and what He has done for him at the Cross, and ask for and receive the Deliverance which He has already afforded. Millions have been set free, and anyone who will so subject his Faith can be set free.

The idea that one can be Saved and continue on in such a lifestyle of homosexuality, or anything else of that nature, is a fool's hope. It cannot be done! Jesus didn't die on the Cross in order to save us in our sins, but rather *"from our sin."* To be sure, homosexuality, along with drunkenness, adultery, stealing, lying, and a thousand and one other things, constitutes sin. If Salvation doesn't save us from sin, then it's not true Salvation, but rather mere religion made up by man.

THE ACT OF HOMOSEXUALITY

"And they called unto Lot, and said unto him, Where are the men who came in to you this night? bring them out unto us, that we may know them" (Gen. 19:5).

The words, *"Know them,"* as was used by the men of Sodom, and as it regarded the two men (Angels) in the home of Lot, referred to knowing them sexually, i.e., *"in a homosexual way."*

Homosexuality is always, after a fashion, predatorial. Actually, predatoriality is the spirit of homosexuality. It is not merely an alternate lifestyle, but rather a perversion of the worst sort.

The fact that the mass of men gathered at the door of Lot's house were all, without exception, involved in this demand is emphatic. It shows the absolute depth to which the citizenship of this city had sunk, at least as it regarded sexual perversion.

Josephus, the Jewish historian, claims that these two men, who were, in reality, Angels, had beautiful countenances, which is, no doubt, true. This tended to excite the lust of the Sodomites and caused them to assault Lot's house with shameful demands.

The sin of homosexuality was exceedingly prevalent among the Canaanites (Lev. 18:22) and other heathen nations as well (Rom. 1:27). Under the Law of Moses, it was punishable by death.

LOT

"And Lot went out at the door unto them, and shut the door after him" (Gen. 19:6).

As we shall see, Lot accomplished nothing, either by pleading or by warning. The more he begged this mob, the more irrational and lustful these reprobates became.

It is impossible to reason with lust, especially this type of lust. As stated, it is predatorial and will respond to no rational appeal.

BRETHREN?

"And said, I pray you, brethren, do not so wickedly" (Gen. 19:7).

The Text marks this sin as unspeakably vile by telling us that they commanded Lot to bring out his guests so that they could seduce them publicly and in the sight of the whole population. They had lost all sense of shame and decency, for they made no attempt at perpetrating this shameful vice in secret. Had the Lord not wiped out this city and the three others similar in the region, this wretched state of affairs would have put an end to all morality and decency in that area. It could very well have greatly hindered God's Plan for Canaan in the coming years, which was Satan's intention all along.

Lot refers to them as, *"Brethren,"* though the correct name should have been, *"Perverts."*

Why did he refer to them as brethren?

COMPROMISE

The very fact of this type of terminology shows that Lot had long since compromised his Testimony. As a result, these vile individuals had not become like Lot, but rather Lot had become like them, at least in many ways. This is always the shame of compromise. It never remains static, but rather suffers deterioration.

We learn from this that while the Bible does not teach isolation, it definitely does teach separation. The admonition of the Holy Spirit through Paul, *"Be not unequally yoked together with unbelievers: for what fellowship has Righteousness with unrighteousness? and what communion has light with darkness? . . . Wherefore come out from among them, and be you separate, says the Lord, and touch not the unclean thing; and I will receive you,"* was definitely not being practiced by Lot (II Cor. 6:14, 17). While the record is clear that he did not partake of their evil and, as well, that it vexed his righteous soul (II Pet. 2:7-8), still, he compromised his Testimony.

THE RESULT OF COMPROMISE

"Behold now, I have two daughters who have not known man; let me, I pray you, bring them out unto you, and do to them as is good in your eyes: only unto these Men do nothing; for therefore came They under the shadow of my roof" (Gen. 19:8).

This Passage proves that not all the men of Sodom were homosexuals; nevertheless, I think one can say without fear of contradiction that the majority was.

The idea of giving one's daughters to this vile mob is beyond comprehension. Lot seeks to appease these animals by a most humiliating proposition, but all in vain. If a man will mingle with the world for the purpose of self-aggrandizement, he must make up his mind to endure the sad consequences. We cannot profit by the world and, at the same time, bear effectual Testimony against its wickedness.

A JUDGE?

"And they said, Stand back. And they said again, This one fellow came in to sojourn, and he will needs be a judge: now will we deal worse with you, than with Them. And they pressed sore upon the man, even Lot, and came near to break the door" (Gen. 19:9).

The terminology used here tells us several things:

• Due to Abraham having rescued many Sodomites from Chedorlaomer, evidently, these homosexuals had declared him off limits. But now, due to Lot's protection of the two Angels, they are breaking their commitment to him.

• Who does he think he is, they contemplate, judging them? They will do whatever they so desire, and his appeals will fall on deaf ears. In other words, they were saying, *"You are not our judge."* Again, by them using the word, *"Judge,"* there is a slim possibility that Lot was actually a judge in the city of Sodom.

THE ANGELS

"But the Men put forth Their hand, and pulled Lot into the house to Them, and shut to the door" (Gen. 19:10).

Observing the situation, the Angels now take charge. Evidently, Lot was standing near the door. The Angels opened it, took him by the arm, and pulled him back into the house. They will now take matters into their own hands.

Little did these perverts know who these men actually were. Little did they realize that they were hours away from total destruction. Let all who walk accordingly understand the following:

As destruction ultimately came upon Sodom and other cities in that region, likewise, destruction will most definitely come upon all who reject God. As fire came upon Sodom, fire is coming upon this world and upon every single soul who rejects Christ.

Now, men can laugh at that, make fun of that, and ridicule and make light of that; nevertheless, that's exactly what is going to happen (II Pet. 3:7).

There is only one way to escape the coming Judgment, and that is to accept the Lord Jesus Christ as one's Saviour. In Him Alone is Salvation. In Him Alone is Redemption. Addressing this very thing, He said:

"I am the Way, the Truth, and the Life: no man comes unto the Father, but by Me" (Jn. 14:6).

This means that every single person in this world who is following Muhammad will die and go to Hell. It means that all who are following Buddha, Confucius, Joseph Smith, or anyone or anything else will die and go to Hell. Jesus Christ is the Only Way because He Alone is God, and He Alone paid the price on Calvary's

Cross in the giving of Himself as a Sacrifice, which cul-
minated in the shedding of His Own Precious Blood.
Faith in that vicarious, Atoning Sacrifice will bring
Salvation, and that alone will bring Salvation.

BLINDNESS

*"And they smote the men who were at the door of
the house with blindness, both small and great: so that
they wearied themselves to find the door"* (Gen. 19:11).

The *"blindness"* mentioned here was not total blindness as we think of such. The word really means a
disturbance of vision caused by the eye not being in its
proper connection with the brain. They could still see
but not see properly. So, now their sight becomes as perverted as their passions, which it, no doubt, remained
until they were all destroyed a few hours later.

Not desiring to make more of this episode than we
should but, at the same time, knowing that we should
not make less either, an analogy can be drawn as to
the protection of the Child of God.

AN EVIL, WICKED WORLD

As Believers, we are in the midst of an evil, wicked,
and ungodly world. It is ruled by Satan exactly as
Sodom was ruled by Satan. In fact, Paul refers to
Satan as *"the god of this world"* (II Cor. 4:4). Whereas
the Angels blinded the eyes of these Sodomites, Satan
has *"blinded the minds of them who believe not, lest
the Light of the Glorious Gospel of Christ, Who is the
Image of God, should shine unto them"* (II Cor. 4:4).

As well, evil spirits working in this maelstrom of
iniquity constantly seek to hinder and oppress the
Child of God.

However, concerning this very thing, the Apostle
John said:

"You are of God, little children, and have overcome them: because greater is He Who is in you, than he who is in the world" (I Jn. 4:4).

The pronoun, *"He,"* as used here by John, refers to the Holy Spirit, Who abides constantly and perpetually in the heart and life of each Believer. However, we must never take Him for granted. Considering how important He is to us and, above all, that He is God, and that we have the privilege of having Him abide with us, we should seek to learn how He functions and works.

THE HOLY SPIRIT

Most Christians, I suppose, think that the Work of the Holy Spirit is automatic. In other words, He just does what He desires to do, etc. Nothing could be further from the truth.

Potentially, all things are possible, and potentially, the Holy Spirit can and will do mighty and great things for us, but only on the premise of our doing a certain thing. What is that?

The Holy Spirit works entirely on the premise of the Finished Work of Christ, which, of course, refers to the Cross (Rom. 8:2). In fact, He will not work outside of those premises.

This means that every Believer must ever make the Cross of Christ the Object of his Faith. In fact, this is the only thing the Holy Spirit actually requires. He does not require the Saint to be a theologian or a scholar. He only requires that one's own Faith be anchored squarely in the great Sacrifice of Christ, for this is where the demands of the Law were satisfied by Jesus giving His Life to atone for all sin (Jn. 1:29).

THE MEANS IS THE CROSS

If the Believer understands that the Cross of Christ

is the Means by which God gives all things to Believers, and that the Holy Spirit works exclusively within the parameters of the Finished Work of Christ and, thereby, anchors his Faith exclusively in that Finished Work, then total and complete victory in every capacity will be ours (Rom. 6:3-5, 11, 14; 8:1-2, 11, 13; I Cor. 1:17-18, 21, 23; 2:2, 5; Gal. 6:14; Eph. 2:13-18; Col. 2:10-15).

What I've just given to you in brief is the single most important thing that you could ever hear or read as a Believer. It is God's Prescribed Order for Victory as it regards His Children.

If we place our Faith and confidence strictly in Christ and what He has done for us at the Cross, ever making the Cross the Object of our Faith, we can rest assured that total and complete Divine Protection will be given to us in every capacity, and Satan will not be able to touch us. Let the Church understand that the Cross, and the Cross alone, is the answer. Unfortunately, far too many preachers seek to project something else as the answer and the solution. Other than the Cross of Christ, there is no other solution because no other solution is needed.

THE FAMILY

"*And the Men said unto Lot, Have you here any besides? son-in-law, and your sons, and your daughters, and whatsoever you have in the city, bring them out of this place*" (Gen. 19:12).

Concerning this, Mackintosh said:

"*To attempt to reprove the world's ways, while we profit by association with it, is vanity; the world will attach very little weight to such reproof and such testimony. Thus it was, too, with Lot's testimony to his sons-in-law; 'he seemed as one who mocked.' It is vain to speak of approaching judgment while finding our*

*place, our portion, and our enjoyment in the very scene
which is to be judged.*"[1]

DESTRUCTION

*"For we will destroy this place, because the cry of
them is waxen great before the Face of the LORD; and
the LORD has sent Us to destroy it"* (Gen. 19:13).

The Lord sent two Angels to destroy Sodom and
Gomorrah, along with two other smaller cities. I wonder, at this moment, are Angels being sent to other
cities in this world, or even America?

Speaking of this present time, perhaps one can say
that there are at least a few Believers in every city in
this world, and there are many in some cities. To be
sure, as we have seen here, even a few carry great
weight. So, I think the following is what the world is
now facing:

Judgment must come, and for all the obvious reasons.
We speak of Judgment on a scale that is beyond present comprehension. However, before this Judgment
comes, Believers must be taken out of this world,
which will be done at the Rapture (I Thess. 4:13-18).
So, the Church presently should be ardently looking
for the Rapture. Is it?

Hardly!

Once again I go back to the Cross. When the Church
properly looks to the Cross, then everything, as it regards
the Word of God, begins to come into proper focus.
Otherwise, the Believer is *"tossed to and fro, and carried about with every wind of doctrine, by the sleight of
men, and cunning craftiness, whereby they lie in wait
to deceive"* (Eph. 4:14). In fact, the Cross of Christ is
the actual dividing line between the true Church and
the apostate church. It is as one views the Cross that
one will view the Truth.

THE TESTIMONY

"And Lot went out, and spoke unto his sons-in-law, who married his daughters, and said, Up, get you out of this place; for the LORD will destroy this city. But he seemed as one who mocked unto his sons-in-law" (Gen. 19:14).

Some claim that the original Hebrew Text addresses these men as the future sons-in-law of Lot, meaning they were only engaged to Lot's daughters, but the wedding had not yet been consummated. Actually, this is probably the case simply because the Scripture plainly says that they had not *"known man"* (Gen. 19:8). So, if they were married, that would not be correct.

It must be understood that engagement in those days meant the same as marriage but without consummation.

Irrespective, his future sons-in-law had no confidence in his Testimony. In fact, they mocked him by claiming that he was mocking them.

The nearer the world approaches the end, the more it laughs at the Divine threats pronounced upon the wicked. Similarly, Noah warned his generation in vain. Now, when we speak, even as I have just spoken, of the next Coming of the Son of God to judge the world and cast unbelievers into the eternal fire of Hell, the ungodly ridicule this as something that is unthinkable. Let us, therefore, beware of despising the Warnings of God, as do the epicureans, who accept only what pleases their flesh and agrees with their reason, though the Divine Truth is manifest to them.

THE ANGELS

"And when the morning arose, then the Angels hastened Lot, saying, Arise, take your wife, and your two

daughters, who are here; lest you be consumed in the iniquity of the city" (Gen. 19:15).

Two things are said here:

1. The day now arrives which will occasion the destruction of Sodom and the other cities of the plain. However, little did its inhabitants know of such a thing, and neither did they believe such a thing. Their cup of iniquity had reached the overflowing point, and God had no choice but to destroy them.

What He did is the same as a surgeon removing a diseased organ from a patient in order that his life be spared. While it occasions pain and suffering, the act of surgery must be regarded as positive, as should be obvious. It is likewise with the Judgment of God.

The Lord does nothing but that, in the long run, it is good for all involved. In fact, the destruction of these cities was an act of Mercy on the part of the Lord as far as the Earth was concerned. Wickedness can become so great that destruction is the only answer.

2. The Angels who were sent by God to carry out this task hastened Lot in his preparations to leave, which were slow, to say the least.

Is the Holy Spirit presently hastening the Church to get ready for the Rapture? I believe He is.

LINGERING

"And while he lingered, the Men laid hold upon his hand, and upon the hand of his wife, and upon the hand of his two daughters; the LORD being merciful unto him: and They brought him forth, and set him without the city" (Gen. 19:16).

Concerning his lingering, Whitelaw says:

"Lot's irresolution would have been his ruin but for his attendants. His heart manifestly clung to the earthly possessions he was leaving. The Angels made *no mention of his attempting to save a portion of his great wealth.*"[2]

The loving insistence of the Angels with this unhappy procrastinator was most touching. Its cause is revealed in the words, *"The LORD being merciful unto him."* His folly in lingering, and further, in preferring his own place of safety to that proposed by the Angels, illustrates the deep unbelief of the human heart.

The Angels did not let Lot linger long. It seems that they literally took hold of his hand, the hand of his wife, and the hands of his two daughters and, in a sense, pushed them out of the city. To be sure, Lot and his family were not acting in Faith or obedience, so bringing them out of the city was pure, unmerited Grace. In essence, it was for Abraham's sake, who interceded on Lot's behalf, whereby, serving as a Type of Christ and His Intercession for us (Heb. 7:25).

ESCAPE

"And it came to pass, when They had brought them forth abroad, that he said, Escape for your life; look not behind you, neither stay you in all the plain; escape to the mountain, lest you be consumed" (Gen. 19:17).

Every city in the plain, which obviously numbered about five, was to be destroyed. So, they were told to *"escape to the mountain unless you be consumed."*

As well, it seems that Jehovah Himself, Who, though not mentioned, has now appeared upon the scene.

The phrase, *"Escape for your life,"* actually says in the Hebrew, *"Escape for your soul."* This means that had he stayed, his soul would have been lost.

The command, *"Look not behind you,"* was not given merely to prevent delay, but it also showed that God demanded of them a total abandonment in heart and will of the condemned cities, hence, the severity with which the violation of the command was visited.

All of this that we are seeing here in this example given proclaims to us the fact that all that's in this world, all that we count so dear, and all which seems to be so valuable, in reality, is going to be totally consumed. That's at least one of the reasons that Jesus said:

"Lay not up for yourselves treasures upon Earth, where moth and rust do corrupt, and where thieves break through and steal:

"But lay up for yourselves treasures in Heaven, where neither moth nor rust does corrupt, and where thieves do not break through or steal.

"For where your treasure is, there will your heart be also" (Mat. 6:19-21).

THE MOUNTAIN?

"And Lot said unto them, Oh, not so, my LORD:

"Behold now, Your Servant has found Grace in Your Sight, and You have magnified Your Mercy, which You have shown unto me in saving my life; and I cannot escape to the mountain, lest some evil take me, and I die" (Gen. 19:18-19).

By Lot referring to this One as *"LORD,"* and when we add Verse 24, it becomes obvious that Jehovah has now joined the two Angels and will direct the Judgment. Lot, as well, knows that this is the Lord.

However, strangely enough, he does not want to obey the Lord as it regards going to the mountain. As we shall see, he wants to go to another city, even as small as it might be.

Lot had functioned in the flesh for so long that even in the face of impending doom, he must continue to do so. The *"LORD"* told him to go to the mountain while the flesh steered him toward the city — any city. However, fear will haunt him there as well.

To be out of the Will of God is to be away from God. Now, let's say that again because it is so very important.

If one is in the Will of God, one is at the same time in the Way of God. However, to be outside of the Will of God is at the same time to be away from God.

How crass for Lot to question God, especially at a time like this!

Why was he afraid of the mountain? If God had told him to go there, and He certainly had, then most definitely the Lord would protect him; however, the *"flesh"* has no *"faith."* It has none simply because it's depending on self and not on the Lord.

THE CITY

"Behold now, this city is near to flee unto, and it is a little one: Oh, let me escape thither, (is it not a little one?) and my soul shall live" (Gen. 19:20).

It makes no sense whatsoever for Lot to disobey the Lord in not going immediately to the mountain, but instead, desiring to go to another city, as small as it might be. But again, when a Believer attempts to function in the realm of disobedience, what he does makes no sense whatsoever because it is nonsensical. People do not do stupid things when they are in the Will of God. It's when they are attempting to function in the realm of disobedience that they become foolish in their direction.

Lot was wrong to begin with in accepting the plain of Jordan, which was toward Sodom. He should have let Abraham decide for him. He was wrong in pitching his tent toward Sodom and wrong for moving into Sodom. As my mother used to say, *"Two wrongs don't make one right."*

WRONG DIRECTION

For the Believer, who is going in the wrong direction, to once again get things straight, he has to cease going in the wrong direction. In other words, he has to make things right with God and then get in the Will of God. That's not difficult to do once we tell the Lord that's what we desire. And then, had it not been for the intercession of Abraham, Lot would have been destroyed along with Sodom, etc.

So, Lot had been going in a wrong direction for a long, long time. He was accustomed to charting his own course, and he still hadn't repented, even at this late hour, so he continued to do the same. Amazingly enough, the Lord would humor him, even as He humors us at times as well.

YOUR REQUEST IS GRANTED

"And He said unto him, See, I have accepted you concerning this thing also, that I will not overthrow this city, for the which you have spoken" (Gen. 19:21).

Evidently, this small city was one of the towns located in the plain, which had also been marked for destruction. So, the Lord gives him that which he desires. It was a prayer that Lot would wish had never been answered in a positive way. It would not at all prove to be satisfactory, and Lot would shortly have to leave there and go to the mountain where the Lord had originally directed him.

Excursions of the flesh never come to a good end simply because it's a course that the Lord hasn't chartered. So, as Lot, we waste our time on these excursions. They may seem right at the moment, but if the Lord hasn't designed them, we will find soon enough that there is no profit in that direction.

THE LORD AND BELIEVERS

"Make haste, escape quickly; for I cannot do anything till you come out of Sodom. Therefore the name of the city was called Zoar.

"The sun was risen upon the Earth when Lot entered into Zoar" (Gen. 19:22-23).

Marvelously enough, the Lord proclaims the fact that He could not send the Judgment until Lot was safely out of Sodom and had gone to the city of his request. What does it mean, the Lord could do nothing?

I think the answer to that question covers far more territory than meets the eye. The Lord doesn't need us. In fact, He doesn't need anything. However, in His Grace and Mercy, He has allowed us to be a part of His Great Plan as it regards Redemption. This means that whatever it is that He does is based a great deal on what we do.

If the church goes in the wrong direction, or even if one Believer goes in the wrong direction, to that extent, whether the entirety of the church or the lone Believer, the Work of God will be hindered. This makes it imperative that we do our very best to ascertain the Will of God and to walk therein.

The Lord, in essence, had given His Word that He would spare Lot. So, until they were safely out of the city, He couldn't bring Judgment on the city, which was so desperately needed. It can work the opposite way as well.

If the Believer doesn't function in Faith, the Lord, Who works through Believers, can little function in the capacity of bringing souls to Himself. Perhaps if we understood this properly, we would be more responsible in our daily walk before the Lord.

JUDGMENT FROM HEAVEN

"Then the LORD rained upon Sodom and upon

Gomorrah brimstone and fire from the LORD out of Heaven" (Gen. 19:24).

Several things are said here:

• The way the Scripture is structured, we have here a distinction of Persons in the Godhead. Jehovah (the Son) rained down from Jehovah (the Father) the destruction upon Sodom and Gomorrah.

• The brimstone and fire, which was burning brimstone that destroyed the cities, did not burst upon them from Hell beneath but from Heaven above.

• The doom of these cities is referred to in the following Scriptures: Deut. 29:23; Isa. 13:19; Jer. 49:18; Zeph. 2:9; Mat. 10:15; II Pet. 2:6; Jude, Vs. 7.

Some claim that it was a violent earthquake which caused this disaster; however, an earthquake can hardly account for the burning of the sulfur. The Bible emphatically attributes the Judgment to the Lord. In other words, the cause was supernatural and not natural.

THE PLAIN

"And He overthrew those cities, and all the plain, and all the inhabitants of the cities, and that which grew upon the ground" (Gen. 19:25).

The entire plain was seared. What was once a verdant garden has now become a desert. This is what sin does!

All the inhabitants of these particular cities died in the inferno. This is proof of their entire corruption.

If it is to be noticed, at least as one reads the Bible, the Lord took an interest only in the countries and cities of the world at that time, and actually, all down through history, which affected His People. At this particular time, He was preparing the family of Abraham for the possession of Canaan even though it would be several hundreds of years before this would actually take place. As Israel finally became a Nation, we find the Lord once again dealing with nations which impacted Israel, especially if they impacted the chosen people in a negative way. There is no record that the Lord dealt with other nations of the world, at least at that time, which were too distant to have had an effect upon the chosen people and the chosen land.

Even during the times of the Early Church, we find the Lord addressing Himself to mighty Rome, which ruled the world of that day, only as it impacted the Church.

THE PLANS OF SATAN

The terrible evil of Sodom and Gomorrah was all planned by Satan to hinder, harm, and corrupt the Work of God. He was successful in drawing Lot into his web, and had it not been for Abraham, he would have been eternally lost. However, his major effort in all of this evil was to stop the coming of the Seed of the woman (Gen. 3:15). I doubt very seriously that he knew exactly how all of this was going to happen, but that it would happen, whatever would be the means or the method, and would spell his doom. So, he set out in several ways to stop the coming of the *"Seed."*

ENDTIME EVENTS

At this particular time, and I speak of 2012, considering the terrorist activity, events are speeding up as it regards the fulfillment of Bible Prophecy. In other words, the Rapture of the Church is near at hand because the Advent of the Antichrist is already being prepared. We know from II Thessalonians, Chapter 2, that the Antichrist cannot be revealed until the Church has first been taken out (II Thess. 2:7-8).

Regrettably, a great part of the modern church has

already apostatized, with the words of Paul already coming to pass. He said:

"Now the Spirit (Holy Spirit) speaks expressly (pointedly), that in the latter times (the times in which we now live) some shall depart from the Faith (depart from the Cross), giving heed to seducing spirits, and doctrines of demons" (I Tim. 4:1).

The Lord has raised up this Ministry (Jimmy Swaggart Ministries), among others, to preach the Cross. The Message of the Cross, and that Message alone, is the very center and core of Christianity. With the Cross removed, Christianity ceases to be Biblical and becomes no more than the other religions of the world, which, at best, is a philosophical quest. Without the Cross, there is no power to deliver (I Cor. 1:18). Without the Cross, captives aren't set free (Lk. 4:18). Without the Cross, lives aren't changed (Gal. 6:14). In fact, as I've already stated, the Cross is the dividing line between the true Church and the apostate church. That and that alone decides the order. Only that which is on the side of the Cross will stand the acid test while all else will be *"burned"* exactly as Sodom and Gomorrah.

PILLAR OF SALT

"But his wife looked back from behind him, and she became a pillar of salt" (Gen. 19:26).

The Seventeenth Verse of this Chapter proclaims the fact that God had pointedly warned Lot and his family not to look back as destruction was brought to bear upon the cities of the plain. Lot and his daughters obeyed, but his wife didn't. The Scripture says that she *"looked back,"* and when she did, *"She became a pillar of salt."*

The words, *"Looked back from behind him,"* as it regards this woman, means in the Hebrew that *"she kept looking back steadily, wistfully, and with desire."* Her heart was in Sodom, so her soul was in Sodom as well. Regrettably and sadly, she is now in Hell and will be there forever and forever.

Jesus reminded the world of this episode by pointedly saying, *"Remember Lot's wife"* (Lk. 17:32). Jesus also said:

"No man, having put his hand to the plough, and looking back, is fit for the Kingdom of God" (Lk. 9:62).

ABRAHAM

"And Abraham got up early in the morning to the place where he stood before the LORD" (Gen. 19:27).

We do not know exactly what Abraham knew at this time as it regards Lot. There is no indication that the Lord had told the Patriarch during the intercessory period that He would spare Lot. However, Abraham's posture at this time proclaims the fact that he believed that the Judge of all the Earth would, in fact, bring out his nephew.

"Standing before the Lord," indicates that Abraham was in prayer. In other words, the indication is that he was still interceding before the Lord as it regarded Lot, even up unto the last minute. As is obvious here, the Lord honored that intercession.

James said:

"The effectual fervent prayer of a righteous man avails much" (James 5:16).

This should encourage every Believer to constantly intercede for their lost loved ones, and even for those who are weak in the Faith, even as Lot.

SODOM AND GOMORRAH

"And he looked toward Sodom and Gomorrah, and toward all the land of the plain, and beheld, and, lo,

the smoke of the country went up as the smoke of a furnace" (Gen. 19:28).

It is believed that these cities were situated at the southern extremity of the Dead Sea.

As the Lord rained brimstone and fire upon these cities, the Scripture says that *"the smoke . . . went up as the smoke of a furnace."*

The violence of the fire is indicated by the word, *"Furnace,"* which is not the ordinary word, but means a kiln, such as that used for burning chalk into lime or for melting ores of metal. In other words, the heat was so intense that everything melted, which means there was nothing left.

Some may argue that a God Who is referred to as *"Love,"* could not do such a terrible thing, which resulted in the deaths of untold thousands of people, even including all the children and babies. My answer to that is as follows:

If God is truly a God of love, as He definitely is, then He had to do this thing, as distasteful as it may have been. Once again I go back to the idea of a surgeon removing a cancer from a patient. Even though it causes pain and suffering, the surgeon is taking such drastic action because if he doesn't, the patient will die. In other words, he performs surgery in order to save the patient.

MAJOR SURGERY

Many times in history, God has had to perform major surgery on this Earth in order to save the patient. Sin is the ruination of all that is good. It is the destroyer of all happiness, all peace, all welfare, and all security. It is the most insidious cancer, one might say, that mankind has ever known. It must be stopped, or all will be ruined.

It can be stopped by Judgment coming upon the sinner or by Judgment coming upon God's Son, Who took our place. In other words, we accept Christ Who suffered Judgment in our place, or we will be judged instead. There is no alternative; sin must be judged, and to be sure, all men are sinners. So, there is no alternative to the statement I've just made. It is either Jesus Christ or eternal Hell. That may be blunt, but it just happens to be true!

GOD REMEMBERED

"And it came to pass, when God destroyed the cities of the plain, that God remembered Abraham, and sent Lot out of the midst of the overthrow, when He overthrew the cities in the which Lot dwelt" (Gen. 19:29).

The words, *"God remembered Abraham,"* proclaim the fact that Abraham's intercessory petition did not go unanswered. This shows that God preserved Lot, not on account of his Righteousness, for Lot sinned by being in Sodom and further sinned by his delay, but because of the intercession of believing Abraham. God so dearly loved the Patriarch that He spared Lot. In this case, as we have previously stated, Abraham was a Type of Christ. He served as a mediator of God and Lot.

Presently, and forevermore, Jesus Christ is our Mediator. The Scripture says:

"For there is one God, and one Mediator between God and men, the Man Christ Jesus" (I Tim. 2:5).

Presently we can certainly pray for others, even as did Abraham, actually interceding on their behalf; however, no human being since Christ can serve as a Mediator, that prerogative being that of Christ Alone. When the Holy Spirit said that there is *"one Mediator between God and men,"* He meant exactly what He said. That means there aren't 10, five, or two, only one, and that One is *"the Man Christ Jesus."*

ONE MEDIATOR

This means that every Catholic priest, and any other person who might label himself as such, is blaspheming. In effect, by their very actions and supposed office, they are saying that Christ did not accomplish the task at Calvary, and human instrumentation is needed. Such thinking is blasphemy, actually undermining the entirety of the Scriptures.

Furthermore, the Scripture tells us that Christ was not always a Mediator. While He has always been God, He has not always been the Mediator. He became that by becoming *"the Man Christ Jesus,"* but, as well, that alone did not make Him the Mediator.

He became the Mediator only after He *"gave Himself a ransom for all"* (I Tim. 2:6). This speaks of the Cross, which gave Christ the right to become and be the Mediator between God and men. He atoned there for all sin by the giving of Himself, and did so as our Substitute and Representative Man (I Cor. 15:45-47).

When it says that God remembered, it doesn't mean that God has a tendency to forget. Since God knows everything, He never forgets anything, with the exception of the sins He has forgiven and put out of existence.

When the Bible speaks of God remembering, it means God now breaks into the situation to do something about it, whatever it might be. God sent His Angels to bring Lot out of Sodom, not because Lot deserved it, but for Abraham's sake. Thus, although Sodom was not spared, the intent of Abraham's intercession was answered.

"In these, the closing days of time,
"What joy the glorious hope affords,

"That soon oh, wondrous truth sublime!
"He shall reign, King of kings and Lord of lords."

"The signs around in Earth and air,
"Are painted on the starlit sky,
"God's Faithful Witnesses declare,
"That the coming of the Saviour draweth nigh."

"The dead in Christ who 'neath us lie,
"In countless numbers, all shall rise,
"When through the portals of the sky,
"He shall come to prepare our Paradise."

"And we who, living, yet remain,
"Caught up, shall meet our Faithful Lord,
"This hope we cherish not in vain,
"But we comfort one another by this word."

ABRAHAM

CHAPTER

21

The Daughters Of Lot

THE DAUGHTERS OF LOT

"And Lot went up out of Zoar, and dwelt in the mountain, and his two daughters with him; for he feared to dwell in Zoar: and he dwelt in a cave, he and his two daughters" (Gen. 19:30).

Lot either fled Zoar because the people there threatened to kill him, perhaps blaming him somewhat for the destruction of the other cities, or else, he was fearful that God might smite this city as well.

Regarding the latter, he had reason to fear. Even though Zoar was but a small town, it was as wicked as Sodom. It was a center of idolatrous worship for the whole area.

The Scripture says, *"He dwelt in a cave."* Let's look at that a moment:

His wealth had once been so great that he and Abraham could not dwell together because of the size of their herds, but he is now living in a cave, with this being his miserable home.

However, wealth or no wealth, there is no profit in living for Satan. Per capita, the suicide rate among the up and out is far greater than it is for the down and out. Let it be understood that all without God, no matter how *"up"* they may be according to the view of the world, are at the same time, *"out."* The only satisfaction in life is living for Christ. That's why Jesus said:

"Take heed, and beware of covetousness: for a man's life consists not in the abundance of the things which he possesses" (Lk. 12:15).

The Scripture says that Lot *"feared."* When one is out of the Will of God, thereby, out of the Presence of God, which means he is devoid of the Leadership of the Lord, fear rules. It is a terrible, disquieting condition for one to find oneself. In that state, it doesn't matter where one goes or what one does; the fear remains. The reasons are obvious or, at least, certainly should be.

LOT'S DAUGHTERS

"And the firstborn said unto the younger, Our father is old, and there is not a man in the Earth to come in unto us after the manner of all the Earth" (Gen. 19:31).

What the two daughters of Lot were about to do constituted a monstrous sin, as is overly obvious. However, family and preservation of the family were important, very important in ancient times. Since Lot was old and now poor, with all his belongings destroyed along with Sodom, his daughters saw no prospect for marriage. As well, and to which we have already alluded, these girls had been adversely influenced by the low morals of Sodom. While they knew God and, in their weak way, served the Lord, one might say, the entirety of their dilemma is not to be blamed on them, but rather their father. While no sin is excusable, still, at times, there are mitigating circumstances.

Considering all of this, it is not strange that the older daughter suggested incest as the only way they could preserve the family line.

Lot had long since ceased trusting God, but rather his own ingenuity, so his daughters followed suit. The Lord could have given them husbands, but they didn't understand the path of Faith, not at all!

WINE

"Come, let us make our father drink wine, and we will lie with him, that we may preserve seed of our father" (Gen. 19:32).

Despondent and full of fear, Lot succumbs to the lure of alcoholic beverage.

This is at least one of the reasons that the world is sated with alcohol, nicotine, and drugs. It is guilt-ridden, and, cut off from God, it seeks a substitute. But alas, such substitutes always put one in bondage, with their situation now the worse instead of the better. How quickly these things cease to be a crutch and now become a slave-master.

As we look at all of this, we find the utter degradation of Lot and his family, which thus ends in his intense shame.

Concerning this, Mackintosh said:

"And then see his end! — his own daughters make him drunk, and in his drunkenness he becomes the instrument of bringing into existence the Ammonites and the Moabites — the determined enemies of the people of God. What a volume of solemn instruction is here! Oh, my reader, see here what the world is! See what a fatal thing it is to allow the heart to go out after it! What a commentary is Lot's history upon the brief but comprehensive admonition, 'Love not the world'! This world's Sodoms and its Zoars are all alike. There is no security, no peace, no rest, no solid satisfaction for the heart therein. The Judgment of God hangs over the whole scene; and He only holds back the sword in long-suffering Mercy, not willing that any should perish, but that all should come to repentance."[1]

THE FIRSTBORN

"And they made their father drink wine that night: and the firstborn went in, and lay with her father; and he perceived not when she lay down, nor when she arose" (Gen. 19:33).

This was no drunken orgy, but still, it was a revolting sin, which should be obvious. As we look into the entirety of this sordid picture, let us see the cause of it.

The means was alcohol while the reason and the cause was a lack of Faith. Dealing with alcohol first, once again, as with Noah, we see the result of intoxicating beverage. Understanding this, how could any Believer place a seal of approval on any type of alcoholic consumption, even so-called moderate drinking? But yet, the real cause of this revolting sin was a lack of faith. In fact, as it regards the Believer, the cause of all sin is a lack of faith. Paul said, *"Whatsoever is not of faith is sin"* (Rom. 14:23). What did the Apostle mean by that statement?

FAITH

As stated, as it regards Believers, if we trace the origin of sin in whatever form, we will always find, without exception, that the cause is a lack of faith.

When Paul speaks of Faith, he is speaking of Christ and what Christ has done for us at the Cross, that ever being the Object of our Faith. If that ceases to be the object, while it still may be faith, it's not faith which God will recognize. So, let the reader understand that always, and without exception, Faith in the Bible refers to *"Jesus Christ and Him Crucified"* as its Object. When the Believer keeps his Faith anchored in the Cross, everything comes into proper perspective. When his faith is moved to other things, then everything is out of place.

When Lot chose the well-watered plains of Jordan, which led toward Sodom, he had moved his faith from the Cross to other things, such as money, etc. Let us say it again:

Sin always begins with our faith being transferred from the correct Object, which is the Cross, to something else, and it doesn't matter what the something else is.

UNDERSTANDING THE CROSS

Having taken this course, Lot ultimately moved into Sodom because now his faith was in his own ingenuity and ability. So, that's what his daughters learned. They knew God, but they knew nothing about trusting God, and, above all, they knew nothing of what this was all about, which would ultimately lead to the coming of the Redeemer and the Cross. They could have known, and Lot could have known. They had the greatest opportunity in the world. Few men in history were given Revelations from God as was Abraham. So, they didn't know because they had little desire to know.

How many Christians presently are like Lot and his daughters? They know God, but they know little about God.

One can know trust and Faith only as one understands the Cross. Otherwise, what one refers to as faith, while it may be faith, it's not faith which God will recognize. In other words, it's not Saving and keeping Faith, which alone comes by one's proper understanding of the Cross, which gives one a proper understanding of the Word.

So, that night, Lot resorted to alcohol because his Faith had long since been misplaced. His daughters committed an even more heinous sin by committing incest with him, and even though he was not a party to that crime, it actually was his fault.

THE YOUNGER

"And it came to pass on the morrow, that the first-born said unto the younger, Behold, I lay yesternight with my father: let us make him drink wine this night also; and you go in, and lie with him, that we may preserve seed of our father" (Gen. 19:34).

The details of this account clearly show that when Lot went to the mountain cave, he endeavored to escape from his problems, not by carrying them to God's Throne, where all Believers should carry them, but by drowning them in dissipation. This wretched man, who had once been a Saint in God's Church, lost his way because he moved his faith from the Cross of Christ, so to speak, to other things.

There is one glimmer of light in the whole thing. The daughters apparently believed that unless their father was drunk, he would never be brought to assent as it regarded their lewd proposal. Twice overcome by wine, he was twice in succession dishonored by his daughters. Twice overcome while in his drunken stupor, he allowed himself to commit an act which almost out-sodomized Sodom. This shows to what depths a Saint may fall when once he turns his back on God!

DESPAIR, DRUNKENNESS, AND DECEPTION

"And they made their father drink wine that night also: and the younger arose, and lay with him; and he perceived not when she lay down, nor when she arose" (Gen. 19:35).

These girls had been in Sodom most of, if not all, of their lives. Consequently, they had been greatly influenced by the low moral standards of the city, which is a gross understatement. So, it is not strange that the older daughter suggested incest as the only way they could preserve the family line.

One can see in this the picture of so many modern Christian families. These girls knew about God, but they were far more influenced by the evil of Sodom than they were the Righteousness of Heaven. In fact, their very position proclaimed where their attachments were, and you can lay all of this at the feet of their father, Lot.

They knew nothing of Faith, of what it meant to really live for God, or what their purpose in life should have been. So, when they found themselves in this dilemma, they turned to their own evil ingenuity instead of trusting the Lord.

As stated, how many modern Christians fall into the same category? The answer is sadly obvious, *"Almost all."*

MODERN CHRISTIANS?

Sometime back, I occasioned to know of a terrible problem which had arisen in a particular family. I suggested to them that they take it to the Lord, especially considering that they loudly proclaimed themselves to be good Christians.

In those days, we were having two prayer meetings a day at the Ministry, and I was hoping they would come to the prayer meetings, at least the ones around which they could arrange their schedule. Their response was tepid, to say the least!

Some days later, it was related to me that the dear lady had actually said in response to my invitation, *"I just don't get anything out of it!"*

That's a strange statement coming from a Christian. What in the world did she mean, that she *"got nothing out of seeking God"?* Was she meaning that she did not want to pray with us, or was she meaning that God didn't answer prayer? Consequently, it was a waste of time!

I don't know the answer to those questions; I only know her response. I also know that in the not too distant future, the thing of which she was greatly concerned went into total wreckage, with all types of sorrow and heartache.

As we've already stated, it is all a matter of Faith. Is our Faith anchored in the Cross, or is it anchored elsewhere?

RESULTS

"Thus were both the daughters of Lot with child by their father" (Gen. 19:36).

After this, Lot disappears from sacred history, with not even his death being recorded.

It is believed by some that Abraham took Lot and his daughters into his home and supported them. There is no record of such; however, one cannot imagine Abraham seeing his nephew homeless and penniless and not helping him. He had risked his life to save him from the heathen king who had taken him and his family captive some years before, so it is certain that he would provide help at this time as well.

THE MOABITES AND THE AMMONITES

"And the firstborn bore a son, and called his name Moab: the same is the father of the Moabites unto this day.

"And the younger, she also bore a son, and called his name Ben-ammi: the same is the father of the children of Ammon unto this day" (Gen. 19:37-38).

"Moab" means, *"From my father,"* while *"Ben-ammi"* means, *"Son of my people."* They are the ancestors of the Moabites and the Ammonites.

Despite their ignoble beginnings, the Lord showed a concern for them as descendants of Lot (Deut. 2:9, 19), but regrettably, they later became enemies of Israel (I Sam. 14:47; II Ki. 3:5; II Chron. 20:1, 22).

As it was then with Sodom and Gomorrah, so it will be soon with this world. The Believer, consequently, must see what Lot failed to see and, regrettably, what many, if not most, modern Christians fail to see as well.

This world and all that it holds is passing and is of short duration. As stated, the Judgment of God hangs heavily over it.

Furthermore, we're living at the very conclusion of the Church Age. The foundation is already being laid for the advent of the Antichrist, so that makes the Rapture of the Church even much closer. While Christ is definitely going to take over this world, it will not be as many preachers claim.

DOMINIONISM

It is claimed by many that Christianity is gradually going to take over the entirety of the world, actually coming to terms with other religions. Then, they say, Christ will come back and the Millennium will begin. Of course, these individuals believe that the Book of Revelation is now history. In other words, they believe that it has already been fulfilled many centuries ago and holds no validity for the future. How anyone could come to that conclusion, at least if they read this Book with any degree of honesty at all, is beyond my comprehension.

The truth is, Jesus Christ is definitely going to take over this world, but it will not be by Christianity gradually changing society. Rather, it will be in a cataclysmic, even violent way. Some 2,600 years ago, the Lord gave a dream to a heathen king by the name of Nebuchadnezzar. In a great statue, he saw the coming kingdoms of this world but did not know what it all meant, even as the world presently knows nothing of futuristic events, which the Bible so boldly proclaims. Daniel interpreted the dream for the man and then said concerning this giant statue which he saw in his dream:

"You saw till that a Stone was cut out without hands (Jesus), which smote the image upon his feet that were of iron and clay, and broke them to pieces . . . and the Stone that smote the image became a great mountain, and filled the whole Earth" (Dan. 2:34-35).

WHAT THE SCRIPTURE TEACHES

As stated, it is definitely true that Jesus is going to rule the entirety of this Earth. However, this will not take place until the Great Tribulation has come upon this Earth, which will conclude with the Second Coming. In fact, the Great Tribulation will be so bad that Jesus said there has never been anything like it and never will there be anything like it again (Mat. 24:21).

The Second Coming will take place at the conclusion of the Great Tribulation, actually in the midst of the Battle of Armageddon. It will be a time of a tremendous display of Power such as the nations and kingdoms of this world have never seen, with the Antichrist and all of his armies being violently overthrown. So, clearly, the Scripture teaches that the rosy picture painted by some preachers is only a fabrication. It's not Scriptural! In fact, the Holy Spirit through Paul said, *"This know also, that in the last days perilous times shall come"* (II Tim. 3:1).

He also said, *"Now the Spirit speaks expressly, that in the latter times some shall depart from the Faith, giving heed to seducing spirits, and doctrines of demons"* (I Tim. 4:1).

So, apostasy is predicted for the church as it regards its closing days. Regrettably, that apostasy is even now upon us. The world not only tries to build its kingdom on Earth, but at the same time, many in the church are attempting to do the same thing.

Our business as Believers is not to build an earthly kingdom, but rather to *"preach the Gospel to every creature"* (Mk. 16:15).

*"There will be a great reunion in the sky,
"When the Saviour comes again,
"Hallelujah, we shall see Him by and by,
"When the Saviour comes again."*

"At the shout, the dead in Christ shall all arise,
"When the Saviour comes again,
"Living ones caught up to meet them in the skies,
"When the Saviour comes again."

"Wonderful, oh, wonderful the day will be,
"When the Saviour comes again,
"Then at last beholding, we His Face shall see,
"When the Saviour comes again."

ABRAHAM

CHARTER

22

Abraham And Abimelech

ABRAHAM AND ABIMELECH

THE SOUTH COUNTRY

"And Abraham journeyed from thence toward the south country, and dwelled between Kadesh and Shur, and sojourned in Gerar" (Gen. 20:1).

We find Abraham often journeying, which he was probably intended by the Lord to do, in that he was to be ever reminded that Canaan was not intended for a permanent habitation but for a constant pilgrimage. However, it seems that Abraham did not exactly seek the Face of the Lord all of the time as to exactly where the journey should lead him. He will once again go south, which will prove exactly as it did before, to be the occasion of another sad spectacle. This time he did not go into Egypt, but he went toward Egypt, which he should not have done. As we have stated, man, if left on his own, cannot learn spiritual lessons. For reasons known only to him, Abraham journeys south and, thereby, forsakes the path of Faith. As such, he will once again sink into a degradation that is contemptible.

We will find here that an old sin is an easy sin.

DECEPTION

"And Abraham said of Sarah his wife, She is my sister: and Abimelech king of Gerar sent, and took Sarah" (Gen. 20:2).

This is the same sin that Abraham committed in Egypt. Exactly as Lot, he left the path of Faith, thereby, trusting in his own ingenuity, which always gets us into trouble. Because it's so important, please allow me to say again what we've said some paragraphs back.

Every sin is always a departure from Faith. Faith in Christ and Him Crucified is the only answer to the sin problem, and we mean the only answer, as it is to every problem. The trouble is, the church all too often deals with symptoms as it regards sin instead of the cause. In fact, the church little knows the cause, so it manufactures its own causes.

One of the primary examples is, if we sin, so the church says, we do so because that's what we want to do. While sin definitely is a matter of choice, it is not a choice as one thinks.

SIN AND ITS CAUSE

There is no true Christian who wants to sin. The Divine Nature is in him, ever propelling him toward Righteousness and godliness, which means that sin is totally and completely an aberration. In other words, as it regards the path of faithlessness, Satan can make a person do something that he doesn't want to do.

I realize that most Christians would disagree with that statement, but it is the truth, and it's happening millions of times each day all over the world. Let's see what the Word of God says:

"For that which I do I allow not (understand not): for what I would, that do I not; but what I hate, that do I" (Rom. 7:15). What in the world did Paul mean by this statement?

ROMANS, CHAPTER 7

Romans, Chapter 7, is the account of the experience of the Apostle Paul immediately after he was Saved, and which continued for several years, at least up unto the time that the Lord gave him the meaning of the New Covenant, which is the meaning of the Cross. Romans, Chapter 7, is not, as many preachers claim, the account of Paul before he was Saved. What good would that do?

From the Passage just quoted, it is easy to understand that Paul is saying here that he is doing things that he doesn't want to do. In other words, he was trying very, very hard not to sin but was failing just the same. He went on to say:

"For I know that in me (that is, in my flesh,) dwells no good thing: for to will is present with me; but how to perform that which is good I find not" (Rom. 7:18).

He plainly tells us here that willpower, within itself, is not enough. While the will is important (whosoever will . . .), still, if that is our means of victory, we will fail. Such an effort constitutes the Christian trying to live for God by his own power and strength, which he cannot do. In fact, the failures will get worse and worse, despite all of his efforts to do and be otherwise.

RESPONSIBILITY?

Consequently, it is very easy to see in these Passages that Christians are not sinning because they want to sin, but rather because they embarked upon a wrong course. This means their faith is in the wrong place, which means that the Holy Spirit simply will not help in that type of situation, and this leaves the individual helpless.

Oh yes, the Believer is definitely responsible for his actions. There is no place or time that he isn't responsible. However, he is not responsible in the way that most in the church claims it to be so. In other words, if a true Christian sins, he is not sinning just because he wants to sin. He is sinning simply because he has left the path of true Faith and is now functioning in the flesh.

As we have stated, no true Christian wants to sin, but yet, at the same time, there may be times that the flesh will want something that is not proper. However, the inner man, which speaks of the Divine Nature, doesn't want anything that's ungodly. Paul also said, *"For I delight in the Law of God after the inward man: But I see another Law in my members, warring against the Law of my mind, and bringing me into captivity to the Law of Sin which is in my members"* (Rom. 7:22-23). In fact, this is the struggle in which all Christians always engage. If the Believer doesn't know or understand God's Prescribed Order of Victory, which is Faith in Christ and the Cross exclusively, failure will always be the end result.

Unfortunately, many preachers, if not most, totally misinterpret the Seventh Chapter of Romans. They do so simply because the things that Paul is saying completely blows to pieces their belief system. So, they try to say that Paul was speaking of his life before Conversion, which is ridiculous. The truth is the following:

After Paul was Saved on the road to Damascus and baptized with the Holy Spirit some three days later, he set out to be the Child of God that he should be. He said:

> **"For I was alive without the Law once** *(Paul is referring to himself personally and his Conversion to Christ; the Law, he states, had nothing to do with that Conversion; neither did it have anything to do with his life in Christ)***: but when the Commandment came** *(having just been Saved and not understanding the Cross of Christ, he tried to live for God by keeping the Commandments through his own strength and power; in his defense, no one else at that time understood the Cross; in fact, the meaning of the Cross, which is actually the meaning of the New Covenant, would be given to Paul)***, sin revived** *(the sin nature will always, without exception, revive under such circumstances, which results in failure)***, and I died**

(he was not meaning that he physically died, as would be obvious, but that he died to the Commandment; in other words, he failed to obey no matter how hard he tried; let all Believers understand that if the Apostle Paul couldn't live for God in this manner, neither can you!)" **(Rom. 7:9).**

MODERN CHRISTIANS

The tragedy is, most modern Christians, and we speak of those who truly know and love the Lord, are trying to live for God in the same manner that Paul did before he was given God's Prescribed Order of Victory, which is the Cross. In other words, Believers are trying to live for God by the means of willpower. As previously stated, while the will is definitely important, within itself, it's not able to carry us through.

GOD'S PRESCRIBED ORDER OF VICTORY

We could write volumes on this particular subject, but hopefully, this short diagram will give you an idea of that which the Holy Spirit gave to the Apostle Paul:
- Jesus Christ is the Source of all things that we receive from God (Jn. 1:1-2, 14, 29; Col. 2:10-15).
- The Cross of Christ is the Means by which all of these wonderful things are given to us (Rom. 6:1-14; I Cor. 1:17, 18, 23; 2:2).
- With Christ being the Source and the Cross being the Means, the Cross of Christ, without exception, must be the Object of our Faith, and the only Object of our Faith (Gal., Chpt. 5; 6:14; Col. 2:10-15).
- With the Cross of Christ as the Object of our Faith, and we speak of what He there did and not of the wooden beam on which He died, the Holy Spirit, without Whom we can do nothing, will then grandly

and gloriously help us, and there's nothing He cannot do (Rom. 8:1-11; Eph. 2:13-18).

TRUE FAITH

That which we are about to say, we have already said many times and will continue to say it many times in this Volume because it's so very, very important. In fact, it is the single most important thing that the Christian could ever hear, read, or know.

Jesus Christ and Him Crucified must always be, as stated, the Object of our Faith. As well, we must always have the Holy Spirit as it regards His Power, and all else that He is, for that matter. If our Faith is anchored in the Sacrifice of Christ, then the Holy Spirit will grandly help us. Otherwise, if we move our faith from the Cross of Christ to other things, we deny ourselves the Help of the Spirit (Rom. 8:1-11). This means that we're left on our own, and failure is going to be the result no matter how hard we might try otherwise.

So, the church, little knowing the reason for failure, only knows to do what the world does if there is failure, and that is to engage in punishment. That's not the answer! It is only adding insult to injury. In the first place, the one doing the punishing may very well be in worse spiritual condition than the one who is being punished. Furthermore, and even more important, for us to seek to punish someone who has failed is, in essence, insulting Christ by saying that Christ was not punished enough on the Cross, and we have to add something to what He has already done. Doesn't the reader understand just how abominable such thinking actually is?

Jesus suffered for us, and His Suffering had to do with sin. Furthermore, there is no way that suffering or punishment on our part can atone for sin. Once again, if we think that such is the case, this means that we do not at all understand the Atonement and, in fact, are making up our own Salvation, which is an abominable in the Eyes of God. It is Jesus Christ and Him Crucified, or it is nothing!

THE PATH OF FAITH

So, Abraham leaves the path of Faith and lies about Sarah. To be sure, his sin this time is far more abominable than it was down in Egypt because the Lord has recently told him that Sarah is going to bear a child. This means that the entirety of the great Plan of God for the human race is placed in jeopardy.

It may be said that this was Satan's second effort to hinder the Birth of the Messiah by the intervention of a heathen father; therefore, he would and could incite Abimelech to this action.

This means that Abraham's failure on this occasion was deeper than when he was in Egypt. As stated, so long as the Christian walks in the path of Faith, he is clothed with dignity and ennobled with courage. However, when directly he leaves that path, he falls even lower than the children of Satan. Nothing but Faith can impart true elevation to a man's character because it alone connects the soul with God. Please remember, when we speak of Faith, always and without exception, we are speaking of Faith in Christ and His Cross.

In the confession of Abraham to Abimelech, there is this painful feature revealed in his character. He starts upon his course with a falsehood and compels his wife to be the degraded sharer of the lie.

INCREDIBLE?

If it is objected that this whole occurrence is incredible because it is claimed that no heathen prince would desire to marry a woman upwards of 90 years of age, or to conceive such a passion for her that to secure her, he would murder her husband — the very fate which Abraham feared for himself — we must understand that God undoubtedly had miraculously renewed the youth of Sarah so that she became sufficiently youthful in appearance to suitably become the wife of this Philistine prince. Even though she was some 90 years of age, she evidently looked like she was 30 years of age, if that. Considering that she was already beautiful, we now see the attraction.

To not believe this is to limit God.

If it is to be noticed, when this Text was written, the Holy Spirit through Moses was careful to delineate that Sarah was Abraham's wife and not his sister, at least in the capacity of which he claims. Once again, Abraham sets out to deceive Abimelech, which was the title of the Philistine prince, exactly as he had tried to deceive Pharaoh in Egypt. Let us say it again, *"An old sin is an easy sin."*

INTERVENTION

"But God came to Abimelech in a dream by night, and said to him, Behold, you are but a dead man, for the woman which you have taken; for she is a man's wife" (Gen. 20:3).

Three things are said here:

1. God revealed Himself to Abimelech in a dream.

2. What the Lord said to Abimelech greatly scared him. In essence, He said, *"If you touch Sarah, you can consider yourself a dead man."*

3. If God had not intervened, Abraham's sin would have been disastrous. If it is to be noticed, Sarah is again referred to by the Holy Spirit as Abraham's wife. The *"sister"* thing was mentioned only by Abraham and

not by the Lord. The truth is, Sarah was Abraham's half-sister, both of them having the same father but not the same mother.

It had been some 20 years since the episode in Egypt, but let us say it again, *"An old sin is an easy sin."*

ABIMELECH

"But Abimelech had not come near her: and he said, LORD, will You slay also a righteous nation?" (Gen. 20:4).

The Lord had intervened with a dream before Abimelech had a chance to come near Sarah.

Already knowing of the destruction of Sodom and Gomorrah, the Philistine prince fears that he and his people are in for the same destruction unless the Lord is pacified quickly.

He refers to God as *"LORD,"* in effect, referring to Him as Deity. The question begs to be asked: considering the Power that the Lord had just unleashed as it regards the destruction of the cities of the plain, which were close to Philistine territory, and considering that God appears to this Philistine prince in a dream, surely that was enough evidence to prove to this man that Jehovah was the True God. Why then would he not serve God?

That same question can be asked presently of the untold millions in this world who know about God, but yet, refuse to serve Him. However, the major problem with most who live in a so-called Christian nation is that they actually think they are serving Him when, in reality, they've never been Born-Again. Deception is an awful thing, and it has many ways in which to plague the human race. Once again, we come back to Faith, or the lack thereof.

Millions have faith in God, but it's in the wrong kind of way. True Faith is always anchored in Jesus Christ and Him Crucified. Otherwise, while it may be very religious, it is not acceptable to God. Regrettably, Faith in Christ and His Cross is not acceptable to much of the world and even not much of the church.

CLEAN HANDS

"Said he not unto me, She is my sister? and she, even she herself said, He is my brother: in the integrity of my heart and innocency of my hands have I done this" (Gen. 20:5).

This heathen prince pleads his innocence before God, at least as far as the matter of Sarah is concerned. Abraham claimed that Sarah was his sister, and Sarah backed up what he had said by claiming that Abraham was her brother. So, on this basis, Abimelech took her into his harem.

In this matter, the man was innocent. It was Abraham and Sarah, as well, who had done wrong.

Forgetting God's Ability to protect his life, he had recourse to the same stratagem which he had adopted in Egypt years before. Here we have the father of the faithful carried away by taking his eye off of God. He is no longer a man of Faith, but rather of craftiness and deception.

How true it is that we are only strong as we cling to God in the sense of our perfect weakness. So long as we are in the path of His Appointment, nothing can harm us. Had Abraham simply leaned on God, the men of Gerar would not have meddled with him, and it was his privilege to have vindicated God's Faithfulness in the midst of the most appalling difficulties. Thus, too, he would have maintained his own dignity as a man of Faith.

DISHONORING GOD

Concerning this, Mackintosh said:
"It is often a source of sorrow to the heart to mark how the Children of God dishonor Him, and, as a consequence,

lower ourselves before the world by losing the sense of His sufficiency for every emergency.

"*So long as we live in the realization of the Truth that all our hope is in God, so long shall we be above the world in every shape and form. There is nothing so elevating to the whole moral being as Faith: it carries one entirely beyond the reach of this world's thoughts; for how can those of the world, or even worldly-minded Christians, understand the life of Faith? Impossible! The springs on which it draws lie far away beyond their comprehension. They live on the surface of present things. So long as they can see what they deem a proper foundation for hope and confidence, so long they are hopeful and confident; but the idea of resting solely on the promise of an unseen God, they understand not.*

"*But the man of Faith is calm in the midst of scenes in which nature can see nothing. In fact, none but those who know God can ever approve the actings of Faith; for none but they really understand the solid and truly-reasonable ground of such actions.*"[1]

PROTECTION

"*And God said unto him in a dream, Yes, I know that you did this in the integrity of your heart; for I also withheld you from sinning against Me: therefore suffered I you not to touch her*" (Gen. 20:6).

Not only does Abimelech assert his position, but the Lord admits the plea. And yet, this Philistine king indulges in polygamy and claims the right of taking the female relatives of anyone passing through his territory to add them to his harem.

However, his words mean no more than that he was not consciously violating any of his own rules of morality and, thus, illustrate the Gospel principle that men will be punished, not by an absolute degree, but equitably, according to their knowledge (Lk. 12:47-48).

Abimelech was doing wrong and was suffering punishment, but the punishment was remedial for his advancement in right-knowing and right-doing. It is thus a means of Revelation that men have attained to a proper understanding of the moral Law. Though often called, *"The Law of Nature,"* yet nature does not give it but only acknowledges it when given.

The inner Light, in fact, is but a faint and inconstant glimmering, for Christ Alone is the True Light; for only by Him does the Law of Nature become a clear rule for Christian guidance (Mat. 6:23; Jn. 1:9; Rom. 2:14-15).

A PROPHET

"Now therefore restore the man his wife; for he is a Prophet, and he shall pray for you, and you shall live: and if you restore her not, know that you shall surely die, you, and all who are yours" (Gen. 20:7).

It should be noticed in this Text that even though Abraham has done wrong, very wrong, his position as a Prophet has not been diminished, nor, in fact, any part of his Calling.

In the history of God's People, whether we look at them as a whole or as individuals, we are often struck with the amazing difference between what we are in God's View and what we are in the view of the world. God sees His People in Christ. He looks at us through Christ; hence, He sees us *"without spot or wrinkle or any such thing."* We are as Christ is before God. We are perfected forever as to our standing in Christ.

THE OTHER SIDE

The fact is, in ourselves, we are poor, feeble, imperfect, stumbling, and inconsistent creatures. Inasmuch as it is what we are in ourselves, and that alone, that the world takes knowledge of, it is that, that the difference seems so great between the Divine and the human estimate. Thus, when Balak seeks to curse the Seed of Abraham, Jehovah's word is, *"I have not beheld iniquity in Jacob, neither have I seen perverseness in Israel."*

He then said, *"How goodly are your tents, O Jacob, and your tabernacles, O Israel"* (Num. 23:21; 24:5).

The outward observance was very obvious that Israel, in the natural, did not measure up to these things, but that's the way God saw them simply because He looked at them through Christ. He does the same with all Believers, again because of Christ.

According to many modern Pentecostal denominations, due to his failure, Abraham would have had to cease all ministry for two years, etc. Now, while such foolishness may sound satisfactory to the carnal ear, such thinking and action are actually an abomination with God. It belittles the Sacrifice of Christ, actually saying that what He did at the Cross is not enough.

When we cease to be Biblical, we become foolish!

CHRIST AND THE CROSS

At the same time, it should be understood that this in no way condones sin in any fashion. It's just that sin and wrongdoing are so evil and so bad that only Christ and what He did at the Cross can cleanse this stain. Man's foolish efforts at punishment, or his own ways and means of atonement, are woefully insufficient. Again I emphasize the fact that when we try to add something to the shed Blood of Christ, we greatly insult the Lord and His Finished Work.

Abraham was a Prophet before the problem, he was a Prophet during the problem, and he was a Prophet after the problem. No, this does not condone the problem, and, in fact, great hurt always accompanies sin, as should be obvious. However, as we've already stated, sin is so awful, so terrible, and so destructive that it took the Cross to address this thing. If we try to use other means or methods other than the Cross to address sin, we sin greatly.

THE OFFICE OF THE PROPHET

In fact, even though Abraham, Moses, and Enoch were Prophets, it was Samuel who first stood in the Office of the Prophet (I Sam. 9:9).

One might say that the Office of the Prophet was twofold:

1. To announce the Will of God to men (Ex. 4:15; 7:1).

2. To intercede with God for men (Jer. 7:16; 11:14; 14:11).

Now, let's go back to Abraham: he might lower himself in the view of Abimelech, king of Gerar, which he did, and Abimelech might rebuke him, which he did, as well; yet, when God comes to deal with the case, He says to Abimelech, *"Behold, you are but a dead man"* and of Abraham He says, *"He is a Prophet, he shall pray for you."*

Yes, with all *"the integrity of his heart and the innocency of his hands,"* the king of Gerar was *"but a dead man."* Moreover, he must be a debtor to the prayers of the erring and inconsistent stranger for the restoration of the health of his household. Such is the Manner of God.

God may have many a secret controversy with His Child on the grounds of erroneous ways, if, in fact, that be the case, but directly the enemy enters a suit against the Child of God, Jehovah ever pleads His Servant's Cause, *"Touch not My Anointed, and do My Prophets no* harm." Then, *"He who touches you, touches the apple of My Eye."* And then, *"It is God Who justifies, who is he who condemns?"*

The idea is: no dart of the enemy can ever penetrate the shield behind which the Lord has hidden the very feeblest lamb of His Blood-bought flock.

THE TESTIMONY

"Therefore Abimelech rose early in the morning, and called all his servants, and told all these things in their ears: and the men were sore afraid" (Gen. 20:8).

The very next morning after the dream that night, Abimelech sought to rectify the situation.

In all of this, Abimelech is taught that he does not himself hold a near relationship to God but requires someone to speak for him. This means he had need of fuller instruction, and he ought to try to attain to a higher level with God. He certainly had the opportunity to do so; however, the following Verses tell us that He allowed Abraham's previous performance to greatly hinder him as it regards this of which we speak.

This is one of the great hurts of failure. It always causes someone to stumble. To be sure, there is no excuse for the stumbling, as there was no excuse for Abimelech; however, the human spirit is fallen as a result of what happened in the Garden of Eden. As a result, it seldom seeks the higher level, but rather uses any excuse to continue to wallow in the mudhole.

ABIMELECH AND ABRAHAM

"Then Abimelech called Abraham, and said unto him, What have you done unto us? and what have I offended you, that you have brought on me and on my kingdom a great sin? you have done deeds unto me that ought not to be done" (Gen. 20:9).

We will find here that the questions which Abimelech posed to Abraham were very similar to those posed by Pharaoh concerning the same sin (Gen. 12:18).

As Abimelech spoke to Abraham, his words were unquestionably designed to convey a severe reproach, which it did.

It seems that Abimelech's conversation stems more so from fear and frustration than anything else.

It is interesting that this heathen king understood the word, *"Sin,"* which means that he had some knowledge of God that was greatly increased after the dream he had.

As well, it is interesting that he really did not accuse Abraham of sin, but rather of Abraham putting him in a position to where he might have sinned, and sinned greatly, which would have affected the entirety of his kingdom. This is what he gathered from what the Lord told him in the dream, and he was right about the matter. When he spoke about what Abraham had done, he merely said, *"You have done deeds unto me that ought not to be done."*

All of this shows that he was greatly afraid of Abraham. To be frank, he conducted himself exactly as he should have, and God rewarded him by healing him and all of his household of the plague, which had caused him great problems.

THE QUESTION

"And Abimelech said unto Abraham, What did you see, that caused you to do this thing?" (Gen. 20:10).

Abimelech asked the question as to what was in Abraham's mind that would have caused him to take this particular position.

He, in effect, is saying, *"We aren't murderers, and furthermore, we treat people right."*

Abimelech seems to take pride in his just rule. Every indication is, he seems to have been a just king, especially considering that his knowledge of the Lord was very sketchy. Unfortunately, his first contact with one who truly knew God, at least as far as we know, did not present the Lord in the best light.

How guilty are all of us in this respect. We are recipients and projectors of His Light, but how so often what we, in fact, project is not entirely that which we have received.

FEAR

"And Abraham said, Because I thought, Surely the fear of God is not in this place; and they will kill me for my wife's sake" (Gen. 20:11).

Abraham speaks of the fear of God, but the truth is, he was operating in human fear and not in faith. So, in his mind, he projected a scenario which, in fact, would never have happened.

How so often we modern Believers operate in the same capacity. We operate from the spirit of fear, rather than the Power of Faith. Even at our highest, too often, we make our plans and then ask God to bless those plans. Such a position is that which God will not take. He blesses only the Plans which He Alone has instituted.

PROPER FAITH

Even though we have explained it several times already, due to the serious nature of the subject, and due to the fact that much error has been propagated in the last several decades, I think it would be difficult for us to address the subject too much.

When we speak of Faith, it must always be understood that it's Faith in Christ and Him Crucified. This must ever be the Object of our Faith, or else, it will be faith that God will not recognize.

We talk about having Faith in the Word, which is certainly correct. However, we should also understand that our claims of having Faith in the Word of God are not valid unless we first understand that everything is based on the Sacrifice of Christ. In fact, the Sacrifice of Christ is the Story of the Bible. It's not the other way around, meaning that the Word of God merely portrays that particular Story. The Word is the Story, and the Story is the Word.

THE FIRST OBJECT LESSON

The first object lesson, as it regards the Word of God and the great Plan of Redemption, which is what the Word is all about, is found in Genesis, Chapter 4. In graphic detail, we have there the illustration of Cain and Abel and the sacrifices offered by these two men. One was accepted by God (the blood sacrifice of Abel), with the other rejected by God (the sacrifice of Cain, which was vegetables or some such work of his own hands). This particular Chapter sets the stage for the entirety of the Bible. It is the Sacrifice of Christ on the Cross versus every other sacrifice of which one can think. All sacrifices are rejected, other than Christ and what He did at the Cross. So, when we speak of Faith, we must always understand that, Biblically speaking, it must be Faith in Christ and what Christ did at the Cross.

Again, even though I am being very repetitious, Christ must never be separated from His Work carried out on the Cross. If we separate Christ from that Work in any way, we are left with *"another Jesus"* (II Cor. 11:4).

What do we mean by that?

ANOTHER JESUS

To be frank, in the modern church, Christ has mostly been separated from the Cross, and we continue to speak of His Work carried out at the Cross. That means that, as it regards Christ, the emphasis is placed on anything and everything except the Cross. That's why Paul said:

"For Christ sent me not to baptize, but to preach the Gospel: not with wisdom of words, lest the Cross of Christ should be made of none effect" (I Cor. 1:17).

He also said:

"If you be circumcised, Christ shall profit you nothing" (Gal. 5:2).

And then:

"Christ is become of no effect unto you, whosoever of you are justified (seek to be justified) by the Law; you are fallen from Grace" (Gal. 5:4).

Paul is not knocking Water Baptism, and neither is he saying that it's a sin for little boys to be circumcised, etc. He is meaning that if we emphasize these things or claim that such has to be in order for one to be Saved, then we have made the Cross of Christ, which refers to all that Jesus there did, of none effect. That's the sin of the modern church — they have made the Cross of Christ of none effect.

The Healing Jesus, as well as the Miracle-working Jesus, is very important. Of course, Jesus in any posture in which we can place Him is very important. Still, the emphasis must always be on Jesus Christ and Him Crucified. As we've said, He must never be separated from the Cross.

WIFE

"And yet indeed she is my sister; she is the daughter of my father, but not the daughter of my mother, and she became my wife" (Gen. 20:12).

If it is to be noticed, Abraham dwells on the fact that Sarah is indeed his half-sister, while the Holy Spirit emphasizes the fact of the lady being his wife (Vss. 2-3, 7).

As stated, Sarah was apparently Abraham's half-sister, being Terah's daughter by another wife. We gather from her calling her daughter Sarai — that is, princess — that Sarah's mother was not a concubine, as Hagar, but belonged to some noble race.

Many Christians, I'm afraid, little think of this which Abraham did in referring to Sarah as his sister; however, the motive was deception. Placing Sarah in this very compromising position was what Satan desired. If he could have impregnated her by Pharaoh or Abimelech, the Plan of God would have been seriously hindered and may have been delayed for a long period of time. In fact, only the Intervention of God stopped this effort by the Evil One.

While we expect Satan to do everything within his power to hurt and hinder, he can only bring his plans to fruition if he can get a Saint of God, as Abraham, to cooperate with him. While Abraham did so unwittingly, still, the danger was the same. The real sin was Abraham leaving the path of Faith, as that is always the real sin with us presently.

SARAH

"And it came to pass, when God caused me to wander from my father's house, that I said unto her, This is your kindness which you shall show unto me; at every place where we shall come, say of me, He is my brother" (Gen. 20:13).

This deception, it seems, was formulated by Abraham at the very beginning of his sojourn, which, of course, was many years earlier. It is somewhat understandable at Abraham doing such a thing in his earliest days even though it was wrong at that time, as well; it is harder to understand these many years later.

Abraham had seen God do great and mighty things for him. As the Lord led and guided them, he and those with him had defeated powerful armies some years earlier, and did so without the loss of a single person. As well, they recovered all that had been stolen and taken. This was a Miracle of unprecedented proportions.

As well, the Lord had appeared to him several times and had even visited him, which was the time before the destruction of Sodom and Gomorrah. At this particular time, Abraham had been given almost the entirety of the Revelation concerning the birth of this Miracle child. He now knew that it would not be Ishmael, but rather the one who would be born to Sarah, even though she had not been able to conceive all of these years.

So, why did he need to lie to Abimelech, especially this late in the day, so to speak?

The answer to this is probably not as complicated as it first seems.

DAILY

The path of Faith is a daily exercise. In other words, the Faith we had yesterday, while sufficient for that time, is not sufficient for today. There must be a fresh enduement of Faith each and every day. Jesus addressed this by saying:

"If any man will come after Me, let him deny himself (deny his own personal strength and ability), and take up his cross daily, and follow Me" (Lk. 9:23).

If it is to be noticed, Jesus spoke of taking up the Cross *"daily."* It's almost as if we start over again each and every day. The idea is this:

As stated, Faith we had yesterday will not suffice for today, and the Lord has designed it that way. In all of this, He is teaching us several things.

They are:

• He is telling us that the Cross is the answer for everything we need. In other words, it was there that

Jesus paid the price and made it possible for God to grant us Grace in every capacity.

• He has so designed it that we will, in essence, help to appropriate Faith each and every day, and we speak of Faith in the Cross. It is done in this manner in order to teach us trust, confidence, and a constant looking to Him.

• All of this is done in this manner that we may learn not to depend on ourselves, but rather to deny our own ability and strength, thereby, depending totally and completely on Christ and what Christ has done for us.

This is the big struggle for the Child of God. Whether we realize it or not, we want to discontinue our trust in Christ and what He has done for us at the Cross, and rather depend on other things. However, let it ever be understood, if our trust is placed in anything other than Christ and Him Crucified, we have then departed from the true path of Faith, and the faith we now have is a pseudo-faith, which God will not recognize, and which will fall out to grave problems exactly as it did with Abraham.

The sin is leaving the path of true Faith, which always falls out to wrongdoing in other ways.

THE GIFTS

"And Abimelech took sheep, and oxen, and menservants, and womenservants, and gave them unto Abraham, and restored him Sarah his wife" (Gen. 20:14).

Once again the Holy Spirit calls attention to the fact that Sarah is Abraham's wife.

Abimelech gave these things to Abraham simply because he recognized the Power of God. In other words, he didn't want to offend the Lord, so he would give His Prophet these gifts, which Abraham took.

His taking the gifts meant that he accepted the apology of Abimelech, and, at the same time, he was saying, *"I am sorry for my actions."* The giving of gifts and the receiving of gifts were very special in those days and held high meaning.

KINDNESS

"And Abimelech said, Behold, my land is before you: dwell where it pleases you" (Gen. 20:15).

Abimelech was a smart man, in fact, a just ruler. While we have little knowledge as to the exact spiritual condition of this man, we do know that he knew and understood that the Blessings of God were upon Abraham. Consequently, he offers him a place in *"his land."* To be sure, this was a smart move on the part of the heathen king, and he, no doubt, experienced great Blessings from God because of this act.

Remember that the Lord had said, *"And I will bless them who bless you, and curse him who curses you: and in you shall all families of the Earth be blessed"* (Gen. 12:3).

To help the Work of God, which Abimelech certainly did, never goes unnoticed by the Lord.

THE REPROOF

"And unto Sarah he said, Behold, I have given your brother a thousand pieces of silver: behold, he is to you a covering of the eyes, unto all who are with you, and with all other: thus she was reproved" (Gen. 20:16).

Abimelech reproved Sarah by referring to Abraham as her *"brother"* when, in reality, all knew that he was her husband. In effect, the heathen prince is telling her, *"Don't do that again. It doesn't become you."*

And then, by using the phrase, *"Behold, he (Abraham) is to you a covering of the eyes (and), unto all who are with you, and with all others,"* he is saying, *"If you openly claim Abraham as your husband, this, to be sure, will be protection enough for you."*

In other words, he was saying to her that God would protect the both of them. What a rebuke!

HEALING

"So Abraham prayed unto God: and God healed Abimelech, and his wife, and his maidservants; and they bore children" (Gen. 20:17).

Evidently, Abimelech related to Abraham the physical problem which had beset them. It seems to have affected him and his wife, as well as all who were of his household, however many that may have been. It seems the women could not conceive, and we know from the next Verse that the Lord had instigated this.

We learn from these two Verses that not only can the Lord heal, but, as well, He can cause physical problems if, in fact, it serves His Purpose.

THE MALADY

"For the LORD had fast closed up all the wombs of the house of Abimelech, because of Sarah Abraham's wife" (Gen. 20:18).

The advent of sickness came about as a result of sin, which caused the Fall. In fact, Satan is the primary author of sickness and disease. In the beginning, God never intended for man to be so afflicted. In fact, had there not been the Fall, there would be no such thing as sickness or disease, or dying, for that matter. Man was originally created to live forever and if the Fall had not occurred, would have done so by partaking of the Tree of Life.

Even though Satan is the author of sickness and disease, still, he can do nothing unless he receives permission from the Lord to do so. In fact, Satan, who is the archenemy of God, and who is the author of all evil, is subject to the Lord in everything. So, when it says here that *"the Lord had fast closed up all the wombs of the house of Abimelech,"* it can mean that the Lord either did this Personally, or else, He allowed Satan to do so. From the way the Text reads, it seems that the Lord did this Personally.

However, God never chastises men, either by affliction or rebuke, for His Pleasure, but rather for our profit. As well, He never pardons sin without restoring Blessing on the sinner. So, He blessed Abraham by answering his prayer regarding healing for Abimelech, and He healed Abimelech, irrespective that he was a sinner.

Horton says that in the midst of all of this, *"God was faithfully watching over Sarah as the mother of the promised son, the one who would carry on the Blessings of God's Covenant."*

> *"Lift up your heads, pilgrims so weary!*
> *"See day's approach now crimson the sky;*
> *"Night shadows flee, and your Beloved,*
> *"Awaited with longing at last draws nigh."*
>
> *"Dark was the night sin warred against us!*
> *"Heavy the load of sorrow be borne;*
> *"But now we see, signs of His Coming,*
> *"Our hearts glow within us, joy's cup runs over!"*
>
> *"O blessed hope! O blessed promise!*
> *"Filling our hearts with rapture divine;*
> *"O day of days! Hail Your Appearing!*
> *"Your Transcendent Glory forever shall shine!"*
>
> *"Even so, come, Precious Lord Jesus!*
> *"Creation waits Redemption to see;*
> *"Caught up in clouds, soon we shall meet Thee,*
> *"O blessed assurance, forever will be!"*

ABRAHAM

CHAPTER

23

Abraham And Isaac

ABRAHAM AND ISAAC

THE MIRACLE

"And the LORD visited Sarah as He had said, and the LORD did unto Sarah as He had spoken" (Gen. 21:1).

Chapter 21 of Genesis presents new Creation. The Divine title *"Elohim"* and not *"Jehovah"* appears throughout, with the exception of Verses 1 and 33. In these Verses, God is *"Jehovah"* because it touches His Covenant Relationship as a Saviour.

The birth of Isaac had to do with the Incarnation of the Lord Jesus Christ. The first Adam had failed, and failed miserably, which plunged the human race into an abyss of wickedness and evil, resulting in death. In fact, sin gave Satan a legal right to hold the entirety of humanity captive, which he did. The only hope for the human race, the fallen sons of the first Adam, was for God to become man and, thereby, die on the Cross. He would be referred to as the *"Last Adam"* because there would never be a need for another one. He was, as well, called the *"Second Man"* (I Cor. 15:45, 47).

THE INCARNATION OF CHRIST

Even though Jesus Christ was God and, in fact, had always been God and would always be God, still, as God, He did not attempt to redeem humanity. As God, He could have done so; however, to redeem man in that fashion would have been against God's Nature and Character, which He will never do. In other words, He had to pay the full price, and that full price would be death, and God cannot die. So, God would become Man.

However, to become man, a line would have to be established, actually beginning with Abraham. As a Prophet, Abraham was a Type of Christ. It would go through the lineage of David, who was king, and would be a Type of Christ in His Kingly Posture. Hence, the Genealogy of Christ opens in Matthew with the words, *"The Book of the Generation of Jesus Christ, the Son of David, the Son of Abraham"* (Mat. 1:1).

So, this lineage had to begin in the Lord and in the Lord only. That's the reason that all hope of the flesh had to die before Isaac could be born. When that hope, or the efforts of Abraham and Sarah, totally and completely died, the Lord would miraculously give life to Sarah's dead womb even though she was 90 years of age. He would empower Abraham, as well, even though he was 100 years of age.

Here we have the accomplished Promise — the blessed fruit of patient waiting upon God. Let it be understood that none ever waited in vain.

FAITH

The soul that takes hold of God's Promise by Faith has gotten a stable reality which will never fail him. Thus was it with Abraham; thus was it with the Faithful from age to age; and thus will it be with all those who are enabled, in any measure, to trust in the Living God.

Even at the risk of such repetition so as to excite the reader, let us once again illuminate the fact that the Faith addressed here is Faith in Christ and what Christ would do at the Cross. Even though Abraham may not have understood the Cross as we do presently, he definitely did have a general idea of all that God was doing in order to bring about the Redeemer. Jesus said so (Jn. 8:56). *"This is the victory that overcomes the world, even our Faith"* (I Jn. 5:4).

God will always do what He has spoken. Of that we can be certain, and of that we can be sure.

THE SET TIME

"For Sarah conceived, and bore Abraham a son in his old age, at the set time of which God had spoken to him" (Gen. 21:2).

God's Word gave Abraham strength to beget, Sarah to conceive, and Isaac to come forth. Three times repeated in two Verses, which is not without meaning, the clause points to the supernatural character of Isaac's birth.

The *"set time"* tells us that God's Timing is all a part of His Will and is just as important as what is done. As we've already stated, the hope of the flesh had to totally and completely die in both Abraham and Sarah before this great Miracle could be brought about. It is the same with us presently.

The work that is carried out in our hearts and lives by the Lord must be totally of the Lord. The biggest problem that He has with Believers, believe it or not, is unbelief. We keep trying to do for ourselves, exactly as did Abraham and Sarah, which only God can do. In this Chapter, we will see exactly why it cannot be done by our own ingenuity and ability.

ISAAC

"And Abraham called the name of his son who was born unto him, whom Sarah bore to him, Isaac" (Gen. 21:3).

A year before, the Lord had told Abraham that Sarah would bear a son and that his name should be called *"Isaac"* (Gen. 17:19). Isaac means, *"Laughter,"* and he was named this for a purpose and a reason.

As stated, Isaac was to be the progenitor and Type of the Messiah, Who would one day come. As such, He would bring Salvation to this hurting world, which would be the occasion of unspeakable joy. *"Laughter"* speaks of Blessing, increase, healing, life, well-being, and of good things, hence Jesus saying, *"I am come that they might have life, and that they might have it more abundantly"* (Jn. 10:10). As Isaac was a Type of Christ, it would not be wrong to say that one of the Names of Christ is *"Laughter."*

> *"It is joy unspeakable and full of glory,*
> *"Full of glory, full of glory.*
> *"It is joy unspeakable and full of glory,*
> *"And the half has never yet been told."*

CIRCUMCISION

"And Abraham circumcised his son Isaac being eight days old, as God had commanded him" (Gen. 21:4).

When the Covenant of Circumcision had been given to Abraham, the Lord commanded that little boy babies were to be circumcised at eight days old (Gen. 17:12). The eight days after birth were for physical reasons. It took this long after birth for the blood to properly develop in that it would properly coagulate. If the little boy was circumcised before this, he could bleed to death.

However, other than that, circumcision was a sign of the Covenant, which, in essence, proclaimed the fact that God would ultimately send a Redeemer into this world, Who would redeem the fallen sons of Adam's race by going to the Cross of Calvary. Many other things played into this Covenant and were very important in their own capacity; however, the end result was ever to be Christ.

ONE HUNDRED YEARS OLD

"And Abraham was an hundred years old, when his son Isaac was born unto him" (Gen. 21:5).

Abraham And Isaac 399

This Verse is placed in the Text so that all may know that Isaac's birth was indeed miraculous. A woman some 90 years old could not conceive, and a man 100 years old could not father a child. So, the conception and birth of Isaac were far beyond the boundaries of human possibility; therefore, God was the One Who brought about this miraculous act, which resulted in this Miracle child.

Concerning this, Paul said:

"Who against hope believed in hope, that he might become the father of many nations; according to that which was spoken, So shall your seed be.

"And being not weak in Faith, he considered not his own body now dead, when he was about an hundred years old, neither yet the deadness of Sarah's womb:

"He staggered not at the Promise of God through unbelief; but was strong in Faith, giving Glory to God;

"And being fully persuaded that, what He had promised, He was able also to perform.

"And therefore it was imputed to him for Righteousness" (Rom. 4:18-22).

While Abraham definitely did not stagger at the Promise of God, knowing that God would ultimately bring this Promise to pass, still, he had some trouble getting there, as the account discloses. The Promise he believed. It was the *"how"* of the Promise which gave him trouble, and it is often the same with us presently. How will the Lord do what He has promised? Then we try to help Him, all ultimately to our chagrin.

SARAH

"And Sarah said, God has made me to laugh, so that all who hear will laugh with me" (Gen. 21:6).

The birth of Isaac, as would be obvious, was an occasion of great joy. However, the joy expressed here was of far greater degree, to which we have already alluded, than the mere fact of what had happened, as wonderful as that was. All of this leads to Christ, and Christ brings an unparalleled joy to all who accept Him and, thereby, know Him.

Sarah had once laughed in unbelief. She now laughs in Faith, a laughter, incidentally, expressing joy which will never end.

Yes, Sarah, even though it has been some 4,000 years since you uttered these words, *"So that all who hear will laugh with me,"* to be sure, I am laughing today the laughter of joy because of what your Faith and the Faith of Abraham brought forth. Of course, I'm speaking of the Lord Jesus Christ.

THE MIRACLE OF FAITH

"And she said, Who would have said unto Abraham, that Sarah should have given children suck? for I have born him a son in his old age" (Gen. 21:7).

This is a poem and could very well have been a song.

The question that Sarah asks in her poem or song refers to the fact that what had happened was beyond human reasoning and most definitely beyond human ability. Who would have thought that Sarah, barren all of her life, at 90 years of age would give birth to a baby boy? However, that's exactly what happened because it was a Work of the Lord.

ISAAC

"And the child grew, and was weaned: and Abraham made a great feast the same day that Isaac was weaned" (Gen. 21:8).

The custom in those days was to nurse children for two or three years before they were weaned, with some children being as much as five years old. When a boy was weaned, he was then turned over to his father for training, at which time his education began.

Isaac was the son of Promise, and through him would come the Blessing, which would ultimately touch the entirety of the world. That Blessing was and is Christ. In view of this, and as was the custom, as well, Abraham made a great feast on the day of the weaning of Isaac.

MURDER

"And Sarah saw the son of Hagar the Egyptian, which she had born unto Abraham, mocking" (Gen. 21:9).

According to the time that Isaac was weaned, Ishmael would now be anywhere from 17 to 20 years old.

The *"mocking"* of Isaac by Ishmael is mentioned by Paul in Galatians 4:29. He uses the word, *"Persecuted,"* which, in the Greek, carries the meaning of a desire to murder. So Ishmael, spurred by his mother, Hagar, wanted to murder Isaac.

The Jewish Targums say that Ishmael had planned Isaac's murder by stealth. He would feign that he was playing a game with the young child, would shoot arrows in the distance, and then have Isaac run and fetch them. The plan was for one of the arrows to hit Isaac and kill him, with it then claimed to be an accident. However, Sarah saw what was happening, whatever it might have been at that time, and demanded the expulsion of the bondwoman, i.e., *"Hagar,"* and her son.

THE ALLEGORY

Paul used this in Galatians, Chapter 4, as an allegory. The word, *"Allegory,"* simply means a symbolic representation.

We have in this example, even as Paul used it, Isaac symbolizing the new nature, i.e., *"the Divine Nature,"* which comes into the Believer at Conversion, and

Ishmael, who represents the old nature. The birth of the new nature demands the expulsion of the old. It is impossible to improve the old nature. In other words, Ishmael must go.

Paul said in Romans 8:7 that the old nature is *"enmity against God: that it is not subject to the Law of God, neither indeed can be."*

George Williams said:

"If therefore it cannot be subject to the Law of God, how can it be improved? How foolish therefore appears the doctrine of moral evolution!"[1]

Regeneration is not a change of the old nature but the introduction of a new. It is the implantation of the nature of Life of the Last Adam by the Operation of the Holy Spirit, founded upon the accomplished Redemption of Christ. The moment the sinner believes in his heart and confesses with his mouth the Lord Jesus, he immediately becomes the possessor of a new life, and that Life is Christ. He is born of God, is a Child of God, and as Paul put it, is a son of the free woman (Rom. 10:9; Gal. 3:26; 4:31; Col. 3:4; I Jn. 3:1-2).

Mackintosh said:

"Nor does the introduction of this new nature alter, in the slightest degree, the true, essential character of the old."[2]

Concerning this, the Scripture says:

"The flesh lusts against the Spirit, and the Spirit against the flesh: and these are contrary the one to the other" (Gal. 5:17).

THE GROUND OF MOST FALSE DOCTRINE

It is in this area that most false doctrine appears. There are some who think that Regeneration is a certain change which the old nature undergoes; and, moreover, that this change is gradual in its operation until, at length, the whole man becomes transformed.

Once again, this is moral evolution, which the Bible doesn't teach.

It rather teaches that it is impossible to improve the old nature. Paul plainly says, *"It is not subject to the Law of God, neither indeed can be"* (Rom. 8:7). If it's not subject to the Law of God, how can it be improved? This is where the struggle commences.

If the Believer doesn't understand the Cross and what Jesus did there, and that his Faith must ever remain in the Cross, which alone is the secret of all victorious living, that Believer will seek to devise means and ways to live a holy life, which God cannot recognize, and in which the Holy Spirit will not function. Therefore, the Believer is left on his own, which guarantees failure. Regrettably, because of having an erroneous understanding of the Cross, most Christians attempt to make Ishmael holy. This means they try to improve the old nature, which is always doomed to failure. It is either Faith in the Cross, or it is failure. God doesn't have 10 ways or even two ways of victory, only one, and that is *"Jesus Christ and Him Crucified"* (Gal. 2:20-21).

> *"There's a blessed time that's coming, coming soon,*
> *"It may be evening, morning, or at noon,*
> *"The wedding of the bride, united with the Groom,*
> *"We shall see the King when He comes."*
>
> *"Are you ready should the Saviour call today?*
> *"Would Jesus say, 'Well done,' or, 'Go away'?*
> *"My Home is for the pure, the vile can never stay,*
> *"We shall see the King when He comes."*
>
> *"Oh, my brother, are you ready for the call?*
> *"To crown your Saviour King and Lord of all?*
> *"The kingdoms of this world shall soon before*
>   *Him fall,*
> *"We shall see the King when He comes."*

ABRAHAM

CHAPTER

24

Abraham
And The Bondwoman
And Her Son

ABRAHAM AND THE BONDWOMAN AND HER SON

"Wherefore she said unto Abraham, Cast out this bondwoman and her son: for the son of this bondwoman shall not be heir with my son, even with Isaac" (Gen. 21:10).

Isaac is a Type of Christ, and in Christ, we have all Life and all Victory. The *"bondwoman,"* which, of course, is Hagar, symbolizes the Law while her son Ishmael symbolizes the old nature (Gal., Chpt. 4).

Sarah rightly said to Abraham, even as we shall see, that this bondwoman and her son had to go. Isaac had now arrived, and if Hagar and Ishmael were allowed to stay, they would only seek to do away with Isaac. There is no compromise here, and there is no ground for reconciliation. One or the other must go.

Bringing it over into the spiritual sense, even as Paul did in Galatians, Chapter 4, this means that we must cast out all efforts of the flesh as it regards the living of a righteous and holy life. Our confidence and Faith must totally and completely be in Christ and what Christ has done for us at the Cross. If we seek to live this life in any other way or manner, we are going against the Bible, and the end result will not be victory, but rather failure, and abject failure at that.

This is not a question of *"maybe," "hope so,"* or *"maybe so,"* but rather *"do or die."*

Due to the fact that this is very difficult for many to understand, please allow us the freedom of being more specific.

ISHMAEL

If you as a Believer think that your Righteousness with God or your holiness, etc., has to do with your belonging to a certain denomination or a certain church, or your doing certain good things or not doing certain bad things, then purely and simply, you are harboring Ishmael, which God can never condone. It must always be Christ and Him Crucified and never anything else.

Sometime back, I had a preacher tell me, in effect, that if a person did not belong to a particular religious denomination, something was wrong with that person, whomever he might be. In fact, untold millions believe the same way.

Such an attitude proclaims the fact that this preacher, and others like him, have placed their faith in that denomination, which means it's not in Christ and Him Crucified. They may claim it is, but it isn't. Anytime we make certain things a condition, other than Christ and His Sacrifice, we have told the Lord that we're going to keep Ishmael, etc. That's why the Holy Spirit through Sarah said, *"For the son of this bondwoman shall not be heir with my son, even with Isaac."*

If you as a Believer want to inherit the great Promises of God, in other words, you want all that the Lord has for you, you can only obtain this by going God's Way. If you want to argue that God has ways other than the Cross, please show it to me in the Bible. You can't show it because it's not there.

THE FRUIT OF THE FLESH

"And the thing was very grievous in Abraham's sight because of his son" (Gen. 21:11).

Ishmael was the fair fruit of Abraham's efforts, and he was loath to give him up.

George Williams says:

"The Divine way of Holiness is to 'put off the old man' just as Abraham 'put off' Ishmael. Man's way of

Holiness is to improve the 'old man' that is, to improve Ishmael. The effort is both foolish and hopeless. Of course the casting out of Ishmael was 'very grievous in Abraham's sight' because there always brings about a struggle to cast out this element of bondage, that is, Salvation by works. For legalism is dear to the heart. Ishmael was the fruit, and to Abraham the fair fruit of his own energy and planning."[1]

So, the Church as a whole doesn't want to give up Ishmael, and Believers as a whole don't want to give up Ishmael.

We have placed a lot of effort, scheming, planning, and sweat, so to speak, in this *"fruit of the flesh,"* and we do not part with it easily or quickly. Now, what exactly am I talking about?

THE OBJECT OF OUR FAITH

I'm speaking of us putting our Faith in all types of things other than Christ and His Cross, thinking this will bring us Righteousness, Holiness, etc.

Most Christians, I think, will read these words and automatically claim that their Faith is in Christ and His Sacrifice. However, the truth is, for most, it isn't. How do I know that? There are two reasons:

1. In the lives of most Christians, there is anything but victory.

2. If our pulpits are silent on a particular subject, it is a cinch that the people in the pew are not going to know anything about that particular subject.

To be sure, as it regards the Cross of Christ, the pulpits have been stone silent for the last several decades. *"Faith comes by hearing, and hearing by the Word of God,"* but if the Word of God on any subject, as stated, is not taught, then it's impossible for *"Faith to come"* (Rom. 10:17).

Most Christians place their Faith and confidence in the Cross as it regards their initial Salvation experience, but when it comes to Sanctification, they don't have the faintest idea how the Cross plays into this all-important aspect of their life and living.

THE CROSS

In Romans, Chapter 6, when Paul set out to explain the sin nature, he immediately took the Believer to the Cross (Rom. 6:3-5). Now, please understand, in these Passages, Paul is not speaking of Water Baptism, but rather the Crucifixion of Christ and our being in Christ.

When Jesus died on the Cross, was buried and then rose from the dead, He did all of this as our Substitute. When we exhibit Faith in that great Sacrifice, in the Mind of God, we are literally placed *"in Christ."* Consequently, all the victory that Christ purchased becomes ours. However, it is only in Christ and His Sacrifice, and our Faith in that Finished Work, that guarantees the Help of the Holy Spirit, which then guarantees victory.

If we maintain our Faith in the Cross of Christ, ever making it the Standard, then the Holy Spirit, through Paul, plainly states, *"Sin shall not have dominion over you"* (Rom. 6:14).

All too often, we Christians love to hold to our *"works."* When told that we must give them up, in other words, stop placing our faith in these things, but rather place our Faith in Christ and Him Crucified, it becomes very grievous to us. As stated, we put a lot of time, energy, and labor into these things, and as Abraham loved Ishmael, we love these particular *"works."* As someone has well said, *"The doing of religion is the most powerful narcotic there is."* Please notice the word, *"Doing."*

IN ISAAC SHALL YOUR SEED BE CALLED

*"And God said unto Abraham, Let it not be griev-
ous in your sight because of the lad, and because of
the bondwoman; in all that Sarah has said unto you,
hearken unto her voice; for in Isaac shall your seed be
called"* (Gen. 21:12).

The birth of Isaac did not improve Ishmael but only
brought out his real opposition to the child of Promise.
He might have gone on very quietly and orderly till Isaac
made his appearance, but then he showed what he
was by persecuting and mocking the child of Promise.

What then was the remedy? Was it to make Ishmael
better? By no means was it to make Ishmael better;
but, *"Cast out this bondwoman and her son; for the son
of this bondwoman shall not be heir with my son, even
with Isaac."*

Here was the only remedy. That which was crooked
cannot be made straight. Therefore, you have to get
rid of the crooked thing altogether and occupy yourself with that which is divinely straight. It is labor
lost to seek to make a crooked thing straight. Hence,
all efforts after the improvement of nature are utterly
futile so far as God is concerned. So, that rules out
humanistic psychology altogether!

THE GALATIANS

The entire Book of Galatians deals with this very
subject. The error into which the Galatian churches
fell was the introduction of that which addressed itself
to works.

*"Except you be circumcised after the manner of
Moses, you cannot be saved"* (Acts 15:1).

Here, Salvation was made to depend upon something
that man could be, man could do, or man could keep.

This was upsetting the entirety of the fabric of Redemption, which, as the Believer knows, rests exclusively upon what Christ is and what He has done. To make Salvation even remotely dependent upon anything in or done by man is to set it entirely aside. When we speak of Salvation, we are including Righteousness, Holiness, Victory, etc. In other words, Ishmael had to be entirely cast out and all of Abraham's hopes be made to depend upon what God had done and given in the person of Isaac.

SALVATION IS ALL OF GOD

As is obvious, this leaves man nothing in which to glory. As well, man has nothing in which he can rightly glory. Salvation is all of God and must ever remain all of God. He is the Creator, and I am the creature; He is the Blesser, and I am the Blessed; He is *"the Better,"* and I am *"the less"* (Heb. 7:7); He is the Giver, and I am the receiver.

This is what makes Christianity unique and distinguishes it from every system of human religion under the sun, whether it be Romanism, Hinduism, Islam, Confucianism, Mormonism, Buddhism, Judaism, or any other *"ism."*

Human religion gives the creature a place, more or less; it keeps the bondwoman and her son in the house; and it gives man something in which to glory. On the contrary, Bible Christianity excludes the Preacher from all interference in the Work of Salvation — casts out the bondwoman and her son, and gives all the Glory to Whom Alone Glory is due.

WHO ARE THE BONDWOMAN AND HER SON?

Let us inquire as to who this bondwoman and her son

really are, and what they represent. Galatians, Chapter 4, furnishes ample teaching as to these two points.

In a word, the bondwoman represents the Covenant of the Law, and her son represents all who are *"of works of Law,"* or on that principle. This is very clear and plain.

The bondwoman only genders to bondage and can never bring forth a free man. How can she? The Law never could give liberty, for so long as a man is alive, it rules him (Rom. 7:1). I can never be free as long as I am under the dominion of anyone, for while I live, the Law rules me, and nothing but death can give me Deliverance from its dominion. This is the Doctrine of Romans, Chapter 7. However, Paul said:

"Wherefore, my brethren, you also are become dead to the Law by the Body of Christ (what Christ did at the Cross); that you should be married to another, even to Him Who is raised from the dead, that we should bring forth fruit unto God" (Rom. 7:4). This is freedom, for *"If the Son shall make you free, you shall be free indeed"* (Jn. 8:36).

So, the first four Verses of Romans, Chapter 7, tell us, if the Believer is attempting to live this Christian life or is placing his faith in that other than Christ and what Christ has done at the Cross, in effect, God looks at that Christian as committing *"spiritual adultery."* This is what the first four Verses of Romans, Chapter 7, reveal to us.

THE SON OF THE BONDWOMAN

"And also of the son of the bondwoman will I make a nation, because he is your seed" (Gen. 21:13).

If it is to be noticed, Hagar is never acknowledged by the Holy Spirit as Abraham's wife; however, her child, as Abraham's son, receives a noble promise for the father's sake. Here the allegory breaks down or, at least partially so, even as do all allegories, types, etc.

However, let us look at this situation in the natural, at least as it regards the *"nation,"* of which the Lord spoke to Abraham.

As we have stated over and over, Ishmael was a work of the flesh. He was a result of the scheming and planning of Abraham and Sarah and was by no means the product of the Holy Spirit, as should be overly obvious. In the natural, in Ishmael, we're seeing the beginning of the Arab world. Even though a half-brother to Isaac, i.e., *"Israel,"* it would be Israel's bitter enemy. It continues unto this very hour.

Out of this *"work of the flesh"* came the religion of Islam, which claims that Ishmael is the promised seed and not Isaac. It also claims that Muhammad is a result of that seed and not Christ. So, anytime a work of the flesh is brought forth, it will always bitterly oppose the Ways of the Lord and, at the same time, will gender much trouble.

THE DEPARTURE

"And Abraham rose up early in the morning, and took bread, and a bottle of water, and gave it unto Hagar, putting it on her shoulder, and the child, and sent her away: and she departed, and wandered in the wilderness of Beer-sheba" (Gen. 21:14).

The Holy Spirit through Paul would use this incident to teach a very valuable spiritual lesson; still, these were actual events. Even though Hagar and Ishmael conducted themselves very wrongly toward Isaac and actually desired to murder him, and would have done so had the opportunity presented itself, still, the scene before our eyes is one of great sadness.

Due to the Command of the Lord, Abraham rises up early in the morning to carry out that which was demanded of him. It would not be an easy situation for the Patriarch. Whatever he thought of Hagar, he greatly loved the boy, and despite what was happening, that love was not diminished. But yet, he knew that the Lord was exactly right in what was being demanded. For Isaac's sake, he must send them away.

This is Abraham's sixth surrender.

- First of all, he surrendered his *"country."*
- Then, his *"family."*
- Then, the *"vale of Jordan."*
- Then, the *"gold of Sodom."*
- Then, he would surrender *"self,"* as recorded in Chapter 15.
- And now, the sixth surrender is *"Ishmael."*
- The last one, as we shall see, will be *"Isaac"* himself.

The sevenfold surrender, which was demanded of Abraham, was a pattern as it regards every single Believer, even unto this hour. These surrenders do not come easily or quickly, as all of us are prone to find out. But yet, if we are to be what the Lord wants us to be, they are surrenders which must be made. Even though they are hard, they are necessary, and then looking back, we see why it was always for the best.

WATER

"And the water was spent in the bottle, and she cast the child under one of the shrubs" (Gen. 21:15).

Irrespective of what Hagar and Ishmael had done, it is hard to conceive of Abraham sending her and the boy into the wilderness as he did. Considering that he was a very wealthy man, it would seem that Abraham would have made provisions for them, as it regards another place, and then seen to their needs, etc.

So, even though the Scripture is silent concerning these matters, we have to come to the conclusion that the Lord told Abraham to do as he did. Otherwise, I hardly think he would have done so, especially considering the feelings he had for Ishmael.

All of this is bigger than life, and the Lord was, no doubt, guiding in all matters, even down to the smallest details.

So, now the water that Hagar had been given is gone. The boy is evidently very thirsty, and the woman sees no way out but death.

I'm sure that she knew what the Lord had said concerning Isaac. He was the promised seed and, therefore, Abraham's true heir. Nevertheless, as it regards Ishmael, she had schemed, wanting him to have that portion, and willing, it seems, to do anything to secure her ends. However, she was fighting against God, and now she faces death.

DEATH

"And she went, and sat her down over against him a good way off, as it were a bow shot: for she said, Let me not see the death of the child. And she sat over against him, and lift up her voice, and wept" (Gen. 21:16).

Evidently, Ishmael was near fainting, and his mother knew that without water, he would die very soon. Actually, both of them would die.

Unable to bear the thought of seeing her son die, she leaves him under a shrub and staggers a distance away, herself, as well, facing certain death. Out of despair, she lifted up her voice and wept.

FEAR NOT

"And God heard the voice of the lad; and the Angel of God called to Hagar out of Heaven, and said unto her, What ails you, Hagar? fear not; for God has heard the voice of the lad where he is" (Gen. 21:17).

It is not said that either Ishmael or his mother prayed to God in their distress. Hence, the Divine interposition on their behalf was due solely to Mercy and to God's Love for Abraham. So, it seems that the Lord did many things for other people for Abraham's sake (Gen. 19:29).

The Lord called to Hagar and said certain things to her.

Despite the fact that she had been a part of the household of the greatest Man of God on the face of the Earth at that time, still, there is no record that Hagar ever actually knew the Lord. She was so close and, at the same time, so far away.

How so many today are in the Church but actually not of the Church. They are religious but lost!

ISHMAEL

"Arise, lift up the lad, and hold him in your hand; for I will make him a great nation" (Gen. 21:18).

Ishmael was between 17 and 20 years old at this particular time. So, when Hagar is told to *"hold him in your hand,"* the Lord is referring to her placing her hand on his shoulder and steadying him, which she did. For the sake of Abraham, the Lord said that He would *"make of him (Ishmael) a great nation,"* and that He did! As stated, Ishmael was the progenitor of the Arabs.

A WELL OF WATER

"And God opened her eyes, and she saw a well of water; and she went, and filled the bottle with water, and gave the lad drink" (Gen. 21:19).

The idea seems to be that, at this juncture, she believed the Lord and when this came about, *"God opened her eyes."* She then saw a well of water. Why she had not seen it before, we aren't told. Perhaps the Lord purposely blinded her to the well until certain things could be made known to her, and she would acknowledge them, which required a modicum of Faith.

THE BLESSINGS OF THE LORD

"And God was with the lad; and he grew, and dwelt in the wilderness, and became an archer" (Gen. 21:20).

Once again, the Lord was with Ishmael, which means that He helped him, despite his murderous attitude toward Isaac, simply for the sake of Abraham. Genesis, Chapter 17, Verse 18, records Abraham seeking the Lord as it regards Ishmael, and Verse 20 records the answer given by the Lord concerning the Blessing of Ishmael. To be sure, God always keeps His Promises.

ISHMAEL

"And he dwelt in the wilderness of Paran: and his mother took him a wife out of the land of Egypt" (Gen. 21:21).

We have here the beginning of the Arab people. In all of this, we notice God's Care even for an Ishmael, who would appear to be outside all Covenant Blessings. He was one whose *"hand was to be against every man, and every man's against him"* (Gen. 16:12). But yet, God manifested care for Ishmael.

"When the trump of the great Archangel,
"Its mighty tones shall sound,
"And, the end of the age proclaiming,
"Shall pierce the depths profound;
"When the Son of Man shall come in His Glory,
"To take the Saints on high,
"What a shouting in the skies,

"From the multitudes that rise,
"Changed in the twinkling of an eye."

"When He comes in the clouds descending,
"And they who love Him hear,
"From their graves shall awake and praise Him,
"With joy and not with fear,
"When the body and the soul are reunited,
"And clothed no more to die,
"What a shouting there will be,
"When each other's face we see,
"Changed in the twinkling of an eye."

"O the seed that was sown in weakness,
"Shall then be raised in Power,
"And the songs of the Blood-bought millions,
"Shall hail that blissful hour;
"When we gather safely home in the morning,
"And night's dark shadows fly,
"What a shouting on the shore,
"When we meet to part no more,
"Changed in the twinkling of an eye."

ABRAHAM

CHAPTER

25

Abraham And
The Philistine

ABRAHAM AND THE PHILISTINE

"And it came to pass at that time, that Abimelech and Phichol the chief captain of his host spoke unto Abraham, saying, God is with you in all that you do" (Gen. 21:22).

The dream that Abimelech had concerning God and what the Lord told him about Abraham, and Abraham praying for the healing of his household, caused Abraham to stand big in the eyes of this heathen prince. As well, he had, no doubt, heard of the birth of Isaac and considered it, as well, as none other than a Miracle. Then he saw the power, strength, and riches of Abraham and concluded by saying to him, *"God is with you in all that you do."*

Though a heathen, Abimelech recognized something in Abraham which he knew to be of Jehovah and, thereby, determined to treat Abraham accordingly. Unfortunately, many modern so-called religious leaders seemingly do not even have the spiritual perception that this heathen prince of so long ago had.

Abimelech wants to stay on the good side of Abraham, which is not a difficult thing to do inasmuch as the Patriarch is a kind, gracious, and considerate man. He wants to let Abraham know, as well, that he intends no harm to him and that he, in fact, wants the two of them to be friends.

A COVENANT

"Now therefore swear unto me here by God that you will not deal falsely with me, nor with my son, nor with my son's son: but according to the kindness that I have done unto you, you shall do unto me, and to the land wherein you have sojourned" (Gen. 21:23).

Abimelech desires a covenant with Abraham that will extend not only to his son but, as well, to his grandson.

As we can see from the terminology being used here, from the time of the victorious sixth surrender, which spoke of the expulsion of Ishmael, all is strength and victory. He no longer fears the prince of this world, in this case, represented by Abimelech, but rather reproves him. Now that Isaac has come, who is Christ in Type, Abraham knows himself to be the possessor, as well, of earthly promises and conducts himself accordingly. Even the heathen prince confesses that God is with him.

THE MODERN BELIEVER

The spirit now possessed by Abraham is the same spirit that the modern Believer should have. Jesus has now come and suffered on the Cross, thereby, providing for us both earthly and Heavenly Promises. However, we can have these possessions only as we know and understand the manner in which they are given to us. Once again, we come back to Christ and His Cross.

God hasn't changed because God cannot change. It is the Cross which has brought about all good things.

Before the Cross, a thrice-Holy God could not allow sinful man to approach Him. Such would have occasioned the death of all who made that attempt. However, the Cross settled that problem by Jesus there atoning for all sin. Due to the Cross, the door is now open for all to come, and actually, the invitation is given (Rev. 22:17).

The reason that sinful man could not approach God before the Cross was just that, man was sinful, and there was nothing that he could do to assuage the sin, to ameliorate the sin, or to remove the sin.

God cannot abide sin in any form. When Jesus died on the Cross, He atoned for all sin, past, present, and future. Now, with an evidence of Faith in Christ and what Christ has done for us at the Cross, sinful man can be justified and actually given the Perfection of Christ. With all sin atoned, God can fellowship with man. How thankful we should be for this, considering we in no way could do this ourselves but that Jesus did it for us, even at great price.

THE COVENANT WAS MADE

"And Abraham said, I will swear" (Gen. 21:24).

Even though Abraham did swear as it regards that for which the heathen prince asked, there was still a present and personal matter to be settled.

However, any matter can be settled if both or all parties will look to the Lord and, thereby, seek to do right. The problem is, without the Lord, this means that rank covetousness stands in the way of any settlement.

THE WELL OF WATER

"And Abraham reproved Abimelech because of a well of water, which Abimelech's servants had violently taken away" (Gen. 21:25).

The ownership of wells in that part of the world was as jealously guarded as the possession of a valuable object, which these wells were! So, the greatest possible injury that could be done to one, at least of a material kind, was the hindering of water supplies. It seems the servants of Abimelech had violently taken over a well that had originally belonged to Abraham. So, Abraham knew that this matter had to be settled, or else, it would quickly get out of hand.

ABIMELECH

"And Abimelech said, I know not who has done this thing; neither did you tell me, neither yet heard I of it, but today" (Gen. 21:26).

Evidently, one of the reasons that Abimelech, along with his chief captain Phichol, came to visit Abraham was because Abimelech had apparently noticed a coolness on Abraham's part. Not knowing the reason for this simply because he had no knowledge of the incident of the well, he came to Abraham in order to ascertain what the problem might be, or if, in fact, there was a problem.

This may not seem like much to us presently, but it was quite an affair at that time. When Abraham explains the situation, Abimelech confesses that he had heard nothing of this situation. Consequently, he definitely was not an accomplice in this situation, the deed having been carried out by his herdsmen.

THE COVENANT

"And Abraham took sheep and oxen, and gave them unto Abimelech; and both of them made a covenant" (Gen. 21:27).

Abraham desired to show this heathen prince and those with him, and especially his chief captain, that he carried no animosity against anyone but only sought to live peaceably. Desiring the friendship of Abimelech and showing that he carried no ill will, he furnished sheep and oxen for both Abimelech and himself. These animals would be used to offer as a sacrifice before God so that the covenant would be binding.

SEVEN EWE LAMBS

"And Abraham set seven ewe lambs from the flock by themselves" (Gen. 21:28).

The seven ewe lambs are to be a gift to Abimelech. If he accepts them, which he did, it shows that the argument has been settled, and the well is returned to Abraham, who dug it in the first place.

ANOTHER COVENANT OF SORTS

"And Abimelech said unto Abraham, What do these seven ewe lambs mean which you have set by themselves?" (Gen. 21:29).

The word in Hebrew for *"swearing"* is a passive verb, literally signifying *"to be sevened,"* that is, done or confirmed by seven. In this ancient narrative, we see a covenant actually thus made binding.

Seven ewe lambs are picked out and placed by themselves. By accepting these, Abimelech bound himself to acknowledge and respect Abraham's title to the well. Apparently this matter of ratifying an oath was unknown to the Philistines, as Abimelech asked, *"What mean these seven ewe lambs?"* As soon as the lambs were accepted, the ratification was complete.

A WITNESS

"And he said, For these seven ewe lambs shall you take of my hand, that they may be a witness unto me, that I have dug this well" (Gen. 21:30).

This is the well, which by now is obvious, that was the cause of the contention. Abraham had dug the well, but the herdsmen of Abimelech had taken it over by force. If Abimelech takes the seven lambs, which he obviously did, this shows that he agrees with Abraham's statements concerning the fact that the well had originally belonged to him and had been fraudulently taken.

BEER-SHEBA

"Wherefore he called that place Beer-sheba; because there they did swear both of them" (Gen. 21:31).

Abimelech took the seven lambs, signifying that he agreed with Abraham, and that the matter was now settled. *"Beer-sheba"* means, *"The well of the oath."*

The well of the oath is witness to Abraham's title in the Earth and to Abimelech's confession of the fact.

THE COVENANT MADE

"Thus they made a covenant at Beer-sheba: then Abimelech rose up, and Phichol the chief captain of his host, and they returned into the land of the Philistines" (Gen. 21:32).

This area ruled by Abimelech is called here the land of the Philistines for the first time. However, the main body of the Philistines, who established their cities in the south coastal plain of Canaan, did not arrive until later.

Abimelech was not as aggressive as the later Philistines since he was willing to make this treaty and allow Abraham to live in his territory.

However, there is a difference now in Abraham, as I think is somewhat obvious. Isaac has now been born and weaned, and Ishmael has been expelled. Abraham now knows that Isaac is the child of Promise. We now find the man who is operating strictly on the path of Faith.

And yet, when we think of his failures, we should not charge him unduly. Would we have done any better? Would we have done even as well? The Cross is now history, which means that all that Abraham looked forward to has now come to pass. As well, we have the Holy Spirit abiding with us. When we consider these facts, it stands to reason that we should presently do much better than Abraham; however, who would be so crass as to place themselves in such a position of superiority?

THE TREE

"And Abraham planted a grove in Beer-sheba, and called there on the Name of the LORD, the Everlasting God" (Gen. 21:33).

In the Hebrew, the word is, *"Tree,"* and not, *"Grove."* Accordingly, he takes possession of the land, thereby, planting a tree. He worships Jehovah, the Everlasting God; for the God Who gave Isaac must be, in truth, the Everlasting God. So, Abraham now dwells where the power of the world had been. Abimelech, as well as Ishmael, withdrew from his land.

All of this is a pledge or a sign of what Israel should have and of the glory and dominion that will be hers in Christ, with Christ as the Everlasting God. This is the Divine definition of Jehovah, i.e., *"Jesus Christ, the same yesterday and today and forever."*

It is believed that Abraham planted a tamarisk tree, a tree that is loaded with beautiful pink blossoms in the spring.

He refers now to Jehovah as *"El'olam."* In Genesis 14:22, Abraham claimed for Jehovah that He was *"El Elyon,"* the Supreme God; in Genesis 17:1, Jehovah reveals Himself as *"El Shaddai,"* the Almighty God; and now, Abraham claims for Him the attribute of eternity. As he advanced in Holiness, Abraham also grew in knowledge of the manifold nature of the Deity. We also more clearly understand why the Hebrews called God not *"El,"* but *"Elohim."* In the plural of appellation, all the Divine attributes were combined. *"El"* might be *"Elyon,"* *"Shaddai,"* or *"Olam."* Elohim was all in one.

SOJOURN

"And Abraham sojourned in the Philistines' land many days" (Gen. 21:34).

The Patriarch would actually live here until he died.

"Great God of wonders!
"All Your Ways are matchless,
"Godlike, and Divine;
"But the fair glories of Your Grace,

"More Godlike and unrivaled shine,
"More Godlike and unrivaled shine."

"In wonder lost, with trembling joy,
"We take the Pardon of our God:
"Pardon for crimes of deepest dye,
"A pardon bought with Jesus' Blood,
"A pardon bought with Jesus' Blood."

"O may this strange, this matchless Grace,
"This Godlike Miracle of love,
"Fill the whole Earth with grateful praise,
"And all the Angelic choirs above,
"And all the Angelic choirs above."

ABRAHAM

CHAPTER

26

Abraham And The Test

ABRAHAM AND THE TEST

"And it came to pass after these things, that God did tempt Abraham, and said unto him, Abraham: and he said, Behold, here I am" (Gen. 22:1).

The word, *"Tempt,"* should have been translated, *"Test,"* or, *"Prove,"* for that's what it means in the Hebrew. God did not *"test"* Abraham that He (God) might know, as we think of such, for He already knew. God is Omniscient, meaning that He knows everything, past, present, and future. He did this that Abraham might know. Faith must always be tested, and great Faith must be tested greatly. To be sure, this was at least one of, if not the greatest, tests that any man had to undergo.

George Williams said:

"It is a high honor to be tested by God. There are various kinds of trials, some from circumstances or some from the hand of Satan, but the highest character of trial is that which comes from God Himself."[1]

THE REASON FOR THIS TEST

Most do not understand the cause or reason for this test. Many think that it's because Abraham loved Isaac too much, etc. While Abraham certainly loved his son, even as he should have, this was not the reason for the test.

The entire framework of the Move of God, as it regarded Abraham, was the part the Patriarch would play, which was great indeed, in bringing the Redeemer into this world. This is the entire Plan of God; He must redeem Adam's fallen race. The way that it would be done, in fact, the way it had to be done, had long since been decided, even before the foundation of the world (I Pet. 1:18-20). God would have to become

Man because it was man who had fallen. God as God couldn't redeem humanity, and neither could Angels, Seraphim, or Cherubim, simply because they were of another creation. As well, tremendous responsibility had been given to the first Adam who, incidentally, failed; so another Adam, so to speak, Whom Paul referred to as the *"Last Adam,"* would have to be brought on the scene (I Cor. 15:45).

GOD IS IN VIEW

In all of this, the Bible student must realize that it is not Satan that is in view here, but rather God. It is God Who has been offended. Consequently, it is God Who will set the Standard for Redemption, in other words, the price that will have to be paid in order for His thrice-Holy Nature and Righteousness to be satisfied. In fact, the price was so high that man could in no way meet the terms. So, God would have to pay the price Himself, and that price would be death. Inasmuch as God cannot die, He would have to become Man in order to make the supreme Sacrifice.

In this object lesson of all object lessons, God will show the Patriarch how He will redeem lost humanity. As stated, it will be through death. However, even though He would show Abraham this much, He wouldn't exactly show him the means by which this death would be carried out, and we speak of the Cross. That would later be shown to Moses (Num. 21:8-9). The reader must remember that anything and everything which God does is always far larger than we can at first contemplate. No, God didn't have Abraham to undergo this tremendous test merely to prove a point. To be sure, many things entered into that which was done, as it always is with God. However, the primary purpose was to show the Patriarch what all of this was all about, and what it would take to redeem the human race. This is at least one of the reasons that Jesus said:

"Your father Abraham rejoiced to see My Day: and he saw it, and was glad" (Jn. 8:56).

GOD'S TIMING

The phrase, *"And it came to pass after these things,"* refers to some years after the expulsion of Ishmael. It could have been anywhere from 15 to 25 years after that particular event. In other words, Isaac could have been between 20 and 30 years of age at this time.

The Lord had spoken to Abraham quite a number of times through the years, but this was to be the most momentous of all. When the Lord called his name, and the Patriarch answered, *"Behold, here I am,"* little did he realize what was about to transpire. As stated, this was undoubtedly one of the greatest tests that God ever asked of any man.

Quite possibly, the Patriarch thought that every test of his Faith had come and gone. The problem with Lot had finally been settled, even though we are not aware of the end result. The terrible situation with Ishmael had finally come to a head and had been the source of great hurt; however, Abraham had passed the test with quick obedience. So, now he is at ease. Having made peace with the Philistines, he and Sarah are enjoying the leisure of old age. And now, the Lord speaks again:

HIS SON, A BURNT OFFERING?

"And He said, Take now your son, your only son Isaac, whom you love, and go into the land of Moriah; and offer him there for a Burnt Offering upon one of the mountains which I will tell you of" (Gen. 22:2).

One can only imagine, but not very successfully, what must have gone on in Abraham's mind upon first hearing this command. What preliminary remarks were made, if any, before this tremendous announcement came forth, we aren't told. Then again, what was required was of such moment, so absolutely mind-boggling, that, really, there is no way to soften the blow. So, it seems that without preliminary fanfare, the Lord simply uttered the command. This would be the seventh of the sevenfold surrender required of Abraham, and, as previously stated, in one way or the other, the one which is required of every Believer. Inasmuch as the Patriarch is the father of us all (Rom. 4:16), his example serves as a pattern for us.

THE TWOFOLD TRIAL

Abraham is commanded to kill his son. The trial was twofold:

1. Human sacrifice was abhorrent to the nature of Jehovah, so the Patriarch must now prove to himself that what he is hearing is definitely from God. Could such a deed really be enjoined upon him by God?

In fact, in the future, some Israelites would offer up their firstborn in trying to atone for their sins (Mic. 6:7); however, instead of such a deed bringing peace, it only brought a deeper condemnation to the soul. Had Abraham, as well, been moved upon by such means, his conduct would have deserved and met with similar condemnation. But, when he convinced himself that this Word definitely did come from the Lord, then obedience was required of him.

2. He now was faced with a trial of his Faith. He was being told to destroy the son in whom *"his seed was to be called."* Several things had to be faced, the least certainly not being his love for his son. Even more

important was the position of Isaac as the appointed means for the Blessing of all mankind. All of this stood arrayed against the command.

As a result of Abraham's obedience, there were great Blessings for both him and Isaac, for Isaac grandly obeyed, as well, in the submitting himself for a sacrifice, which we must not overlook.

SOMETHING HIGHER

However, there was something even higher than all of this in that the act, or rather the command for the act to be performed, contained a great typical value. As we've already stated, there was in it the setting forth of the mystery of the Father in the giving of His Son to die for the sins of the world. In that, we have the greater purpose. While all things played their part, God would show the Patriarch the reason for all that he had thus far gone through. To be sure, even though this would be the greatest test of his Faith, it was by no means the only test of his Faith, with many milestones already having been passed. So, now the Heavenly Father will relate to a greater degree the *"why"* of all of this.

Abraham was to go to *"the land of Moriah."* The very name means, *"Jah,"* or, *"Jehovah is Provider."*

ONLY!

As we have stated, it is believed that this mountain where Isaac was to be offered is the same place where the Temple would later be built. Actually, it is believed that the large stone over which the modern Muslim Dome of the Rock is now built was the actual site of the proposed sacrifice and, as well, the site where the Holy of Holies was located in Solomon's Temple.

To this command that Isaac be offered up as a *"Burnt Offering"* and that the Promise would still, in some Divine manner, be fulfilled in him, the only answer that Abraham could come up with was that God would raise the boy from the dead.

Concerning this proposed sacrifice, God used the word, *"Only,"* as it referred to Isaac. *"Only"* means only in the sense of unique, one-of-a-kind, and special. In other words, Isaac was Abraham's only hope for the fulfillment of God's Salvation-Promise. Isaac, being Abraham's *"only"* son, whom he loved, thus became a Type of God's *"Only"* Son, Who is also called His *"Beloved Son"* (Mat. 3:17).

The *"Burnt Offering,"* or *"whole Burnt Offering,"* as it was sometimes called, means literally, *"An ascent."* It went up completely in smoke, which means it was consumed totally, and was a type or illustration of complete surrender to God and a complete exaltation of Him.

OBEDIENCE

"And Abraham rose up early in the morning, and saddled his ass, and took two of his young men with him, and Isaac his son, and clave the wood for the Burnt Offering, and rose up, and went unto the place of which God had told him" (Gen. 22:3).

As in the prior Chapter concerning Ishmael, so here, there is, as well, prompt obedience. Abraham rises early in the morning. There is no record that he told Sarah what he was doing, possibly for fear that she would try to stop him.

Why didn't God tell the Patriarch to take one, or even many, of his lambs out of his great flocks and offer them up? Why the human sacrifice episode, especially considering that God hated such?

As we've already stated, among other things, this was a Type of what God would do in the giving of His Only Son to redeem lost humanity.

The human sacrifice was demanded because the blood of bulls and goats cannot take away sins (Heb. 10:4). As well, God hated human sacrifice, which made the giving of His Only Son an even greater thing. Human sacrifices could not take away sins in any fashion. There is only One Human Sacrifice that could carry forth this great Work, and that was and is the Sacrifice of the Lord Jesus Christ, the Son of the Living God. That's why John 3:16 is perhaps the most beloved Scripture in the entirety of the Bible:

"For God so loved the world, that He gave His Only Begotten Son, that whosoever believes in Him should not perish, but have Everlasting Life."

FAITH?

What must have been the thoughts of the Patriarch when he was cutting the wood which would provide the fire for the Burnt Offering? How his heart must have broken a thousand times over. How so much the stifled sobs choked him as he endeavored to carry out the Command of God. Let me make the following statements and ask a question:

We look at the modern, so-called Faith prima-donnas, who, in reality, have no faith at all, who boast of their $5,000 suits, claiming that their faith obtained such for them. In reality, the money was wheedled out of stupid Christians, with the lure that the stupid Christians are going to get far more in return. When we place such abominations up beside the Faith of Abraham, I will ask the reader, *"How does it compare?"*

This stuff that passes today for Faith, and stuff it is, is, in reality, no more than a religious con game. It is in street parlance, *"A scam."* And yet, millions of Christians fall for these *"scams"* simply because there seems to be enough greed in all of us to keep the con game alive.

Let the reader understand that when we speak of Faith, it must be Faith in Christ and His Cross, or else, it's not Faith that God will recognize. In other words, any other type of so-called faith is bogus (Rom. 6:1-14; 8:1-11; I Cor. 1:17-18, 21, 23; 2:2, 5; Gal. 6:14; Eph. 2:13-18; Col. 2:10-15).

Concerning obedience, the Scripture says that Abraham *"rose up, and went."* It is just that simple! As well, he went to *"the place of which God had told him."*

THE THIRD DAY

"Then on the third day Abraham lifted up his eyes, and saw the place afar off" (Gen. 22:4).

This was, no doubt, the longest three days of Abraham's life. What were his thoughts when he *"saw the place afar off"*? How many temptations did he endure, which prompted him to turn around and go back? Did he sleep any during these three days and nights?

Some folk think that perfect Faith never has a question, never has a second thought, and never experiences any qualms; however that is wishful thinking only and not reality. In fact, were there no struggle, there would be no faith. What kind of test would it be if, in fact, there was no question?

WORSHIP

"And Abraham said unto his young men, Abide you here with the ass; and I and the lad will go yonder and worship, and come again to you" (Gen. 22:5).

We learn at least two very important things from this particular Verse:

1. We learn some things about worship. Praise is what we do while worship is what we are. In other words, every part and particle of our life and living should be worship of the Lord. While all worship is not praise, all praise definitely is worship.

If it is to be noticed, even though no one but Abraham knew what actually was to happen at this place of sacrifice, still, he knew what was supposed to happen. His son was to be sacrificed; and yet, he calls it *"worship."*

2. By him using the phrase, *"And come again to you,"* he was stating that he believed that God would raise the boy from the dead. In essence, he said, *"I and the lad will go yonder,"* and *"I and the lad will come again to you."*

THE CROSS

"And Abraham took the wood of the Burnt Offering, and laid it upon Isaac his son; and he took the fire in his hand, and a knife; and they went both of them together" (Gen. 22:6).

In Isaac carrying the wood on which he was to be sacrificed, we discern a Type of Christ carrying His Cross (Jn. 19:17).

This was the seventh of the sevenfold surrender of Abraham and, by far, the hardest. There is no way that we can put ourselves in his shoes. There's no way that we really can even begin to understand what he was going through as he and Isaac walked up this mountain together. Was he having second thoughts?

Whatever his thoughts were, nothing slowed his advancement in his obedience to God. In all of this scenario, he never slacked, nor did he slow. His demeanor seemed to be that of Christ when Isaiah said of Him, *"For the Lord GOD will help Me; therefore shall I not be confounded: therefore have I set My Face like a flint, and I know that I shall not be ashamed"* (Isa. 50:7).

THE LAMB

"And Isaac spoke unto Abraham his father, and said, My father: and he said, Here am I, my son. And he said, Behold the fire and the wood: but where is the lamb for a Burnt Offering?" (Gen. 22:7).

Isaac now speaks with his father, inquiring as to where the lamb was. The question must have broken Abraham's heart all over again.

The Sacrificial system was obviously explained to Adam and Eve by the Lord, and was meant to serve as a Type and Symbol of the coming Redeemer. There is evidence of sacrifices being offered all the way from the beginning, with that of Abel being the first recorded case (Gen., Chpt. 4).

As well, there is every evidence that the ones offering up the sacrifices knew that they represented the coming Redeemer, with the first prediction being given in the Garden of Eden (Gen. 3:15). Naturally, they would not have had as much knowledge as we presently have, due to the fact that the Cross is now history. However, they were well aware that the sacrifices were a substitute until the Seed of the woman would come, Who would redeem the fallen sons of Adam's lost race.

GOD WILL PROVIDE

"And Abraham said, My son, God will provide Himself a lamb for a Burnt Offering: so they went both of them together" (Gen. 22:8).

What exactly did Abraham mean by the statement, *"God will provide Himself a lamb for a Burnt Offering"*? Was he speaking prophetically of the Work of the Father and the Son as it regards Redemption, or was he, by the use of the word *"lamb,"* meaning Isaac, thus showing that it was not he who chose the victim, but God? I think, in a sense, it was probably both.

I think the Holy Spirit, by the mouth of Abraham, predicted the Lamb of God, which would be provided, and which would take away the sin of the world (Jn. 1:29).

I think in order to act on this which God has commanded, by now, Abraham knows his own Faith. He knows not, however, if Isaac personally has the Faith to endure what is about to happen. As we shall see, Isaac will pass the test with flying colors.

THE ALTAR

"And they came to the place which God had told him of; and Abraham built an Altar there, and laid the wood in order, and bound Isaac his son, and laid him on the Altar upon the wood" (Gen. 22:9).

The Lord, as is obvious here, had told him exactly to where he should come. As stated, about 1,000 years into the future, Solomon would build the Temple on this spot.

As Abraham built the Altar, he was drawing ever closer to the fatal moment. Was God asking too much of him? Was it possible for a human being to stand such a thing? Such thoughts must have gone through his mind.

But yet, Isaac would yield unreservedly to that which his father was about to do. Sometimes we have a tendency to overlook Isaac. Sandwiched between his father and his grandfather Jacob, he doesn't draw the attention of the other two. Even though his test did not compare with that of Abraham, still, his yielding as he did shows the Faith he had in both God and Abraham. By this time, Abraham has resigned himself to the death of Isaac, and Isaac has resigned himself to serve as the sacrifice.

THE KNIFE

"And Abraham stretched forth his hand, and took the knife to kill his son" (Gen. 22:10).

Isaac, as the unresisting Burnt Offering, is a striking Type of Him Who said, *"I delight to do Your Will, O My God"* (Ps. 40:8).

When Abraham took the knife in his hand and raised his arm, he fully intended to punch the knife deep into his son's chest. He would then ignite the wood with fire and, thereby, reduce Isaac's body to ashes. He then expected the Lord to raise Isaac from the dead. In other words, if there was ever a man committed, this man was committed.

In his mind, how could it be otherwise! The Lord had promised to establish His Covenant with Isaac (Gen. 17:19) and had even said, *"In Isaac shall your seed be called"* (Gen. 21:12). So, the only thing that Abraham could see was that God would raise the boy from the dead.

However, the Lord wasn't wanting to portray at this time His Miracle-working Power to Abraham, but rather the object lesson of the Plan of Redemption, which would require the Death of God's Son. The entire scenario, as well, would prove, beyond the shadow of a doubt, Abraham's love for the Lord and his trust in the Lord.

ABRAHAM, ABRAHAM

"And the Angel of the LORD called unto him out of heaven, and said, Abraham, Abraham: and he said, Here am I" (Gen. 22:11).

He Who said, *"Abraham, Abraham,"* was the same One Who said, *"Martha, Martha,"* *"Simon, Simon,"* and *"Saul, Saul."* The repetition denotes urgency.

Horton said, *"When Abraham took the knife, his surrender was complete."* His Faith and consecration had now been demonstrated totally and completely, and so God stopped him by calling his name twice.

As the Lord called out to Abraham at this time, to be sure, the Voice of God never was so welcomed, never so sweet, and never so seasonable as now. Concerning this, Matthew Henry said:

"It was the trial that God intended, not the act. It was not God's intention that Isaac should actually be sacrificed. In this it was shown that nobler blood from that of animals, in due time, was to be shed for sin — even the Blood of the Only Begotten Son of God. But in the meanwhile God would not in any case have human sacrifices used."[2]

FAITH TESTED

"And He said, Lay not your hand upon the lad, neither do you anything unto him: for now I know that you fear God, seeing you have not withheld your son, your only son from Me" (Gen. 22:12).

All of this portrays the fact that it's not so much the act but the intent of the heart which God sees. Abraham didn't have to kill the boy to prove himself to God, but he had to fully intend to do so, and that he did! He did it even though he did not understand why God would ask such a thing, or why it was necessary for God to ask such a thing. In other words, he knew he had heard the Voice of God, and he knew what God had told him to do. In his mind, even though the questions loomed large, the answer to those questions was not really his affair, that being in the

Domain of Jehovah. His business was to obey, and obey he did.

We aren't told the exact manner in which God revealed Himself to Abraham. The Scripture merely says, *"And it came to pass after these things, that God did tempt Abraham, and said unto him . . . Take now your son, your only son Isaac, whom you love, and go into the land of Moriah; and offer him there for a Burnt Offering . . ."* (Gen. 22:1-2).

To be sure, Abraham had to be doubly certain that the voice speaking to him was definitely that of God and not the Evil One. We are given precious little information as it regards Abraham's actions and thoughts. At any rate, whatever transpired, he, in fact, knew beyond the shadow of a doubt that it was God speaking to him. Therefore, he obeyed!

OMNISCIENCE

How do we reconcile the statement as given by the Lord, *"For now I know that you fear God,"* with the Omniscience of God, which means that He knows all things, past, present, and future?

Some have claimed that God had to know the situation by experience as well as foreknowledge; however, that would make His Word less than experience, which we know is not the case.

Others have claimed that this is merely an anthropomorphism, which means that the Holy Spirit spoke in human terminology in order that we might understand. That is not plausible either because, were that the case, that would mean the Holy Spirit is not telling the truth.

The Hebrew word here for *"know"* is, *"Yada,"* and means, *"To observe, to care, to recognize, to instruct, to designate, or even to punish."*

A root of *"yada"* is, *"Yiddehonee,"* and means, *"The knowing One."* As well, this is the meaning of the word, *"Know,"* in Verse 12. So, it can be translated as the following to help us understand it better:

"For I the Knowing One knew that you feared God, and that you would not withhold your son, your only son from Me."

THE DOCTRINE OF SUBSTITUTION

"And Abraham lifted up his eyes, and looked, and behold behind him a ram caught in a thicket by his horns: and Abraham went and took the ram, and offered him up for a Burnt Offering in the stead of his son" (Gen. 22:13).

As stated, here we have the Doctrine of Substitution plainly laid out. The ram was offered up in sacrifice instead of his son.

As is clearly observed, the Lord Jesus Christ became our Substitute. It would have done no good to have actually sacrificed Isaac simply because, as all, with the exception of Christ, Isaac was born in sin. However, the ram, which was an innocent victim, could be a Type of Christ and could be offered up in the place of Isaac, which it was. Faith in what that sacrifice represented would definitely cover sin even though the blood of bulls and goats could not take away sin, that remaining until the Cross of Christ (Heb. 10:4).

THE DOCTRINE OF SUBSTITUTION
AND IDENTIFICATION

As stated, even though the Doctrine of Substitution is clearly set forth here, its corresponding Doctrine of Identification is not so clearly stated, that awaiting Moses (Num. 21:9). Still, we are seeing here the very heart of the Salvation Plan.

Jesus Christ is our Substitute, meaning that He did for us what we could not do for ourselves. This refers to satisfying the demands of a thrice-Holy God, which Christ did by dying on the Cross. We are then to identify with Him in this which He has done.

All of this is clearly laid out in Romans, Chapter 6. First of all, we are baptized into the Death of Christ, then buried with Him, and then raised with Him in Newness of Life (Rom. 6:3-5), which all comes by Faith.

When the Scripture speaks of our being baptized into His Death, it is not speaking of Water Baptism, as many believe, but rather our identification with Christ. It means this:

THE BELIEVING SINNER

Whenever the believing sinner exhibits Faith in Christ, in the Mind of God, the believing sinner is literally placed into the very Crucifixion, Death, and Resurrection of Christ. Christ was our Substitute, and our Faith in Him so identifies us with Him that God looks at us as though what was done was done by us, even though it was done by Christ.

We were then buried with Him, which refers to the old life and all that we once were. Being buried means it is no more, meaning that the old you died (Rom. 6:7-8).

We were then raised with Him *"in Newness of Life,"* which means that we are now New Creations, with old things having passed away and all things having become new (II Cor. 5:17).

This that we have given is the very heart of Salvation, which pertains to all that we are in Christ. In fact, the very words, *"In Christ,"* portray this great Plan more so than anything else. The Apostle Paul uses *"in Christ,"* *"in Him,"* or one of its several derivatives some 170 times, it is said, in his 14 Epistles. Due to what

Christ did at the Cross, all on our behalf, and our Faith and confidence in Him and what He has done, we are literally *"in Christ."* That is the Doctrine of *"Substitution and Identification."*

JEHOVAH-JIREH

"And Abraham called the name of that place Jehovah-jireh: as it is said to this day, In the Mount of the LORD it shall be seen" (Gen. 22:14).

As stated, *"Jehovah-jireh"* means, *"The Lord will provide."* The question may be asked, *"Provide what?"*

He would provide a Saviour, a Redeemer, Who would be the Lord Jesus Christ, God's Only Son, of Whom both Isaac and the ram were a Type.

While this *"provision"* pertains to everything that the Believer needs, whether it is domestical, physical, or material, it is primarily the Spiritual addressed here. Man needs a Redeemer, which is his primary need, and that Redeemer is the Lord Jesus Christ.

From all of this, the Jews coined a proverb which states, *"In the Mount of the Lord it shall be seen,"* which is a Prophecy of the Manifestation of Christ. It might be said that on this very mountain, the Sacrifice would be offered, which would take away the sin of the world (Isa. 53:5; Jn. 1:29).

Unfortunately, at the present time, this *"provision,"* which, incidentally, is by far the greatest provision ever known, has been perverted, or one might say, *"Inverted."* The emphasis at the present time is placed by many on the provision of material things, when the primary cause of this provision pertains to God providing a Saviour from sin. This is what Paul was speaking of when he said:

"For many walk, of whom I have told you often, and now tell you even weeping, that they are the enemies of the Cross of Christ:

"Whose end is destruction, whose god is their belly, and whose glory is in their shame, who mind earthly things" (Phil. 3:18-19).

ENEMIES OF THE CROSS

Paul told us to *"mark those"* who conduct themselves in that fashion, which means to point them out. The phrase, *"Whose god is their belly,"* points to their own self-will, with the *"earthly things"* pointing to that which money can buy. Considering this, their *"glory"* is not in the Cross of Christ, but rather in themselves, which is *"their shame."*

These Passages mean that everyone who places other things ahead of the Cross of Christ, or rather looks to other things than the Cross of Christ, has to be put down as *"enemies of the Cross."* This pertains to those who follow after the psychological way, as well as those who subscribe to the Word of Faith doctrine.

Concerning *"glory,"* Paul also said:

"But God forbid that I should glory, save in the Cross of our Lord Jesus Christ, by Whom the world is crucified unto me, and I unto the world" (Gal. 6:14).

He also said:

"For Christ sent me not to baptize (not to place the emphasis on Water Baptism, or anything else for that matter), but to preach the Gospel: not with wisdom of words, lest the Cross of Christ should be made of none effect" (I Cor. 1:17).

THE MODERN CHURCH

In truth, sadly, the modern church has all but rejected that which God has provided, which is the Cross of Christ, and has substituted other things to take its place. The modern church is, for all practical purposes, a Cross-less church; consequently, it is *"Christian"* in name only. If we remove the Cross, ignore the Cross, fail of belief regarding the Cross, or even shift our Faith from the Cross to other things, we have denied that which God has provided and are substituting other things to take its place. In other words, we blaspheme!

When we speak of the Cross, we aren't speaking of the wooden beam on which Jesus died, as should be obvious, but rather what Jesus there did in order to purchase the New Covenant.

This of which we speak here has been the battleground of the Plan of God from the very beginning. Abel has offered up the lamb as a sacrifice, which God provided, and Cain has offered up something else and grows very angry because God will not accept it. It hasn't changed from then until now. Religious men keep trying to offer up things other than Christ and Him Crucified and then when God rejects it, which shows itself up in a lack of victory in their hearts and lives, they seek to kill those who trust in God's Way. In our land the law will not allow such, so they do the second best thing, which is try to kill one's reputation, or use any tactic at their disposal to destroy the ministry of those whom they do not like.

It began that way, it continues that way, and will be that way until the Lord comes.

TOTALLY CORRUPT

Concerning the church in these days, the last days, Jesus said:

"Another Parable spoke He unto them;
The Kingdom of Heaven is like unto leaven
(invariably presented in Scripture as a symbol

of evil), **which a woman took** *(frequently in Scripture the woman, as well, is presented as an agent of idolatry),* **and hid in three measures of meal** *(the meal is the Word of God),* **till the whole was leavened** *(more tares than wheat)"* **(Mat. 13:33).**

The phrase, *"Till the whole was leavened,"* tells us the condition of the church in these the last days.

A PERSONAL EXPERIENCE

It was the late winter of 1992, if I remember the time frame correctly. It was our morning prayer meeting, which convened at 10:00 a.m. There were not many there, possibly seven or eight.

As we went to prayer that morning, after a few moments, the Spirit of God settled over me in a great way. I was praying for myself, but then the Lord gave me a great burden for the church as a whole.

He said to me, *"I will help you, but you must know that the entirety of the church is in terrible condition."* He then gave to me the words of Isaiah, which were given so long ago.

"Why should you be stricken anymore? you will revolt more and more: the whole head is sick, and the whole heart faint.

"From the sole of the foot even unto the head there is no soundness in it; but wounds, and bruises, and putrefying sores: they have not been closed, neither bound up, neither mollified with ointment" (Isa. 1:5-6).

Then the Lord spoke again, saying, *"I am going to start a Work at Family Worship Center that will girdle the entirety of the globe."*

The Spirit of God lingered for a great period of time, actually, almost to the noon hour.

I knew that the Lord had spoken, and I knew what he said, but I wondered how in the world would such happen. What did he mean, *"Girdle the globe?"*

Now I know what He meant. When He spoke unto my heart, it would be some five years before He would give me the great Word of the Cross. But now, that Message by radio, television, and the Internet is going out all over the world from FAMILY WORSHIP CENTER exactly as the Lord said it would, and it's only the beginning. I believe that the Lord is going to effect a Move which will result in millions of souls being Saved. I realize those numbers are big, but I believe in my heart this is exactly what the Lord is going to do. In fact, the preparation stages have already begun.

REVELATION

"And the Angel of the LORD called unto Abraham out of heaven the second time" (Gen. 22:15).

The first time the Lord spoke to Abraham, at least after they had arrived at the mountain, regarded substitution, as we've already explained. This time, it would be for Revelation, meaning that God will reveal to Abraham what He is going to do for him. However, let the reader understand that the *"Revelation"* is entirely dependent upon the *"Substitution."* No Substitution, no Revelation! To make it simpler, no Cross, no Revelation!

The modern church stumbles along with little or no Revelation, or else, a borrowed Revelation, simply because it has ignored the Substitution, i.e., *"the Cross."*

All Revelation depends in some way on the Cross of Christ. In fact, anything and everything that God does for us, to us, of us, with us, and in us is done exclusively by and through Christ and what He did at the Cross. If we deny the Cross or ignore the Cross in any way, we cut God off and open ourselves up to deceiving spirits.   So, anything and everything that one hears from preachers who have denied the Cross or ignored the Cross is not of God and, in fact, is made up out of their own minds, or else, given to them by Angels of light (II Cor. 11:13-15).

FOUNT OF BLESSING

"And said, By Myself have I sworn, says the LORD, for because you have done this thing, and have not withheld your son, your only son" (Gen. 22:16).

Taking this statement through to its ultimate conclusion, it, in effect, is saying exactly what I have just said.

While Isaac wasn't sacrificed, actually, in a figure, he was, and, as well, in a figure, he was raised from the dead (Heb. 11:18-19). This means that although he was of Christ, he was a figure of Christ.

The point of this statement is, the great Blessing that God pronounces upon Abraham and his seed, which, in effect, includes not only Israel but also every Believer who has ever lived (Rom. 4:16), comes exclusively by and through the Cross of Christ. In fact, it could not be any clearer.

VICTORY

"That in blessing I will bless you, and in multiplying I will multiply your seed as the stars of the heaven, and as the sand which is upon the seashore; and your seed shall possess the gate of his enemies" (Gen. 22:17).

This Passage tells us three things:

1. It is no longer a promise but a solemn contract ratified by an oath. God said, *"By Myself I have sworn"* (Vs. 16).

2. It assures Abraham's seed of ultimate victory. This refers to victory over the world, the flesh, and the

Devil, which all comes by what Jesus did at the Cross our Faith in that Finished Work. This gives latitude to the Holy Spirit to exhibit His Power on our behalf.

3. It transfers to Abraham's offspring the Promise of being the Means of Blessedness to all mankind, which refers not only to Israel but, as well, to the Church, all in Christ.

CERTAIN VICTORY

In the last phrase of this Verse, He didn't say, *"And your seed may possibly possess the gate of his enemies,"* but rather, *"Your seed shall possess the gate of his enemies."*

This pertains to Christ and what He did at the Cross. Paul outlined this by saying:

"Blotting out the handwriting of Ordinances that was against us, which was contrary to us, and took it out of the way, nailing it to His Cross;

"And having spoiled principalities and powers, He made a show of them openly, triumphing over them in it" (Col. 2:14-15).

"Possessing the gate" refers to taking the city or defeating the enemy. It pertains to certain victory. The idea is this:

If you, the Believer, go God's Way, which is the Way of the Cross and is perfectly outlined in this Chapter, then you are guaranteed certain victory over the world, the flesh, and the Devil, as coined by the Early Church fathers.

To the contrary, if the Believer's Faith is in anything other than the Cross of Christ, then victory is impossible. The very word, *"Believers,"* refers to believing in Jesus Christ and Him Crucified (I Cor. 1:23). Failure to believe in the Cross, which means to put one's Faith totally and completely in the Sacrifice of Christ, puts one in the ranks of *"unbelievers."* No matter how religious the other things may be in which one may place his Faith, it is that which God cannot recognize. He recognizes the Cross alone!

OBEDIENCE

"And in your seed shall all the nations of the Earth be blessed; because you have obeyed My Voice" (Gen. 22:18).

Obedience from Abraham in every respect, even the most difficult things, was that which the Lord desired.

For the modern Saint, we find two things which are absolutely necessary:

• We are to obey the Word of God in every respect, understanding that it is our guide through life. Truly as the Psalmist said:

"Your Word is a Lamp unto my feet, and a Light unto my path" (Ps. 119:105).

The first question for anything must be, *"Is it Scriptural?"*

• On a personal basis, the Lord desires to lead us in all things and will definitely give us personal Guidance and Direction, if we will only seek His Face as it regards this of which we speak. Regrettably, many Christians only seek the Lord in times of crisis and little consult Him, if at all, as it regards the everyday directions of life. However, the Lord wants to be involved in every aspect of our lives and living, and unless He is involved in every aspect, He cannot ascertain our obedience.

FAITH

As it pertains to a Believer, everything, irrespective as to what it is, has to do with our Faith and our obedience. In fact, Faith and obedience are twins. If there is little faith, there will be little obedience, and, of necessity, great Faith demands total obedience.

Once again, even though we are being repetitious, when we speak of *"Faith,"* always and without exception, we are speaking of Faith in Christ and what Christ did for us in His Suffering. Those two things are to never be divorced.

Please notice, the *"Blessing"* which was given to Abraham was all predicated on his obedience. It is no less with us presently.

Incidentally, the Promise that all the nations of the Earth should be blessed in the Promised Seed predicts primarily the Salvation of the Gentiles, as such. This is proof that the *"mystery"* revealed in the Epistle to the Ephesians, and revealed there for the first time, is not the Blessing of the Gentile nations per se, but rather Christ and the Church (Eph. 3:3-4, 9; 5:32; 6:19).

THE RETURN TO BEER-SHEBA

"So Abraham returned unto his young men, and they rose up and went together to Beer-sheba; and Abraham dwelt at Beer-sheba" (Gen. 22:19).

The leaving of Beer-sheba with Isaac and the others some three days before was, without a doubt, the most horrifying three days journey that Abraham had ever undertaken. Likewise, but in the opposite direction, the three days journey back to Beer-sheba was, without a doubt, the most wonderful journey in which the Patriarch had ever engaged. He left with Isaac, and he came back with Isaac. At the same time, he fully obeyed the Lord.

The phrase, *"And Abraham dwelt at Beer-sheba,"* indicates that he probably spent the balance of his life in this place, with the exception that he may have visited Mamre, near Hebron, from time to time.

POINTING TO CHRIST

"And it came to pass after these things, that it was told Abraham, saying, Behold, Milcah, she has also born children unto your brother Nahor;

"Huz his firstborn, and Buz his brother, and Kemuel the father of Aram,

"And Chesed, and Hazo, and Pildash, and Jidlaph, and Bethuel.

"And Bethuel begat Rebekah: these eight Milcah did bear to Nahor, Abraham's brother.

"And his concubine, whose name was Reumah, she bore also Tebah, and Gaham, and Thahash, and Maachah" (Gen. 22:20-24).

This Chapter concludes with an account of Nahor's family, who settled at Haran (Gen. 12:1-5). None of this would have been given but for the connection which it had with the Work of God on Earth. From these people mentioned here, both Isaac and Jacob took wives; and preparatory to the account of those events, this genealogy is recorded.

All of this was for the sake of bringing Christ into the world. God must become Man, and as Man, He would redeem the human race, and do so by dying on the Cross.

THE LORD JESUS CHRIST

Isaac was a Type of Christ, and had he actually died at the time of the proposed sacrifice, it would have been with inward peace and without extraordinary pain. However, Christ actually tasted death and all of its bitterness. He died surrounded with contempt and insult, treated with indignity and cruelty, and loaded with the weight of our iniquities, while *"it pleased the LORD to bruise Him, and to put Him to grief, and even to make His Soul a Sacrifice for sin"* (Isa. 53:10).

Hereby we perceive the Love of Christ in that He gave Himself a Sacrifice for our sins. Behold He dies, yet rises; He lives, ascends, and intercedes for us! He calls the sinners to come to Him and partake of His Blood-bought Salvation.

Whatsoever is dearest to us upon Earth is our Isaac — happy are we if we can sacrifice it to God. The only way for us to find comfort in any earthly thing is to surrender it in Faith into the Hands of God.

Yet, we shall do well to remember that Abraham was not justified by this action regarding Isaac, but by the infinitely more noble Obedience of Jesus Christ — his Faith receiving this, relying on this, and rejoicing in this. This means that his Salvation was by Faith in Christ and the Suffering of Christ, and so is every other soul who has ever made Christ the Lord of their lives. It is all by Faith, as it has all been by Faith.

So, the closing Verses of this Twenty-second Chapter, which seem to be insignificant, with the casual reader wondering why they were even included, are extremely important because they ultimately point to Christ. Anything connected with Christ is the single most important thing there is.

"I can see far down the mountain,
"Where I have wandered many years,
"Often hindered on my journey,
"By the ghosts of doubts and fears."

"Broken vows and disappointments,
"Thickly strewn along the way,
"But the Spirit has led unerring,
"To the land I hold today."

ABRAHAM

CHAPTER

27

Abraham And
The Death Of Sarah

ABRAHAM AND THE DEATH OF SARAH

"And Sarah was an hundred and twenty-seven years old: these were the years of the life of Sarah.

"And Sarah died in Kirjath-arba; the same is Hebron in the land of Canaan: and Abraham came to mourn for Sarah, and to weep for her" (Gen. 23:1-2).

Sarah is the only woman in the Bible whose age, death, and burial are recorded.

No doubt, this is significant partly because she is the mother of the Hebrew Nation, and partly because the promised heir having come, the vessel of the promise, that is, Sarah, i.e., *"the first Covenant,"* necessarily passes away.

This means that Isaac was 37 years old when his mother Sarah died, and Abraham was 137.

"Arba" is the old name of *"Hebron."* Abraham must have temporarily moved here from Beer-sheba.

Regarding the place of Sarah's death, perhaps the phrase, *"In the land of Canaan,"* is given in order that we might know that she did not die in the country of the Philistines, but rather in the *"Promised Land."* Upon coming into the Promised Land, which took place about 400 years later, Caleb took *"Kirjath-arba"* as his possession (Josh. 15:13-14).

The sadness of Abraham in losing Sarah was, I think, to a greater degree than normal.

She had fought this good fight of Faith with him every step of the way; consequently, in a sense, as he was the *"father of us all"* (Rom. 4:16), Sarah was the *"mother of us all"* (I Pet. 3:6).

FAITH

"And Abraham stood up from before his dead, and spoke unto the sons of Heth, saying,

"I am a stranger and a sojourner with you: give me a possession of a buryingplace with you, that I may bury my dead out of my sight.

"And the children of Heth answered Abraham, saying unto him,

"Hear us, my lord: you are a mighty prince among us: in the choice of our sepulchres bury your dead; none of us shall withhold from you his sepulchre, but that you may bury your dead" (Gen. 23:3-6).

Love weeps for Sarah, but Faith *"stood up from before his dead,"* in essence, meaning that Abraham most definitely believed in a coming Resurrection. It hasn't happened yet, but it's due at any time.

With Abraham's statement to the sons of Heth that he was *"a stranger and a sojourner among you"* was a confession that he sought, as his real inheritance, a better country, even an Heavenly (Heb. 11:13).

The request for a *"buryingplace"* for Sarah is the first mention of a grave in Scripture.

The Patriarch's request of the sons of Heth that he might purchase a gravesite for Sarah was a sign of his right and title to the land of Canaan, which the sons of Heth would not have understood.

They offered to give him a buryingplace without cost, but, likewise, for reasons these individuals would never have understood, the Patriarch could not accept their largesse. With perfect courtesy, though, likewise, with respectful firmness, he declines their offer.

ABRAHAM

"And Abraham stood up, and bowed himself to the people of the land, even to the children of Heth" (Gen. 23:7).

The sons of Heth offered Abraham the choicest of their sepulchres, but in death, as in life, the man of Faith would be a pilgrim. He would have no fellowship with the children of darkness and would not be indebted to them even for a grave. Accordingly, he insisted upon this purchase.

They had no idea that Abraham was looking forward to the possession of the whole land. Because he did so look forward, the possession of a grave was by no means a small matter to him.

Hebrews, Chapter 11, states, *"These all died, not having received the Promises; but in dying, as in living, they found the Promises real and satisfying."*

The Patriarch felt out these sons of Heth as to how they felt about him securing a gravesite among them for Sarah. Once he ascertained that they were agreeable, he would now proceed to speak of a specific place. As is obvious, not any place would do. It must be *"the cave of Machpelah."*

THE CAVE OF MACHPELAH

"And he communed with them, saying, If it be your mind that I should bury my dead out of my sight; hear me, and entreat for me to Ephron the son of Zohar,

"That he may give me the cave of Machpelah, which he has, which is in the end of his field; for as much money as it is worth he shall give it to me for a possession of a buryingplace among you" (Gen. 23:8-9).

As previously stated, in the purchasing of Machpelah for a burying place, Abraham gave expression to his Faith as it regards the coming Resurrection. *"He stood up from before his dead."* Faith cannot long keep death in view; it has a higher object. Resurrection is that which ever fills the vision of Faith, and in the power thereof, it can rise up from before the dead.

There is much conveyed in this action of Abraham. We want to understand its meaning much more fully because we are much too prone to be occupied with death and its consequences. Death is the boundary of Satan's power; but where Satan ends, God begins.

Abraham understood this when he rose up and purchased the cave of Machpelah as a sleeping-place for Sarah. This was the expression of Abraham's Faith, though in reference to the future. He knew that in the ages to come, God's Promise about the land of Canaan would be fulfilled, and he was able to lay the body of Sarah in the tomb *"in sure and certain hope of a glorious Resurrection."*

THE HITTITE

"And Ephron dwelt among the children of Heth: and Ephron the Hittite answered Abraham in the audience of the children of Heth, even of all who went in at the gate of his city, saying,

"No, my lord, hear me: the field give I to you, and the cave that is therein, I give it to you; in the presence of the sons of my people I give it to you: bury your dead.

"And Abraham bowed down himself before the people of the land" (Gen. 23:10-12).

The sons of Heth knew nothing about Salvation and Resurrection, which means that the thoughts which filled the Patriarch's soul were entirely foreign to them. To them, it seemed a small matter where he buried his dead, but it was by no means a small matter to Abraham.

The finest traits and characteristics of Faith are those which are the more incomprehensible to the natural man. The Canaanites had no idea of the expectations which were giving character to Abraham's actions on this occasion. They had no idea that he was looking forward to the possession of the land, even the entirety of the land, while he was merely looking for a spot in which, as a dead man, he might wait for God's Time and God's Manner.

This is a truly glorious feature in the Divine Life. Those *"witnesses"* of whom the Apostle is speaking in Hebrews, Chapter 11, did not merely live by Faith, but even when they arrived at the close of their lives, they proved that the Promises of God were as real and satisfying to their souls as when they first began.

MONEY

"And he spoke unto Ephron in the audience of the people of the land, saying, But if you will give it, I pray you, hear me: I will give you money for the field; take it of me, and I will bury my dead there" (Gen. 23:13).

This is the first time that money is mentioned in the Bible as a medium of exchange.

Why was Abraham so particular about this purchase? Why was he so anxious to make good his claim to the field and cave of Ephron on righteous principles? Why was he so determined to weigh out the full price *"current with the merchant"*?

"Faith" is the answer. He did it all by Faith. He knew the land was his in prospect, and that in Resurrection-Glory, his seed should yet possess it, but until then, he would be no debtor to those who were yet to be dispossessed.

THE PURCHASE

"And Ephron answered Abraham, saying unto him,

"My Lord, hearken unto me: the land is worth four hundred shekels of silver; what is that between me and you? bury therefore your dead.

"And Abraham hearkened unto Ephron; and Abraham weighed to Ephron the silver, which he had named in the audience of the sons of Heth, four hundred shekels of silver, current money with the merchant" (Gen. 23:14-16).

Abraham was a mighty prince among these people, and they undoubtedly would have been very glad to have done him the favor of giving him the land free of charge. However, Abraham had learned to take his favors only from the God of Resurrection. While he would pay *"them"* for Machpelah, he would look to *"Him"* for the entirety of the land of Canaan, which most certainly one day would be his.

The truth is, looking at things in this light, the cave of Machpelah was worth much more to him than it was to them. Faith conducts the soul onward into God's Future. It looks at things as He looks at them and estimates them according to the Judgment of the Sanctuary.

As stated, even though the sons of Heth did not understand these things, Abraham was purchasing this buryingplace, which significantly set forth his hope of Resurrection and an inheritance founded thereon.

THE POSSESSION

"And the field of Ephron, which was in Machpelah, which was before Mamre, the field, and the cave which was therein, and all the trees that were in the field, that were in all the borders round about, were made sure.

"Unto Abraham for a possession in the presence of the children of Heth, before all who went in at the gate of his city.

"And after this, Abraham buried Sarah his wife in the cave of the field of Machpelah before Mamre: the same is Hebron in the land of Canaan.

"And the field, and the cave that is therein, were made sure unto Abraham for a possession of a burying-place by the sons of Heth" (Gen. 23:17-20).

Thus, we may view this beautiful Chapter in a two-fold light:

1. As setting before us a plain, practical principle, as to our dealings with the world, such dealings must always be aboveboard, forthright, and honest.

2. We should do everything with the idea in mind that the Blessed Hope is ever before us and should ever animate the Man of Faith.

Putting both of these points together, we have an example of what the Child of God should ever be. The Hope set before us in the Gospel is a glorious immortality. While it lifts the heart above every influence of nature and the world, it furnishes a high and holy principle with which to govern all of our dealings with those who are without. *"We know that, when He shall appear, we shall be like Him; for we shall see Him as He is"* (I Jn. 3:2).

What is the Scriptural effect of this?

"Every man who has this Hope in Him purifies himself, even as He is pure" (I Jn. 3:3).

In the cave of Machpelah, his own remains and those of Isaac, Rebekah, Jacob, and Leah were deposited. Of the great Patriarchal family, Rachel alone was not buried here.

DISCREPANCY?

Some have claimed that there is a discrepancy in the account given in Genesis, Chapter 23, concerning the cave of Machpelah, and the statement made by Stephen in Acts 7:16. That particular statement says:

"And were carried over into Sychem, and laid in the sepulchre that Abraham bought for a sum of money of the sons of Emmor the father of Sychem."

There is no discrepancy.

The reference here is given by Stephen as to the burial of the 12 Patriarchs, who were Jacob's sons. Jacob was buried in the cave of Machpelah near Hebron where Abraham and Sarah had been buried (Gen. 23:17, 19; 50:13). Joseph was buried in Shechem (Josh. 24:32).

Genesis 33:19 and Joshua 24:32 indicate that Jacob did the actual buying of the plot in Shechem.

However, Abraham was still alive at the time, and it was undoubtedly purchased in the name of Abraham as the head of the clan, as things were done in those days. So, there is no discrepancy in the account given by Moses in Genesis, Chapter 23, and the account given by Stephen in Acts 7:16.

Incidentally, Shechem is about 75 miles north of Hebron where the cave of Machpelah is located.

"Thanks to God for my Redeemer,
"Thanks for all You did provide!
"Thanks for time now but a memory,
"Thanks for Jesus by my side!
"Thanks for pleasant, cheerful springtime,
"Thanks for summer, winter, fall!
"Thanks for tears by now forgotten,
"Thanks for peace within my soul!"

"Thanks for prayers that You have answered,
"Thanks for what You did deny!
"Thanks for storms that I have weathered,
"Thanks for all You do supply!
"Thanks for pain, and thanks for pleasure,
"Thanks for comfort in despair!
"Thanks for Grace that none can measure,
"Thanks for love beyond compare!"

"Thanks for roses by the wayside,
"Thanks for thorns that stems contain!
"Thanks for homes and thanks for fireside,
"Thanks for hope, that sweet refrain!
"Thanks for joy and thanks for sorrow,
"Thanks for Heavenly peace with Thee!
"Thanks for hope in the tomorrow,
"Thanks through all eternity!"

ABRAHAM

CHAPTER

28

Abraham And
A Bride For Isaac

ABRAHAM AND A BRIDE FOR ISAAC

"And Abraham was old, and well stricken in age: and the LORD had blessed Abraham in all things" (Gen. 24:1).

In fact, the Patriarch was now about 140 years old and would actually live to the age of 175 (Gen. 25:7). He lived some 35 years after Isaac was married and lived to see Esau and Jacob nearly grown up.

In the Bible, Genesis, Chapters 22 through 24, present a startling picture. In Chapter 22, the son is offered up. In Chapter 23, Sarah is laid aside. In Chapter 24, the servant is sent forth to procure a bride for him who had been, as it were, received from the dead in a figure.

When we turn to the New Testament, we see a remarkable similarity:

- The Rejection and Death of Christ.
- The setting aside of Israel after the flesh.
- The calling out of the Church to occupy the high position of the Bride of the Lamb.

So, in this Chapter, we shall see a portrayal of that just mentioned.

Some may ask if we are, in fact, to view this particular Chapter as a *"type"* of the calling out of the Church by the Holy Spirit. Perhaps, as Mackintosh says, it would be better to look at it as an illustration of that Glorious Work. He went on to say:

"We cannot suppose that the Spirit of God would occupy an unusually long Chapter with a mere detail of a family compact, were that compact not typical or illustrative of some great truth."[1]

I personally believe that it furnishes us with a beautiful illustration or foreshadowing of the great mystery of the Church. It is important to see that there is no direct Revelation of this mystery in the Old Testament, in other words, stating that the Church is not really referred to in the Old Testament. There are, nevertheless, scenes and circumstances that, in a very remarkable manner, shadow it forth, which are portrayed in this Chapter.

THE CHURCH IN THE OLD TESTAMENT

In essence, Israel was the Church of the Old Testament. Actually, as stated, there is only a dim shadow of the Church in the Old Testament. Why is that?

The Church actually was not the Will of God for the world. It was God's Will and Plan that Israel would be raised up, which they were, would bring forth the Word of God, which they did, and serve as the Womb of the Messiah, which they did. They were to accept Him as Saviour and Lord and then be a blessing to the entirety of the world. In fact, Jesus introduced the Kingdom with His First Advent. Regrettably, Israel would have none of it. She would not accept her King, and we speak of Jesus; therefore, she forfeited the Kingdom. As the result, Israel was scattered all over the world and will not regain her rightful place and position until she accepts Jesus Christ as Saviour and Lord. This she will do in the midst of the Battle of Armageddon, in other words, at His Second Advent. So, the Church was morphed in to take the place of Israel, which she did. In fact, the time of the Church is just about over because Israel will soon be restored.

That's the primary reason that the Church is not mentioned in the Old Testament, except in distant shadow.

ISAAC

"And Abraham said unto his eldest servant of his house, who ruled over all that he had, Put, I pray you, your hand under my thigh:

"And I will make you swear by the LORD, the God of heaven, and the God of the Earth, that you shall

not take a wife unto my son of the daughters of the Canaanites, among whom I dwell:

"But you shall go unto my country, and to my kindred, and take a wife unto my son Isaac" (Gen. 24:2-4).

The *"eldest servant"* mentioned here must be none other than Eliezer of Damascus, for he is referred to in that manner throughout the entirety of this Chapter. It is done so for a particular reason if, in fact, this Chapter is also meant to portray the Holy Spirit seeking a bride for Christ, which is the Church. I believe this Chapter is meant to portray exactly that.

The Business of the Holy Spirit is not to glorify Himself, even though He is God, but rather to glorify Christ (Jn. 16:13-14).

ELIEZER

Before Eliezer went on this all-important journey, he had to swear by the Lord, the God of Heaven, that he would not choose one of the daughters of the Canaanites as a wife for Isaac. He was instructed to go to Abraham's country, from whence the Patriarch had come. In this case, we speak of Nahor, which was near the city of Haran. It was about a 700 mile journey from Beer-sheba.

The placing of the hand of the servant under the thigh of the Patriarch seems to be an origination of Abraham inasmuch as nothing similar can elsewhere be found.

The thigh, as the source of posterity, has been regarded as pointing to Abraham's future descendants, and in particular, to Christ, the Promised Seed. So, the oath was the equivalent to a swearing by Him Who was to come, namely Christ.

Abraham knew that his Calling and purpose in life were to bring about the promised son, which had now been done, through whom the great Nation of Israel would come forth. It was all for the intended purpose of bringing the Son of God into the world. So, not only was Isaac of extreme importance as a person, as would be obvious, but the young lady to whom he would be married would figure prominently in that importance as well. She must not be a daughter of the Canaanites, but rather of his own people.

CANAANITES!

What was the difference between the Canaanite women and those of his own family back in Haran?

There were at least three reasons that Abraham demanded that Eliezer not choose a woman of the Canaanites:

1. It is undoubtedly correct that the Lord moved upon Abraham to do what he did (Vs. 7). Abraham's entire family were descendants of Shem, of whom the Prophecy declared that the Blessing (Christ) would come (Gen. 9:26).

2. There is a good possibility that the Canaanite races or people were already being infiltrated by fallen Angels, bringing forth a race of giants, with the entirety of some tribes totally contaminated in some way. Genesis 6:4 says:

"There were giants in the Earth in those days (before the Flood); and also after that (after the Flood), when the sons of God came in unto the daughters of men, and they bore children unto them."

As well, the Canaanites were descendants of Ham who had been cursed (Gen. 9:25).

3. Due to the Revelation given to Abraham by God, the entirety of his family, whomever they might have been, knew God in some fashion whereas the Canaanites knew Him not at all.

THE COMMAND OF THE LORD

"And the servant said unto him, Peradventure the woman will not be willing to follow me unto this land: must I needs bring your son again unto the land from where you came?

"And Abraham said unto him, You beware that you bring not my son thither again.

"The LORD God of Heaven, which took me from my father's house, and from the land of my kindred, and Who spoke unto me, and Who swore unto me, saying, Unto your seed will I give this land; He shall send His Angel before you, and you shall take a wife unto my son from thence" (Gen. 24:5-7).

Several things are said here:

• Not being the one to whom the Word from the Lord was given concerning this thing, Eliezer foresees potential problems. But yet, he would totally submit to Abraham's Faith, despite these potential difficulties. Blessed is the Pastor who has men like this in his Church, who can recognize Faith.

• By no means was Isaac to be taken to the particular land where his wife was to be found. The Promised Land was his home, and opportunity for temptation must not be put in his way. His Calling is Canaan Land, even though he, as his father Abraham, will not live to see the Promise brought to pass.

• According to Verse 7, every indication is that the Lord had given Abraham instructions as to what to do.

• The Lord would send an Angel who would precede Eliezer and, thereby, prepare the way.

FAITH

"And if the woman will not be willing to follow you, then you shall be clear from this my oath: only bring not my son thither again.

"And the servant put his hand under the thigh of Abraham his master, and swore to him concerning that matter" (Gen. 24:8-9).

Even though Abraham mentions the possibility of the particular woman chosen by the Holy Spirit not being willing to follow, this is said only to placate Eliezer. Abraham knows that the woman chosen by the Lord will, in fact, be willing to follow Eliezer back to the land of Canaan in order to be the wife of Isaac. However, under no circumstances was the idea to be entertained that Isaac himself was to go to Haran, even if the woman demanded she meet him before such a journey be undertaken. The instructions were specific: Isaac was to remain in Canaan, and the woman was to come to Canaan to be with him.

Eliezer realized such was a tall order and wondered in his mind if he could get a woman to do such a thing, considering that she had never met Isaac, didn't know what he was like, but yet, she would be committing her entire life to this unseen man. However, Eliezer had Faith.

Regarding these conditions, Eliezer did as Abraham commanded him as it regards his putting his hand under the thigh of the Patriarch and, in effect, swearing to an oath.

Far more here was at stake than meets the eye. I think that Eliezer completely understood what was at stake, at least as much as one could at that particular time. In fact, the entirety of the Plan of God hinged on this being carried out, and being carried out exactly as the Lord had told Abraham that it must be carried out.

ALL THE GOODS

"And the servant took ten camels of the camels of his master, and departed; for all the goods of his

master were in his hand: and he arose, and went to Mesopotamia, unto the city of Nahor" (Gen. 24:10).

Camels were the largest beasts of burden, at least in that particular area. *"Ten"* in the Bible is the number of completion. So, a little bit of everything that Abraham had was placed on those camels. No doubt, Eliezer also had many other servants with him in order to help him on this long journey and, as well, to serve as protection.

Abraham had 318 trained soldiers in his retinue, so to speak. No doubt, some of these men, if not the majority, went with Eliezer.

If we follow the narrative through, believing that this portrays Abraham as a Type of God the Father, Isaac as a Type of Christ, and Eliezer as a Type of the Holy Spirit, with Rebekah being a type of the Church, i.e., *"the Bride of Christ,"* then we must come to the conclusion that all that the Father has actually belongs to Christ but has been placed in the Hands of the Holy Spirit, Who will dispense it as He sees fit. The reader must remember that Isaac, in a figure, has already been offered up in Sacrifice and resurrected, hence, a Type of the Exalted Christ, Who has sent the Holy Spirit into the world to seek a Bride for the Son of God.

While Eliezer was under strict orders from Abraham, still, he could dispense these goods as he saw fit. However, to be sure, the goods would be dispensed only to the right people.

THE CAMELS

"And he made his camels to kneel down without the city by a well of water at the time of the evening, even the time that women go out to draw water" (Gen. 24:11).

The long journey of some 700 miles, which probably took several weeks, has now been completed.

Eliezer has arrived at the city of Nahor, which is very near Haran.

Inasmuch as he has now arrived, he will immediately begin his requests for a bride for Isaac.

Where Eliezer would begin his quest should provide us food for thought. He didn't go to a place of amusement, but rather to a *"well"* where the women draw water, which, needless to say, was a laborious task. In other words, he was looking for a young lady who was industrious, zealous, not afraid of hard work, and who was responsible. He could only find her at such a place as this.

PRAYER

"And he said O LORD God of my master Abraham, I pray You, send me good speed this day, and show kindness unto my master Abraham.

"Behold, I stand here by the well of water; and the daughters of the men of the city come out to draw water:

"And let it come to pass, that the damsel to whom I shall say, Let down your pitcher, I pray you, that I may drink; and she shall say, Drink, and I will give your camels drink also: let the same be she that You have appointed for Your Servant Isaac; and thereby shall I know that You have showed kindness unto my master" (Gen. 24:12-14).

Let's look at what is done here:

• Eliezer is looking to the Lord to lead him and guide him. He does not at all trust his own instincts or personal wisdom. He needs Leading from the Lord, so he will seek the Lord. How much this should be a lesson to all of us as well.

Also, we should understand as Believers that due to the fact that Abraham is the *"father of us all"* (Rom. 4:16), everything that happened to him in some way applies to us. We speak, of course, in a spiritual sense.

- If it is to be noticed, Eliezer does not for a moment forget that the mission on which he has embarked is for Abraham.
- He is specific in his prayer, asking for a certain thing; consequently, it is obvious that he believes that God hears and answers prayer.
- Camels drink a lot of water. Consequently, anyone who would slake their thirst, much less 10 of these animals, would have to draw a lot of water, which, within itself, is a big task. So, he put the following before the Lord:

The young lady whom he would approach, asking for a drink of water, and she would graciously give it to him, and then, as well, would offer to give the camels water, would be the one *"appointed for Your Servant Isaac."*

As is obvious, Eliezer certainly didn't make it easy. Asking that the Lord would impress upon her to water the camels, as well, narrowed down the field considerably. What young lady would want to draw that much water, especially for a stranger?

REBEKAH

"And it came to pass, before he had done speaking, that, behold, Rebekah came out, who was born to Bethuel, son of Milcah, the wife of Nahor, Abraham's brother, with her pitcher upon her shoulder" (Gen. 24:15).

Did Rebekah know that when she arose that morning, she was being guided by an Angel, for this is exactly what happened? Maybe the girl had been praying for months that the Lord would give her the right husband. Little did she know and realize how that prayer would be answered, and how important her part and position would be in the great Plan of God. It was a Plan that pertained to Redemption and would touch the entirety of the world for all time. This was the young lady chosen by the Lord. Incidentally, she was the second cousin of Isaac.

As the Church, of which Rebekah was an Old Testament type, are we this agreeable? Do we volunteer for hard manual labor, to use an expression? Is our attitude as obedient as that of Rebekah's? Can the Holy Spirit deal with us with the same favorable results as Eliezer, a Type of the Holy Spirit, dealt with Rebekah?

BEAUTIFUL

"And the damsel was very fair to look upon, a virgin, neither had any man known her: and she went down to the well, and filled her pitcher, and came up" (Gen. 24:16).

The girl was beautiful, and, as well, she was a virgin. Also, she was industrious, as is obvious here.

This is a picture of what the Lord expects the Church to be. In His Eyes, the Church is beautiful. As well, the Lord expects the Church to follow Him exclusively, i.e., the Holy Spirit, and not depend on self or other people, which He will always look at as *"spiritual adultery"* (Rom. 7:1-4). If, in fact, Rebekah is a type of the Church, then it is plain to see that the Lord expects the Church to be industrious, i.e., *"busy in the Work of the Lord."*

Even though this young girl was beautiful, she did not think herself too good to perform this task of drawing water from the well, which was not easy, to say the least.

Most of the wells in those days were fed by a spring, with a series of steps that led down to the well. Consequently, to walk up those steps carrying one or two goatskins full of water was no easy task.

THE SIGN

"And the servant ran to meet her, and said, Let me, I pray you, drink a little water of your pitcher" (Gen. 24:17).

Eliezer will now put the first part of his plan into operation. Rebekah evidently was the first girl to show up at the well, and apparently came up at the very time he was arriving. Seeing the girl but still not knowing who she was, he would ask for a drink of water from her pitcher.

I would say the request was unusual, especially considering that a man was asking such of a woman. She could easily have told him to draw his own water, but she didn't, responding exactly as he hoped she would.

DRINK

"And she said, Drink, my lord: and she hasted, and let down her pitcher upon her hand, and gave him drink" (Gen. 24:18).

Rebekah not only acquiesced to his request, but she did so gleefully and promptly.

As she gave him to drink, we, as members of the Body of Christ, are to give the Water of Life to a hurting, dying world. As she drew from the well, we are to draw from the Well, i.e., *"Christ."* Jesus said, *"If any man thirst, let him come unto Me, and drink"* (Jn. 7:37).

Every Believer in the world is to be a Light and a preservative to the world.

The SonLife Broadcasting Network, consisting of radio, television, and the Internet, was designed by the Holy Spirit to touch the entirety of the world. Of course, in this mix, television reaches far, far more than any other medium. To be sure, those to whom the Lord has given the privilege and the responsibility of being a part of this effort are privileged indeed!

Rebekah could not remotely know or understand her part in this great Plan of God, but, to be sure, it was a part that was vastly significant for the entirety of the world and for all time, even unto the present.

Likewise, you who are with the SonLife Broadcasting Network cannot know or understand, and neither can we as its leaders, the vast significance of all that is being done. However, to be sure, it is far, far bigger than meets the eye.

THE SECOND PART OF THE SIGN

"And when she had done giving him drink, she said, I will draw water for your camels also, until they have done drinking" (Gen. 24:19).

Without him asking her to do so, she immediately volunteered to draw water for the camels, exactly as he had asked the Lord that the chosen girl would do.

As stated, camels drink a lot of water. So, the girl had to make quite a few trips down the stairs to the well and then bring back those heavy goatskins full of water.

To be sure, what the Lord asks us to do is not glamorous all of the time. There was nothing glamorous about this young lady taking goatskins down to this well, filling them with water, and then climbing those steps with that heavy load on her shoulders, and having to do so many times. However, she did it without complaint!

Little did she realize that her doing this would have such eternal consequences.

We must ever understand that anything we do for the Lord, no matter how menial it might be, is never without tremendous consequences. Unfortunately, it seems that none of us quite understand that as well as we should.

HER CONDUCT

"And she hasted, and emptied her pitcher into the trough, and ran again unto the well to draw water, and drew for all his camels" (Gen. 24:20).

Eliezer had servants who might have spared Rebekah her labor, but he interfered not, so that he might observe her conduct and await the answer to his prayer.

Her conduct, in itself, so amiable and so exactly in unison with his wishes, struck him with a kind of amazement, accompanied with a momentary hesitation, as to whether all could be true.

Recovering from his astonishment and being satisfied that the Lord had indeed heard his prayer, as we shall see, he now will present her with gifts, which must have been a surprise to her.

THE LORD

"And the man wondering at her held his piece, to witness whether the LORD had made his journey prosperous or not" (Gen. 24:21).

"Wondering at her" means that he *"eagerly or carefully watched her."*

Eliezer keenly observed all that Rebekah said and did, and then carefully came to the conclusion that this beautiful and kind maiden was the destined bride of the son of his master. The Lord had answered his prayer.

It should be noticed here the degree that Eliezer sought the Lord, looked to the Lord, and depended on the Lord. I cannot overemphasize the fact that this should be a great lesson to us as Believers. Presently, due to what Christ has done at the Cross, the Holy Spirit gives us this help constantly, or at least He desires to do so, whereas such help afforded in Abraham's day was sporadic at best. Presently, the Holy Spirit abides permanently (Jn. 14:16-17).

Modern Christians are constantly proclaiming that they wish that the Lord would give them the type of help that He gave Eliezer. The truth is, He will do even more because He now has greater latitude, due to the Cross. The problem is not with the Holy Spirit, as the problem is never with the Holy Spirit. The problem is us! Most Christians have very little prayer life whereas it is obvious that Eliezer had a very personal relationship with the Lord. He had allowed Abraham's Faith to become his Faith. Likewise, Abraham's consecration was also his consecration.

The modern Believer can get as close to the Lord as he so desires. It's never up to the Lord; He is always ready. The slackness is always on our part.

THE CROSS

As I dictate these notes on June 19, 2012, I have been living for the Lord about 69 years, but the following I can say, I think, without reservation:

In 1997, the Lord began to open up to me the Message of the Cross, in effect, what the Cross actually means, which is the meaning of the New Covenant. As it refers to living for God, I think I've learned more in this last several years than all the rest of my time put together. I have found out that the Cross is the Foundation of all Biblical Doctrine. In other words, every single Doctrine in the Word of God must stem from the Cross, which has made it all possible, or else, it will be perverted in some manner. It should be obvious, if the foundation of anything isn't right, then what's built on that foundation cannot be right either. However, if the foundation is correct, irrespective of what is built on the foundation, even if it's wrong, it can be corrected. So, it's absolutely imperative that each and every Believer understand the Cross even as the Word of God sets it forth. In fact, the Story of the Bible is the Cross of Christ even as the Cross of Christ is the Story of the Bible.

UNDERSTANDING THE CROSS

Regrettably, most Believers automatically think they understand all about the Cross. I remember a letter someone sent to me a short time back. It was cryptic and to the point. The man said, *"Why do you keep talking about the Cross? We already understand all about the Cross."*

The truth is, this man didn't understand anything about the Cross. Unfortunately, most of Christendom falls into the same category.

Many modern Christians dismiss the Cross out of hand, and if they think of it at all, they do so only in a sentimental way. Others place value on the Cross as it regards their initial Salvation experience, but it stops there. Precious few Christians understand the Cross as it regards their Sanctification experience, and that can cause the Believer untold problems. Please note the following:

• Chapter 1 of Romans proclaims to us the plight of the Gentiles. It's not a very pretty picture.

• Chapters 2 and 3 of Romans proclaim the Jewish situation, and, in effect, they are placed in the same category as the Gentiles, desperately needing a Redeemer.

• Chapters 4 and 5 of Romans proclaim the solution to man's lost condition, which is Jesus Christ and that which He offers through the Cross, which is *"Justification by Faith."*

• Chapter 6 of Romans tells us how to have victory over the sin nature.

• Chapter 7 of Romans proclaims the Believer trying to live this life by the means of the flesh, which always brings defeat.

• Chapter 8 of Romans explains the Sanctification process of the Holy Spirit, as to how He works within our hearts and lives. He works exclusively within the parameters of the Finished Work of Christ, i.e., the Cross. He doesn't demand much of us, but He does demand that our Faith be exclusively in Christ and the Cross. That being done, He can and will do for us what nothing else can do.

• Chapters 9 through 11 of Romans proclaim a solemn warning to the Church. If we, as Israel of old, seek to develop our own Righteousness, which means we ignore the Cross, the end result of the Church will be the same as it was with Israel.

• Chapters 12 through 16 of Romans proclaim the practical aspect of Christianity, in other words, how we are to live after we understand God's Prescribed Order of Victory.

IN CHRIST

In a very abbreviated way, I will attempt to proclaim what the Holy Spirit is telling us through the Apostle Paul regarding this all-important aspect of the Believer's life. As stated, Paul takes us to the Cross and tells us that, as Believers, when we were Saved, we were *"baptized into His Death."* We were then *"buried with Him by Baptism into Death."* Please understand, Paul is not speaking here of Water Baptism, but rather the Crucifixion of Christ. As well, we were raised with Christ *"in Newness of Life"* (Rom. 6:3-4).

Regrettably, most Christians completely miss the meaning of the Sixth Chapter of Romans because they think that Paul is speaking of Water Baptism. He uses the word, *"Baptized,"* in these Passages in a figurative sense instead of their literal sense. He does it because it explains the experience of the Believer, as it regards our *"in Christ"* experience, greater than anything else. This means that Christ was our Substitute, and all that He did for us at the Cross now becomes ours upon our simple

Faith evidenced in Him. We are placed into Christ by our Faith, at least in the Mind of God, Whose Mind Alone actually matters. In other words, we simply believe, and the Work is done (Jn. 3:16). However, please remember, it must be Faith in Christ and what Christ has done for us at the Cross. This Faith is to remain with us and be practiced by us every day of our lives until the trump sounds, or the Lord calls us home (Lk. 9:23; 14:27).

Now, please remember that Paul is speaking here to Believers, in other words, people who have already been Saved, some of them for many, many years. But still, he takes these Believers, plus you and me, to the Cross, always to the Cross.

He tells us that when we evidenced Faith in Christ, and I continue to speak of the moment we were Saved, at that particular time, we *"died with Christ"* (Rom. 6:7-8). This means that we died to the old life, to the sin nature, etc. While the sin nature didn't die, we died to it. The way we stay dead, and this is very important, is to continue, even on a daily basis, our Faith in the Cross and not allow it to be moved to anything else.

The Holy Spirit works exclusively within the parameters of the Finished Work of Christ, i.e., the Cross. Continuing to anchor our Faith in Christ and His Cross gives the Holy Spirit latitude to work within our hearts and lives, and to work as He Alone can work. As stated, the Holy Spirit, Whom we must have, works entirely within the parameters of the Cross of Christ. In other words, it is the Cross, rather what Jesus there did, which gives the Holy Spirit the legal means to work with us and in us (Rom. 8:1-11).

WALKING AFTER THE SPIRIT

Paul said:
"There is therefore now no condemnation to them

who are in Christ Jesus, who walk not after the flesh, but after the Spirit" (Rom. 8:1).

What is *"walking after the Spirit"*?

It is not doing spiritual things. Unfortunately, most Christians think that's what Paul is talking about. He isn't!

"Walking after the Spirit," which, of course, refers to the Holy Spirit, means that we place our Faith exclusively in Christ and what Christ did for us at the Cross. That is *"walking after the Spirit."* Incidentally, the word, *"Walk,"* or, *"Walking,"* refers to the manner in which we order our behavior, in other words, how we live for God, how we have victory over the world, the flesh, and the Devil, and how we grow in Grace and the Knowledge of the Lord.

If our Faith is properly placed in the Cross, which gives the Holy Spirit latitude to work within our lives, this will give us total victory over the *"Law of Sin and Death,"* i.e., *"the sin nature."*

If the Believer has his Faith properly placed in the Cross, and maintains it in the Cross, ever making this the Object of his Faith, he need never worry about the sin nature. He is dead to that particular factor. However, if the Believer attempts to live for God by means other than constant Faith in Christ and the Cross, the Believer will see the sin nature once again beginning to dominate him exactly as it did before he was Saved. This is a miserable experience for any person to undergo. Regrettably, that's where most modern Christians actually are. They know little about the Cross as it regards their Sanctification and, therefore, try to live for God by other means, which cannot be done.

GIFTS

"And it came to pass, as the camels had done drinking, that the man took a golden earring of half a shekel

weight, and two bracelets for her hands of ten shekels weight of gold" (Gen. 24:22).

The *"golden earring of half a shekel weight"* would be worth presently (2012) about $1,000. Incidentally, it was a nose-ring instead of an earring.

Whether the two bracelets weighed *"ten shekels"* each, or both weighed *"ten shekels,"* we aren't told. At any rate, *"ten shekels weight of gold"* would be worth, in today's money, about $13,000.

In the spiritual sense, these gifts, which came from Eliezer, are types of Gifts of the Spirit and, in fact, all good things which the Lord does for us. The fact that these were items of *"gold"* proclaims the fact that they are all of God.

I suspect that Rebekah was somewhat taken aback when she was given these very expensive gifts.

THE BLESSINGS OF THE LORD

When the believing sinner comes to Christ, the Holy Spirit immediately begins to give good, beautiful, and wonderful things to us, which, in fact, never ends all the days of our lives. To be sure, what He gives us is of far greater value than the symbolism of gold suggested here. While He takes care of us financially and materially, as well, His Greater Blessings are in the spiritual sense. The mature Christian soon finds that out.

As well, the gifts presented to Rebekah by Eliezer were in no way meant to pay her for the work she had done. In fact, Eliezer could have asked someone to water his camels for a tiny, tiny fraction of what he gave Rebekah. No! These were gifts because Eliezer suspected that this was the one whom God had chosen. He was right!

In living for God, we soon learn that we really cannot earn anything from Him. In other words, He has nothing for sale. If He did, we certainly would never be able to afford such wonders. His Gifts are free and freely given. As well, they are lavishly given because He is rich in the things we desperately need and, in fact, rich in everything.

THE PRESENCE OF THE LORD

Oh, how I sense His Presence even as I attempt to elaborate on this gesture of Eliezer, which took place so long, long ago. How much the Lord wants to give us good things! How much He longs to lavish His Largess on us! Then again, how so very valuable are His Gifts, and they just keep on coming. It's like we are admitted into a treasure house. We go into one room, which is filled with all types of riches. But then, we see a door, which leads to another room with even more riches. It seems that the rooms never end, and the riches just keep getting greater and greater.

Rebekah now only has these token gifts. She will soon be wed to Isaac, which means that all he has, and, to be sure, that is bountiful, will then become hers in totality.

When we come into Christ, we become *"heirs of God, and joint-heirs with Christ"* (Rom. 8:17).

QUESTIONS

"And said, Whose daughter are you? tell me, I pray you: is there room in your father's house for us to lodge in?" (Gen. 24:23).

Two questions are here asked:

1. *"Whose daughter are you?"* Considering that the signs requested by the Lord by Eliezer have now been granted, he must know who the young lady actually is. The question will gender a positive response, even as we shall see, and at the same time, as it follows the *"Type,"*

is meant to point to identification with Christ. Rebekah will soon belong to Isaac, who is a Type of Christ, even as the believing sinner is soon to belong to Christ.

2. *"Is there room in your father's house for us to lodge in?"* presents the question that the Holy Spirit asks of every believing sinner. We must make room for Christ. In fact, the Holy Spirit is constantly asking untold millions around the world, *"Is there room for Me?"*

IDENTIFICATION

"And she said unto him, I am the daughter of Bethuel the son of Milcah, which she bore unto Nahor" (Gen. 24:24).

Rebekah mentions her father's mother to show that she was descended from a highborn wife and not from a concubine. However, Eliezer would welcome the information as proving that not only on the father's side, but also on the mother's, she was Isaac's cousin, Milcah being the daughter of Haran, Abraham's brother.

This is probably the time that he gave her the jewels which he was holding in his hand.

ROOM TO LODGE IN

"She said moreover unto him, We have both straw and provender enough, and room to lodge in" (Gen. 24:25).

Her answer was in the positive. It was exactly that for which Eliezer had hoped. In essence, she was saying that they would give Eliezer and those with him everything that they had, regarding hospitality, and, as well, would make room for them as it regarded their lodging.

Little did she know or understand how important and how significant the words she was saying were. Little did she realize where this invitation would lead or that individuals would be talking about her thousands of years into the future because of her saying,

"Yes," to the Lord Jesus Christ, for that's exactly what she was doing.

When the great invitation comes to us, in whatever capacity, may our answer be as open and as broad as that of Rebekah.

WORSHIP

"And the man bowed down his head, and worshipped the LORD" (Gen. 24:26).

It is obvious that Eliezer had a close walk with the Lord. It is obvious that the Faith of Abraham was his Faith as well! It is obvious that he was accustomed to being led by the Lord. His demeanor, his attitude, and his response all point to total consecration.

Abraham had entrusted to his hand the future of the entirety of the Plan of God. What a responsibility he had, and how so much with dignity, responsibility, and forthrightness did he carry out this which he was assigned to do. May we do as well!

In the Hebrew language, the words, *"Bow down,"* express reverent inclination of the head. The second verb, *"Worship,"* proclaims a complete prostration of the body. This means that Eliezer fell prostrate on the ground, worshipping the Lord in thankfulness to Him for the Guidance and the Leading which had been given at this time.

A PRAYER OF THANKSGIVING

"And he said, Blessed be the LORD God of my master Abraham, who has not left destitute my master of His Mercy and His Truth: I being in the way, the LORD led me to the house of my master's brethren" (Gen. 24:27).

This prayer of Eliezer proclaims the fact that this man knew and understood the Grace of God, which he exclaims by mentioning the Mercy of the Lord and, as well, *"His Truth."* Mercy, being a product of Grace, proclaims the fact that Eliezer understood this great Doctrine. To be sure, if Grace is properly understood, *"truth,"* as well, will be understood.

The short phrase, *"I being in the way,"* refers to his being in the way of Mercy and truth, which is the place that every Believer ought to be and, in fact, can be.

As well, if Mercy and truth are properly understood and entertained, there will, at the same time, be Leading and Guidance by the Lord, which refers to a place of deep consecration.

THE WITNESS

"And the damsel ran, and told them of her mother's house these things.

"And Rebekah had a brother, and his name was Laban: and Laban ran out unto the man, unto the well" (Gen. 24:28-29).

How far Rebekah lived from the well, we aren't told; however, it must have been only a short distance, possibly several hundreds of yards.

The indication is that she first went and told her family what had just transpired. Even though this is the logical narration of the story, still, it is that which every Believer should do. We should witness first to our family and then to all others, as well. A story so wonderful, so grand, and so glorious begs to be told. To be sure, the Gospel Message is the grandest story ever told. How right was the songwriter:

"What a wonderful Light in my life has been shone,
"Since Jesus came into my heart!"

OBSERVATION

"And it came to pass, when he saw the earring and the bracelets upon his sister's hands, and when

he heard the words of Rebekah his sister, saying, Thus spoke the man unto me; that he came unto the man; and, behold, he stood by the camels at the well" (Gen. 24:30).

Every true Christian has Gifts given to him by the Lord, which should be an obvious sign to the world. The Bible said that Laban *"saw"* and *"heard."* He saw the gifts, and he heard the words which his sister said.

As it regards our lives, the world should *"see"* what the Lord has done for us, and then they will *"hear"* what we have to say concerning that tremendous Miracle which has transpired.

Laban then went to Eliezer.

PREPARATION

"And he said, Come in, you blessed of the LORD; why do you stand without? for I have prepared the house, and room for the camels.

"And the man came into the house: and he ungirded his camels, and gave straw and provender for the camels, and water to wash his feet, and the men's feet who were with him" (Gen. 24:31-32).

Laban was an idolater (Gen. 31:30); however, by him referring to Eliezer as *"blessed of the LORD,"* we know that he had some knowledge of the Lord. In fact, the original Revelation given by God to Abraham had, no doubt, instituted the worship of Jehovah in the household. But yet, they were still clinging to their idols, which, regrettably, is indicative of many modern Christians.

Many presently serve God, but, at the same time, the things of the world prove to be an allurement. In fact, Israel had the same problem, hence, the Prophet Samuel saying to them, *"Prepare your hearts unto the LORD, and serve Him only"* (I Sam. 7:3).

The idea was, they were serving the Lord and Baal at the same time. Regrettably, that problem didn't die with Israel.

THE MESSAGE

"And there was set meat before him to eat: but he said, I will not eat, until I have told my errand. And he said, Speak on" (Gen. 24:33).

We are witnessing here a perfect example of proper responsibility. That which was uppermost on his mind was not his own wants and needs, but rather the very purpose for which he came, which was to relay the message that Abraham had given him to relay.

All of this has to do with the protocol of that day, which was rigidly observed at that particular time.

Continuing to stand on protocol, Eliezer will request that he be given permission to speak even before the hospitality of food is enjoyed. If Laban had not conceded, he would not have entered his house. However, Laban did concede.

Incidentally, we will hear more of Laban, and I speak of the time of Jacob. He was a man of greed, and through greed, he lost Jacob. As well, as we shall see, it seems to be greed which forces his attention at this present time with his sister Rebekah and with Eliezer.

THE BLESSING

"And he said, I am Abraham's servant.

"And the LORD has blessed my master greatly; and he is become great: and He has given him flocks, and herds, and silver, and gold, and menservants, and maidservants, and camels, and asses" (Gen. 24:34-35).

Eliezer identifies himself but does so by promoting Abraham, which the Holy Spirit always does as it regards God the Father and God the Son. In fact, it is said of the Spirit:

"Howbeit when He, the Spirit of Truth, is come, He will guide you into all Truth: for He shall not speak of Himself; but whatsoever He shall hear, that shall He speak: and He will show you things to come.

"He shall glorify Me: for He shall receive of Mine, and shall show it unto you" (Jn. 16:13-14).

This is exactly what Eliezer is now doing!

He gives praise and glory to the Lord for all the good things which had happened. He credits the Lord with blessing Abraham with material things, which Laban would have readily understood.

THE BELIEVER

Let the reader know and understand that the Lord will do the same presently as He did then. He is no respecter of persons, and what He has previously done, He definitely will continue to do.

So, every Believer ought to believe the Lord for the Blessings of God regarding all things, as well as financial and material things. Our problem is, *"We have not because we ask not."* Then, far too often, *"We ask, and receive not, because we ask amiss, that we may consume it upon our lusts"* (James 4:2-3).

However, if we genuinely desire to bless the Work of the Lord, should the Lord place material things into our hand, to be sure, the Lord will definitely bless. In fact, He desires to bless! He wants to bless! If we will ardently seek His Face, consecrate ourselves fully to Him, and look to the Cross for all things, understanding that it was there that the price was paid, to be sure, God will bless us spiritually, physically, domestically, and financially.

I can sense the Presence of the Lord even as I dictate these words, and I believe that you the reader can sense the Lord as well. He loves you! He wants to bless you! He will do so in all things because He has all things. God is good, and as the song says, *"He's not good just some of the time, but God is good all of the time."*

ISAAC WAS GIVEN ALL

"And Sarah my master's wife bore a son to my master when she was old: and unto him has he given all that he has" (Gen. 24:36).

In this short sentence, so much is said.

Isaac was the Miracle child born to Sarah when she was 90 years old, and Abraham was 100. This proclaims the Miracle-working Power of Almighty God.

Even though Eliezer did not mention this here, this *"son"* was to be the seed who would bring the *"Seed of the woman"* into the world, which had been predicted immediately after the Fall in the Garden of Eden (Gen. 3:15).

Isaac is now a grown man, and Abraham has given to him all of his riches, which means that he was a very wealthy man.

Laban would have been little impressed by the great spiritual riches, which, in fact, had made all the other things possible, so they were not mentioned. However, he was greatly impressed by the material riches, so this is what Eliezer addressed. As a point of information, this is what he should have addressed because Laban could little have understood spiritual things.

Likewise, the Heavenly Father has given all things unto the *"Son."* The Son has given all things to us exactly as everything that belonged to Isaac would be given to Rebekah, who was a type of the Church.

Some would claim that she was a type of Israel, in fact, being the mother of Israel, so to speak. While the latter is true, we must go to Romans 4:16, where the Holy Spirit through Paul proclaims the fact that

Abraham is the *"father of us all,"* and he is speaking of Israel and the Church. So, I think the ground referring typology is safe regarding my conclusions respecting the symbolism.

A WIFE

"And my master made me swear, saying, You shall not take a wife to my son of the daughters of the Canaanites, in whose land I dwell" (Gen. 24:37).

As everything was to be a certain way regarding Isaac, likewise, it is the same for the Christian presently. The Lord has a Will for all things, and it's our business to find what that Will is, and then wholeheartedly obey that Will.

THE ANGEL

"But you shall go unto my father's house, and to my kindred, and take a wife unto my son.

"And I said unto my master, Peradventure the woman will not follow me.

"And he said unto me, The LORD, before Whom I walk, will send His Angel with you, and prosper your way; and you shall take a wife for my son of my kindred, and of my father's house" (Gen. 24:38-40).

As we have stated, the Lord had already informed Abraham that He would prepare the way before Eliezer, even by sending an Angel to protect him and to prepare for his arrival. It is obvious that this is exactly what was done.

THE OATH

"Then shall you be clear from this my oath, when you come to my kindred; and if they give not you one, you shall be clear from my oath" (Gen. 24:41).

As is obvious, the Lord had so ingrained into Abraham the necessity of what was to be done that he is fearful lest it not be carried out exactly as the Lord wanted. He even made his trusted servant, Eliezer, take an oath that he would strictly follow all directions.

The reason Abraham was adamant in this is because it was the Word of the Lord. Even though they didn't have a Bible in those days, with the first Books yet to be written by Moses some 400 years later, still, what the Lord told the Patriarch was very exact and, in fact, would be written by Moses at the later time mentioned.

We should be so zealous presently to follow the Word of the Lord exactly as it is given. The first question that should be asked about anything and everything is, *"Is it Scriptural?"*

PROSPERITY

"And I came this day unto the well, and said, O LORD God of my master Abraham, if now You do prosper my way which I go" (Gen. 24:42).

The prosperity of which Eliezer speaks refers to the petition he will lay before the Lord, and he prays that God will answer his prayer, which He most definitely did.

As real as the Lord was to Eliezer, even more real He is with us today because of the Cross.

The Cross of Christ atoned for all sin, past, present, and future, at least, for all who will believe (Jn. 3:16). This made it possible for the Holy Spirit, Who is God, to function in our hearts and lives to a far greater degree than what you're reading here in Genesis, as it regards Eliezer. The reason that we do not have the Fellowship, the Leading, the Guidance, and the Counsel we ought to have is because our minds and hearts are tuned elsewhere. The Holy Spirit, Who always glorifies Christ and always pleases the Father, will be just as real to us as we will allow Him to be.

THE PETITION

"Behold, I stand by the well of water; and it shall come to pass, that when the virgin comes forth to draw water, and I say to her, Give me, I pray you, a little water of your pitcher to drink;

"And she say to me, Both you drink, and I will also draw water for your camels: let the same be the woman whom the LORD has appointed out for my master's son" (Gen. 24:43-44).

Eliezer has reason that he will stand by the well inasmuch as women come during the day to draw water. As men generally did not perform this task, he felt this would be the best place to begin, and so it was.

However, as it concerned this girl, she first had to be a virgin and, second, she had to be a part of Abraham's family. He could not tell by looking at her as it regarded these things. So, his petition was this:

He would ask her for a drink of water, and if she willingly gave him the water and, at the same time, also offered to draw water for his camels, this would be the woman.

Considering that he had men with him who could easily have drawn the water and, as well, that this was a very hard task, it would have to be the Lord for this young lady to offer her kindness in this regard. However, that was the petition he put before the Lord. Anyone would have to agree, if it was met, it would have to be the Lord. In other words, Eliezer didn't make it easy.

No young lady out of the blue, so to speak, would volunteer to make many trips down the stairs to the well, thereby, carrying the heavy load back in order to water camels. So, I think you get the point!

THE ANSWER

"And before I had done speaking in my heart, behold, Rebekah came forth with her pitcher on her shoulder; and she went down unto the well, and drew water: and I said unto her, Let me drink, I pray you.

"And she made haste, and let down her pitcher from her shoulder, and said, Drink, and I will give your camels drink also: so I drank, and she made the camels drink also" (Gen. 24:45-46).

Eliezer silently prayed, and before he had even finished, Rebekah appeared on the scene. He asked her for a drink of water, and she immediately acquiesced to his request. She also instantly volunteered to water the camels as well.

This is an answer to prayer that is so astounding that it defies description. And yet, we must remember, this which was taking place beside that water well that particular day nearly 4,000 years ago was the single most important thing on the face of the Earth at that particular time. Mighty empires may have been raising their heads, and mighty armies may have marched, but in the Eyes of God, Whose Eyes Alone matter, this meeting between Eliezer and Rebekah was the next step. What an important step it was to bringing this great Salvation to the entirety of the world. When we read the Bible, especially the Old Testament, we should understand that everything that happened was pushing ever a little closer toward the great Redemption Plan being formulated.

That day that the Apostle Paul heard the Macedonian Call, which would be the first excursion of the Gospel into Europe, was so significant, so important, and so far reaching that there is no way that words could describe how important it actually was. In fact, it resulted in my Salvation and your Salvation, plus the other millions who have come to Christ from then until now.

But, as we shall see, Eliezer had one more hurdle to cross.

FAMILY

"And I asked her, and said, Whose daughter are you? And she said, The daughter of Bethuel, Nahor's son, whom Milcah bore unto him: and I put the earring upon her face, and the bracelets upon her hands" (Gen. 24:47).

Lo and behold, when asked about her family, he found to his joy that she was a member of the family of Abraham, exactly that for which he was seeking.

Why was Abraham so adamant about the wife of Isaac being a member of his own family?

He understood exactly what all of this meant. It was leading up to the Coming of the Redeemer into the world, in effect, the Incarnation, God becoming Man. Now, how much knowledge that Abraham had as it regards all of this, we aren't told; however, Jesus did say:

"Your father Abraham rejoiced to see My Day: and he saw it, and was glad" (Jn. 8:56).

The short phrase, *"My Day,"* means, in essence, that the Lord gave Abraham a complete picture of Who Christ would be and what Christ would do, and we speak of the Cross. So, a bride for Isaac was extremely important.

Also, the land of Canaan was so infested with giants, which were a product of fallen Angels and women (Gen. 14:5-6), that it was not known in that part of the world as to which family was contaminated, and which wasn't. So, the Lord bluntly tells the great Patriarch that the wife of Isaac must come from his own family, which she did.

So, when Eliezer asks, *"Whose daughter are you?"* the answer forthcoming was exactly what he wanted to hear.

WORSHIP

"And I bowed down my head, and worshipped the LORD, and blessed the LORD God of my master Abraham, which had led me in the right way to take my master's brother's daughter unto his son" (Gen. 24:48).

If it is to be noticed, Eliezer is not at all ashamed to confess before these men his dependence on the Lord. We should presently, as well, be so forward.

Here is a man who took full advantage of the Move of God in his master's life, and, of course, we speak of Abraham. It is obvious that Eliezer knew the Lord in a real and personal way. So, although a servant, he is given a place in Biblical history and in the great Plan of God that was and is important beyond description.

May we, as well, be so faithful.

THE ANSWER

"And now if you will deal kindly and truly with my master, tell me: and if not, tell me; that I may turn to the right hand, or to the left.

"Then Laban and Bethuel answered and said, The thing proceeds from the LORD; we cannot speak unto you bad or good.

"Behold, Rebekah is before you, take her, and go, and let her be your master's son's wife, as the LORD has spoken" (Gen. 24:49-51).

After Eliezer relates these things to these men, they are quickly made to see that all of this is entirely beyond their scope of comprehension. They do not attempt to elaborate on the subject or, it seems, to even ask any questions. Their statement, *"The thing proceeds from the LORD,"* in effect, said it all. They immediately give their consent for Rebekah to go with this man back to the home of Isaac, some 700 miles distance.

This was a very long journey in those days, and, in fact, they would never see Rebekah again.

THANKS TO THE LORD

"And it came to pass, that, when Abraham's servant heard their words, he worshipped the LORD, bowing himself to the earth" (Gen. 24:52).

For every victory, Eliezer worships the Lord, and does so openly, which speaks volumes of this man. As well, his worship was not merely a silent *"thank you,"* but he was very physical, at times even prostrating himself on the ground.

Of course, when we understand how important all of this was, we can understand Eliezer's reaction. I think he realized its vast significance, at least as far as it was possible then.

THE GIFTS

"And the servant brought forth jewels of silver, and jewels of gold, and raiment, and gave them to Rebekah: he gave also to her brother and to her mother precious things.

"And they did eat and drink, he and the men who were with him, and tarried all night; and they rose up in the morning, and he said, Send me away unto my master" (Gen. 24:53-54).

The gifts now were lavish. The gifts were, as well, expensive. Considering how rich Abraham was and how important this event, the worth of all of this was undoubtedly staggering.

In other words, the jewelry and, no doubt, the silver and the gold, could easily have been as much as $250,000 in 2012 dollars.

Little by little, the family of Rebekah surely was beginning to understand just how rich and how powerful that Abraham actually was, but yet, despite this knowledge, they still only knew in part.

TARRY NOT

"And her brother and her mother said, Let the damsel abide with us a few days, at the least ten; after that she shall go.

"And he said unto them, Hinder me not, seeing the LORD has prospered my way; send me away that I may go to my master.

"And they said, We will call the damsel, and inquire at her mouth" (Gen. 24:55-57).

Perhaps a little different than the custom, Eliezer wants to depart immediately. His mission is all-important, and he cannot rest until the young lady is safe by Isaac's side.

There is no doubt that the Holy Spirit was working as it regarded the situation, not only as it pertained to Eliezer, but, as well, as it pertained to Rebekah and her family.

Eliezer had one mission to carry out, and this mission was now complete, with the exception of getting this young lady to Canaan and by the side of Isaac. So, Eliezer is very antsy to get this show on the road, so to speak.

THE GREAT QUESTION

"And they called Rebekah, and said unto her, Will you go with this man? And she said, I will go" (Gen. 24:58).

One can certainly understand the feelings of this family, taking into consideration that they would probably never see Rebekah again. This could not be easy for her mother and father, as well as her brother. So, they asked for 10 days in order to say their goodbyes, which would include all of the relatives.

However, Eliezer felt in his spirit that he must leave immediately, so Rebekah is given the choice as to what she wanted to do.

She was asked the great question, *"Will you go with this man?"* Her answer seems to be without hesitation. She said, *"I will go."*

Whenever we come to Christ, we, in effect, must give up our families, our friends, and everything, for that matter. That certainly doesn't mean that we cease to love them. Not at all! In fact, we love them even more, but Christ comes first.

To be sure, when the Holy Spirit poses the question to each of us, *"Will you go with this man?"* speaking of Christ, our answer must be as quick as was the answer of Rebekah. *"I will go!"* It is a journey that, in fact, will never end.

THE BLESSING

"And they sent away Rebekah their sister, and her nurse, and Abraham's servant, and his men.

"And they blessed Rebekah, and said unto her, You are our sister, be thou the mother of thousands of millions, and let your seed possess the gate of those which hate them" (Gen. 24:59-60).

No doubt, the blessing they posed upon Rebekah was standard; however, little did they realize that the staggering numbers they presented would, in fact, come to pass. Every single person who has ever come to Christ is a part of these *"thousands of millions."*

As well, through Jesus Christ, victory in every capacity has been won, and victory in every capacity will continue to be won.

When the Lord is in the mix, there is no limit to what can be done. He is a Miracle-working God. I might quickly add that He desires to make Himself real and to show Himself real on behalf of those who will dare to believe Him. To be sure, Eliezer believed the Lord!

FOLLOW THE MAN

"And Rebekah arose, and her damsels, and they rode upon the camels, and followed the man: and the servant took Rebekah, and went his way" (Gen. 24:61).

Not only did Rebekah's nurse go with her but other young ladies, as well, as represented by the word, *"Damsels."* This showed that her family was quite wealthy also.

The Scripture says that they *"followed the man,"* speaking of Eliezer.

We are to follow the Holy Spirit in all of His Leading. Always, and without exception, He will lead us to Christ.

Rebekah said, *"Goodbye,"* to all of her loved ones, knowing that, more than likely, she would never see them again. Despite the jewels that were given unto her and the explanation of Eliezer concerning the power and position of Abraham, which would belong to Isaac, still, there had to be an urging in her heart placed there by the Holy Spirit, which caused her to do what she did. Isn't that what Jesus said that we must do?

"He who loves father or mother more than Me is not worthy of Me: and he who loves son or daughter more than Me is not worthy of Me" (Mat. 10:37).

PRAYER

"And Isaac came from the way of the well Lahai-roi; for he dwelt in the south country.

"And Isaac went out to meditate in the field at the eventide: and he lifted up his eyes, and saw, and, behold, the camels were coming" (Gen. 24:62-63).

It is beautiful that Isaac has laid his eyes on his bride-to-be while in prayer.

Evidently, he had gone out to a place of solitude to seek the Face of the Lord, possibly about the mission of Eliezer concerning the obtaining for him a wife.

It is doubtful that he expected Eliezer back so soon. He knew the long distance to where his father Abraham had sent Eliezer, and about how long it would take to get there and to get back. However, he had no idea how long Eliezer would be once he arrived there. So, I doubt very seriously that he was expecting the servant back this soon.

No doubt, thoughts filled his mind. Would Eliezer be successful? If so, what would she look like?

He was not to be disappointed, not in the least! The Lord would arrange this match, and that which the Lord does is always beautiful and glorious. While in prayer, he happened to look up, and behold, the camel train was coming.

REBEKAH

"And Rebekah lifted up her eyes, and when she saw Isaac, she lighted off the camel.

"For she had said unto the servant, What man is this who walks in the field to meet us? And the servant had said, It is my master: therefore she took a veil, and covered herself" (Gen. 24:64-65).

All the thoughts that Isaac had, no doubt, were present in the mind of Rebekah as well. What would he be like?

In a sense, her commitment was even greater than that of Isaac. While he would be able to remain with his family to the end of his days, she had left her family back in Haran, and actually would never see them again. She had left all for this man, whom she had never seen, but, to be sure, she definitely was not to be disappointed.

Again, the Lord has arranged all things, and His Arrangements are always perfect.

We aren't told what the thoughts of Isaac were or those of Rebekah at the moment of their meeting. Perhaps it was too personal for the Holy Spirit to divulge this meeting.

However, this one thing is certain: both were very pleased at what the Lord had chosen.

ELIEZER

"And the servant told Isaac all things that he had done" (Gen. 24:66).

After Isaac had met Rebekah, Eliezer then related to him the Blessings of God upon his journey. God had moved wondrously, and the mother of Israel, for that's actually what Rebekah would be, would be everything that Isaac could ever want. To be sure, Isaac would be everything Rebekah would ever want or desire.

In fact, this meeting of Isaac and Rebekah, and the fact that she would be his wife, is a type of the meeting that will take place when the Trump of God sounds, and every Believer will meet Christ in the air (I Thess. 4:13-18).

HIS WIFE

"And Isaac brought her into his mother Sarah's tent, and took Rebekah, and she became his wife; and he loved her; and Isaac was comforted after his mother's death" (Gen. 24:67).

Incidentally, in those days, the primitive marriage ceremony consisted solely of the taking of a bride before witnesses.

If it is to be noticed, the word, *"Death,"* is added by the translators. It was not in the original Text. In other words, when Moses wrote it, it actually stated, *"And Isaac was comforted after his mother."*

It is as if the Holy Spirit would not conclude this beautiful and joyful narrative with a note of sorrow.

Isaac being comforted by Rebekah after his mother's death shows that he did not make comparisons between his mother and Rebekah, which allowed his wife to be the queen of the home, even as she should have been. In other words, she didn't have to compete with Sarah, meaning that Isaac did not constantly compare the two.

So is told this beautiful love story, which symbolizes Christ and the Church, represented by Isaac and Rebekah. However, the emphasis seems to be on Eliezer, who symbolized the Holy Spirit, as he obtained the bride for Isaac. Likewise, the Holy Spirit is presently making up the Church as a Bride for Christ.

> *"Lo! He comes, with clouds descending,*
> *"Once for favorite sinners slain;*
> *"Thousand Saints attending,*
> *"Swell the triumph of His Train.*
> *"Hallelujah! Hallelujah!*
> *"God appears on Earth to reign."*
>
> *"Every eye shall now behold Him,*
> *"Robed in dreadful majesty!*
> *"Those who set at naught and sold Him,*
> *"Pierced, and nailed Him to the tree,*
> *"Deeply wailing, deeply wailing,*
> *"Shall the true Messiah see."*
>
> *"Yea, Amen; let all adore Thee,*
> *"High on Your Eternal Throne:*
> *"Saviour, take the Power and Glory;*
> *"Claim the Kingdom for Your Own.*
> *"Oh, come quickly, oh, come quickly!*
> *"Everlasting God come down."*

ABRAHAM

CHAPTER

29

Abraham,
The Father Of Us All

ABRAHAM, THE FATHER OF US ALL

"Then again Abraham took a wife, and her name was Keturah" (Gen. 25:1).

Sarah having waxed old and vanished away (Heb. 9:13), that is, the Jewish Covenant of works, Keturah, the Gentile, now appears with her sons. Thus is the future picture.

This having been accomplished, the nations of the Earth (represented by Keturah and her sons) will be raised up as children of Abraham and receive their inheritance, which, of course, speaks of the Church.

Abraham not only laid the groundwork for Israel but, as well, for the Church. So, everything that happened to him was of utmost significance as it regarded the entirety of the Plan of God, hence, Abraham was referred to as *"the father of us all"* (Rom.4:16).

To say it again, if it is to be noticed, Sarah, while representing us all, was more so the mother of Israel. Keturah, Abraham's second wife, and we're speaking of this union taking place after Sarah's death, represents the Church and, therefore, the Gentiles. So, when Paul said that the Patriarch *"was the father of us all,"* this statement actually covered the entirety of the Plan of God.

Abraham was 137 years of age when Sarah died. He probably married Keturah not long thereafter. He died at 175 years of age. So, he was married to her 35 or more years.

GENTILE SONS

"And she bore him Zimran, and Jokshan, and Medan, and Midian, and Ishbak, and Shuah.

"And Jokshan begat Sheba and Dedan. And the sons of Dedan were Asshurim, and Letushim, and Leummim.

"And the sons of Midian; Ephah, and Epher, and Hanoch, and Abidah, and Eldaah. All these were the children of Keturah" (Gen. 25:2-4).

Abraham was probably between 140 and 150 years old when these sons were born.

Of course, it would be obvious that it is beyond nature for a man 100 years old to have a son. How much more improbable, even impossible, must it have become after 40 years had passed! So, we must conclude that the rejuvenation given to Abraham by the Lord, as it regarded the birth of Isaac, carried over for many more years, which it, no doubt, did. With God, all things are possible!

It is believed that Midian is the one son of Keturah who had a great future before him inasmuch as his race became famous traders. As well, it is believed that Medan and Midian grew together into one tribe. Jethro, the father-in-law of Moses, belonged to this tribe (Ex. 2:15-16).

If it is to be remembered, Gideon won a great victory over the Midianites, as recorded in Judges, Chapters 6 through 8.

A PERSONAL TESTIMONY

As it regards the touch that God gave Abraham, which made it possible for him to father a child at 100 years of age, and, as well, more sons at 140 years of age plus, we must reckon this as an astounding Miracle.

The Lord healed me when I was about 10 years of age. I stayed nauseous constantly and then would just simply go unconscious. This happened several times at school, with my parents having to come and pick me up. To be sure, my parents took me to the best doctors in the area, but after giving test after test, they could not find anything wrong. I personally believe that the Devil was trying to kill me. He knew that the Lord would use us to touch the world for Evangelism, so he was trying to stop this process.

The last time that I went unconscious at school, the principal spoke to my mother and dad and said to them, *"If something is not done for Jimmy, you are going to have to take him out of school."* His exact words were, *"We don't want him dying on our hands."*

To be sure, my parents, along with the Pastor of our Church, plus others, prayed for me any number of times but, seemingly, to no avail.

It was a Sunday. Church had just ended, and my mother and dad were going to take the Pastor and his wife out to lunch, but first, they had to stop and pray for one of the parishioners.

After praying for the brother, all walked to the front room of the little three-room, shotgun house. They were standing there talking when, all of a sudden, my dad said to our Pastor, *"Brother Calbreith, would you anoint Jimmy with oil and pray for him again? If something is not done, we are going to have to take him out of school."*

The Pastor smiled, and I can still remember that. He walked across the small room with a bottle of oil in his hands that he had just used to pray for the dear brother.

He touched my head with oil, and all began to pray. Then I felt it:

It was about the size of a softball. As well, it was hot; not burning hot, but healing hot. It started at the top of my head and very slowly went down through my body, out my legs, and out my feet. I knew beyond the shadow of a doubt that I was healed. I never was nauseous again, and, in fact, I haven't really been sick at all, with the exception that in January, 2001, I had a mild heart attack. Of course, that is serious, but that's it.

I've never had a headache in my life; I've never had a stomach ache in my life; and I've never had a backache in my life. As Jeremiah said, *"Heal me, O LORD, and I shall be healed; save me, and I shall be saved: for You are my praise"* (Jer. 17:14).

I had been prayed for many times in the past several months by the same Pastor, but with no visible results. So, why did the Lord wait this long to do it, and why did He do it in this fashion? That I cannot explain! As stated, I believe that Satan was trying to kill me, and when the Lord effected the task, it was done completely.

HEIR OF THE PROMISE

"And Abraham gave all that he had unto Isaac" (Gen. 25:5).

That alone, which is born of the Spirit, can be partaker of the Promises. The flesh cannot inherit such. In the spiritual, what does that mean?

Everything that is truly of God is born strictly of God. That means that all of Salvation and all of Sanctification are totally and completely of God. When the Believer understands this and functions accordingly, the Promises in all of their abundance are his, and we speak of victory and prosperity.

God's Way is the Cross, whether for Salvation or Sanctification. When man attempts to bypass God's Way and thereby attempts to manufacture his own Salvation or his own Sanctification, the problem begins. Regrettably, untold millions of the unsaved and millions of Christians do this every day.

The Cross is the Means by which God gives all things to the fallen sons of Adam's lost race. Whether it be Salvation for the sinner or Sanctification for the Saint, without exception, all come by Means of the Cross.

It is only when the Believer takes his eyes off the Cross, thereby, placing them on something else, that the problem begins. This means that his faith is transferred from the Cross to something else.

GOD'S PRESCRIBED ORDER OF VICTORY

While all of this sounds very complicated, in reality, it isn't. Please note carefully what I've already given in this Volume, but due to its vast significance, I want it clearly understood, hence, the repetition:

• Jesus Christ is the Source of all things and everything that we receive from God. He Alone is the Way to the Father, meaning that no man comes to the Father except by Christ (Jn. 1:1-3; 14:6; Col. 2:10-15).

• The Cross of Christ is the Means by which all of these wonderful things are given to us. In other words, the Cross makes it all legal. There, Jesus atoned for all sin, and I mean all sin, at least for those who will believe (Jn. 3:16). Sin is the legal means by which Satan holds man captive, but with all sin atoned, Satan has no more legal right to hold anyone captive. If he does, and, regrettably, he does with most of the world, it is because that man, whether Believer or unbeliever, does not take advantage of that which Jesus did at Calvary's Cross. Millions of unredeemed are seeing their bondages instantly broken when they place their Faith exclusively in Christ and what He did for us at the Cross. Likewise, millions of Believers have seen their bondages broken and now enjoy the *"more Abundant Life"* promised by our Saviour, all because of the Cross (Rom. 6:1-14; Gal., Chpt. 5; 6:14).

• With the Cross of Christ being the Means by which all of these great things are given to us, this demands that our Faith be exclusively in Christ and the Cross, and maintained exclusively in Christ and the Cross. In fact, the Object of Faith, which must be the

Cross, is one of the single most important Doctrines in the entirety of the Word of God (I Cor. 1:17-18, 23; 2:2; Col. 2:10-15).

• With Christ as our Source and the Cross as our Means, and with the Cross being the Object of our Faith, then the Holy Spirit, Who works exclusively within the parameters, so to speak, of the Finished Work of Christ, will work mightily on our behalf. It is impossible for us to be what we ought to be without the Help, Leading, Guidance, and Power of the Holy Spirit. However, if we place our faith in anything other than the Cross of Christ, which, in reality, is placing it exclusively in the Word of God, we frustrate the Grace of God (Gal. 2:21). For the Holy Spirit to do what He Alone can do and which we must have done, that is, if we are to live a victorious life, this demands that our Faith be exclusively in Christ and what He did for us at the Cross. Again, please note the following very carefully:

1. The only way to God the Father is through the Lord Jesus Christ (Jn. 14:6).

2. The only way to Jesus Christ is through the Cross. If we try to come to Christ any other way, we conclude with *"another Jesus"* (Lk. 9:23; II Cor. 11:4).

3. The only way to the Cross is a denial of self (Lk. 9:23-24).

Abraham was very, very rich! If it is to be noticed, he gave everything he had to Isaac, which tells us that the Lord will give everything He has to those who are true heirs of the Promise.

SEPARATION

"But unto the sons of the concubines, which Abraham had, Abraham gave gifts, and sent them away from Isaac his son, while he yet lived, eastward, unto the east country" (Gen. 25:6).

There is a vast difference in mere *"gifts"* and the entirety of the inheritance.

While the Believer might receive some small *"gifts"* as it regards ways other than the Cross, which, to be frank, has characterized all Believers, that is a far cry from the totality of the inheritance. So, the modern crowd, regarding the modern church who has repudiated the Cross, might receive a few *"gifts,"* but the truth is, what they are getting is a far cry, as stated, from the inheritance.

The *"inheritance"* involves spiritual things while the *"gifts,"* at least as represented here, involve only material things, which are temporal at best. So, the Believer can have the inheritance, or he can settle for temporary gifts. I think it is obvious as to the correct way.

INSTRUCTIONS

As well, Abraham was instructed by the Lord to separate Isaac from the sons born to Keturah. While the Bible definitely teaches separation, as is proclaimed here, it does not teach isolation. Let it be ever understood that the two definitely cannot coexist. I speak of that which is born of the Spirit and that which is born of the flesh.

The Way of Faith is the Way of the Cross, just as the Way of the Cross is the Way of Faith. In the literal or the spiritual sense, it can have no fellowship with the flesh.

Taking the latter first, *"the bondwoman and her son,"* must be cast out, even as Paul used Hagar and Ishmael as an allegory (Gal. 4:30-31). The Holy Spirit in our lives is ever struggling against the flesh and ever seeking to cast it out (Gal. 5:16-17).

In the natural or literal sense, the same holds true. Those who follow the Way of the Cross can have no fellowship with those who follow the way of the flesh. In fact, those who are of the flesh, which refers to trusting in things other than Christ and what He did at the Cross, will always persecute those who are after the Spirit (Gal. 1:23).

So, even though the sons of Keturah are, at the same time, the sons of Abraham, they are not heirs of the Promise, that alone joined to Isaac.

"Christ's Coming now is nearing,
"Blest day of His Appearing,
"This tho't my heart great joy affords;
"Millions around are sighing,
"For this release are a crying,
"Hasten Your Glorious Coming, Lord."

"Sorrow and sin prevails,
"In pain the Earth travails,
"Darkness abounds in every land;
"But in Earth's darkest hour,
"He'll come in mighty Power,
"Hasten Your Glorious Coming, Lord."

"So when the trumpet sounds,
"And He from Heaven descends,
"To claim the Church, His Spotless Bride;
"With boundless joy we'll greet Him,
"As we arise to meet Him,
"Hasten Your Glorious Coming, Lord."

ABRAHAM

CHAPTER

30

Death Of Abraham

DEATH OF ABRAHAM

"And these are the days of the years of Abraham's life which he lived, an hundred threescore and fifteen years.

"Then Abraham gave up the ghost, and died in a good old age, an old man, and full of years; and was gathered to his people" (Gen. 25:7-8).

It is believed that Abraham may have been born about two years after the death of Noah, and was actually contemporary with Shem, Noah's son, for many years.

So, if, in fact, that was the case, he was in a position to receive the facts affecting the antediluvian world. As stated, he was born of the Spirit at 75 years of age and departed to be with Christ at 175.

Few men in history, if any, have affected the world as did Abraham. That which characterized his person and his life was that of Faith.

By that, we speak of Faith in Christ and what Christ would do to redeem the fallen sons of Adam's lost race.

As with Paul, this giant *"fought the good fight, finished the course, and kept the Faith,"* and there was definitely laid up for him the Crown of Righteousness.

The phrase, *"Then Abraham . . . was gathered to his people,"* implies the belief in a future life. He was satisfied not merely with life and all of its Blessings, but with living, which characterizes all who are of Faith. He was now ready for the transition to a higher sphere. He died in the hope of a better country, even an heavenly (Heb. 11:13-16).

Abraham died a natural death, apparently, without pain. He simply breathed his last and went to be with his people.

ISAAC AND ISHMAEL

"And his sons Isaac and Ishmael buried him in the cave of Machpelah, in the field of Ephron the son of Zohar the Hittite, which is before Mamre" (Gen. 25:9).

It is so very pleasant to read that Isaac and Ishmael stood side by side at their father's grave, which speaks to us of prophetic overtones.

In the year 2012 A.D., which is the time of this writing, the animosity between the two is at a fever pitch, as it has been all of these many centuries. However, one day, that's going to change, and we speak of the Coming of the Lord.

On that Glad Day, it will be obvious to all that Jesus Christ is the Son of God, the Messiah of Israel, Isaac's *"Seed,"* and, as well, the True *"Seed of the woman."* At that time, both Isaac and Ishmael will accept Him, Who is Lord of all.

It is ironic: the True *"Seed"* is rejected presently by both Isaac and Ishmael. Israel believes that Jesus Christ was an imposter, with the Muslims denying His Divinity. That will soon be rectified, and both Isaac and Ishmael will stand side by side, with the hate and the war forever gone. This alone, and we speak of the Coming of the Lord, is the hope of humanity.

This doesn't mean that Jesus Christ will recognize Islam, for that will never be done. It does mean that, at that time, many Muslims will accept Jesus Christ as Saviour and as Lord. As well, from that time forward, they will no longer be Muslims.

Also, the greatest Miracle of all will be that the Jews to a person, and from all over the world, will accept Jesus Christ as Saviour and as Lord. Finally, spiritually speaking, they will come home! They will realize then that the One they crucified was and is their Messiah and their Saviour.

THE PURCHASED FIELD

"The field which Abraham purchased of the sons of Heth: there was Abraham buried, and Sarah his wife" (Gen. 25:10).

This plot of ground in which Abraham and Sarah were buried was that alone which Abraham actually owned in Canaan when he died, as far as land was concerned. And yet, that burial place proclaimed to all that one day the entirety of the land, which would ultimately be called *"Israel,"* would belong to him. So, his burial place was of far greater significance than the sons of Heth, from whom the land was purchased, ever knew. It signified Abraham's Faith in the Promises of God, and yet, was far broader than the mere land itself.

Actually, the land was but a means to an end, which would support a people, who would ultimately bring the Messiah into the world, Who would give His Life in order that man might be Saved. So, the greatness of Abraham can be summed up in the following short statement:

"He believed God, and God counted it to him for Righteousness" (Gen. 15:6).

When it says that he *"believed God,"* it is speaking of what God would do to redeem fallen humanity. It would be the giving of His Only Son, of Whom Isaac was a Type, Who would give Himself as a Sacrifice, which would effect the Salvation of all mankind (Gal. 1:4). This is the type of Faith which characterized Abraham. His Faith was in a Prophetic Jesus, while ours is in a Historic Jesus.

THE BLESSING

"And it came to pass after the death of Abraham, that God blessed his son Isaac; and Isaac dwelt by the well Lahai-roi" (Gen. 25:11).

If it is to be noticed, it says that God blessed Isaac, but it doesn't mention anything about God blessing the other sons of Abraham. If we desire the Blessing, we can have the Blessing as well. In fact, all who make Christ and His Cross the Object of their Faith are guaranteed the *"Blessing of Abraham."*

Paul said so:

"That the Blessing of Abraham might come on the Gentiles through Jesus Christ; that we might receive the Promise of the Spirit through Faith" (Gal. 3:14).

The *"Blessing of Abraham"* is predicated on what Christ did for us in order to *"redeem us from the curse of the Law."* He did this by *"being made a curse for us,"* which took place by Him *"hanging on the tree"* (Gal. 3:13).

The *"curse of the Law"* was death, which means that all who broke the Law were subject to its penalty. Sadly, the whole of the human race, other than Christ, broke the Law and, thereby, came under its curse.

However, when Jesus came as our Substitute and took the penalty for us, the curse, which was death, was satisfied, and satisfied in every respect. He Alone could be our Substitute and take the penalty for us because He was the Son of God, thereby, the Perfect Sacrifice. In other words, all sin was atoned, both past, present, and future. This made it possible for the *"Blessing of Abraham,"* which, incidentally, is *"Justification by Faith,"* to come upon the Gentiles, and the Jews, as well, for that matter.

As a result of what Jesus did for us at the Cross and our Faith in that Finished Work, the Holy Spirit now abides permanently within our hearts and lives, which is the present end result of the *"Blessing of Abraham."*

"Marvelous Message we bring,
"Glorious carols we sing,

"Wonderful Word of the King:
"Jesus is coming again!"

"Forest and flower exclaim,
"Mountain and meadow the same,
"All Earth and Heaven proclaim,
"Jesus is coming again!"

"Standing before Him at last,
"Trial and trouble all past,
"Crowns at His Feet we will cast:
"Jesus is coming again!"

BIBLIOGRAPHY

CHAPTER 4

C.H. Mackintosh, *Notes on the Book of Genesis*, Loizeaux Brothers, New York, 1880, pgs. 138-139.

Matthew Henry, *An Exposition of the Old and New Testaments, Volume 1*, Henry C. Sleight, New York, 1833, pg. 68.

Ibid., pg. 44.

CHAPTER 5

Mackintosh, C.H., *Notes on the Book of Genesis*, Loizeaux Brothers, New York, 1880, pg. 140.

Ibid., pgs. 140-141.

Ibid., pg. 142.

Ibid., pg. 142.

CHAPTER 6

C.H. Mackintosh, *Notes on the Book of Genesis*, Loizeaux Brothers, New York, 1880, pg. 147.

Ibid., pgs. 147-148.

H.D.M. Spence, *The Pulpit Commentary: Vol. 1*, Grand Rapids, Eerdmans Publishing Company, 1978, pg. 197.

CHAPTER 8

George Williams, *The Student's Commentary on the Holy Scriptures*, Grand Rapids, Kregel Publications, 1949, pgs. 18-19.

C.H. Mackintosh, *Notes on the Book of Genesis*, Loizeaux Brothers, New York, 1880, pgs. 156-157.

CHAPTER 9

C.H. Mackintosh, *Notes on the Book of Genesis*, Loizeaux Brothers, New York, 1880, pgs. 158.

CHAPTER 13

George Williams, *The Students Commentary on the Holy Scriptures*, Grand Rapids, Kregel Publications, 1949, pg. 20.

CHAPTER 14

George Williams, *The Students Commentary on the Holy Scriptures*, Grand Rapids, Kregel Publications, 1949, pg. 20.

C.H. Mackintosh, *Notes on the Book of Genesis*, Loizeaux Brothers, New York, 1880, pgs. 174-175.

George Williams, *The Students Commentary on the Holy Scriptures*, Grand Rapids, Kregel Publications, 1949, pgs. 20-21.

Charles John Ellicott, *Ellicott's Commentary on the Whole Bible*, Zondervan, Grand Rapids, 1970, pg. 70.

CHAPTER 15

C.F. Keil & F. Delitzsch, *The Pentateuch*, T&T Clark, Edinburgh, 1885, pg. 223.

George Williams, The Students Commentary on the Holy Scriptures, Grand Rapids, Kregel Publications, 1949, pg. 21.

C.J. Ellicott, An Old Testament Commentary for English Readers, Cassell, Petter, Galpin & Co., London, 1882, pg. 71.

CHAPTER 16

H.D.M. Spence, *The Pulpit Commentary: Vol. 1*, Grand Rapids, Eerdmans Publishing Company, 1978, pg. 233.

Charles John Ellicott, *Ellicott's Commentary on the Whole Bible*, Zondervan, Grand Rapids, 1970, pg. 72.

CHAPTER 17

George Williams, *The Students Commentary on the Holy Scriptures*, Grand Rapids, Kregel Publications, 1949, pg. 22.

CHAPTER 19

Matthew Henry, *Matthew Henry Commentary: Genesis to Esther*, Thomas Nelson, Tennessee, 1979, pg. 53.

CHAPTER 20
C.H. Mackintosh, *Notes on the Book of Genesis*, George Morrish, London, pg. 189.
Rev. T. Whitelaw, *The Pulpit Commentary: Genesis*, C. Kegan, Paul & Co., London, 1881, pg. 255.

CHAPTER 21
C.H. Mackintosh, *Notes on the Book of Genesis*, Loizeaux Brothers, New York, 1880, pg. 209.

CHAPTER 22
C.H. Mackintosh, *Notes on the Book of Genesis*, Loizeaux Brothers, New York, 1880, pgs. 211-212.

CHAPTER 23
George Williams, *The Students Commentary on the Holy Scriptures*, Grand Rapids, Kregel Publications, 1949, pg. 25.
C.H. Mackintosh, *Notes on the Book of Genesis*, Loizeaux Brothers, New York, 1880, pg. 200.

CHAPTER 24
George Williams, *The Students Commentary on the Holy Scriptures*, Grand Rapids, Kregel Publications, 1949, pgs. 25-26.

CHAPTER 26
George Williams, *The Students Commentary on the Holy Scriptures*, Grand Rapids, Kregel Publications, 1949, pg. 27.
Matthew Henry, Matthew Henry Commentary: *Genesis to Esther*, Thomas Nelson, Tennessee, 1979, pg. 62.

CHAPTER 28
C.H. Mackintosh, *Notes on the Book of Genesis*, Loizeaux Brothers, New York, 1880, pg. 225.

NOTES